Selling the Silver Bullet

Texas Film and Media Studies Series, Thomas Schatz, Series Editor

Selling the Silver Bullet

The Lone Ranger and Transmedia Brand Licensing

AVI SANTO

University of Texas Press *Austin*

Printed in the United States of America
First edition, 2015

Requests for permission to reproduce material from this work should be sent to:
Permissions
University of Texas Press
P.O. Box 7819
Austin, TX 78713-7819
http://utpress.utexas.edu/index.php/rp-form

♾ The paper used in this book meets the minimum requirements of ANSI/NISO Z39.48-1992 (R1997) (Permanence of Paper).

Library of Congress Cataloging-in-Publication Data
Santo, Avi, author.
Selling the Silver Bullet : the Lone Ranger and transmedia brand licensing / Avi Santo. — First edition.
pages cm — (Texas film and media studies series)
Includes bibliographical references and index.
ISBN 978-0-292-77253-3 (cloth : alk. paper)
ISBN 978-0-292-77254-0 (pbk. : alk. paper)
ISBN 978-1-4773-0396-2 (library e-book)
ISBN 978-1-4773-0397-9 (non-library e-book)
1. Lone Ranger (Fictitious character) 2. Product management. 3. License agreements. 4. Character merchandising. 5. Branding (Marketing). I. Title. II. Series: Texas film and media studies series.
HF5415.15.S36 2015
658.8′27—dc23

2014040041

doi:10.7560/772533

To my favorite cow folk—Estelle and Hedy—You've finally made me admit to myself that I do in fact love the Lone Ranger

Contents

Acknowledgments

This book took far longer to complete than I ever could have anticipated. I hope it is because I had a lot of insightful things to say and not because I am longwinded. Either way, the book is long (but a quick read, I promise), so these acknowledgments will be short. Let me begin by thanking the archives and their wonderfully helpful staffs, without whom I'd never have found and gathered the materials needed to write a book of this sort: the Detroit Public Library's Burton Historical Collection, the American Heritage Center at the University of Wyoming, the William H. Hanon Library at Loyola Marymount University, the Howard Gotlieb Archival Research Center at Boston University, and the Donnelley and Lee Library at Lake Forest College.

I am also appreciative of the opportunities I have been given by several scholarly journals and online platforms to publish parts of this research: *Cinema Journal* (then editor Heather Hendershot), *Critical Studies in Media Communication* (then editors Kent Ono and Ronald Jackson), *In Media Res* (then editor Alisa Perren), *Journal of Consumer Culture* (editor Steven Miles), *Popular Communication* (then-editors Jonathan Gray, Lee Harrington, and Cornell Sandvoss), and *Television & New Media* (editor Vicki Mayer). In each case, my argument was greatly improved by submitting to the peer review process. I am also grateful for the guidance and patience I have received from the University of Texas Press, and in particular, series editor Tom Schatz, as well as for the helpful feedback I've received from the anonymous reviewers of this manuscript.

Also, a special shout-out to the undergraduate and graduate research assistants who spent time—some of it unpaid—creating a database of scanned documents, searching for obscure bibliographic information, copyediting, and trolling the Internet: Tyler Deatley, Lynn Feigenbaum,

Timothy Kines, Amberly Pescek, Katherine Skophammer, and Lisa Webster.

Thanks to the colleagues and mentors who took many hours of their time to brainstorm ideas, read (multiple) drafts, offer critical feedback and words of encouragement, share intel, and otherwise serve as inspiring role models: Jenifer Alonzo, Hector Amaya, Tim Anderson, Robert Arnett, Kyle Barnett, Mary Beltran, Alexis Carreiro, John Downing, Gary Edgerton, Kathleen Fitzpatrick, Jonathan Gray, Hollis Griffin, Karen Gustafson, Fran Hassencahl, Dana Heller, Catherine Johnson, Derek Johnson, Jeffrey P. Jones, Michael Kackman, Mary Celeste Kearney, Derek Kompare, Christopher Lucas, Jason Mittell, Afsheen Nomai, Roberta Pearson, Allison Perlman, Alisa Perren, Jennifer Petersen, Margaret Pitts, Burton Saint-John III, Thomas Schatz, Greg Smith, Janet Staiger, Craig Stewart, Joseph Straubhaar, and David Uskovich.

Finally, a special thank-you to the people in my life who have shared their love, offered me repose, and never snickered at the work I do or lost faith in my ability to do it well. When this project began, I was in a relationship with Joan Miller of Austin, Texas. I am so very pleased that we remained friends even after I moved away (we even got married on the same day, but to different people). As I finish this project, I am so grateful to have Nikki Kilgore be a part of this moment. She has made the past five years—with its many ups and downs—joyful, and she has put up with the insanity that comes with being married to an academic (plus she plays a mean electric bass).

Selling the Silver Bullet

CHAPTER 1

Hi-Yo Licensing

Introduction

In October 1940, Armstrong's Linoleum Floors took out a full-page color ad in *Better Homes & Gardens* (see Figure 1.1) promoting a new bedroom design modeled after the Lone Ranger. He was the masked cowboy hero who, along with his Native American companion, Tonto, and his powerful steed, Silver, defended the Old West against criminals and charlatans, always leaving behind a silver bullet as his calling card. Originating as a radio series in 1933, by 1940 the Lone Ranger had become a cross-media star, appearing in comic strips, comic books, adult and juvenile novels, and film serials. The "Masked Man"—as he was consistently called—was also a marketing phenomenon, rivaling Mickey Mouse as one of the most successfully licensed and merchandised children's properties in the United States.

As pictured, Armstrong's Lone Ranger–inspired room featured walls painted blue with an accompanying oversized fluorescent portrait print of the cowboy hero astride Silver and a green-checkered-linoleum floor with a close-up of Silver's head as the center square. The remainder of the room was decked out in a Western motif, with a wicker chair, plaid sheets, a bullhorn-shaped curtain rod, and various accoutrements befitting a cowboy enthusiast neatly placed throughout, including boots, a handkerchief, a leather belt, a Stetson hat, a horse whip, a banjo, a white horse figurine, and some spurs. Each of these items corresponded with Lone Ranger merchandise sold by licensees other than Armstrong. In fact, upon closer inspection, the visible tag for the cowboy boots clearly marked it as an official Lone Ranger product. Much more clearly marked as Lone Ranger paraphernalia was the framed Lone Ranger Safety Club certificate hanging on the back wall.

Figure 1.1. Armstrong Linoleum Lone Ranger flooring ad, *Better Homes & Gardens*, October 1940. Author's collection.

The Lone Ranger Safety Club was affiliated with *The Lone Ranger* radio program and paid for by its sponsors. The Masked Man's corporate owners, the Lone Ranger Incorporated (LRI), used the Safety Club ingeniously to promote a Lone Ranger lifestyle that gave meaning to the hundreds of licensed products bearing the Lone Ranger's likeness. These included Armstrong's Linoleum flooring and wall art. Not insignificantly, the ad features two radio sets, one prominently bathed in sunlight underneath the bedroom window and the other breaking up the ad's copy. The second radio image is accompanied by a drawing of a small boy decked out in Western attire playing with the dial as the words "Hi-Yo-Silver," the Lone Ranger's trademarked catchphrase, literally exit the box and cross over into the material world. Armstrong's tagline mimics this movement from ethereal fantasy to lived experience, informing mothers, "Now your Lone Ranger can live in the West . . . right in his own room." In this manner, Lone Ranger licensed merchandise was positioned as the conduit for making the Masked Man's radio adventures real by allowing enthusiasts to embody their hero's attributes.

Radios are not the only doubled images in the ad. Directly underneath Armstrong's tagline is a second image of the Lone Ranger riding Silver, this one in color and bearing LRI's corporate copyright. It is the very image that adorned the vast majority of Lone Ranger licensed products and packaging in the late 1930s and early 1940s. Originally distributed as a giveaway to radio listeners in 1936, the drawing was repurposed by LRI to serve as an easily recognizable unifying brand image. Since many children likely first acquired the drawing by writing in to their local radio station, its subsequent appearance on hundreds of products likely made these objects seem like natural extensions of the radio adventures. In 1938, LRI embarked on a "cooperative consumer advertising campaign," with twenty-three manufacturers all producing goods under the licensed title "Trading Post" and bearing the Lone Ranger brand image.[1] By February 1939, the number of product licensees had grown to sixty-two, and by 1941, LRI had negotiated an impressive seventy-four separate merchandising licenses for the Lone Ranger.[2] Lone Ranger Trading Posts were set up in department stores like Gimbel's in New York City, aggregating merchandise from multiple manufacturers under a unified banner while also providing shoppers with both immersive and extractable experiences. Gimbel's set up a makeshift silver mine where shoppers could see the Lone Ranger's "helpers" forge his mythic silver bullets and could pose for a photo with a nine-foot wooden likeness of the Masked Man, available for pickup "right beside the counter selling Lone Ranger outfits from $1.98 to $6.98, complete with masks."[3]

Meanwhile, LRI encouraged radio sponsors and other third-party media licensees for Lone Ranger comic strips and film serials to work with retailers in promoting new Lone Ranger experiences.[4] This generated what Eileen Meehan has termed a "commercial intertext" in which

Figure 1.2. A drawing of the Lone Ranger riding Silver was initially distributed as a giveaway item to radio listeners. Author's collection.

Figure 1.3. The 1936 Lone Ranger giveaway drawing was used as a branded image on radio sponsor marketing and sales materials throughout the late 1930s and early 1940s. This 1938 cutout for Schultze's Bakery's Butter-Nut Bread was used as a display item in grocery stores. Author's collection.

the radio program was the key to generating interest in a much more expansive Lone Ranger lifestyle brand.[5] The end result was a kind of paratextual synergy in which every encounter with the brand prepared consumers for the next one and in many instances guided them toward that next encounter (see Figures 1.2–1.9).[6]

At this point, you might be asking why this book begins with a description of an advertisement for Lone Ranger–branded merchandise rather than with the radio text that seemingly inspired this ancillary product. Simply put, the Lone Ranger's value for LRI exceeded his popular radio adventures. In fact, the cowboy icon was imagined almost from the outset as a lifestyle brand whose textual exploits were primarily a means of generating exposure for the property, which in turn opened up sponsorship and merchandising opportunities for its owners. While accounts of the Lone Ranger's popularity and iconic status typically approach the figure as embodying a particular—if also malleable—set of mythic/ideological qualities that resonated (or failed to resonate) with the American public,[7] very few accounts exist that assess the Lone Ranger's popularity as intellectual property (IP).[8]

It is often assumed that increasing trends toward horizontal integration and technological convergence within our media industries, dating

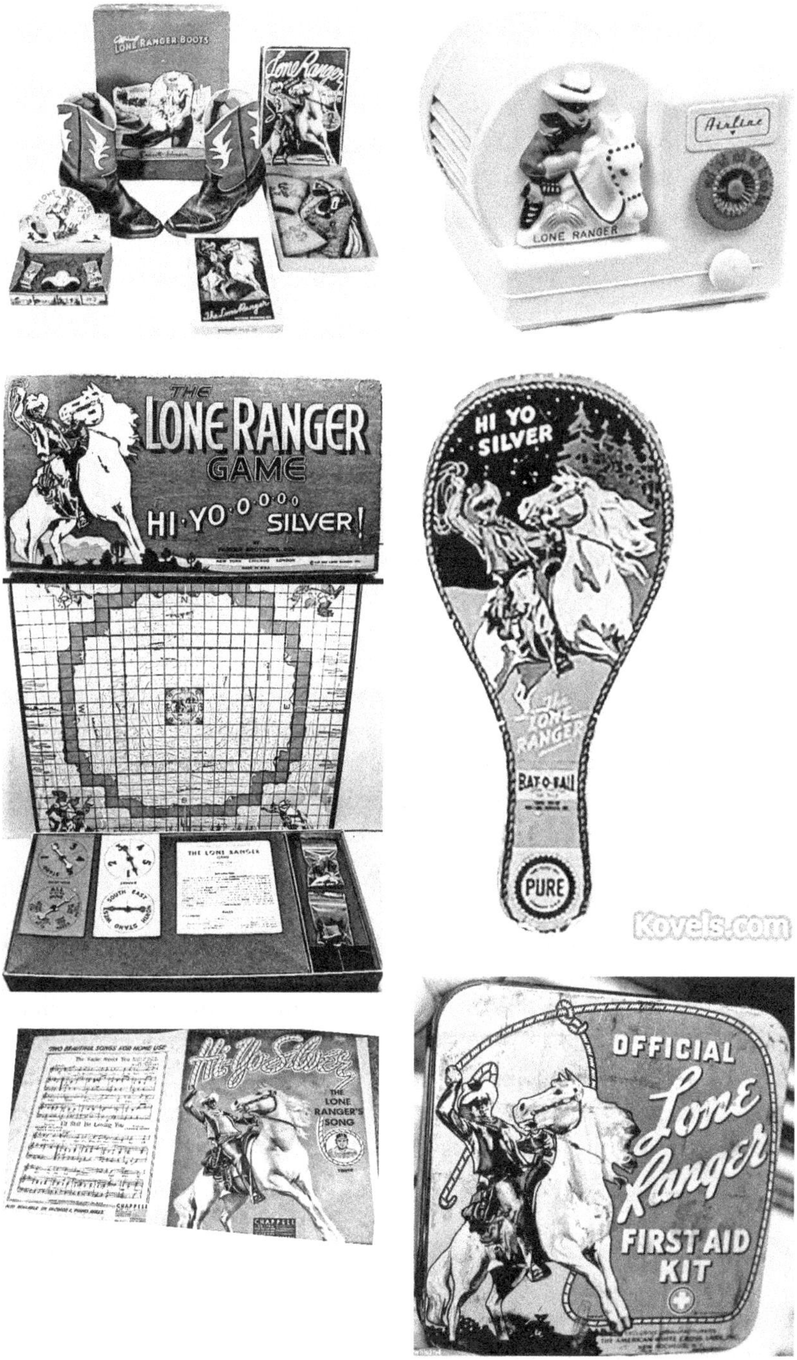

Figures 1.4–1.9. The same image was used as a unifying brand for the 1938 "Trading Post" Cooperative Consumer Advertising Campaign and was featured on a wide array of products, including Lone Ranger boots, gun holsters, printing sets, viewfinders, board games, sheet music, radio sets, bat-o-ball paddles, and first aid kits. Several of these items can be seen strewn around the room in the Armstrong Linoleum Lone Ranger bedroom advertisement.

back to the late 1960s and early 1990s respectively, drive IP management strategies. Scholars have argued that during this period, media conglomerates shifted away from producing medium-specific texts toward investing in "content" that could traverse previously bounded media forms.[9] Yet as the Lone Ranger/Armstrong Linoleum example suggests, IP was both extended and coordinated across media and merchandising platforms long before conglomeration and convergence became industry buzzwords. Though conglomeration and convergence have made cross-media brand extension more common (and perhaps more commonsensical), many efforts to cultivate investment among both consumers and licensees in cross-media entertainment franchises, in which stories told across a range of media forms are linked together by a shared affiliation with a brand, can be found throughout the first half of the twentieth century.

The Lone Ranger was by no means an isolated instance of carefully orchestrated brand management and cross-media marketing in the 1930s. In 1933–1934, John Dille, president of the National Newspaper Syndicate, had a special Buck Rogers short film screened at the World's Fair. He generated dozens of new licenses by promoting his futuristic brand at a venue celebrating the wonders of new technologies.[10] In 1936, Dille had another Buck Rogers short film made and screened in several department store windows where Buck Rogers merchandise was sold.[11] In 1935, under the guidance of Herman "Kay" Kamen, head of Walt Disney Enterprises, the company's licensing and merchandising arm, Disney released Snow White and the Seven Dwarfs merchandise two years before the actual film as advance promotion for the company's first feature-length motion picture.[12] In 1937, licensor Stephen Slesinger engineered a cross-property promotional campaign by having a licensee selling Tarzan-branded ice cream give away original Buck Rogers, Tailspin Tommy, and Ella Cinders storybooks in exchange for collecting and sending in a dozen ice cream lids, effectively introducing fans of one property to the others that Slesinger managed.[13] Slesinger and his wife Shirley Slesinger-Lasswell were also responsible for introducing Winnie the Pooh products to American audiences through the creation of radio (1933) and later live action television projects (1960) intended to call attention to the character's merchandisable personality and distinguish it from the myriad teddy bears marketed to children and their parents.[14] In fact, the list of "innovations" and "innovators" in the management of character brands in the first half of the twentieth century is so long, at some point we must accept that this was less a series of unique experiments than a routine set of business practices commonly adhered to by a loosely organized licensing field.

Selling the Silver Bullet offers a sustained case study of the Lone Ranger as character license from 1933 to 2013 in order to trace how the fields of licensing, merchandising, and brand management have operated within shifting industrial and sociohistorical conditions that continue to redefine how the business of entertainment functions. Through the prism of the Lone Ranger, this book makes the case that in order to understand how iconic characters gain and retain their status as cultural commodities, scholars must pay greater attention to the work done by so-called peripheral consumer product and licensing divisions in (selectively) extending iconic characters' reach and in cultivating investment in these characters among potential stakeholders. In doing so, this book productively instructs readers on the shifting value and roles of character licensing across a number of intertwining cultural industries—most notably, radio, television, film, comic books, comic strips, and toys—from the prenetwork to the postnetwork eras, and from the studio system to industrial conglomeration.

Complicating Licensing

Through licensing, IP owners are able to extend a property's reach into almost every area of consumer life without having to invest in manufacturing infrastructure or distribution networks. Licensing agreements typically involve a contract signed between a minimum of two parties, in which licensors give the licensee(s) permission to use the name and/or image of their intellectual property for a specified purpose, for a limited amount of time, and within agreed-upon geographic and product market boundaries. In exchange for an upfront fee, a guaranteed minimum payment, and a royalty percentage of either the net or gross profits, licensees reap the benefits of associating their wares with a recognizable icon that comes with a built-in fan base, which in turn helps their product stand out within a competitive marketplace. The licensor does not relinquish ownership over the intellectual property.

While anything that is proprietarily owned can be licensed, ranging from artwork and music to fashion labels and trademarks (e.g., the Coca-Cola insignia, which generated $850 million in branded merchandise retail sales in 2010),[15] entertainment and character brand licensing is particularly profitable. In 2011, character and entertainment brand licensing, at $48 billion, accounted for 43.86 percent of all retail sales of licensed merchandise while earning property owners $2.48 billion in royalty revenue.[16] Overall, in 2011 the strongest product categories for character and entertainment licenses were toys/games (25.5% of royalty revenue, or $632.4 million), software/video games (13.5% or $334.8 million), apparel (10% or $248 million), food/beverage (8% or $198.4 million), and gifts/novelties (7% or $173.6 million).[17] Other licensing categories include accessories, footwear, home décor, health/beauty, housewares, music/video, infant products, promotions, publishing, sports goods, paper/school supplies, and other. A company like Disney is capable of extending its character and corporate brands into almost every one of these markets, ranging from toys, games, and apparel to "non-character products with subtle inspiration drawn from either motion pictures or Walt Disney's lifestyle aura," including high-end fashion and jewelry lines and home furnishings.[18]

When media scholars talk about licensing, the usual refrain is less than flattering. It is viewed as lucrative but essentially noncreative, leeching off the popularity of established and successful characters and texts—and largely concerned with contract oversight. Jane Gaines refers to licensing as a "parasitic industry," a description intended to call attention to how it profits off of the creative labor performed by others.[19] Offering a more literal but no less negative description of the field, Norma Pecora suggests that while the claim that licensing is paramount to stealing is simplistic, it is "nonetheless the 'philosophical' foundation to licensing."[20] Though it is not my aim in this project to recuperate licensing as a benevolent and heroic profession, it is clear that efforts to paint licensors as villains and opportunists greatly oversimplify the work they do in popularizing IP with licensees. In suggesting that only the pursuit of profit governs how the field operates, scholars risk overlooking the myriad ways that cultural systems shape economic activities, imbuing both products and processes with social value well beyond (but also intrinsic to) their monetary value.

Licensing has historically served as a key site for transforming intellectual properties into cultural commodities. As a 1935 article in the *New Yorker* detailing the phenomenal popularity of Winnie the Pooh succinctly exclaims, "if the image and the name of Winnie-the-Pooh today are unforgettable, the blame rests not so much with [the character's creator] Mr. Milne as with [the property's licensor] Mr. Slesinger."[21] Indeed, Slesinger was the one who dressed up Pooh in his iconic red shirt in an effort to distinguish the character from other teddy bears on the market, a tactical marketing decision with decidedly creative and cultural impact.

Most historical accounts of the character-licensing field begin with the phenomenally successful 1977 Star Wars merchandising campaign. Star

Wars is generally seen as having changed everything, supposedly breaking so radically with past licensing and merchandising endeavors that they are now scarcely worthy of mention. As Karen Raugust puts it, "Many observers point to the licensing program surrounding the movie *Star Wars*, released in 1977, as the start of the licensing business as we know it today . . . people began to think of this business as a career opportunity."[22] While Star Wars was—and still is—an incredible merchandising success, earning nearly $13 billion in retail sales of licensed merchandise alone from 1977 to 2007,[23] it is important not to assume that its unprecedented market accomplishments are proof that merchandising and licensing strategies had been undeveloped previously. The occupational purviews and tactics embraced, imagined, and fought over by licensors prior to the field's emergence as a power player were essential to crystallizing assumptions, now taken for granted, about the value that character brands possess as cultural commodities.

There is practically no scholarly history analyzing character licensing and entertainment brand management practices prior to *Star Wars*. Jane Gaines, Gary Cross, Mark C. Rogers, and Ian Gordon each acknowledge the significance of licensing and merchandising to the development of the American film, toy, comic book, and newspaper comic strip syndication industries in the late nineteenth and early twentieth centuries.[24] Other rare and valuable exceptions to the dearth of in-depth analysis on this topic include Jason Scott's work on the promotion and exploitation of character-oriented media franchises in the first half of the twentieth century, Chris Anderson's work on Disneyland as commercial intertext, Mary Celeste Kearney's analysis of how *A Date with Judy* and *Corliss Archer* were promoted across media markets in the 1940s, Michael Kackman's work on the international expansion of the Hopalong Cassidy brand by William Boyd Enterprises in the 1950s, and Cathy Johnson's work on BBC Radio's licensing and merchandising programs in the 1940s and 1950s.[25]

Selling the Silver Bullet aims to show how many of the transmedia experiences documented and celebrated by contemporary scholars of convergent media find their generative precursors in the tactical work done by character licensors many decades earlier. These range from opportunities to drill down into a story through extra-textuals that provide dedicated fans with additive comprehension possibilities, to the development of participatory brand communities and immersive world-building experiences.[26]

My goal, however, is not to make a facile point about contemporary brand management strategies having historical parallels. Derek Johnson is correct in his assertion that it is misleading to read the coordinated media extension of 1930s properties like Little Orphan Annie, Popeye, or Dick Tracy through the lens of contemporary discourses.[27] Still, it would also be a mistake to think that such concepts do not find their genealogical roots in earlier moments. In contrast to prevailing assumptions that brand management practices were born of conglomeration and convergence, Johnson's own work demonstrates how contemporary media franchise development strategies are less the outcome of conglomeration than the impetus for industry restructuring.[28]

Hence, my intention in *Selling the Silver Bullet* is to situate the development of character licensing and entertainment brand management practices within their proper historical, institutional, and cultural contexts and to unravel the economic, legal, industrial, and social mechanisms that shaped the practices character licensors employed pre-conglomeration and pre-convergence, always with an eye to how such tactics would later become commonsense strategies for extending IP. While LRI's brand extension arsenal included variations on what today might be called transmedia storytelling, branded entertainment, additive comprehension, and commercial intertexts, such precursors to the contemporary moment developed as tactical maneuvers rooted within their particular historical and industrial contexts. Indeed, LRI's greatest innovations often came in response to crises that threatened the entity's autonomy, authority, and market share and were intended to leverage its position against competitors. As such, in drawing comparisons between past and present tactics, surface-level similarities must be contextualized to identify their very different generative mechanisms. Though contemporary brand management practices are informed by past iterations, these typically take the form of residual inspirations rather than a direct lineage. Tracing the Lone Ranger's career as IP allows for a nuanced assessment of the ways that character-licensing firms and consumer product divisions have responded to changing cultural and economic conditions over the past eighty years, in turn altering perceptions about the creative and managerial authority these so-called ancillary units wield.

As intellectual properties eclipse the products bearing their names and become the primary purveyors of both meaning and value, there needs to be an accompanying shift in focus among scholars toward investigating licensing sites as contested spaces for delineating and negotiating creative authority. Corporate authorship is not merely a dogmatic assertion of control over IP via contractual and legal instruments (though these are certainly effective tools), but also a valuable form of brand stewardship. Even as corporations displace human authors and artists as the primary legal owners and economic beneficiaries of branded characters and stories that circulate under their imprimatur, they stake their authority on their managerial acumen. They do so by seeking to redefine categories of authorship in the legal sphere, but also by presenting themselves to consumers and creative laborers as the ultimate trustees of a character brand's essence.

Brand management is never simply or only about successful profit maximization strategies (though, to be certain, making money is always the desired outcome), but also about historically and socially contingent beliefs about what "values" are economically valuable. In his critique of Horkheimer and Adorno's economic determinism in studying the "culture industry," Bernard Miège argues that scholars need to pay greater attention to the cultural dimensions of the production process as shaping the often incoherent ideologies of media products. Miège suggests that cultural and social dynamics not only outweigh economic factors in creating cultural commodities, but these contentious and varied cultural and social interactions often also shape economic rationales.[29] Meanwhile, Paul Du Gay asserts, "The production of culture cannot be reduced to a question of 'economics' alone. Processes of production are themselves cultural phenomena in that they are assemblages of meaningful practices that construct certain ways for people to conceive and conduct themselves in an organizational context."[30] Licensing agents play key cultural roles in helping licensees understand both the value of character and entertainment properties among consumers as well as how to translate that value for different market conditions.

Most of the cultural managerial work that licensors "do" hides in plain sight, distilled through various overt and mundane practices. It is only by treating what seem like run-of-the-mill economic and promotional practices common to the licensing profession—drawing up contracts, assembling merchandising guides, taking out ads in industry press organs, etc.—as tactical and cultural resources that we can begin to recognize how these sites of inter- and intra-industry exchange shape expressive culture and define the occupational identities that licensors embrace.

For example, by the early 1950s, LRI had developed a fairly standardized licensing agreement template that could be adapted for any number of Lone Ranger products and productions—ranging from branded flashlights to public appearances and from comic books to television—merely by filling in different licensee names, dates, dollars, and percentages and referencing the appropriate subclauses pertaining to the particular item being commissioned. Also included in every contract was "Schedule B: Descriptions," which contained detailed information on the Lone Ranger, Tonto, and the rest of the supporting characters' appearances and habits, which licensees were expected to adhere to in their representational strategies. The Lone Ranger's height, weight, age, and facial structure, the look in his eyes, the shape of his nose, the color and cut of his hair, the sound of his voice, the way he walked, and the types of clothing he wore were all spelled out. Of course, some of the details about the Lone Ranger's appearance had changed from earlier contracts. In the late 1930s the Masked Man was described as 5′11″ and 170 pounds, rugged yet also clean-shaven.[31] By 1951, the Lone Ranger was expected to be between 6′ and 6′2″ and 190–210 pounds with "no fat; broad shoulders and lean hips." Though still described as clean-shaven, this version of the Lone Ranger was no longer rugged, but "well-groomed, does not wear chaps. Wears high-heeled cowboy boots with trousers tucked into the tops."[32]

These small representational changes not only demonstrate how brand formulas are often adjusted in response to changing sociohistorical and production contexts; they also complicate the perception that licensing agreements are merely transactional and legal documents. To be certain, LRI's numerous contracts with its licensees were filled with their fair share of sometimes indecipherable and often dry jargon about payment methods and schedules, but far from being *only* economic agreements, they were also clearly sites of cultural and creative deliberation. Schedule B not only structured licensee creative practices; the changing descriptions of the Masked Man and his colleagues also reveal how licensors sought to simultaneously regulate and adapt properties in accordance with shifting cultural ideals. As such, these documents are also often sites of struggle and debate between licensors and licensees over creative authority and third-party authorial rights to both property and profit.

Above all else, licensors are in the business of cultivating investment among stakeholders in a property's attributes and value. Much as in agricultural work, cultivating investment involves not only planting seeds with potential licensees and convincing them that a property can be made to work within differentiated markets, but also teaching licensees how to properly extract value from the property. While the value of planting apple trees is obvious (you get apples), variations in climate, soil type, or the intended use of the fruit (for juice, applesauce, or as produce, etc.) require different cultivation techniques. Planting the trees in the wrong soil or too close together, irrigating improperly, or picking the apples too early all risk spoiling the fruit. The same holds true for how licensors go about their jobs of establishing value for their properties. Licensors often work to teach licensees, whether via the stick or the carrot, the contract or consult, how to properly (and improperly) take advantage of brand attributes.

According to a December 1966 article published in *True* magazine, character licensors play many different roles in extending intellectual property across markets: "The licensing agent acts as legal advisor, salesman, merchandising expert, package designer, promoter, advertising consultant, brusher-offer, whooper-upper and Dutch Uncle."[33] Though offered up somewhat comically, this list of licensor activities suggests a fairly complex relationship with licensees, who are seen as needing occasional "brushing off" and substantial oversight. This perspective hints at the ways licensing can, at times, be a contested terrain, wherein contracts are not only violated, but their interpretation is the subject of heated debate. Under such conditions, licensors' authority is repeatedly challenged, and they must readjust their tactics in response to licensee feedback.

Licensors stake their creative authority not only on their ability to mediate between IP and licensees but also on their skill in translating, and hence monetizing, a character brand's appeal with consumers. Licensors present themselves as being uniquely positioned to help licensees understand what makes a particular character brand popular with consumers. Put another way, licensors' creative authority is a function of their status as cultural intermediaries, acting as both brand interpreters and advocates for (imagined) consumers, translating the brand's (still inherent) social and cultural value for licensees.

Often this means imposing "commonsense" cultural assumptions onto economic processes. For example, in an interview, Jay Emmett, former president of the Licensing Corporation of America, who in the 1960s was responsible for negotiating merchandising rights for James Bond, Batman, and Superman, dismissed my suggestion to license Superman's name and image for a line of prophylactics (tagline: "for the man of steel") as my somehow misunderstanding the property's "true" consumer appeal with children and parents. Though Emmett acknowledged that there was likely a market for such a product, he saw associating Superman with sexuality as ultimately harmful to the brand's overall value, both economic and social.[34] In rejecting my offer, Emmett revealed how the Superman brand's economic value was directly correlated with its perceived social value as superimposed onto an imagined consumer group. And yet his attempt to correct my misunderstanding of why Superman was popular never deviated from the premise that the qualities and attributes that Superman possessed were inherent, rather than selectively imposed by either him or the property's corporate owner. Instead, Emmett continued to maintain that he was just there to ensure that the Man of Steel's meanings were being properly translated across markets: Superman sold himself.

Licensors see themselves as protecting both brand and consumer from those would-be-licensees who cannot appreciate the property's popular attributes. As Nicole Garrison-Sprenger notes regarding licensing Superman merchandise, "a clothing manufacturer that puts the [Superman] logo on a cheap pair of pants that rips or frays after a few wears is negating the 'strength' aspect [of the character], essentially throwing Kryptonite at the Superman brand."[35]

Within licensor trade rituals, or the mechanisms through which licensors construct certain truths about their properties as well as their own occupational identities, the brand is often described as possessing qualities that inspire acts of creative expression and consumption. According to this division of labor, the licensor merely appears to chaperone the brand on its journey, performing a series of secondary tasks designed to facilitate a pleasant and profitable experience. Yet it is through these "accompaniments" that the licensor emerges as brand advocate, guardian, and steward, authorized to teach licensees how to decipher a property's attributes and entrusted with both safeguarding and rearranging brand formulas to best take advantage of their market appeal. Where Pierre Bourdieu saw the "charismatic ideology . . . of creation" as the chief stumbling block in conducting rigorous research into the production of cultural goods, when it comes to understanding how IP accrues value, the difficulty actually lies in the constant erasure of its authorial markers.[36]

Licensor authority resides in its ability to provide licensees with the right interpretive framework for gaining inspiration from licensed source material. Presented as "common sense," such responses demonstrate what Timothy Havens identifies as the impact of "industry lore" on cultural production and distribution. According to Havens, industry lore refers to "the conventional knowledge among industry insiders about what kinds of media culture are and are not possible, and what audiences that culture will and will not attract."[37] Industry lore encompasses the educative stories that media industry professionals tell one another about what makes for a successful product. Appearing in trade press interviews and self-serving biographies, circulating at industry parties, trade shows, and closed-door meetings, and even finding their way into merchandising guides and licensing agreements, these shared cautionary and celebratory stories about consumer tastes and desires often guide licensor assessments of appropriate expansion outlets, providing interpretive frameworks for making sense of market conditions.

Whether through legal battles against trademark infringers or through the array of merchandising and writer's guides it produced, LRI repeatedly linked its corporate authority to a deep-seated understanding of the Lone Ranger and its skill in guiding licensees to extract the Masked Man's merchandisable attributes. Through their managerial acumen, corporate entities like LRI positioned themselves as cultural intermediaries capable of translating brand attributes for differentiated industrial and cultural contexts and channeling consumer needs and desires into appropriate production outlets.

Why LRI?

While this is certainly a book about the Lone Ranger as IP, LRI is the true star of this particular project. It was first formed in 1935 as an independent licensing operation and still exists today, albeit as a subdivision within a subdivision of DreamWorks Entertainment's DreamWorks Classics. In between, the company has also been owned and operated by the Jack Wrather Corporation (1954–1985), the Southbrook International Television Company (1985–1994), Broadway Video (1994–2000), and Classic Media Incorporated (2000–2012). LRI's longevity and multiple permutations allow for a sustained and nuanced analysis of how the character-licensing field has changed over the past eighty years, from semi-autonomous and existing at the interstices of different media and manufacturing industries, to integrated within media conglomerates (while being subordinate to other divisions within those conglomerates). Indeed, one of the primary reasons that I selected LRI and the Lone Ranger as case studies is that they offer a unique opportunity to trace how character licensing, brand management, and consumer product extension practices have been rationalized and operationalized within the entertainment industries at different historical junctures.

I have also chosen to focus on LRI precisely because it is not Disney or Warner Bros.—companies whose continued successes often obscure the complex managerial labor that goes into cultivating investment in character brands not named Mickey Mouse or Superman—although in the early 1940s, the Lone Ranger's popularity easily rivaled that of the Man of Steel or the Mouse House's trademarked mascot. Whereas most scholarship on contemporary convergence culture and branding tends to celebrate successful franchises and thus oversimplifies innovation as a causal argument, the Lone Ranger's struggles over the past half century make possible an analysis of brand management tactics in adverse conditions. The divergent paths taken by LRI, DC Comics (acquired by Warner Communications Inc. in 1971), and Disney reveal a great deal about how the consolidation of industrial practices around character brands in the second half of the twentieth century and beyond have made it increasingly difficult for independent IP owners to operate from positions of strength. The Lone Ranger's rise to prominence as a national cultural icon starting in the late 1930s through the early 1960s, as well as its protracted devaluation over the past five decades, owes much to the ways the property has been managed by LRI's various owners as well as to their respective positions within the entertainment industries at different historical moments, including their diminishing direct control over production and distribution outlets for promoting the property. The Lone Ranger's topsy-turvy career reveals how the licensing field has both shaped and been shaped by the growing centrality of IP to entertainment industry expansion. It situates the field of character licensing within broader shifts in the entertainment business, from corporate capitalism to conglomeration to contemporary brand networks and the knowledge economy.

Perhaps most importantly, LRI is a corporate entity that at different junctures has been both typical and exceptional in how it went about its business. Over time, LRI's position within the entertainment industry landscape has shifted from emergent to dominant to residual, in turn generating very different position-taking strategies on the parts of its various owners.[38] LRI's shifting status and reputation have informed its brand management practices.

In the late 1930s, LRI bucked the trend toward centralized, national media sponsorship, instead embracing localization and resource recycling as an alternate means of developing the Lone Ranger into an American icon and merchandising phenomenon. LRI used Lone Ranger giveaways, premiums, and other extra-textual materials to cultivate investment in and prepare licensees and consumers for future encounters with the Lone Ranger brand. The Lone Ranger Safety Club was designed to promote an expansive Lone Ranger lifestyle brand that not only linked together the Masked Man's myriad licenses, but also struck a balance between the civic values the Lone Ranger advocated and the property's commercial value. Most importantly, Lone Ranger Safety Clubs taught licensees and Lone Ranger fans how to create local franchise outposts that were linked together as part of a broader Lone Ranger brand community (see Chapter 3).

In the 1940s, LRI established its managerial acumen and cultural/creative authority through a range of practices, from drafting contracts and writer's guides to merchandising packets and trade advertising, all of which repeatedly positioned the company as best able to speak on behalf of the Lone Ranger and translate the character's appeal with consumers for licensees. LRI also established its corporate authority through a series of legal battles linking its marketing efforts and management strategies with its ownership rights (see Chapter 4).

By the 1950s, LRI held a dominant position in the field and deployed a much more conservative managerial style, aimed at controlling how the Lone Ranger was portrayed across platforms and eliminating any potential negative associations. The company exemplified the ways that cultural containment within the United States would produce a set of managerial strategies and styles that would both stabilize character brands and attempt to fortify the positions of their corporate owners in the face of social and industrial reconfigurations. LRI's yearlong 1948 Frontier Town marketing campaign demonstrates how the company responded to cultural containment anxieties by offering parents and children a safe haven *within* the Lone Ranger storyworld (see Chapter 5).

In 1954, the Jack Wrather Corporation (JWC) acquired LRI as well as all rights to the Lone Ranger IP for a then-record $3 million (that's 24.4 million in 2010 dollars, according to the Consumer Price Index converter). Billing the Lone Ranger as a defender of the American heritage, JWC emerged from the postwar period managing a valuable but aging heritage brand. In the 1970s, the Lone Ranger encountered an identity crisis as the attributes that had made the property so valuable for three decades began to lose their luster. The Lone Ranger's failed comeback efforts during this period were, however, less the result of brand stagnation than of overdetermined attempts to rejuvenate the masked hero that misunderstood the continued consumer power of an older generation of brand loyalists. Though the Lone Ranger would see its least successful iterations during this period, culminating in the disastrous *Legend of the Lone Ranger* (1981) blockbuster, the period was actually characterized by tremendous innovation spurred by the need to reboot the property. As other properties—now overseen by powerful conglomerates—eclipsed the Lone Ranger's merchandising prowess, efforts to revitalize the property would produce some ideas that were truly ahead of their time, but also a fair amount of misguided replication of competitor strategies. JWC's struggles to translate the property for changing industrial conditions and consumer tastes in the 1970s and 1980s ultimately resulted not only in the Lone Ranger's diminished reputation as a licensable commodity, but also in JWC's diminished reputation as brand steward (see Chapter 6).

By the new millennium, the Lone Ranger had joined the ranks of hundreds of underperforming heritage brands still perceived by stakeholders as possessing value but lacking a clear path toward being effectively monetized. As the property's status has diminished, so too has the creative and managerial authority previously held by its corporate overseers. Indeed, Classic Media Incorporated (CMI) would grant licensees significant leeway in updating the property. This was certainly the case with the 2013 Lone Ranger feature film—produced by Jerry Bruckheimer, distributed by Disney, and starring Johnny Depp as Tonto—where CMI ceded both script approval and merchandising rights to its more powerful clients. As such, the current configuration of the industry has shaped how the property might be marketed and managed. In spite of the Lone Ranger's diminished—but by no means vanquished—status, many of the tactics employed by LRI in popularizing and extending the property from the 1930s through the 1970s have now achieved "commonsense" status within the character-licensing field (see Chapter 7).

In many ways, the Lone Ranger's future success now seems to rest on the shoulders of the star talent attached to the property rather than the Masked Man serving as the star attraction, although as the final chapter of this book argues, in the end, character brands retain their symbolic capital even when talent fails to monetize them. Accordingly, despite the 2013 film's box office failings, no one in Hollywood argued that the Lone Ranger brought down Bruckheimer and Depp. Rather, it was they who failed to draw the right kind of inspiration from the property, or so industry trade talk has rationalized the matter. In analyzing the fallout from *The Lone Ranger*'s box office failure, I focus on how reviewers selectively framed the film's shortcomings as simultaneously rooted in efforts to diverge from the property's formula as well as the supposed incommensurability of said formula with contemporary audience sensibilities. I also analyze the lessons learned by Hollywood from the film's failure, which might have far-reaching implications for future tentpole films, which currently serve as the centerpiece of multimedia- and merchandise-driven franchises. Of paramount importance is the lesson never learned: that the Lone Ranger possesses insufficient symbolic capital in today's consumer market. While the entertainment industry seeks out new ways to monetize heritage brands, the assumption remains that the value of these intellectual properties is intact, just untapped (see Chapter 8).

A Note on Materials and Method

A significant challenge in a project tracing character licensing pre-conglomeration and pre-convergence is the lack of public records that identify a particular IP owner's or property's comparable market share. The licensing industry did not start tracking such numbers until the mid-to-late 1980s, when the field finally began to organize as a professional community under the auspices of the International Licensing and Merchandisers' Association (LIMA), formed in 1985. Prior to that point, licensing divisions and IP owners saw one another as competitors and were reticent to share data (though they were certainly not above co-opting successful campaign strategies). And while individual IP management firms like LRI accumulated all sorts of statistics about the power and popularity of their properties, these numbers were rarely placed within a broader industrial or consumer context. Because the primary purpose of these statistics was to promote the Lone Ranger to potential licensees, LRI often came across as self-aggrandizing and oblivious to the existence of other licensed IP except for wanting to show how the Lone Ranger bested them. As such, any claims made about LRI's position within an "industry" that did not truly exist, or the Lone Ranger's market share within that industry, are hard to substantiate through earning statements or consumer sales records.

Instead, the Lone Ranger's success and failure as IP needs to be measured by a different yardstick, one that looks to the character's presence across a wide array of media forms and merchandising categories, not to mention within a broader cultural and symbolic landscape of Americana.

The introduction to this chapter suggests that the Lone Ranger rivaled Mickey Mouse as a cross-media and merchandising phenomenon. Comparing any property to the Disney juggernaut is a risky proposition, so let me be clear: by the late 1930s, the Lone Ranger rivaled Mickey Mouse as licensed IP, but by 1942, Disney already had forty-six separate characters that it licensed, which means that Disney earned substantially more revenue than did LRI. Nevertheless, by 1940, both the Lone Ranger and Mickey Mouse were cross-media stars appearing in films (Mickey starred in 104 animated shorts from 1928 to 1940; the Lone Ranger appeared in two fifteen-part film serials by Republic Pictures), radio (870 *Lone*

Ranger episodes versus 20 episodes of the 1938 *Mickey Mouse's Theatre of the Air*), comic strips (both distributed by the King Features Syndicate), magazines, and novels, with comic books debuting for each in the early 1940s. Both were also merchandising machines. A 1935 article marveled at Mickey's expansion into consumer products, listing fifty-seven separate items available for purchase:

> Shoppers carry Mickey Mouse satchels and briefcases bursting with Mickey Mouse soap, candy, playing cards, bridge favors, hairbrushes, chinaware, alarm clocks and hot water bottles wrapped in Mickey Mouse paper tied with Mickey Mouse ribbon and paid for out of Mickey Mouse purses with savings hoarded in Mickey Mouse banks. They wear Mickey Mouse caps, waists, socks, shoes, slippers, garters, mittens, aprons, bibs, and underthings, and beneath Mickey Mouse rain capes and umbrellas. They go to school where Mickey Mouse desk outfits turn lessons into pleasure. They play with Mickey Mouse velocipedes, footballs, baseballs, bounce balls, bats, catching gloves, boxing gloves, doll houses, doll dishes, tops, blocks, drums, puzzle games, paint sets, sewing sets, drawing sets, stamping sets, jack sets, bubble sets, pull sets, pull toys, push toys, animated toys, tents, camp stools, sand pails, masks, blackboards and balloons.[39]

Comparatively, in 1939, LRI released a list of sixty-four Lone Ranger products available for retailers to stock. Items ranged from toys, board games, and novelty items to clothing and accessories, school supplies, food products, and everything in between (such as first aid kits, bandages, tumblers, flashlights, silver-plated spoons, cups, knives, table glassware, combs, toothbrushes, brushes of all types, books to retail at no more than fifty cents, stationery, and novelty bars of soap).[40] Perhaps most tellingly, in 1934, Disney earned $200,000 in royalties from all the characters it licensed, which at the time included Mickey, Minnie Mouse, Clarabelle Cow, Horace Horsecollar, Donald Duck, Goofy, and Pluto. In 1939, LRI netted $310,000 from licensing only the Lone Ranger and his companions Tonto and Silver.

To celebrate the Lone Ranger's twentieth birthday in 1953, Michigan senator Homer Ferguson honored the hero by entering into the congressional record heartfelt thanks for all the public service work the brand had performed on behalf of children. The Lone Ranger's ubiquity by 1953 caused one author to comment, "The impression that had been accumulated by the twentieth anniversary of the Lone Ranger's creation might reasonably have been that the 'masked man of justice' had become, as his creators put it, 'an American institution.'"[41] This is admittedly a nonscientific gauge that relies more on perception than facts, but in many ways it also captures the essence of how character licensing operates: by cultivating investment among licensees in the symbolic power of particular properties as evidence of their potential sales power with consumers.

In analyzing these cultivation techniques, *Selling the Silver Bullet* draws on a number of archival sources. Chief among them are the George W. Trendle and Raymond Meurer papers housed at the Detroit Public Library as well as the Jack Wrather and Anita Granville Wrather papers housed at Loyola Marymount University. Other collections consulted include the Harold Gray papers and Hank Ketcham papers housed at Boston University (Gray and Ketcham were the creators of Little Orphan Annie and Dennis the Menace), the William Dozier papers at the American Heritage Center at the University of Wyoming (Dozier held the TV rights to the 1960s Batman and Green Hornet), and the NBC papers at the University of Wisconsin at Madison. I analyzed trade correspondence, internal memos, and contracts and merchandising guides assembled to license various character-based and entertainment brands. Additionally, a wide range of popular and industry press sources were consulted, including the licensing industry's internal organ, *License Global!* I reviewed articles about licensing as well as advertisements featuring licensed properties aimed at both consumers and future licensees.

While I extracted information from all of these sources about the business of character licensing at various historical moments, it is their contribution to a cultural analysis of the licensing field that is of greater interest. As such, I read these documents for what they reveal about ever-shifting norms and values guiding economic practices, as well as tensions and anxieties about maintaining authority over a property's core values and markets amid changing economic, industrial, legal, technological, and cultural conditions.[42]

I treat the inter- and intra-industry exchanges between licensors and potential licensees—produced through marketing materials, memos, and other correspondence—as sites of discursive struggle over production meanings and occupational identity formation.[43] These interactions shaped sociohistorical and industrial understandings of cultural commodities and their translation across markets. Exchanges between licensors and licensees also serve as sites where the creative authority vested in licensors is affirmed, contested, or negotiated. They offer "tactical responses" (i.e., reactive and contingent) to shifting "socio-historical and industrial conditions."[44]

In applying some of the sociological tenets advocated by production studies scholars[45] to historical analyses of particular media work cultures, *Selling the Silver Bullet* seeks to answer the call for more historical work investigating the roles of older cultural intermediaries in shaping cultural production and circulation.[46] The underlying goals of production studies are valuable in assessing how particular occupational communities came to define and refine their roles within ever-changing institutional and societal structures. Job categories like "licensor," "licensee," or "brand manager" do not simply get created, but rather, their occupational purviews and functions are negotiated in relation to the material conditions of their practice. Similarly, Paul Du Gay and Michael Pryke assert, "Techniques of 'economic management' do not come ready-made. They have to be invented, stabilized, refined and reproduced."[47] LRI's creative and cultural authority as licensor and steward of the Lone Ranger brand has had to be repeatedly reproduced through the tactical discursive exchange of what Caldwell labels "trade stories" designed to establish its "career capital."[48]

Writing history in such a manner generates a far less stable explanatory framework of successes and failures, as accounts of overarching strategies are displaced by a focus on contingent and fluctuating tactics, in turn revealing how the positions and dispositions held by licensors are always in a state of "becoming" through their labor rather than preceding it. As such, while LRI's managerial labor is the key to understanding how the Lone Ranger became such an iconic cultural commodity, the licensor's actions were often less prescient or ingenious than anxious and reactionary, with tactical innovations and managerial purviews formulated in response to both market instabilities and the need to rationalize shifting societal tastes and values.

The remainder of the book follows a loose chronological order that begins in the early 1930s with the creation of *The Lone Ranger* radio series and ends in the first decades of the twenty-first century with efforts to revive the property. Each chapter is also organized thematically to elucidate a particular set of practices, beliefs, concerns, or struggles central to understanding the importance of character licensing to cross-media interactions and how the field has changed over an eighty-year period. Thus, each chapter looks backward as well as forward in tracing how and why character-licensing strategies change. While all chapters use the Lone Ranger as an anchor, the property and its management exist in a mutually constitutive relationship with other IP extension efforts. Hence, each chapter also situates the licensing of the Lone Ranger in relation to other dominant iconic brands during the same time period.

By the time readers get to the book's final chapters, they will have little doubt about how powerful consumer product extensions and character licensing are to current industrial practices and how important the work done by companies like LRI has been in forging these practices. Along the way, readers will gain important insights into how these seemingly ancillary and peripheral operations accrued and leveraged their managerial acumen at distinct sociohistorical moments and under shifting industrial configurations. By repositioning licensing, merchandising, and character brand management as constitutive of myriad creative and economic practices from the pre- to the postnetwork eras, *Selling the Silver Bullet* tracks the tactical ways corporate authorship over intellectual property has been deployed and negotiated over the past eighty years. Now, let us return to "those thrilling days of yesteryear."

CHAPTER 2

Putting on the Mask: Character Licensing before the Lone Ranger

Introduction

In 1953, George W. Trendle, president of LRI, reminisced about his inspiration for creating the Lone Ranger twenty years earlier, nostalgically recalling his own childhood obsession with dime store Western novels written by the likes of Zane Grey (*The Lone Star Ranger*, 1915) and Clarence E. Mulford (Hopalong Cassidy first appeared in short stories beginning in 1904).[1] Not only were Westerns popular reads during the first decades of the twentieth century, but cowboys were also a popular theme for merchandise, with toy guns and rocking horses inspired by (and inspiring) Western play. What this suggests is that Trendle may have taken inspiration not in the Western as a genre per se, but in the dime store Western as offering a formula that could be exploited in developing a merchandisable character brand. After all, Trendle's ingenuity was in tying together Western-themed entertainment and merchandising through the creation of a cowboy hero whose personality could be branded onto a wide range of products and productions.[2]

This brief chapter establishes the generative mechanisms that led to the creation of both the Lone Ranger and LRI, with a particular focus on the crafting of the Lone Ranger's radio formula. To get to LRI's role in cultivating and managing investment in the Lone Ranger IP, we must first review the development of character licensing in the United States in the late nineteenth and early twentieth centuries. The period from 1880 to 1930 was characterized by tremendous innovation as well as uncertainty over how character brand extensions were to proceed and who possessed the creative and legal authority to craft such merchandising campaigns. LRI and the Lone Ranger's arrival on the scene in the mid 1930s did not kick off the character-licensing craze, but rather, it emerged in response to both popular trends as well as correctives to industrial and social anxieties over managing the popularization of character-based intellectual properties. The chapter serves as a bridge between the theorization of licensing put forward in the introduction and the historically grounded case studies of IP management from the 1930s through today that follow in subsequent chapters.

Character Licensing before the 1930s

The earliest known example of character licensing in the United States—in which a creator's characters were used with permission and compensation to sell someone else's goods—is attributed to Palmer Cox's *The Brownies* (1881), an illustrated set of diminutive characters prone to adventuring, which on November 13, 1883, appeared on the cover of *Harper's Young People* advocating on behalf of Proctor & Gamble's Ivory soap.[3] Indeed, The Brownies were a merchandising phenomenon throughout the 1880s and early 1890s, appearing in over forty ads for Ivory soap; over-the-counter advertising booklets and pamphlets for products as diverse as Pond's Extract, Tarrant's Seltzer, A. No. 1 Chocolate Cream Drops, Willimantic Cotton, and Little Grains for Little People; giveaway trading card inserts for Hawley & Hoops' cocoa and chocolate candy, Armour's Mincemeat, and Upton's Fish glue; and giveaway paper dolls for Lion Coffee and Bee Soap. The Brownies were also licensed as toys and novelties, including dolls, stationery, school supplies, and decidedly more adult products like cigar holders.

As early as 1885, Cox began copyrighting all of his illustrations, retaining rights to his work instead of signing them over to the commercial entity employing his characters. The Brownies were so popular that in 1889, Edward Bok, newly appointed editor of *Ladies Home Journal*, signed Cox to an exclusive contract to draw a full-page Brownies adventure with each issue. Significantly, Bok saw *The Brownies* not just as a draw for readers but as a way to entice advertisers to purchase magazine space.[4] Wayne Morgan has argued, "From articles and books, through advertising, products and the theatre, Palmer Cox and his Brownies achieved the comprehensive approach to marketing that characterizes such modern creations as Harry Potter."[5]

Morgan attributes The Brownies' popularity to their exuberance for exploring modern cultural practices like roller skating and hot-air ballooning—whereas most stories directed at children during this period tended to sentimentalize the past.[6] They presented a vision of a harmonious American urban society at a moment when ethnic and class tensions were on the rise.[7] Their celebration of modern life also appealed to American manufacturers, who faced new pressures to mass-produce and distribute goods at an accelerated pace and sought ways to offset risk by differentiating their products. Gary Cross claims that The Brownies were precursors to "modern character sets" like The Smurfs or Care Bears: their physical appearances remained consistent, but each Brownie was differentiated through their accessories or other surface-level decorative elements.[8] This made them relatively affordable to reproduce while also ensuring that licensees could mix and match dozens of different characters. Character-based dolls and other toys also helped American manufacturers loosen the European stranglehold on the U.S. toy market, which stood at 90 percent until 1914.[9]

While The Brownies may have been the first documented example of character licensing, they were by no means an isolated case. Cartoon illustrations and newspaper comics were popular sources for merchandising and media adaptation in the late nineteenth and early twentieth centuries, as can be attested to by the popularity of Kewpie Dolls, based on Rose O'Neill's *Kewpies* (1909) illustrations (The Kewpies repped for Jell-O, much as The Brownies did for Ivory soap), and Buster Brown shoes, based on illustrator Richard Outcault's 1902 comic strip. Donald Crafton refers to Outcault as "the originator of tie-in merchandising; he licensed Buster and his dog Tige to advertise everything from cigars to shoes."[10] Meanwhile, film production companies like the one owned by Thomas Edison acquired the rights to produce film series based on popular comic strips, seeking to parlay their presold qualities into opportunities to cultivate filmgoing audiences. In 1903, Edison licensed the rights to produce eight short films featuring Buster Brown.[11]

For toy manufacturers and retailers, the appeal of these recognizable characters was also tied to their extended market presence. Until the 1930s, toy sales were still largely seasonal, peaking around the Christmas holidays.[12] Comic strip characters like Mutt and Jeff, the Katzenjammer Kids, and Moon Mullins appeared weekly—sometimes daily—in newspapers in many parts of the country. While comic strips primarily helped sell newspapers, their regularly scheduled appearances also served as free promotional fodder for retailers, keeping these figures in front of consumers all year round.[13] Ian Gordon argues that these early forms of cross-promotion helped to transform comic strip characters into brands, wherein the characters became the inspiration for the products rather than sales agents for them.[14]

And there can be little doubt that branded merchandise also increased the popularity of the core texts it was based upon and offered important ancillary revenue sources for their owners. Jason Scott demonstrates how newspaper publishers like Hearst launched film subsidiaries with the express purpose of promoting the company's comic strips.[15] In 1916, Hearst launched the International Film Service with the explicit goal of exploiting the popularity of syndicated comic strips like *Krazy Kat* and *The Katzenjammer Kids*.[16] Giannalberto Bendazzi claims that these "films served to support the more lucrative field of comic strips, by reminding the audiences of their favorite characters."[17] Scott notes that while early "character-oriented franchises" often adapted comics and literary works (for example, the world of L. Frank Baum's Oz) to motion pictures, by the late 1920s the trend was beginning to reverse itself, with animated film subjects like Felix the Cat getting their own comic strips and merchandise lines.[18]

While there were considerable efforts and success at exploiting character-based licenses before 1930, this period was also characterized by confusion over the legal rights and creative authority that licensors and licensees possessed, greatly constraining how IP circulated across media platforms and product lines. Both Cox and Outcault had tremendous difficulties controlling unauthorized uses of their creations.[19] Perhaps the most significant use of Cox's creations was by Kodak, which released its mass market Brownie camera in 1900. Kodak neither asked Cox's permission nor paid him for the right to use the name.[20] Similarly, William Donahey, creator of *The Teenie Weenies* comic strip, was denied trademark ownership over his creation when he attempted to extend his characters into the canned goods market by licensing their name and likeness to Reid-Murdock & Company for a line of pickles. Another manufacturer had already claimed the "Teenie Weenies" name for its canned goods line.[21] As will be discussed in Chapter 4, trademark law in the United States prior to 1946 had yet to recognize how consumers came to associate brands with particular corporate entities rather than specific products (e.g., that the name "Mickey Mouse" is intrinsically linked to the Disney Corporation for many consumers, not just a set of cartoons), making it a challenge to extend character brands across different markets.

As I've argued elsewhere, early character-licensing endeavors prior to the 1930s were also fraught with uncertainty over what roles licensors and licensees were expected to play in creatively exploiting and managing licensed properties.[22] In part, this stemmed from disagreement over where the true value and consumer "goodwill" in the licensed property was generated. For example, when Donahey asked toy distributor Geo. Borgfeldt & Company in 1921 to pay him an up-front sum of money to license his Teenie Weenies, reasoning that the property had accrued a positive reputation among potential consumers based on the creative labor Donahey had put into the comic strip, Borgfeldt balked, retorting, "We would not, under any circumstances . . . pay any general flat consideration in advance or otherwise for the mere right to use Teenie Weenies, or their presumptive value and any goodwill connected therewith. The only reason they interest us at all, as a commercial proposition, is the fact that they have some publicity, on the strength of which we hope, with hard work, to get some business."[23] While the company admitted that the cartoon's existing popularity was attractive, it essentially reframed the concept of "goodwill" as derived from Borgfeldt's labor in producing and distributing quality merchandise bearing the Teenie Weenies name, not from the property's established reputation. Since Borgfeldt would be doing all the work in extending the Teenie Weenies beyond the newspaper page, the company reasoned that it was really the licensee who was helping Donahey by associating the property with established product lines already popular with children.

It is also worth noting that early attempts to extend characters across markets in the first decades of the twentieth century were both abetted and hindered by the growing social and industrial investment in celebrity culture. Citing cultural historian Warren Susman, Gordon argues that the early twentieth century was characterized by an ongoing cultural struggle between notions of character building and a growing fascination with a celebrity culture built on personality, with comic strip characters serving as bridging agents from the former to the latter.[24] In other words, comic strip and cartoon characters could achieve popularity based on their antics and appearance but were often also accused of undermining Victorian mores by failing to serve as appropriate role models for children to emulate. Buster Brown's mischievousness was often lamented as overshadowing any punishment doled out by his parents for misbehaving. According to Gary Cross and Lisa Jacobson, the first decades of the twentieth century saw the emergence of two seemingly contradictory yet interwoven ideas about children's play culture: on the one hand, the arrival of name-brand fantasy toys that indulged children's imaginations as well as parents' newfound sentimentality toward children; on the other hand, a virulent child-improvement ethos advocating for educational toys that taught creativity and skill development and would help bring the classroom into the playroom.[25] The successful toy manufacturer was one who could draw from popular cultural forms such as comic strips while tempering their harmful effects by channeling their personalities in order to sell character-building playthings. This was not always an easy balance to strike, and potential licensees were just as easily scared off by these popular characters as they were eager to join forces with them.

Celebrities have long been the subjects of licensing arrangements. Gregory J. Battersby and Danny Simon assert that celebrity endorsement can be traced to eighteenth-century British nobility, who allowed a cosmetics company to use their names on its products in exchange for a percentage of the revenues.[26] Cross elaborates on how the teddy bear was named—with permission—after President Theodore Roosevelt in 1902.[27] In the early 1920s, Hollywood celebrities like Charlie Chaplin and Mary Pickford also had licensed dolls fashioned in their likenesses. Cross states, "Like the mythical comic-strip characters, these celebrities represented exciting new images that made the ordinary doll or mechanical figure more appealing."[28] Charles Eckert notes that starting in the late 1920s, Hollywood began working with the fashion industry to ensure that the outfits worn by celebrities on screen and in the pages of magazines would also be made available for sale in department stores—an early form of organic product placement that indirectly extended star power into lifestyle brands.[29] While character and celebrity licensing would continue to blossom in the decades to come, both would also be subjected to more scrutinized oversight, intended to purge them of their potentially negative associations.[30] After all, in 1929, notorious child-hater W. C. Fields had a licensed doll marketed to children, as too did Fatty Arbuckle, whose implication in a 1921 sex and murder scandal undercut his happy-go-lucky public image as well as his viability as the model for a licensed kids' toy.

While early efforts to license popular personalities drawn from fictional characters and real-life celebrities were to some extent mutually constitutive, in many ways, character licensing offered instant solutions to the risks associated with flesh-and-blood stars. Comic strip characters never aged, or did so incrementally, granting them longer shelf lives for licensed merchandise than Mary Pickford, Jackie Coogan, or the Our Gang kids, who simply outgrew their childlike associations. Moreover, while comic strip creators like Harold Gray, whose *Little Orphan Annie* debuted in the *New York Daily News* in 1924, could on occasion be the subjects of public scrutiny, their creations' antics were much easier to reel in than those of film stars.

An archconservative, Gray vehemently opposed FDR's New Deal legislation. He repeatedly used his comic strip to wage an open attack on the government, while singing the praises and virtues of industry. Throughout 1934–1935, the serialized adventures focused on the trials and troubles of Annie's benevolent benefactor, Daddy Warbucks. In the strip, Warbucks faced trumped-up charges of tax evasion orchestrated by a government eager to make an example of the wealthy philanthropist (even though they secretly admitted that they knew he was innocent).

Reviews appearing in *Time* magazine and the *New Republic* pointedly accused the cartoonist of propagandizing. On September 9, 1935, *Time* magazine reprinted an editorial by the publisher of the Huntington, West Virginia, *Herald-Dispatch*, a self-identified progressive conservative, calling the strip a "vehicle for a studied, veiled, and alarmingly vindictive propaganda" promoting "rugged individualism." The publisher asserted, "The creator of the comic strip *Little Orphan Annie* has violated his sacred reader trust. . . . In the latest instance, all political leaders, and it follows every public official, are at once indicted as 'crooks' and to accept such a sweeping indictment is to permit the creator of *Little Orphan Annie* . . . and Chicago's Tribune Syndicate, to attack and condemn all persons, all institutions, and all ideas save those they choose to label acceptable." The *New Republic* warned that the strip is "distributed to 135 daily and 100 Sunday papers, and thence to millions of citizens" and, more alarmingly, "has its greatest influence on the youngsters, the voters of the next generation."[31] When threats of pro-business propaganda directed toward children led several newspapers, including the *Herald-Dispatch*, to cease printing the comic strip, the Chicago Tribune Syndicate quickly issued a statement that Gray had been ordered by them to stop editorializing and get back to entertaining.

So, by the 1930s, when the Lone Ranger would come to prominence (alongside a wide range of lasting iconic characters including Dick Tracy, Donald Duck, Flash Gordon, Little Orphan Annie, Mickey Mouse, Popeye the Sailorman, Superman, and Winnie the Pooh), there was already a vibrant if chaotic market for licensed character brands. Licensing experts throughout the 1930s would help restructure the various media and merchandising environments they worked within to better account for the successes that character brands had achieved in the four previous decades, as well as develop strategies to mitigate against the struggles many of those early franchising and extension efforts also encountered.

While people like Herman "Kay" Kamen, who joined Disney in 1932 and would be nicknamed by industry insiders the "Father of Modern Day

Licensing," are celebrated as innovators in the "great man" tradition, it is perhaps more important to recognize the social, industrial, and legal environments that inspired the tactical changes they initiated. As I expand upon in Chapters 3 and 4, the 1930s would prove to be a boon for character licensing in part because the Great Depression necessitated that manufacturers embrace new strategies and new spokespersons who would counter declining sales and anticorporate sentiments. The decade would also see increased tensions between national and regional/local identities crystallized in the expansion of the mass market through technologies like radio, both celebrated and feared for its ability to unite Americans. Once again, licensed characters would prove important mediators in these matters, as licensing agents developed carefully scripted rhetorical responses to accusations that mass culture was undermining traditional values. These agents began to strategically implement guidelines for licensees intended to align economic interests and social values in ways that positioned character brands as inculcators of consumerism's positive potential. Licensed properties often served as linking pins that could join local and national aspirations and markets. Meanwhile, congressional deliberations over revising trademark law—ongoing throughout the 1930s and culminating in the 1946 Lanham Trademark Revision—would be informed by the legal battles waged by property owners throughout the decade, out of which new conceptualizations of corporate authorship as stewardship would emerge.

The Lone Ranger Arrives

The Lone Ranger radio series debuted on January 30, 1933. It was originally created to help attract sponsors to the fledgling Michigan Radio Network, owned by George Trendle and John Kunsky,[32] though it quickly became a platform for cultivating investment among both consumers and licensees in a more expansive Lone Ranger–inspired lifestyle brand.

On the surface, the Lone Ranger formula is fairly straightforward. Set in the Old West (1850–1865), the Lone Ranger is a masked rider who hunts down criminals with the help of his Indian companion, Tonto. The Lone Ranger rides a white steed named Silver and shoots silver bullets from his silver-handled revolvers. His true identity remains a mystery, though he is believed to be the lone Texas Ranger to survive an ambush by the Butch Cavendish gang. It was Tonto who found the wounded ranger and nursed him back to health. While these elements have become canonical, they in fact developed over multiple radio episodes and through trial and error. For instance, Tonto was not actually introduced until the fourth *Lone Ranger* episode. His introduction was motivated by the need to convey plot exposition without the hero talking to himself. In the first three episodes, the Lone Ranger usually disguised himself among a crowd of people to discuss plot points.[33] The Cavendish gang as well as the story of Tonto and the Lone Ranger's initial partnership was introduced years after the radio series first went on the air.[34]

The formula for the Lone Ranger's adventures was also developed over many years (see Chapter 4), but by the late 1930s was fairly standardized. The Lone Ranger would ride into a town, uncover a nefarious plot, help the kindly but helpless and hapless town folk capture the villain, and would ride off again. Seeking to capitalize on the child consumer market by promoting a positive role model whom parents and sponsors could rally around, Lone Ranger plots were purposely devised to be straightforward and unambiguous. The audience for the series was often aware of the villain's identity and plans before the Lone Ranger was, though rarely was the Masked Man depicted as caught off guard by a villain's scheme. There were very few mysteries or cliffhangers. Though technically operating outside the law, the Lone Ranger was a law-abiding hero who often partnered with local law enforcement officers on his adventures. Lone Ranger villains were usually greedy and cruel, with few redeeming motivations for their actions, though the series would on occasion have the Masked Man show felons the error of their ways. Though the Lone Ranger is clearly the hero of these stories, he is also the least developed character in them, initially possessing no backstory or obstacles to overcome. With a virtually infallible hero and a plot that always resolved with the guilty party either caught or repentant, Trendle presented the Lone Ranger to would-be radio sponsors as guaranteed to appeal to both children and their parents.

A practicing lawyer specializing in film booking and property rights, Trendle first joined forces with Kunsky, one of Detroit's most powerful movie theater owners, in the late 1920s and helped broker a deal with Adolph Zucker in 1928 to sell Kunsky's twenty theaters to Paramount for $6 million.[35] The deal came with the caveat that neither Kunsky nor Trendle could reenter the film exhibition business.

In 1930, Trendle and Kunsky (later King) formed the Kunsky-Trendle Broadcasting Company (later King-Trendle; henceforth referred to as KTBC) and bought radio station WGH in Detroit, Michigan, rechristening it WXYZ. At the time, WXYZ was Detroit's CBS affiliate, but in 1932, Trendle canceled the station's contract with the national network, opting instead to create a regional network, the Michigan Radio Network (MRN), with WXYZ as the flagship station. To this end, he bought up seven additional radio stations in the state. While later self-aggrandizing publicity would label Trendle a "pioneer" and a "rebel" for these decisions,[36] his choice to go independent was rooted in simple economics. In 1932, CBS implemented a new policy by which it would pay affiliates to take its programming, both sponsored and sustaining (an industry term used to describe as-yet-unsponsored programming), but this required that affiliates take all or nothing. Trendle saw greater profit margins in reserving evening hours for locally sponsored programming. Yet, without CBS's steady influx of programming, WXYZ initially lost four thousand dollars a week.[37] Trendle needed programming that could compete with NBC and CBS and attract audiences, who, in turn, would lure sponsors.

Knowing that MRN could not afford the production budgets that NBC and CBS were investing in variety programming featuring celebrity hosts and Hollywood guest stars, KTBC opted to create dramas because they were cheap to produce and could employ an anonymous set of actors who would work on various programs. In the absence of any real stars, the characters themselves had to stand out. To this end, Trendle hired Fran Striker to write radio scripts for dramatic series featuring dynamic characters who could capture audience interest in the same manner as other celebrities of the era, at a fraction of the cost. KTBC also decided to focus on developing children's content, since Trendle believed that this group was less discerning than adult listeners and would forgive poor production values in exchange for action and adventure.[38] *The Lone Ranger* was one of dozens of series Striker developed for KTBC, including the urban crime series *The Green Hornet* (1936–1955) and a juvenile police series set in northern Canada, *Sergeant Preston on the Yukon* (1940–1955). While Striker may have formalized *The Lone Ranger*'s plot structure, all KTBC employees were required to sign contracts that prohibited them from making any ownership claims on characters or stories that they might have helped develop.[39]

Though Chapter 4 argues that the Lone Ranger's origins are best understood as corporate and that KTBC purposely rendered opaque the process leading up to the character's creation, there are nonetheless several likely influences that contributed to the initial idea of developing a Western series featuring a masked hero. While both Striker and Trendle would later claim that the Lone Ranger was inspired by characters like Robin Hood and Zorro as well as by the rugged and virtuous qualities displayed by B-Western star Tom Mix,[40] in all likelihood, it was a combination of the Western genre's ubiquity, popularity, and relative inexpensiveness coupled with its successful adaptation as sponsored radio content that proved economically appealing.

In his review of Hollywood business practices during the 1930s, Tino Balio asserts that Westerns, particularly the low-budget, quickly produced "B" variety, were considered to be a reliable genre, with up to two hundred produced annually and distributed primarily to independent theaters unaffiliated with the major studios and in search of content that could produce a "quick payoff" and a quick turnover.[41] Balio also notes that B-Westerns were directed primarily at juvenile audiences, often sacrificing characterization and plot development for fast-paced action.[42] As longtime owners of an independent theater chain who were now in search of inexpensive, reliable content that would capture a young listenership for their fledgling radio network, Trendle and Kunsky likely thought the Western was the kind of low-risk, high-reward genre KTBC was in search of.

Lone Ranger fans have long pointed to the appearance of a recurring masked character on Striker's 1931–1932 *Covered Wagon Days*, a radio series he developed for local Buffalo radio station WEBR before joining KTBC. Of equal note, however, might be the success fellow Buffalo radio writer Herbert L. Rice had in 1932 when contracted by the Hecker H-O Company to create a Western series that would help sell their breakfast cereal. Rice's *H-Bar-O Rangers starring Bobby Benson* along with the 1932 BBD&O-produced *The Tom Mix Ralston Straight Shooters*, which was created to sell the dog food manufacturer's hot cereal to kids, both preceded the Lone Ranger and demonstrated how Westerns could attract sponsorship.[43] So too did the 1932 CBS series *Lone Wolf Tribe*, sponsored by Wrigley's Spearmint Gum, which told stories of the Old West from the Native American perspective while encouraging kids to trade in their "wampum," or gum wrappers, for premiums.[44] Premiums were cheap mass-produced giveaway items that usually bore the brand's insignia and were offered to radio listeners in exchange for their writing in and, occasionally, providing proof of purchase of a sponsor's item.

The Tom Mix Ralston Straight Shooters series offered listeners tons of opportunities to acquire Tom Mix paraphernalia in exchange for sending in proofs of purchase of Ralston Cereal.[45] The show's success likely contributed to Trendle and Striker's drawing inspiration for the Lone Ranger from Tom Mix, though KTBC had no desire to pay a celebrity to lend their name to any series it created (Mix did not star on his own radio show). To this end, the Lone Ranger's mask was intended to make him an object of fascination similar to Tom Mix but with no purse strings attached. The mask also made for a cheap giveaway item that could be mass-produced at minimal cost to the company.

Trendle also settled on developing a Western series because he believed it offered more opportunities for inexpensive premiums and giveaways than other genres. Cross notes that the science fiction genre, headlined by character brands like Buck Rogers and Flash Gordon, likely provided a more novel set of giveaway ideas,[46] though producing ray guns was certainly pricier than making generic pistols. Like many other radio programs, the Lone Ranger first established its value for sponsors through premiums and other giveaway items. As early as June 1933, five months after the radio series debuted, KTBC boasted to potential sponsors that the Lone Ranger had provided "radio's most spectacular incident" to date when WXYZ received 24,607 letters in response to a single announcement offering "genuine Lone Ranger Six Shooters" to the first three hundred people who wrote in.[47] Significantly, though the promotional brochure sought to establish the Lone Ranger radio series' popularity, KTBC's efforts hinged on the enormous response to the giveaway offer, not the content of the show. In other words, premiums were not only used by sponsors to measure audiences, but were an important marketing tool for property owners seeking sponsors, serving as "a handy index to the popularity of the program."[48]

KTBC's strategy paid off when the Gordon Bakery, makers of Silvercup Bread, became the program's sponsor on November 27, 1933 (it would remain a major sponsor of the show until March 1939).[49] Gordon reaped immediate success with the program—a promotional ad in *Grocer's Spotlight* newspaper stated, "Our Best Salesman Rides a Horse."[50]

From the outset, premium and merchandising possibilities were built directly into the Lone Ranger narrative formula. The Lone Ranger's use of silver bullets was settled upon before the series debuted because KTBC wanted the program to have identifiable signature giveaways that could be used to entice a sponsor.[51] Scripts emphasized the Lone Ranger's most merchandisable attributes, which, in addition to silver bullets, included the hero's mask, guns, his horse Silver, and his sidekick Tonto. For example, episode 805 of the series, "Revenge of Mendoza," airing March 25, 1938, begins with a gang of bandits robbing Hank and Maggie Kumert of their life savings. The announcer provides exposition up front that clearly identifies for the audience who the villains are. The Lone Ranger and Tonto arrive after the bandits depart, promising to capture the thieves.

While the plot of "Revenge of Mendoza" was fairly straightforward, it did allow for several showcase moments for Silver. On three occasions in the story, robbery victims mention that the bandits cannot be caught because they ride the fastest horses in the county. Yet Silver is able to overtake them easily, much to the amazement of both the bandits and the posse in pursuit of them, who marvel at Silver's powerful strides. The functions of the radio series in foregrounding the Lone Ranger brand's merchandisable attributes are further discussed in Chapter 3.

Bucking the common trend in the 1930s of turning over radio programming production to ad agencies,[52] KTBC maintained strict control over content production and instead licensed the rights to build sponsored campaigns around the radio series. The company supplied licensees with a comprehensive merchandising package that encouraged radio sponsors to partner with other licensees to generate premiums. For sponsors, premiums were an important way of measuring both the size and consumer-friendliness of a given program's audience. For KTBC, premiums were not only a significant revenue source, but they also extended the Lone Ranger's reach beyond the radio set into children's lived daily experiences. Though Lone Ranger sponsors and their ad agencies were permitted to come up with their own merchandising schemes, any new marketing initiative required approval as well as contractual consent that KTBC would thereafter own the rights to the initiative. By maintaining control over series production and retaining ownership of sponsored merchandising practices, KTBC was able to ensure a coherent relationship between Lone Ranger stories and Lone Ranger merchandise.

On January 31, 1935, Trendle incorporated the Lone Ranger as a separate business enterprise: the Lone Ranger Incorporated (LRI). Trendle became LRI's president and primary shareholder at 70 percent. Trendle's other collaborators on the business end were Alan H. Campbell and Raymond Meurer.[53] Campbell began as head of sales at King-Trendle in 1936, but quickly became Trendle's right-hand man and eventual business partner. Meurer was Trendle's chief legal counsel from the late 1930s onward, and also became a copartner in the mid-1940s. The incorporation gave LRI the right to lease the characters and stories featured under that title for any promotional or production purpose. Trendle's decision to establish LRI as a distinct corporate entity separate from his radio production and regional network operations, and moreover, to position LRI above these other businesses in terms of corporate hierarchy—LRI's first licensee was KTBC, which it granted, for the cost of one dollar, the right to continue producing the radio series—not only dislodged the Lone Ranger from its radio confines but also elevated the Lone Ranger IP as the primary asset that drove all other undertakings.

In this regard, LRI was quite unique. While Disney had set up Walt Disney Enterprises as the company's licensing and merchandising arm in 1929,[54] the unit was subordinate to the company's animated film production assets (even though it earned more) and largely intended to help the company finance future films. Where Douglas Gomery has noted that licensing deals for toys based on Disney's Mickey Mouse and other Silly Symphony characters earned the struggling company hundreds of thousands of dollars in 1930—money that both kept the company out of the red and was used to finance more animation projects—Richard DeCordova has demonstrated that Disney's goal was to promote its films through merchandising: "The sale of a doll to any member of a household is a daily advertisement in that household for our cartoons and keeps them all 'Mickey Mouse Minded.'"[55]

LRI's management team quickly understood that the Lone Ranger was far more than a popular radio program that might yield ancillary revenue from licensing and merchandising deals. They also recognized that the radio program could serve as a promotional catalyst for extending the Lone Ranger's market reach and cultural significance among consumers. Even as the cowboy hero was franchised out across a vast swath of media and merchandise, LRI worked to ensure that these various franchise outposts collectively and coherently promoted the Lone Ranger brand.

Conclusion

Though the Lone Ranger would emerge as a merchandising phenomenon only in the late 1930s, much of the groundwork was laid in the first five years of the character's existence. LRI not only perfected a formula for showcasing how the Lone Ranger's merchandisable attributes were linked to his powerful personality, but also established the Masked Man's ability to compete with celebrities for listener attention. Most important, LRI successfully demonstrated the inextricable link between the radio series' popularity and listener desires for extractable trinkets based on the Lone Ranger's adventures.

By no means original or groundbreaking in its development of a character brand, LRI drew from myriad sources in conceptualizing its masked cowboy hero, while reconceiving the tactics introduced by other IP owners in the first decades of the twentieth century in response to the emerging sociohistorical and industrial contexts of Depression-era American popular entertainment. While this chapter has offered a broad overview of early character licensing and the Lone Ranger's origination, the next chapter digs deep into LRI's approach to building the Lone Ranger into a national cross-media hero and lifestyle brand through coordinated merchandising efforts with local licensees, retailers, and consumer advocates.

CHAPTER 3

Building the Franchise One Market at a Time: The Lone Ranger's Extra-Textual Career in the Late 1930s

Introduction

In 1935, two full years after *The Lone Ranger* radio series first debuted—and not coincidentally, just after the character was incorporated—LRI finally told the story of how the Masked Man had initially formed his special bond with Silver. For several years, listeners had been treated to adventures that emphasized Silver's unique appearance, great speed and strength, and enhanced senses, all helping the Lone Ranger defeat his enemies. As the story goes, the Lone Ranger first encountered the untamable stallion engaged in a fierce battle with a wild buffalo—and saved his life. The horse became the Lone Ranger's devoted companion, permitting the Masked Man to be the first rider he didn't buck.

Though not terribly original, what was remarkable about *How the Lone Ranger Captured Silver* was how it was disseminated (see Figure 3.1). This integral bit of the Lone Ranger mythos was not heard over the radio, but instead was initially distributed as a multipart illustrated short story giveaway by local grocers in exchange for the purchase of a three-day-old loaf of bread from series sponsor Gordon Bakery. At the culmination of the seven-week event, children (and adults) collecting the story were invited to join a newly formed Lone Ranger Safety Club, which in addition to promising more opportunities to discover the Masked Man's secrets, was also promoted as an important means of working alongside the Lone Ranger to ensure healthy and harm-free play opportunities.[1] In telling part of the Lone Ranger's backstory off radio, the promotion generated what Neil Young has termed "additive comprehension," which Henry Jenkins has in turn defined as the "expansion of interpretive possibilities that occurs when fictional franchises are extended across multiple texts

Figure 3.1. A bound copy of *How the Lone Ranger Captured Silver*, ca. 1938.

and media," enriching the experiences of devoted fans without detracting from more casual consumer engagement.[2]

Of course, both Young and Jenkins are referring to the contemporary media landscape, which encourages innovative transmedia storytelling across multiple franchise outposts, each one adding a layer of story comprehension best told through that particular medium's conventions. *How the Lone Ranger Captured Silver* seems to suggest that extending story worlds across media platforms is not a particularly new idea, though the additive comprehension possibilities offered by Lone Ranger giveaways in the 1930s came to fruition under very different cultural and industrial circumstances. Meanwhile, the Lone Ranger Safety Club (LRSC) functioned as a variation on what is today called a "brand community," wherein club members were offered an array of opportunities to extend their Lone Ranger experiences beyond the radio product and share with one another their mutual investment in the Masked Man. When properly marshaled, LRSC members were also important participants in spreading the Lone Ranger gospel to new consumers and licensees.

Many radio histories acknowledge the very large numbers of premiums, giveaways, and other extra-textual ephemera that circulated during the 1930s and 1940s, but these items are almost always treated as ancillary to the radio content that spawned them.[3] Premiums and giveaways are usually addressed as designed to measure the size and receptiveness of a given program's audience to commercial messages as well as indirectly stimulating sales of sponsored products by offering "free" trinkets in exchange for proof of purchase. Jonathan Gray has encouraged media scholars to look beyond the text as the central site of meaningful encounter for readers and, building on the work of Gerard Genette, to analyze how paratexts such as DVD extra features, preview trailers, toy packaging, and other promotional materials actually prepare consumers for future encounters with the work itself (the film, the TV series, etc.).[4] Gray's work is also largely focused on the contemporary media landscape and primarily on how paratexts are engaged by consumers. Yet his provocations can also push scholars to explore the central roles that supposedly ancillary products played in attracting would-be licensees and in preparing them for how to effectively exploit these brands.

In its deployment of extra-textual materials to cultivate deeper investment in the Lone Ranger, LRI was both typical of other entertainment property owners of its day and exceptional in its recognition of these materials as central, not peripheral, to the business of extending the Lone Ranger. Extra-textuals were key to LRI's intersecting goals in the 1930s of extending *The Lone Ranger* radio series market-by-market; linking together Lone Ranger–branded merchandise and Lone Ranger media, including a nationally syndicated comic strip and two fifteen-part film serials produced by Republic Pictures, as part of a commercial intertext; and establishing the Lone Ranger as a lifestyle brand. Throughout the late 1930s, LRI used Lone Ranger giveaways, premiums, and other extra-textual materials to cultivate investment in and prepare both licensees and consumers for future encounters with the Lone Ranger brand. Yet even as LRI worked to convince potential sponsors that the Lone Ranger could be a powerful spokesperson for its products, the company also saw the radio series and its various giveaways as promotional vehicles and launching points for extending the Lone Ranger as a branded icon into new markets. From the outset, *The Lone Ranger* radio series was devised as a vehicle for creatively showcasing the property's most merchandisable attributes. While sponsors paid for the rights to attach their names to the radio series and its extra-textual accoutrements, the radio series primarily sold the Lone Ranger as a lifestyle brand by imbuing the myriad commodities that bore its name and image with cultural meanings and storytelling possibilities drawn from the protagonist's powerful personality. Extra-textuals were essential linking pins in cultivating a Lone Ranger brand community that grew out of the radio series but ultimately looked beyond it in crafting a Lone Ranger–inspired lifestyle.

To establish the Lone Ranger as a lifestyle brand attainable through acquiring so-called "peripherals," LRI chose to pursue localizable merchandising initiatives, working with regional sponsors, local radio and movie theater operators, retailers, and community leaders to integrate the Masked Man into every new market. LRI embraced customization, localization, and other standardized variation tactics designed to adapt the Lone Ranger's image and message to the particular cultural and market conditions that sponsors and merchants were working within. During the Depression years, manufacturers and retailers often encountered resistance from local consumers as well as threats of increased federal oversight by way of FDR's New Deal initiatives. The Lone Ranger was often presented to clients as a potential bridge figure that could repair the relationship between big business and local communities and promote alliances among them to ward off the imposing presence of big government. Importantly, the 1930s would prove to be the decade when national institutions employing modern technologies began to challenge the autonomy and authority vested in local identities. The Lone Ranger would serve as a mediating presence between local and national interests, with LRI establishing a variation on what might now be described as a franchisor/franchisee relationship with its various local partners.

While LRI permitted licensees to tinker with the merchandising formula, its reliance on recycling testimonials and tactics gleaned from successful local merchandising campaigns fostered the impression that licensees could speak to one another in spreading the Lone Ranger gospel. In this regard, the Lone Ranger's paradoxical path to national iconic status complicates Michele Hilmes's assertion that radio in the 1930s and 1940s was regarded as a technology that would "unite a far-flung and disparate nation."[5] The Lone Ranger emerged as a national icon precisely by allowing local communities to speak to one another through their shared but discrete investments in the property.

The most important extra-textual initiative that LRI spearheaded was the LRSC, which functioned as a means of cultivating and managing localizable Lone Ranger brand communities that would advocate on the property's behalf and integrate the hero into its lived daily rituals. Yet these local outposts were also understood as nodes in a broader network that worked to promote the Lone Ranger lifestyle brand while providing potential investors with on-the-ground evidence of the Masked Man's popularity that could then be used to extend the property into new markets.

Following a brief discussion of the central roles that peripherals played on radio in the 1930s, I turn to analyzing how LRI developed *The Lone Ranger* radio program as a form of branded entertainment meant to call attention to the hero's merchandisable attributes. I then demonstrate how LRI made use of customizable and localizable extra-textuals to extend the Lone Ranger across markets while helping licensees set up franchise outposts for the property that could be organically integrated into particular social milieus. Aside from bridging geographically dispersed markets, LRI also sought to teach licensees within the same geographic market to work together in the hopes of generating localized merchandising synergies. I end the chapter with a focused case study of efforts to develop the LRSC into a brand hub that guided members toward embracing and extolling the virtues of a Lone Ranger–inspired lifestyle.

Recentering Peripherals

To understand how something like the *How the Lone Ranger Captured Silver* giveaway came about, it is imperative to situate it within the cultural-industrial matrix of children's radio in the 1930s.

As unemployment rose from 1.55 million in 1929 (3.2% of the American workforce) to over 12.3 million in 1933 (24.9%), never dropping under 7.7 million (14.3%) throughout the 1930s, American businesses were forced to seek new ways of selling not only goods but also the virtue of consumption in an era of scarcity.[6] Gary Cross argues that many Americans began to see continued displays of wealth and excess that had characterized the 1920s as un-American.[7] New approaches would be found in the coalescence of radio technologies, branding practices, and marketing directed at children. Combined, these sites would help many businesses recover both their profit margins and their public reputation, but they would also open up new concerns, particularly over the exploitation of children.

While many businesses were hit hard during the Depression, radio blossomed. Providing a cheap means of entertainment and information, sales of radio sets actually doubled between 1929 and 1933.[8] Roland Marchand argues that by the 1930s, advertising agencies believed that the public was better reached through entertainment than edification and that promotion should be conducted through showmanship.[9]

While radio programs targeted consumers of all ages, one group that was especially identified was children. As Cross argues, by the 1930s, advertisers learned that children were attentive and loyal listeners and thus excellent targets for commercial messages.[10] In addition, the Depression had pushed many adolescents into the workforce. Many boys between ten and twelve years old now earned extra money at part-time jobs, a portion of which could be spent on cheap toys and other consumer goods marketed directly to them by enterprising manufacturers.[11] While marketing to and through children had been a common practice among toy manufacturers since the early 1900s, it accelerated during the 1930s.[12]

With personal consumption of toys dropping from an estimated $336 million in 1929 to $181 million in 1933 and at least ninety-six different toy makers going out of business, enterprising firms turned to radio to give them an added boost, manufacturing low-cost playthings usually associated in some manner with either the characters or plots of particular radio programs.[13] Premiums were championed as an indirect means for sponsors to gauge both the size of a program's radio audience and its receptiveness to commercial messages without directly marketing their wares. Though it is commonly assumed that children's radio programs sold sponsored goods to kids, it is more accurate to say that these programs sold interactive play experiences built around cheaply produced and narratively motivated trinkets that were tied to the purchase of sponsored goods. Premiums and giveaways were bridges between a sponsored program and the products that sponsors wanted listeners to buy.

Children's radio in the 1930s did not typically tell stories that directly incorporated sponsored products into their plots (though other genres like soap operas often did), but they did make regular use of branded characters on loan to sponsors. Indeed, though radio premiums often identified a series' sponsor by name, they rarely bore any direct relationship to sponsored products. Instead, giveaways were usually tied directly to ongoing plot devices or props used by the series' protagonists. For example, *Dick Tracy* giveaways were often presented as either allowing listeners to own a piece of the famous copper's repertoire, such as his gun, badge, or two-way radio wristwatch—all used in the pursuit of criminals—or to acquire items that would help them follow along with a particular plot, such as a map Tracy was using to track down his latest perp.

In one *Radio Orphan Annie* episode, seven and one-half minutes (out of a total of fifteen) are dedicated to describing the grandeur of a ring Daddy Warbucks has given Annie for her birthday while offering children the opportunity to "get a ring just like Annie's" in exchange for ten cents and an Ovaltine box top.[14] Never once does the announcer make any direct pitch for Ovaltine. Instead, the birthday ring is presented as an opportunity to become part of Annie's inner circle of friends—an inner circle that just happens to drink Ovaltine, but also participates in other Orphan Annie–related activities.

In choosing to link giveaways to story elements, many radio programs regularly blurred the line between their entertainment and commercial functions. In one infamous case, the protagonist of *Jack Armstrong, the All American Boy*, a program created by General Mills in 1933 explicitly to sell Wheaties cereal, directly asked children to send in money and proof of purchase of the sponsor's product in exchange for a special stamp book giveaway, implying that these returns would go toward a life-saving operation for Jack's ailing mother. On the series, Jack was also in pursuit of a rare $20,000 stamp that would be used to save his mother's life. Hence, the promotional giveaway encouraged the perception that children could directly assist Jack in saving his mother's life by getting their parents to purchase the sponsor's product. The Federal Trade Commission intervened and forced the show to end the promotion.[15]

Beyond accusations that it took advantage of children's naiveté and their desire for the "free" trinkets used by their heroes other complaints lobbed against children's radio programming included that its "blood and thunder" content promoted bad behavior, such as talking back to one's parents, exalted criminality and other immoral actions, and distracted children from their schoolwork and chores. Significantly, the serialized cliff-hanger endings of many episodes, which left their heroes imperiled, were singled out for causing high levels of anxiety and distress among children, producing nightmares and other irritations that offered no avenues for resolution outside of consumer purchases and continued filial devotion to the program.[16]

Lisa Jacobson notes, however, that though the emerging consumer culture was often lamented as destroying Victorian notions of childhood innocence and upsetting traditional family hierarchies, some experts believed that its "ethos of salesmanship and enticement" could also be harnessed by parents and educators to prepare children for successful integration into modernity.[17] These experts also believed that media and other forms of popular culture could, in the right hands, be valuable character-building tools for teaching children how to imaginatively navigate consumer culture without sacrificing their moral compass. Or, as Nicholas Sammond asserts, "arguments about regulating harmful media gave rise to arguments for media beneficial for the development of children into socially productive adults."[18] Furthermore, responding to cultural concerns that personality was eclipsing character in determining social mores,[19] many children's radio programs advocated for the ability of their powerful and popular personalities to help build/instill character in children through listener engagement with both the program and its various extra-textuals.

As such, premiums and giveaways were often rhetorically positioned as wholesome commercial outlets that taught children important civic and moral lessons even as they required acquisition of sponsored products. For example, in 1933, in conjunction with Orphan Annie's radio adventure in search of a treasure island, the Wander Company and advertising agency Blackett, Sample & Hummert issued a cardboard game giveaway titled "The Ovaltine Way to the Treasure Isle of Health & Happiness," which required children to traverse various unhealthy islands before reaching their final destination, including the "Land of Lost Appetites," "Skinny Land," "Fidgidy Isle," "Isle of No Pep," and "Sissies of Cry Baby Land." Each of these "bad" locations corresponded to a social or medical ill that Ovaltine supposedly helped cure (Ovaltine was marketed as an energy booster that could help underweight children grow "husky, happy, and full o' pep"). Though the game board explicitly told children to "Drink Ovaltine and Help Keep Orphan Annie on the Radio," it was also peppered with other life lessons like "Don't Use Slang," "Don't Talk Back," and "Wash Your Hands and Face," which were intended to appease parents and position the series and its sponsor as contributing positively to child-rearing efforts by instilling respect for (rather than challenging) parental authority.[20]

More than mere afterthoughts, giveaway items were often constitutive of creative decision making, providing inspirational fodder for developing storylines that effectively cultivated desire for these items among listeners. Cross has identified 1930s radio as not merely a conduit for selling products, but as fundamentally reshaping children's play culture by providing a story backdrop into which products could be fit.[21] Even as radio stories offered listeners scenarios that could be reenacted through the acquisition of premiums, premiums also offered listeners (and sponsors) means of extending the radio experience by delivering visual aids that enhanced storytelling in an aural medium, providing opportunities to dig deeper into ongoing storylines or to learn important bits of character backstory. Premiums were also designed to offer participatory opportunities for children to shape the radio narrative. Children's radio regularly held contests where listeners were asked to send in recommendations for things like their choice of names for a newly discovered island that Little Orphan Annie had claimed for the USA, which gave listeners structured and limited opportunities to affect the story. Comic strips offered similar opportunities such as when readers were asked in 1941 to write in with names for Dagwood and Blondie Bumstead's daughter, eventually named Cookie.

LRI also encouraged radio promotions in which the ultimate reward was rhetorically presented as not the acquisition of Lone Ranger–branded merchandise, but the opportunity to gain notoriety among one's friends for one's Lone Ranger prowess. Several LRI merchandising guides for potential sponsors recount the good fortune of young Jimmy Pountain, whose talent at seamlessly imitating the Lone Ranger's famous catchphrase, "Hi-Yo Silver! Away!" won him first prize in a radio contest for the best Lone Ranger sound-alike.[22] Though the contest was promoted as both proof of the Lone Ranger's popularity and a viable way for sponsors to connect directly with child consumers, LRI explained to would-be investors that the real prize was that Jimmy was now assured of being selected to play "the mysterious rider" in his weekly game of cowboys and Indians, since every play session now required that someone assume the role of the Masked Man. In this manner, even as premiums generated indirect sales for sponsors, they also contributed to promoting branded lifestyles that moved beyond the radio series.

Lone Ranger Radio as Branded Entertainment

LRI saw *The Lone Ranger* radio series as primarily a vehicle for building a story around the Lone Ranger's merchandisable attributes. Even as LRI worked to convince potential sponsors that the Lone Ranger could be a powerful spokesperson for their products, the company primarily saw the radio series and its giveaways as launching points for extending the Lone Ranger as a branded icon—a lifestyle brand imbued with cultural meanings and storytelling possibilities drawn from the protagonist's powerful personality. In this regard, LRI's premium strategies differed from those of other children's radio properties like Little Orphan Annie or Dick Tracy. With few exceptions, Lone Ranger stories were almost never serialized, which meant that premiums and other giveaways were rarely tied to particular plots, but instead to the more generic aspects of the Lone Ranger's appearance and activities.[23] While this decision was largely driven by LRI's business model for licensing the radio series market-by-market (see next section), and would change in the early 1940s once national sponsor General Mills became LRI's primary licensee (see Chapter 5), stand-alone episodes allowed for greater investment in the character and offered more room for children to invent their own Lone Ranger stories by making use of branded merchandise.

Jonathan Gray suggests that toys and other merchandise help both to prepare consumers for textual encounters and to keep their attention focused on a particular media franchise.[24] LRI inverted the functions of texts and paratexts, however, in having the radio series serve as a platform that prepared children for further encounters with branded merchandise through a narrative formula that repeatedly foreground the Lone Ranger's merchandisable attributes as well as how to integrate them into play scenarios and other daily rituals. Thus, *The Lone Ranger* radio series might be understood as a precursor to contemporary branded entertainment initiatives in that its primary value for LRI resided in its ability to attract interest from potential sponsors, product manufacturers, and consumers in a more extensive Lone Ranger product line linked to the property's personality and adventures. Branded entertainment is a contemporary media practice wherein companies create content showcasing their brand rather than paying for advertising time. The goal is to entice consumers to seek out branded content, generating buzz that contributes to a brand's reputation.[25] A contemporary example like Hasbro's *Transformers* film franchise largely consists of a series of action-packed set pieces designed to show off the various characters and their abilities to audiences, in turn encouraging certain types of engagement with product lines that have pre-existed the movies (and are also revitalized through them). The films' formulaic dimensions ensure that the property's merchandisable attributes are repeatedly foreground.

That *The Lone Ranger* radio series followed a formula cannot be refuted. Every episode began the exact same way: with the sound of gunshots, the cry "Hi-Yo Silver!" and the William Tell Overture. An announcer would then set the mood: "A fiery horse with the speed of light, a cloud of dust and a hearty Hi-Yo Silver!—the Lone Ranger!" The Lone Ranger himself would then cry out to his horse, "Come on Silver! Tonto is waiting for us in [insert varying locations from Texas through Wyoming]. Hi-Yo Silver, Away!" Thus, within the first three minutes of every episode, many of the property's recurring story elements, and all of its trademarked ones, were introduced. LRI trademarked the names "The Lone Ranger," "Silver," and "Tonto," which along with the catchphrase, "Hi-Yo Silver!" appeared prominently in the company's licensing and merchandising campaigns as early as 1935. The revolving set of meeting points where Tonto was waiting for the Lone Ranger were also integral to extending the radio series into new markets.

Radio plots typically focused on the Lone Ranger's actions in thwarting the villain's schemes, which placed repeated emphasis on a recurring set of merchandisable devices used by the Lone Ranger to defeat the bad guys. The repetitiveness of plot structures allowed these attributes to be showcased in every episode. Head writer Fran Striker was encouraged to make use of a recurring set of props in his scripts rather than find new methods for the Lone Ranger to defeat his adversaries or announce his presence. The Lone Ranger might find a thousand different ways to demonstrate his marksmanship skills and call attention to his silver-handled six shooters that fired silver bullets, but rest assured, he would use his guns in some capacity in almost every episode.

Similarly, *Lone Ranger* plots foreground the hero's masked identity. Within each episode, characters repeatedly referred to the Lone Ranger as the "Masked Man." In fact, in the four dozen episodes from 1938 that I listened to, the Lone Ranger was never once referred to as "the Lone Ranger," except by the radio announcer, and even he often identified the character by his most recognizable feature. Many plots included moments where the hero would remove his mask in order to disguise his identity (unlike many comic book superheroes, the Lone Ranger had no secret identity, making the removal of his mask a plot device most often used for disguising rather than revealing who the character truly was). Upon first encountering new characters, the Lone Ranger would often have to explain that though he wore a mask, he was not a criminal. It was a common plot device that the Lone Ranger and Tonto were initially mistaken for the villains they were hunting, though this was usually resolved quickly. All of this, of course, made the mask a prominently mentioned feature of every episode—and a "most spectacular giveaway" for children to wear while enacting Lone Ranger exploits. LRI advertised the mask giveaway as generating unprecedented attention for sponsors, with up to 350,000 requests made in a single day.[26]

The radio adventures were designed so that the Lone Ranger's personality and values would be defined through the various character props he employed. LRI's goal was to create an assemblage of merchandisable components that, when combined, captured the character's essence. In addition to his mask, *Lone Ranger* stories usually included multiple mentions of his marksmanship skills as well as his super-horse Silver's unique appearance and talents. In the episode "The Theft of Silver," horse thieves whom the Lone Ranger has been tracking steal Silver.[27] Over the course of the episode, Silver is described by the thieves as a "devil on four legs," "strong as a dozen horses," "we've caught the most famous horse in the world," and "solid Silver . . . I never seen none like him." Meanwhile, upon learning of Silver's abduction, the Lone Ranger exclaims, "If only I could shoot to kill." Later in the episode, when he and Tonto are mistaken by the townspeople for the horse thieves, he warns, "I'll shoot the gun from anyone who tries [to shoot]."

Such statements worked to establish the character's prowess and his code of conduct. When gunplay ensued, opponents were always heard crying out, "My hand!" calling attention to the Masked Man's refusal to shoot to kill and his pinpoint accuracy in disarming his opponents. More than merely embellished ornaments, the Lone Ranger's silver-handled six shooters are described as embodying both his expert marksmanship skills and his moral code. The Lone Ranger formula sutured the hero's code of conduct to the righteousness of commodity consumption by insinuating that a Lone Ranger–branded gun was not just a toy but also a conduit for channeling the Lone Ranger's values. All Lone Ranger toys were vested with the hero's personality and, in turn, would teach children important character-building lessons.

Sammond's analysis of Disney in the 1930s reveals how the company also carefully positioned itself as bridging commercial and moral values through its products: "But behind the company's skill at producing popular, well-made cartoons, is also demonstrated an impressive ability to align itself, its founder, and its products with prevailing discourses about an ideal American culture, and to suggest that Disney was actually purposely contributing to the national good."[28] Cross similarly contends that Disney was careful to license only appropriate merchandise—rejecting, for example, a Mickey Mouse ashtray, regardless of how much money it might have brought, because it projected the wrong company image vis-à-vis children.[29]

Repeated emphasis on the Lone Ranger's shooting prowess and other attributes was intended to generate a merchandisable itch that could only be scratched through the acquisition of extra-textuals like *How the Lone Ranger Captured Silver*, *Life of Tonto*, or *How the Lone Ranger Makes his Silver Bullets*, which promised to deepen consumer knowledge about the masked cowboy hero.

Not surprisingly, LRI's sales brochures repeatedly talk about the added value for sponsors investing in premium development for the radio series. A percentage of every premium ordered by sponsors went back into LRI's coffers. While sponsors paid the entire cost of manufacturing and promoting Lone Ranger premiums, LRI collected a royalty from the manufacturer for each item sponsors purchased, exponentially increasing its earnings. Over 60 percent of LRI's net income in 1939 came from merchandising ($100,000), premium development ($50,000), or third-party media adaptation licenses ($100,000 for the comic strip alone). In total, the LRI's net worth was estimated as $400,000 (that's $62.7 million in 2008 dollars).[30]

While LRI saw *The Lone Ranger* radio series as a promotional vehicle for the myriad licensed products bearing its brand insignia, the company also sold potential sponsors on *The Lone Ranger* radio series via the merchandising strength of its extra-textuals. In other words, Lone Ranger merchandising helped sell *The Lone Ranger* radio series market-by-market, which, in turn, helped sell Lone Ranger merchandise within each new market. In order to accomplish this feat, however, LRI first had to convince potential clients that the Lone Ranger could be successfully adapted for local consumer needs.

Merchandising the Masked Man Market-by-Market

Historical accounts of the popularization of early twentieth-century icons like the Lone Ranger, Little Orphan Annie, and Buck Rogers tend to presume that these properties successfully took advantage of the national distribution possibilities emerging out of the radio and publishing industries to become overnight "American" heroes.[31] In actuality, the Lone Ranger's path to becoming a national icon was quite literally forged town by town, or more accurately, market-by-market, and not through a centralized national delivery system.

The second half of the 1930s was a tremendously diverse period for the commercial broadcasting industry in terms of content production, distribution, and the implementation of revenue-generating models. While Susan Smulyan has stated that by the early 1930s radio had become a nationally sponsored medium,[32] this is true only of NBC and CBS, and as Victoria Johnson reveals, even with these networks, national sponsorship was often more of a rhetorical flourish than a fait accompli.[33] Throughout the 1930s, these so-called national networks competed with locally owned and operated independent radio stations as well as regional and quasi-national networks. As the self-proclaimed national networks sought to expand their coverage by growing their affiliate ranks, NBC and CBS vied with geographically discrete stations and networks for market hegemony and sponsor dollars. As early as 1932, CBS had begun paying its affiliates to carry its complete lineup of star-studded "quality" programming, featuring both sponsored and sustaining series. Prior to this, affiliates had paid the national network per program and were usually required to carry only sponsored fare, leaving them free to fill their schedules with either locally produced or regionally inflected programming and to pursue local sponsorships that brought in direct revenue. Thus, local affiliates struck what Alex Russo calls a "Faustian bargain" in entering into relationships with national networks, trading much of their autonomy and authority over content selection and scheduling practices for guaranteed revenue and "quality" programming.[34]

Though some local and regional sponsors saw the national networking system as an opportunity to expand their market reach, many others worried that important outlets for promoting their products would disappear or that their autonomy in selecting sponsorship opportunities would dwindle. Their concern was that the national networks would co-opt local stations and either require them to carry programming that was already nationally sponsored or only make available for sponsorship a limited number of programs that were not suited for local or regional markets, or worse, were skewed toward East Coast and urban sensibilities.

Quasi-national networks like the Mutual Broadcasting System offered local stations greater autonomy and flexibility when it came to content selection and scheduling. Mutual affiliates could opt out of airing unsponsored programming in favor of local fare or could customize programming to suit their scheduling needs. Rather than adjust to a centralized production and promotion process, individual radio stations were encouraged to develop their own programming, which could also be sold to other Mutual affiliates via transcription recordings.[35] As Christopher Sterling and John Kittross explain, "This procedure permitted stations in smaller and more remote towns to have professional drama without network dependency."[36]

Regional networks positioned themselves as offering solutions for both locally based and national sponsors seeking to tap into particular communities, arguing that they provided content tailored toward the interests of their listeners as well as greater flexibility in customizing marketing campaigns. They also assured local and regional sponsors that their content could compete with the extravagant programming produced by the national networks, and at a fraction of the cost. This was the Michigan Radio Network's (MRN) rhetorical gambit when it initially sought a sponsor for the newly launched *Lone Ranger* radio series in 1933. MRN bragged that the 24,607 letters received by station WXYZ over the course of three days in response to a one-time Lone Ranger toy gun giveaway was a postal record exceeded only by the 22,000 letters delivered in one day to Father Coughlin's Detroit-based Shrine of the Little Flower radio program.[37] The promotional brochure added, however, that the Lone Ranger's letters were statistically more significant because Coughlin's program was broadcast coast to coast whereas WXYZ only served the Detroit area. The same brochure also pointed out that *The Lone Ranger* episode that received all this attention was aired at 9:30 p.m., "when radio audiences are at peak and listeners have settled down to mostly one point on the dial. . . . When coast-to-coast broadcasters are in full swing. . . . When world famous orchestras, entertainers and stars are said to be holding the center of interest."[38]

Though Lone Ranger marketing situated the property's success alongside national celebrities and coast-to-coast programming, MRN's appeal was geared toward local and regional sponsors. As the brochure concluded, the Lone Ranger's unprecedented gun giveaway success showed not only the series' popularity, but also the potential for sponsors to successfully reach listeners through independent stations like WXYZ or regional networks like MRN: "Advertisers who want the most return for their radio dollars will find listener coverage of the Michigan Radio Network profitable. It gives concentrated listener coverage to the 50% [of the total radio audience in Michigan] devoted to local offerings."[39] Of course, the company was careful not to suggest that it was MRN that had made the Lone Ranger popular, nor that the Lone Ranger's popularity was some sort of aberration unrelated to the regional network on which the series aired. Rather, it argued that the Lone Ranger's popularity served as evidence of MRN's success at winning over local listeners.

Throughout the late 1930s, LRI went market-by-market, contracting independent radio stations to license the transcribed radio program on a sustaining basis while offering them marketing assistance to procure a sponsor. Transcriptions were radio recordings made on wax cylinders that were sold via syndication directly to local and regional radio stations, bypassing the centralized live network model. The Lone Ranger was produced by KTBC for WXYZ under contract from LRI, all owned by Trendle. LRI contracted independent radio stations that purchased the transcribed radio program in blocks of thirteen, twenty-six, or fifty-two weeks, while searching for a local sponsor. In exchange for a net payment usually equivalent to 30–50 percent of the highest-priced half-hour drama on a station's schedule, LRI supplied three fifteen-minute episodes per week, along with publicity and advertising materials, lists of preferred premium manufacturers (i.e., those that LRI collected a healthy royalty on), and other merchandising management expertise.[40]

By 1937, WXYZ earned most of its revenue through the sale of programming to other stations rather than the selling of ad time to sponsors.[41] By 1938, the Lone Ranger was heard coast to coast on 107 different radio stations without the benefit of a national network and had procured 42 separate sponsors, mostly regional bakeries in noncompeting markets.[42] In 1939, LRI's gross receipts from licensing the rights to *The Lone Ranger* radio series exceeded $1 million.[43]

KTBC was not alone in rolling out its properties market-by-market via transcription recordings, though it was perhaps the most successful at doing so, as well as the most invested in maintaining this practice throughout the 1930s. Perhaps the most infamous radio program to establish its success in a similar manner was *Amos 'n' Andy* (1926–1950), which originated on Chicago's WMAQ in 1928 and was syndicated to thirty other stations around the country by the *Chicago Daily News*. NBC bought WMAQ in 1929 and placed the series on the network.[44] Ziv Television Programs Inc., one of the most successful producers of first-run syndicated television programming in the 1950s, began as a producer of syndicated radio programming in the 1940s, suggesting the continued importance of transcription sales to local and regional stations even after the network era officially took hold. Ziv produced radio programming in a wide range of genres, including action adventure series like *The Cisco Kid* and *Boston Blackie*, targeting both children and adults.[45] According to Hilmes, Ziv distributed 24 shows in 1947 across 850 stations and grossed $10 million.[46]

LRI marketed *The Lone Ranger* as a radio series capable of outdueling national programming in local markets and as a popular alternative in any market, small or large, rural or urban. LRI repeatedly pointed out to potential sponsors that the Lone Ranger had successfully entered into the national lexicon and was a popular cultural phenomenon. To this effect, a 1939 sales packet states, "Jack Benny, Fred Allen, Phil Baker and Phillip Morris programs mention 'the Lone Ranger' and play upon the words 'Hi Yo Silver.' . . . National magazines such as NEW YORKER, JUDGE, LIFE and prominent radio journals quote in picture and in story of 'the Lone Ranger' and the cry, 'Hi Yo Silver.' No matter where you go, you'll hear remarks referring to the great radio character."[47] LRI recycled these pop culture references as a means of demonstrating the Lone Ranger's national recognition as well as associating the property with other nationally recognized celebrities and media outlets. Yet the same packet also meticulously lists all of the station call signs broadcasting the radio series, along with their varying locations. While this list certainly helped potential sponsors identify whether the series was already carried in their market or where the closest broadcast was emanating from, its unstated effect was to call attention to the volume and diversity of local stations, from small towns like Enid, Oklahoma, and Coffeyville, Kansas, to urban centers like New York and Chicago, that had invested in the series.

Frontier Franchising

Merchandising tactics built around premiums and giveaways were key to LRI's expansion efforts. Where sponsors looked to premiums as a means of measuring audience size, LRI used these items to cultivate investment in *The Lone Ranger* radio property by demonstrating how successful merchandising campaigns could not only be replicated across diverse markets but also customized to meet differentiated social and business climates.

LRI's approach to extending the Lone Ranger brand constitutes an early form of media franchising. According to Thomas S. Dicke, franchising is "a method of organization that combines large and small business into a single administrative unit. In a franchising system, one large firm . . . grants or sells the rights to distribute its products or use its trade name and processes to a number of smaller firms."[48] Essentially, a parent company like McDonald's grants franchisees the rights to use its brand logo as well as exclusive access to its distribution, marketing, and merchandising services in exchange for a fee and a contractual guarantee that franchisees will maintain certain standards and practices that consumers have come to associate with the corporate brand. While McDonald's supplies franchisees with raw materials and a host of promotional services, franchisees are expected to do the actual work of (re)producing McDonald's-branded products.

Though he situates its development in the 1980s, Derek Johnson argues that media franchises are similar to traditional retail franchises like McDonald's in that they reproduce an "iconic cultural product available across a number of markets" and consist of "a network of production based in partnerships within and across media sectors . . . [that are constituted and maintained through] licensed partnerships, where independent parties from across media sectors enter into contractual relationships that allow intellectual property to be shared."[49]

Though both media and retail franchisees acquire a prepackaged set of materials established by the franchisor, success is often dependent on franchisees' abilities to customize those materials to meet the wants of particular constituencies. Koichi Iwabuchi identifies an increased reliance on "glocalization" strategies by transnational corporations seeking to extend their brands globally by adapting them to the cultural tastes and values of local economies.[50] Accordingly, in franchising its brand globally, a corporation like McDonald's would conform its product to suit the particularities of local markets—like replacing its usual beef products with McLentil burgers in India, or ensuring that Kashrut and Halal religious dietary laws are observed in Middle Eastern countries. Though part of its overarching global expansion strategy, the corporation's approach to every new market is decidedly tactical, responding to existing practices as much as attempting to impose new ones, "culturalizing" its standardized commodities as much as commodifying the cultural differences it encounters. The end result allows McDonald's to integrate global commodities with local customs and values.

In return, McDonald's not only gains a foothold in new markets but can also recycle successful glocal adaptations as part of its continuing expansion efforts, so that popular products or promotional campaigns initially tied to specific markets become part of its larger repertoire. As such, the El Maco burger, which originated in Australia and features salsa and sour cream condiments, is also a regular or seasonal menu item at McDonald's franchises in Norway, Sweden, and Finland, while halal-and-kosher-friendly McDonald's franchises can be found in India, Pakistan, Indonesia, the United Kingdom, and Argentina as well as in U.S. locations where there are significant Muslim and Jewish populations.

Similarly, international television format exchanges are providing a customizable alternative to syndicating existing TV series in foreign markets.[51] Sixteen countries around the world have adapted *So You Think You Can Dance*, a reality dance competition that originated in the United States. Format changes range from using local judges and contestants to incorporating local dance styles into the competitions.

Though reality television and game shows are the most commonly adapted formats internationally, character-based entertainment franchises have also been given the "glocal" treatment. Sitcoms like *Bewitched* (ABC, 1964–1973), *The Golden Girls* (NBC, 1985–1993), and *The Nanny* (CBS, 1993–1999) have all been sold as locally adaptable formulas around the world, from India to Turkey. The format for the Colombian telenovela *Yo Soy Betty La Fea* (RCN TV, 1999–2001), which revolved around the exploits of an unattractive yet brilliant girl working as an accountant in the fashion industry, has been franchised to twenty-one countries, including the United States. So too have the Israeli series *Betipul* (2009–2011) and

Hatufim (2010–2012), which have been adapted in the United States by pay cable networks HBO and Showtime as *In Treatment* (2009–2011) and *Homeland* (2011–). Meanwhile, children's programs like *Barney and Friends* (1988–) have been adapted in Israel and South Korea, and *Sesame Street* (1969–) has worked with international coproducers in thirty-one countries to develop localized variations of popular characters like Big Bird and Oscar the Grouch.

There were also earlier efforts to franchise media formats both locally and internationally. In the 1950s, the Hopalong Cassidy format was licensed to Cuban radio to produce a Spanish-language version of the hero as a platform for merchandising the property in Latin America.[52] And the franchising of the Baltimore-based children's program *Romper Room* in the 1950s was an example of licensors bypassing network television in favor of selling the format directly to local stations.[53] As part of the franchising process, *Romper Room*'s creators, Bert and Nancy Claster, allowed local communities to select the show's hosts, but insisted on training them. Within six years of its debut, *Romper Room* was franchised to 119 separate local TV stations across the United States as well as Australia and Japan.[54] Similarly, throughout the 1950s, *Bozo the Clown* was franchised to thirty-three local TV stations in the United States and adapted internationally in Brazil, Canada, and Mexico, with each locale featuring its own variation on Bozo and his sidekicks.[55]

Though comparisons with global fast food and television format franchising might seem far afield from character-based entertainment licensing in the 1930s, LRI applied many of the localization, customization, and recycling practices that contemporary franchises engage in to extend the Lone Ranger market-by-market. Though the content of the radio program remained static, the materials that surrounded it were malleable and capable of being tactically adjusted to fit varying markets differentiated by size, location, degrees of urbanity, and social values.

Attracting multiple local and regional sponsorships required LRI to devise a replicable and customizable marketing plan that could be recycled region by region, market-by-market. Marketing materials encouraged new sponsors to join the merchandising fold by simultaneously stressing both uniformity and variation in the Lone Ranger formula across markets. Seeking to replicate the Lone Ranger's successful first sponsorship with Gordon Bakery (1933–1939 over MRN stations), LRI often targeted bakeries as potential sponsors, ensuring that much of the Lone Ranger sales and merchandising packet could be implemented with only minor revisions (and assuring sponsors that the Lone Ranger was already a successful spokesperson for that particular product). The company was sensitive, however, to the needs of sponsors to distinguish themselves from their competitors. This balance was essential in convincing sponsors that the Lone Ranger could help sell their product through a standardized tie-in packet designed primarily for bread manufacturers as well as their corporate image by demonstrating how minor differentiations allowed each sponsor to align the property with their particular brand.

For example, a 1937 sales packet sent to potential sponsors included a four-page layout reprinting multiple versions of Lone Ranger sponsor tie-in items, already adopted by five different sponsoring bakeries.[56] The items reprinted in the brochure included Lone Ranger Safety Club membership application forms, envelopes, pledge cards, badges, and letters to local grocers stocking the sponsor's products. Arranged as a collage, the desired effect was to convince potential sponsors that these reusable tactics had already been successfully adopted by other similar manufacturers yet adjusted to meet each individual sponsor's needs.

Some differentiations amounted to surface level changes in font or design layout—for example, allowing a sponsor's name to appear at the top or bottom of the Lone Ranger newsletter. Others were more substantial. While each sponsor's pledge card listed ten promises made by Lone Ranger Safety Club members, these promises varied in scope, with some placing exclusive emphasis on obeying traffic safety rules while others encompassed larger civic responsibilities and moral values. While all the cards included the promise that children not play in the streets, Kilpatrick Bakery's pledge card included nine other related traffic safety rules, such as not crossing the street except at designated crosswalks and not riding one's bicycle on the wrong side of the street. In contrast, both Kobako's and Gordon's pledge cards were far more expansive, asking that children promise to always tell the truth, be kind to birds and animals, study hard, have good hygiene, and most importantly—seeing as it was both the final pledge and in larger print—"obey [their] father and mother" (see Figure 3.2).

The Safety Club pledges varied according to local community concerns over commercial radio's influence on children and sponsor desires to promote a positive impact within those markets. Pledge cards could be adapted for either environment, in some cases promoting how the sponsor and the Masked Man together taught children to be mindful of the dangers of automobiles, in other cases emphasizing how the sponsor actually reinforced traditional values through bringing the Lone Ranger to the local airwaves.

Figure 3.2. Lone Ranger Consumer Tie-In foldout featuring multiple customizable premiums, ca. 1937. Courtesy of the Burton Historical Collection, Detroit Public Library.

Merchandising wasn't the only flexible or customizable element of the Lone Ranger that LRI tried to sell to potential sponsors. Since it was a transcribed series, LRI argued that *The Lone Ranger* could be successfully inserted into a radio station's schedule at any time of day. Indeed, on WXYZ, the series ran Monday, Wednesday, and Friday evenings, alternating between 7:00 and 9:30 p.m. On WCKY in Cincinnati, however, the Lone Ranger aired at 7:30 p.m. on Tuesdays and Thursdays and at 4:30 p.m. on Sundays. LRI's 1939 sales manual states on its front cover that the series is "designed for early evening broadcasting," but inside, under the section titled "Distinction Won 'The Hard Way,'" the licensor brags that the Lone Ranger's audience continued to grow despite multiple schedule changes between 1934 and 1936, during which time the series could be heard as late as 8:00 p.m.[57] Though transcriptions may have allowed radio stations to flexibly insert the series into their schedules, LRI had to first convince them that *The Lone Ranger* could be successful at any hour of the day and with listeners of any age.

LRI's sponsorship cultivation strategies in the late 1930s were purposely open-ended enough to attract clients targeting more than just children and selling more than just bread. A fluff piece appearing in the *Detroit Saturday Night* newspaper boasts, "Elsewhere, [the Lone] Ranger may be working as a salesman of gasoline, pickles, milk or breakfast food."[58] In Baltimore, the Lone Ranger Ice Cream Company offered listeners multiple premiums, both over the radio and in retail stores stocking their products, including Lone Ranger matchbooks, a decidedly adult giveaway that suggests the sponsor was seeking either a dual audience for the series or a less direct way of getting parents to purchase ice cream cones for their kids. Indeed, an oft-cited 1941 survey used by LRI estimated that 63 percent of the Lone Ranger's total audience consisted of adults.[59]

LRI contracts also stipulated that any promotional materials or premium giveaways devised by sponsors needed to be copyrighted in the name of "The Lone Ranger Inc.," granting LRI not only ownership of said promotional materials, but the right to reproduce and sell those ideas to other potential licensees.[60] The company habitually recycled successful local marketing initiatives and merchandising campaigns as part of the overall Lone Ranger package.[61] More than this, however, LRI repeatedly acknowledged the inspired efforts of local franchisees as part of its own marketing, which contributed to an overall sense that the Lone Ranger was not just a localizable national brand, but that local communities had an active hand in shaping its national appeal.

A promotional pamphlet intended to drum up summertime sponsor-

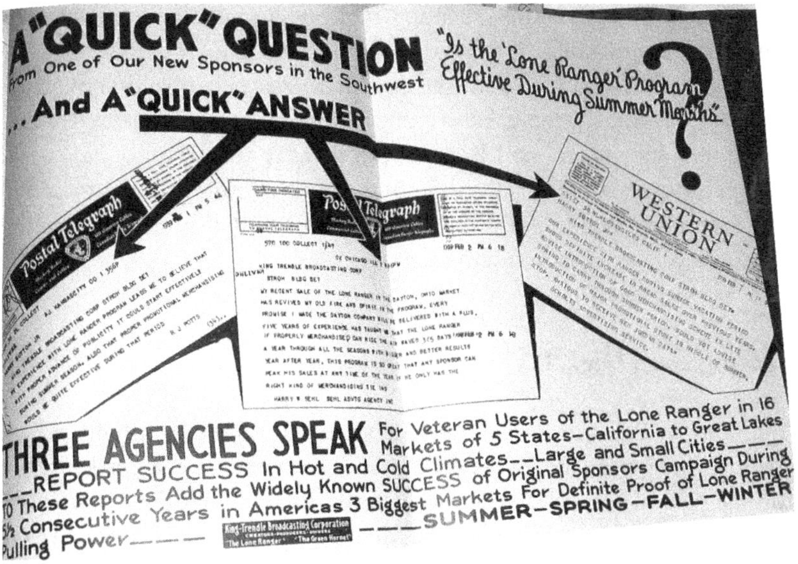

Figure 3.3. LRI recycles correspondence and allows local licensees to "tell one another" how successful the Lone Ranger was. Courtesy of the Burton Historical Collection, Detroit Public Library.

ships for the radio series took the rhetorical tack of answering a "quick question from one of our new sponsors in the Southwest" about the Lone Ranger's hot weather success by reproducing three distinct telegrams from ad agencies developing marketing campaigns built around the series. Described by LRI as input from "veteran users" representing clients in sixteen markets consisting of both large and small cities across five states from California to the Great Lakes, the pamphlet answered a temporal question—what is the best season to sponsor the series—with a spatial response that allowed potential and existing sponsors to hear about the Lone Ranger's success directly from one another, lending "authenticity" to LRI's marketing efforts.[62] In essence, by permitting clients to sell the virtues of the radio program to one another, LRI's marketing established the Lone Ranger's national reputation for localized success (see Figure 3.3).

Recirculating sponsor and ad agency kudos also helped LRI establish its managerial function as coordinator between stations and sponsors, facilitating various local parties' ability to share strategies and success stories with one another (even as the company openly recycled successful merchandising campaigns as part of its marketing arsenal). Though sponsors and ad agencies all talked about the Lone Ranger, they spoke to one another through LRI. In the process, LRI's own labor of selectively foregrounding certain merchandising practices over others and convincing licensees to adopt comparable strategies went largely unnoticed. Though the letters and telegrams LRI reproduced were real testimonials to the Lone Ranger's success, it is how the licensor organized these materials that inevitably established the property's local reputation while still building its status as a national cultural icon.

Tapping Local Markets

LRI argued that *The Lone Ranger* radio series could not only help local stations and regional networks compete against national network fare but also help sponsors extend their reach into local markets, especially where resistance existed toward outsiders. Merchandising guides instructed local content distributors and sponsors on how to use Lone Ranger giveaways to better their relationships with existing local retailers and cultivate business from other retailers on their route. For instance, "Plans should be made for intensive dealer contact by salesmen co-incident with advertising announcements for the free [Lone Ranger] photograph. Obviously, near every retailer stop there should be at least another retailer, who having had calls for the advertised product could be easily induced to sell the merchandise."[63]

From the start, the Lone Ranger's radio appeal mattered most to Gordon Bakery in terms of how it could be converted into grocers' stocking Silvercup Bread. As one ad aimed at this occupational community asks, "Who's asleep at the switch? Only the grocer who doesn't take advantage of this amazing radio advertising by *featuring* SILVERCUP in his store."[64]

As the Depression set in, sponsors looked for any advantage they could muster to distinguish their products from those of their competitors. Branded products provided an important intervention. As Cross notes, "The media personality put a 'child's friend' on an ordinary sand pail or pull toy. These toys stood out from the generic version and in effect sold themselves. Retailers then had an incentive to seek a specific line of goods. . . . This gave manufacturers who used licensed characters leverage over store owners."[65]

LRI assembled numerous manuals on how to exploit *The Lone Ranger* effectively for "maximum retail results." Lone Ranger sales kits included detailed suggestions on how to "build up" the importance of merchandising products with retailers.[66] A section titled "Internal Propaganda" cautioned licensees to answer every fan letter because "every letter represents a family. Every family represents potential consumption of product."[67] Strategies for getting sales staff on board included playing a sample episode of the radio program "to give a definite idea of entertainment and use of commercials."[68] Sales staffs were also encouraged to don Lone Ranger cowboy hats and greet retailers with the cry "Hi-Yo Silver" as ways to build sales.[69]

While such suggestions ranged from the obvious to the ridiculous, LRI's recommendations were designed to cultivate investment in the Lone Ranger as an inspirational muse for marketers while also teaching appropriate extraction techniques for maximizing the property's value. A letter from Lloyd George Venard, director of sales for station WCKY in Cincinnati, reporting on the sales campaign on behalf of the Schultze Baking Company, attests to this inspirational function. Venard recounts, "We furnished cowboy entertainment and then played a transcription of the program after which we held a sales meeting which lasted until 12 o'clock and which did not drag for one minute. It was the most remarkable sales meeting I had ever seen because the officials of the Schultze outfit kept firing inspiration to an extremely responsive group of 100 salesmen."[70] Unsurprisingly, LRI reprinted excerpts from this letter in numerous merchandising manuals.

Attracting retailer cooperation required sponsors to provide them with participation incentives. LRI developed detailed merchandising plans designed to help sponsors in assisting retailers with making the Lone Ranger *their* salesman. Every retailer was instructed to let customers know that free Lone Ranger masks were "his own give-away and not the sponsor's."[71] This masked the overt sales function of such premiums and built goodwill for retailers, particularly with children, that then transferred into increased orders of a sponsor's products. Of course, the insistence that every mask be accounted for—"make it forcefully plain . . . the number of unsold products must correspond with the number of masks on hand"—also suggests a certain degree of mistrust between manufacturers and retailers that licensors worked to arbitrate through such detailed merchandising plans.[72]

Cross-Promoting the Cowboy

The Lone Ranger's reputation throughout the 1930s was not merely established market-by-market, but also across differentiated product markets. In addition to the radio series' 42 sponsors and 107 broadcast station licensees,[73] the King Features Syndicate sold a daily *Lone Ranger* comic strip to 80 newspapers across the country.[74] Several Lone Ranger novels were already in print from Grossett & Dunlap (for young adults) and Whitman Publishing (Big Little Books for children), and a comic book published by Dell would debut in 1940. By 1939, Republic Pictures had also released two fifteen-part movie serials. The first film serial won the 1938 Exhibitor Award for Best Serial of the Year and quickly became the top-grossing serial of its time.[75] Billed by Republic as the first movie serial to use a fictional character invented on radio (many serials of the era adapted content from comic strips and pulp novels), *The Lone Ranger* earned $594,137 at the box office (the 1939 sequel, *The Lone Ranger Rides Again*, earned $523,026), for which LRI received $18,750 up front plus 10 percent of all film rental fees in excess of $390,000.[76] The actual revenue LRI received for the film is difficult to measure, in part because the above-mentioned 10 percent came out of Republic's share of the profits (which was 60 percent of the film rentals, the rest going to distributors and exhibitors), but LRI estimated its revenue at around $60,000.[77]

Since Republic did not own a fleet of theaters as did the Hollywood majors, the studio was reliant upon local exhibitors booking its films. In fact, Republic insisted that it could only effectively sell *The Lone Ranger* film serial in markets where the radio series was already on the air, contributing to LRI's expansion push in the late 1930s. As Trendle explained, "After we got the Republic production on the market, we found out from Republic that wherever the picture played, if there was no radio program, the picture died; and they were on our necks all the time to be ahead of the [film] with the radio program. . . . We expanded the radio program just as rapidly as possible for our own selfish interests, but the Republic people withheld the release of their motion picture until after we got into the territory with the radio program, in order to boost their own grosses."[78]

Where the content of the radio series, comic strip, and film remained germane to their respective media, LRI considered Lone Ranger extratextual materials to be rife for "cooperative exploitation."[79] LRI encouraged its licensees to think of the materials surrounding each of these texts, including spot advertisements, contests, and giveaways, as shared property that could be utilized to direct Lone Ranger fans across media sites. Radio sponsors were encouraged to set up promotional lobby displays in theaters in exchange for special radio announcements alerting listeners to the film serial. LRI reasoned, "If the radio station 'plugs' the movie and vice versa, the result will be added program interest for the sponsor; increased attendance at the theatre; and a final result of excellent audience gain for the station."[80] Meanwhile, film exhibitors were prompted to set up counter and window displays in local retail shops that interspersed film stills from Republic's serial with Lone Ranger licensed merchandise available for sale.[81] Finally, LRI advised radio sponsors to furnish store owners carrying their products with film tickets, so they could talk up the serial with customers.[82] In encouraging local licensees to put aside their differences and focus instead on their shared interest in promoting the Lone Ranger brand, LRI worked to establish merchandising frenzies in their communities.

Even as LRI regularly encouraged licensees to see the benefits of working together, it also sought to teach clients the importance of respecting one another's particular turfs. Hence, while Republic's merchandising guide for local film exhibitors extols the virtues of tying in *The Lone Ranger* film release with local radio sponsor initiatives, it also warns exhibitors not to buy ad space on radio without first seeking the approval of local sponsors. "All tie-ups and announcements on or about 'the Lone Ranger,' either with radio stations carrying the program or those not carrying the program, must be made with or okayed by, the concerns sponsoring said program in the district in which the theater playing the serial is located."[83] In this manner, LRI ensured that its various third-party media licensees were not working at cross-purposes with one another, and more importantly, were not undermining the apparent omnipresence of the Lone Ranger brand.

A Friendly Outsider?

In order to cultivate these localizable synergies, however, LRI often had to demonstrate that the Lone Ranger could become a valuable contributing member of the communities it sought to profit from. LRI encouraged sponsors and broadcasters to build anticipation for the radio series by letting listeners know several weeks out that "the Lone Ranger is coming" to town. In this manner, the promotional campaign for the radio series mimicked its plot structure, which saw the Masked Man ride to the rescue of a new town every episode. Though the series formula repeatedly emphasized the Lone Ranger's outsider status, the Masked Man always fought on behalf of small-town values, not to upend or displace them. Even as extra-textual materials continued to serve as promotional vehicles for the Lone Ranger (and its sponsors) and as sites of consumer contact with the brand, many of these items were also designed to offset concerns over consumerism and help sponsors come across as good corporate citizens deeply invested in local community matters.

In their sociological studies of how "average Americans" were responding to changes at the onset of the twentieth century brought about by the emergence of an increasingly centralized mass culture, Robert and Helen Lynd noted that though many middle-class interviewees were excited about the ways new technologies, production practices, and consumer choices were making daily routines easier and more efficient, there was also significant trepidation over the threat to local value systems.[84] As Sammond (2005) summarizes, the Lynds' *Middletown* studies revealed that "with the rise of mass production—and mass culture—came the apparent loss of local control over the production of daily necessities, and with it a seeming loss over patterns of consumption . . . local meanings and practices were being replaced with mass meanings and practices."[85] In particular, an emerging nationally networked mass media system was viewed as potentially detrimental to the maintenance of local autonomy.

Hence, promotional and merchandising materials for the Lone Ranger often advocated for sponsors to engage in what Sharon Marie Ross identifies as "invitational strategies" designed to encourage local participation in shaping the Lone Ranger's meanings.[86] For example, an oft-repeated promotional tie-in for *The Lone Ranger* radio program was to have local newspapers conduct interviews with "leading townspeople" about their childhood heroes, canvassing their "views and opinions on how the Lone Ranger stacks up with their particular favorites," which provided opportunities for different communities to define heroism differently and required marketers to adapt the Masked Man's attributes accordingly.[87] Meanwhile, Republic Pictures rallied local film exhibitors to team up with area schools in promoting *The Lone Ranger* serial, encouraging them to "work with history teachers in the school. Offer free tickets to those winning essay contests on the Civil War, Texas after the Civil War, or any other suitable topic. Let the teachers pick the winners. . . . Make your Masked Ranger one of the most prominent characters in town."[88] Jacobson argues that early twentieth-century advertisers regularly supplied schools with "enrichment materials" designed to raise brand awareness among both pupils and educators.[89] LRI and Republic's goal was not only to have the Lone Ranger become a valuable member of every community he entered, but to empower locals to participate in spreading his gospel. By having teachers select winning essays and reward students with free tickets to *The Lone Ranger*, the promotion unified the property's social and commercial value while also handing over to local educators the power to choose the types of work that should be rewarded. All of this furthered sponsor goals of offering products that appeared to reflect the community's values back onto itself.

Nowhere was this interweaving of national and local identities more evident than in LRI's efforts to establish local chapters of the national Lone Ranger Safety Club. As I argue in the following section, the club was essential to connecting radio sponsors to local communities and to LRI's goals of building loyal brand communities seeking to lead a Lone Ranger lifestyle.

The Lone Ranger Safety Club

The first Lone Ranger Safety Club was launched on October 14, 1935, sponsored by Gordon Bakery and implemented by Gordon's advertising agency, Sehl Advertising.[90] It is unclear how much LRI might have influenced Sehl and Gordon's initial Safety Club initiative, though the idea of a Lone Ranger club had been bandied about since before the radio series debuted. Letters between Fran Striker and WXYZ's talent director, James Jewell, confirm that *The Lone Ranger* was indeed targeted to children, in particular fourteen- and fifteen-year-olds, and that from a very early stage, the possibilities for cultivating and effectively measuring this audience were conceptualized in terms of socially engineering fan communities built around the character's cult of personality. As Striker wrote on January 6, 1933, "I think there will be splendid possibilities in this character of the Lone Ranger . . . the thought struck me as I was writing the play that you might organize a LONE RANGER CLUB of boys, and ask them to write in for their membership cards, etc." Striker's very next sentence establishes the connection between such a fan club and the potential for commercial exploitation. "There might be good commercial possibilities too, for a concern that is selling something that is designed especially for growing boys, clothes, breakfast food, or something of that sort."[91]

Gordon's and Sehl saw the club as a way of gauging the size of its audience by encouraging write-ins to MRN radio stations for membership cards. They also saw the club as fostering good business relations with local retailers to whom they supplied baked goods. Pledge cards were made available only at participating groceries, both necessitating point-of-purchase contact between child consumers and retailers and providing a valuable sales incentive to attract new retailers to stock their products. LRI would recycle both of these ideas in its merchandising campaigns to attract local and regional sponsors in noncompeting markets. Sponsors were strongly encouraged not only to launch the clubs but also to invest resources in starting up neighborhood versions, which would "intensify the club spirit" and "furnish a means of added sales strength to retailers in each zone."[92]

In many respects, the Lone Ranger Safety Club (LRSC) was not unique. Many brands directed at children tried to tap into the popularity of burgeoning boys' and girls' clubs that were popping up all over the United States in the 1920s. Little Orphan Annie, Jack Armstrong, and almost every other radio personality whose sponsor targeted children had some sort of club that listeners could join. Sammond reveals that as early as 1930, Disney "attempted to join the network of clubs and organizations to which children belonged, creating the Mickey Mouse Club, precursor to the company's famous television program two decades later."[93] According to DeCordova, the Mickey Mouse Club boasted 150,000–200,000 members in 1930 and over one million by 1932.[94] In comparison, LRSC membership was estimated at 1.5 million children in 1938.[95]

While Little Orphan Annie used club membership to generate sales for Ovaltine by tying in club activities with sponsored products, and Disney's club was designed to generate a "consumption community" built around Mickey Mouse movies and toys,[96] the LRSC mentioned sponsors only indirectly and almost never promoted particular products as the locus of club activities. Instead, the LRSC transformed the Lone Ranger from a mere set of products and texts that children could consume into a friend and community leader children could build their daily experiences around (see Figure 3.4).

In essence, LRI sought to engineer a Lone Ranger "brand community" that could be mobilized to advocate on the Masked Man's (and his sponsors') behalf and would integrate the Lone Ranger into its daily rituals. According to Albert M. Muniz and Thomas C. O'Guinn, a brand community is "a specialized, non-geographically bound community, based on a structured set of social relationships among admirers of the brand . . . marked by a shared consciousness, rituals and traditions, and a sense of moral responsibility . . . [to integrate and retain] members [and assist] brand community members in the proper use of the brand."[97] By definition, brand community members share an affinity with a particular brand and form bonds through their shared investment in its meanings and values, forging what Muniz and O'Guinn refer to as a sense of "we-ness."[98] Henry Jenkins asserts that "brand loyalty is the holy grail of affective economics . . . reshap[ing] our emotional bonds with brands" in

Figure 3.4. Cover of the *Lone Ranger Safety Club Official Manual* sponsored by Weber's Bread. Note that this is the same image used on Lone Ranger-branded merchandise. Author's collection.

order to generate "emotional capital."[99] James H. McAlexander, John W. Schouten, and Harold F. Koenig argue that "the existence and meaningfulness of the community inhere in customer experience rather than in the brand around which the experience revolves."[100] In other words, "the link is more important than the thing."[101] McAlexander, Schouten, and Koenig also assert that while brand communities often form organically, "marketers can strengthen brand communities by facilitating shared customer experiences."[102] They also suggest that brand communities are constituted by "a fabric of relationships in which a customer is situated," including relationships with the brand and with other customers, as well as with the firm controlling the brand.[103]

Based on the above definition, it seems evident that LRI sought to engineer a far more expansive brand community than just Lone Ranger consumers—one that included the company's many stakeholders as well. LRI's franchising work facilitated an imagined shared consciousness among licensees, a sense of "we-ness" spurred on by local and regional clients communicating with one another through LRI about their successful Lone Ranger merchandising experiences, which in turn constituted a shared set of rituals and traditions built around exploiting the property's merchandisable attributes. LRI's recycling practices allowed local and regional clients to feel as though they had a collective hand in shaping the Masked Man's national reputation, making them "participants in the brand's larger social construction and play[ing] a vital role in the brand's ultimate legacy."[104] Through recycled success stories, LRI's licensees demonstrated a "moral responsibility" to help LRI build its client base and teach future Lone Ranger licensees how to properly exploit the property. In a sense, LRI sought to use its licensees as brand advocates even as it also sought to teach licensees how to cultivate Lone Ranger brand advocates from among their localized consumer bases. This, in turn, suggests a fairly complex and important relationship between the non-geographically bound nature of brand communities and their rootedness in familial, communal, and other spatially bounded practices.

While Jenkins is undoubtedly correct in his assertion that online social networking sites allow brand community members to "sustain their connections over long periods and thus to intensify the role the community plays in their purchasing decisions," digital tools are by no means the only nor even the primary way to connect consumers and intensify their investment in a particular brand.[105] Indeed, even as Muniz Jr. and O'Guinn argue for the increased importance of social networking and other online tools for sustaining brand community activities and interactions, their study begins with interviewing members of the Fairlawn community in Bloomington, Indiana, about their consumption habits and observing how brand loyalties are enacted within family and neighborhood settings.[106] While the experiences community members share with one another certainly circulate online, digital brand communities continue to rely on local stories to reinforce a sense of "we-ness" manifested through similarities and variances in practiced rituals and traditions.

The LRSC was designed to accomplish similar goals through the formation of localized neighborhood chapters that made Lone Ranger brand activities an essential part of children's daily rituals, in the process creating a visible brand presence within actual communities. This strategy was perfectly in tune with the needs of the Lone Ranger's multiple sponsoring bread manufacturers, whose sales strategies often included home delivery and partnerships with local retailers, making them visible members of many of the communities in which their products were sold.

Getting child consumers into retail shops and movie theaters in the late 1930s was no easy feat. Vivianna Zelizer and Lisa Jacobson have documented mounting efforts to protect children against the perceived ill effects of both commercial and industrial culture arising throughout the late nineteenth and early twentieth centuries, often resulting in attempts to sequester children's spaces and limit their mobility. Zelizer points to the rising panic in the late 1920s over traffic-related fatalities from children playing in the streets, which led to greater efforts to promote gated parks, fenced backyards, and walled playrooms as ideal spaces for children to safely inhabit.[107] Jacobson suggests that these confined areas were also imagined as protecting middle-class children from the emerging consumer culture that threatened their moral compass.[108]

In response, LRI sought to develop extra-textual materials that facilitated acceptable opportunities for children to traverse "dangerous" commercial spaces between home and school. The LRSC addressed parental concerns over traffic-related accidents by encouraging children to be more proactive in teaching one another how to play safely outdoors. In so doing, safety clubs proposed an alternative solution to limiting children's mobility by instead offering to teach them how to successfully navigate modern landscapes.

Hence, the Lone Ranger Safety Clubs actually were designed to deflect attention away from sales efforts directed at children, and instead provide sponsors with associative value by promoting the corporation's civic-mindedness. Ostensibly, the LRSC supported traffic safety, healthy living, and respect for authority by encouraging boys and girls to form local club chapters and earn Lone Ranger citations. In this sense, the LRSC was designed to draw children's attention away from the actual radio program and refocus it on the positive activities and values that the Lone Ranger promoted with sponsored assistance.

Exploitation strategies devised by LRI encouraged sponsors to get local authorities to endorse the initiative (and, indirectly, the sponsor). In the 1939 manual *The Lone Ranger: Details of Procedure in Handling the Exploitation of the Program for Maximum Retail Results*, LRI devoted several pages to ideas for maximizing the positive publicity the LRSC might generate for sponsors. Among them are instructions to "Enlist support of local authorities on safety, such as Mayor, Chief of Police, Superintendent of Schools."[109] LRI also supplied sponsors with prepackaged publicity into which the names of interchangeable community leaders could easily be inserted:

> *LONE RANGER WINS PRAISE*
> Parents, educators, and others keenly interested in children's radio programs have been quick to recognize the healthful influence of this great radio feature which now is broadcast coast to coast . . .
> Among those who have commented on the outstanding nature of THE LONE RANGER have been John Doe, Superintendent of Schools of ____________; Richard Blank, President of _________ Chamber of Commerce; Mrs. Jane Roe, President of _______ Women's Club; and Mrs. John Jones, Chairman of the Parent-Teacher Association.[110]

Though clearly formulaic, endorsement opportunities such as these were intended to ingratiate the Lone Ranger and its sponsors into local communities by aligning corporate and small town civic values. The effectiveness of privileging civic duty over commercial sales and then garnering official support from local authorities for these initiatives can be summarized by a January 11, 1941, article in the *New Republic*, which extolled LRI's socially valuable achievements. "The Safety Clubs give the necessary check on popularity and secure the type of local support for which publicity men give their shirts. The mayor or at least the local police chief will always sound off for safety, sales of (insert name of product) go up, and accidents go down in the community. 'Hi-Yo Silver! Away . . . !'"[111]

The LRSC would prove key to LRI's efforts to cultivate investment in the property within new markets, not only offering licensees "a ready-made audience" where "every member is an enthusiastic Lone Ranger booster" who could be counted on to purchase branded products, but also generating goodwill among civic leaders and parents for its character-building activities.[112] Promoting an image of community service through sponsorship of the Lone Ranger and his Safety Club helped offset accusations of greed and claims that businesses were out of touch with consumer needs and concerns during the Depression. It also reframed the terrain of struggle away from national opposition between corporations and government toward local partnerships between the two. Even as the federal government sought to implement New Deal legislation that would give it unprecedented oversight of corporate spending and local economic development programs, the LRSC offered an alternative vision of American citizenship—one that stressed individual efforts, emphasized safeguarding home and community, and was rooted in a complicated and paternalistic relationship between corporate sponsors and local governments.

While appearing on the surface to be "blandly civic," Lone Ranger Safety Clubs often indirectly promoted private enterprise as inherently American.[113] For instance, the 1939 Safety Club Manual produced for Weber's Bread makes several references to the Lone Ranger's desire for boys and girls to "grow up to be happy, healthy and useful citizens" and is filled with patriotic content, including the words to "The Star-Spangled Banner" and a statement that "Almost everything this country has is the result of people pulling together for good and worthy causes."[114] Yet what sort of citizenship did the Safety Club advocate? Decidedly, it endorsed one that limited federal intervention; encouraged local, communal, and individual initiatives; and praised the historic role that free enterprise and corporate sponsorship have played in promoting progress.

While Daniel Czitrom has argued that media constructs contemporary needs through nostalgic appeals to a mythical past,[115] William L. Bird has pointed to the ways that American corporations during the Depression sought to invoke a "usable past" in order to justify their continued appeals for consumption in the face of economic hardship. Corporations stressed the historic continuity between the growth of the American corporation and America itself, with the Depression as an anomaly that would be countered so long as the market was left free to pursue its natural course.

Similarly, Lone Ranger Safety Clubs confirmed that their hero's mission began when "The West of old was fraught with dangers of many kinds: highwaymen, land sharks and roving bands of outlaws were found everywhere. This condition was, in large measure, due to the fact that the US government was unable to establish army posts except in strategic places, because of lack of funds."[116] Where the government was unable to help local communities grow, corporations could. Without ever directly attacking the New Deal, the Lone Ranger Safety Club offered an alternative vision of American citizenship.

Sammond (2005) argues that as communities like the one studied by the Lynds began to lose control over local means of production, they placed increased emphasis on regulating consumption in an attempt to transform consumer impulses—especially among children—into productive activities. Sammond suggests that many corporations sought to shape this "productive consumption" discourse by aligning corporatist and parental interests in managing the behaviors of those in their charge.[117] The LRSC positioned the Masked Man and his corporate benefactors as providing local communities with opportunities for self-management through their participation in club-sponsored initiatives.

Tellingly, the organization of neighborhood chapters took on a corporate structure. Under the heading "Constitution and By-Laws," the LRSC guide explained, "At the first meeting a *temporary* chairman and secretary should be elected. Regular officers would not be elected until after the constitution is formed and adopted. . . . all future business of your club will be managed by these laws."[118] Further along, the guide proposes, "Although it is not necessary for a club to adopt a regular order of business, most clubs do follow a regular business procedure in order to save time and effort."[119] In promoting efficient time management skills and work hierarchies as essential to club "business," the LRSC transposed corporatist ideals onto productive consumption practices by teaching children to consume efficiently and productively.

Moreover, traffic safety was positioned as entirely the responsibility of individual children, not rooted in the need for safer car manufacturing standards or stricter government regulations for drivers. After providing shocking statistics about automobile-related deaths involving children in the streets, the LRSC guide argued, "COURTESY PREVENTS ACCIDENTS. So let's be courteous—everyone of us—all the time!"[120] and then resorted to scare tactics, scolding, "How would you feel, Safety Ranger, if it was copying your careless dash into the street playing, or some other thoughtless action, that caused one of these smaller boys or girls to be injured or killed? ALWAYS REMEMBER THAT YOUR CARELESS EXAMPLE MAY CAUSE A SMALLER CHILD'S INJURY OR DEATH! PLAY SAFE FOR THE SAKE OF OTHERS."[121]

Even as the LRSC seemingly offset the Lone Ranger's commercial functions as a branded spokesperson, the clubs offered sponsors an array of marketing tools that grew directly out of its civic and educative imperatives. Besides transforming community leaders into pitchmen for the solid work that sponsors were doing in positively influencing children, the LRSC encouraged all of its members to ritualistically wear their Lone Ranger citation badges as proof of their dedication to the cause of promoting traffic safety. "It is an honor to be seen wearing this badge, so make good use of it. Besides the distinction it gives you, always bear in mind that when others see you wearing the Lone Ranger Safety Badge it will remind them to be cautious about accidents."[122] Of course, since badges prominently featured the sponsor's name, they also transformed LRSC members into walking billboards. Thus, rather than counteracting the Lone Ranger's commercial appeal, the LRSC actually expanded it, endorsing corporate sponsors and products under the guise of promoting civic duty.

While the LRSC was designed with sponsor interests in mind, the real beneficiary was LRI. The licensor profited handsomely from all of the extra premiums and promotional materials that sponsors had to order as part of the package, including pledge cards, badges, merit citations, and Safety Club guide books. In each instance, LRI would collect a royalty on a sponsor's order. Moreover, the LRSC was a particularly effective tool in attracting new radio sponsors and other third-party media licensees. Perhaps the greatest reward LRI received, however, was free publicity for the Lone Ranger brand. Though radio sponsors paid all the promotional costs for—and dedicated radio time to—launching the LRSC, club activities rarely tied directly back to either the radio series or its sponsors. Rather, the series was merely a pretext for cultivating Lone Ranger fan clubs and deepening fan investment in the masked rider. In turn, the LRSC prepared Lone Ranger fans for an expansive brand experience that far exceeded the scope of the radio program. In this sense, it acted as a precursor to Disney's experiments with television in the mid-1950s, which Chris Anderson describes as "propelled by a centrifugal force that guided the viewer away from the immediate textual experience toward a more pervasive sense of textuality, one that encouraged the consumption of further Disney texts, further Disney products, further Disney experiences."[123]

LRSC members were imagined as a non-medium-specific brand community that would seek out opportunities to engage with the Lone Ranger across an array of media and merchandising outlets. Thus, Republic Pictures described the LRSC as "one of the largest juvenile clubs ever organized for publicity purposes" and promised exhibitors that "Lone Ranger Safety Clubs boasting over one and one-half million members means money in the box office—and assures exhibitors of child patronage."[124] The LRSC was rarely used as a forum for any direct advertising or merchandising of Lone Ranger productions of any sort. Instead, it coordinated efforts to let club members in on the Masked Man's secrets with select merchandise available for sale at local retail stores.

For example, a feature in the 1939 LRSC manual for Weber's Bread titled "the Lone Ranger's Equipment" describes how each aspect of the Lone Ranger's attire contributed to his success, including how the Masked Man's "brightly colored bandana neckerchief, when pulled over his face, protects the Lone Ranger's nose, throat and lungs against the overpowering dust clouds stirred up by the big cattle round-ups, and has often protected his face from stinging sand particles in driving wind storms."[125] The feature provides similarly detailed and evocative explanations for the functions of the Lone Ranger's Stetson hat, mask, vest, revolvers, holsters, chaps, and boots. Adjacent to these descriptions of the Masked Man's "colorful regalia" is a drawn re-creation of each of these wardrobe components, laid out head to toe as if worn by an invisible mannequin.

While the manual makes no mention of where club members might acquire such "equipment," the bodiless pieces align almost perfectly with the fully decked-out child featured in the Collegeville Flag & Manufacturing Company's promotional display for the Lone Ranger playsuits it was licensed to manufacture. The Collegeville playsuit also featured a Lone Ranger–branded Stetson hat, mask, neckerchief, vest, gun and holster set, and trouser chaps, each sold separately but capable of being assembled to re-create a fully embodied Lone Ranger.[126] The LRSC manual thus served as an important link in the chain between the radio series as branded entertainment and Lone Ranger merchandise (see Figures 3.5 and 3.6).

LRI envisioned the LRSC as extending the Lone Ranger experience into almost every aspect of a child's daily life, transforming the property from an entertainment vehicle into a lifestyle brand through the promotion of a set of mundane rituals that LRSC members were expected to perform. The LRSC's advocacy of a "clean, healthy, active life" certainly helped sponsors offset parental concerns over commercialism, but it also helped LRI establish a set of Lone Ranger–inspired and recommended activities that had "good Safety Rangers" brushing their teeth, washing themselves carefully, eating the right foods, engaging in sports, and getting enough sleep to ensure that they had the energy to succeed in school.[127] All of these areas also conveniently corresponded with Lone Ranger–branded merchandise like soap, dishes, baseball caps, jumpsuits, bed linens, and school supplies. Rather than advertise a bar of soap sculpted to look like the Lone Ranger (see Figure 3.7), the LRSC promoted cleanliness as an essential part of being a Safety Ranger. Silver and Tonto soap bars were also available at local retail outlets.

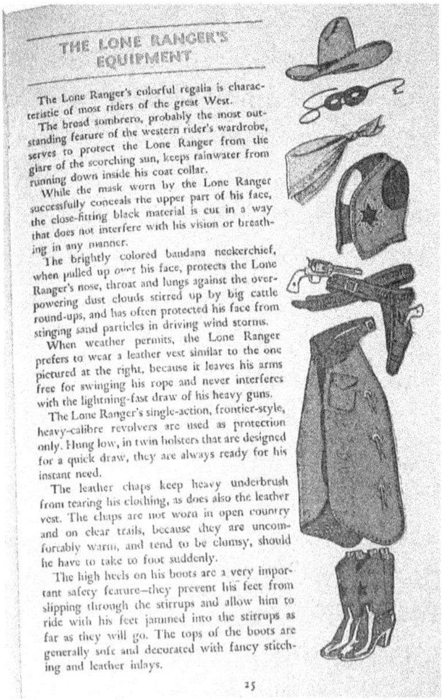

THE LONE RANGER'S EQUIPMENT

The Lone Ranger's colorful regalia is characteristic of most riders of the great West.

The broad sombrero, probably the most outstanding feature of the western rider's wardrobe, serves to protect the Lone Ranger from the glare of the scorching sun, keeps rainwater from running down inside his coat collar.

While the mask worn by the Lone Ranger successfully conceals the upper part of his face, the close-fitting black material is cut in a way that does not interfere with his vision or breathing in any manner.

The brightly colored bandana neckerchief, when pulled up over his face, protects the Lone Ranger's nose, throat and lungs against the overpowering dust clouds stirred up by big cattle round-ups, and has often protected his face from stinging sand particles in driving wind storms.

When weather permits, the Lone Ranger prefers to wear a leather vest similar to the one pictured at the right, because it leaves his arms free for swinging his rope and never interferes with the lightning-fast draw of his heavy guns.

The Lone Ranger's single-action, frontier-style, heavy-calibre revolvers are used as protection only. Hung low, in twin holsters that are designed for a quick draw, they are always ready for his instant need.

The leather chaps keep heavy underbrush from tearing his clothing, as does also the leather vest. The chaps are not worn in open country and on clear trails, because they are uncomfortably warm, and tend to be clumsy, should he have to take to foot suddenly.

The high heels on his boots are a very important safety feature—they prevent his feet from slipping through the stirrups and allow him to ride with his feet jammed into the stirrups as far as they will go. The tops of the boots are generally soft and decorated with fancy stitching and leather inlays.

25

COLLEGEVILLE SUIT CAMPAIGN

The Collegeville Flag & Manufacturing Company is promoting The Lone Ranger Cowboy Suit. The suit is a complete outfit and is excellent as a prize offer for stunts and contests. Still of Sammy McKim shown above available from home office as Still SMLR-5. Prices of the various articles comprising the outfit are as follows:

Neckerchief .... $ .54 a dozen — Mask .... .27 a dozen

Lariat Rope .... .20 a dozen — Holster, belt and gun .... 6.00 a dozen

Trousers .... 12.00 a dozen

On the small items as neckerchief, rope, and mask, orders must total at least one dozen each.
For list of local dealers or orders contact:

Earle Hoyt—COLLEGEVILLE FLAG & MFG. COMPANY
200 Fifth Avenue — New York City

Figures 3.5, 3.6. A page from the 1937 *Lone Ranger Safety Club Official Manual* describing the Lone Ranger's equipment, juxtaposed with a page from Republic's merchandising guide for *The Lone Ranger* 1938 serial showing a Collegeville Lone Ranger playsuit. Author's collection.

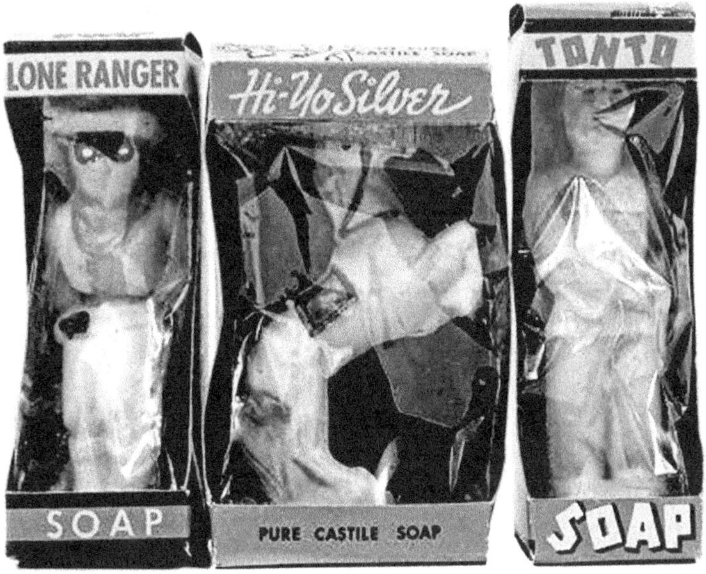

Figure 3.7. Lone Ranger, Silver, and Tonto soap bars, ca. 1937. Author's collection.

Herein lay the LRSC's ultimate success. It not only provided potential licensees with visible evidence of a localizable Lone Ranger fan base, but it promised that club members would seek out Lone Ranger licensees in order to integrate new products and productions into their brand community activities. Thus, local chapters served as both a bull's-eye for targeted merchandising and as proactive brand advocates for the Lone Ranger franchise.

Conclusion

By the end of the 1930s, the Lone Ranger had attained both coast-to-coast coverage and national iconic status. It did so by utilizing the radio series as a platform for showcasing the Lone Ranger's merchandisable attributes, which included the property's localizability and its civic-mindedness. LRI licensed *The Lone Ranger* radio series to local and regional sponsors and radio stations, and more importantly, it franchised out a customizable merchandising program that allowed licensees to adapt the property's appeal to local market conditions and allowed LRI to recycle successful merchandising endeavors as part of its expansion efforts. The Lone Ranger Safety Club was central to LRI's merchandising program, providing a means of transforming the Lone Ranger from a series of loosely connected products and media productions into a lifestyle brand sustained by a proactive brand community. As I argued in the previous section, while the LRSC served as the public face for Lone Ranger brand advocacy, LRI's efforts at cultivating investment in its property were far more expansive, generating a brand community that included both consumers and customers, namely the company's licensees, who often performed the behind-the-scenes work (through LRI's careful orchestration) of singing the Lone Ranger's praises and helping to convince new licensees to join the fold.

From using the radio series as a promotional vehicle to foreground the Lone Ranger's merchandisable attributes, to customizing the Lone Ranger's appeal for different markets, to coordinating a cross-media brand community, many of the practices LRI pursued were exceptional for their moment, but were not necessarily prescient. Instead, I have argued that they are best understood as indicative of an alternative set of practices for developing cultural commodities that emerged out of the particular position LRI and KTBC held within the radio industry. Nonetheless, many of these tactics are now commonplace practices within the contemporary entertainment industry, suggesting a residual trace that ought to be acknowledged as indirectly inspiring current assumptions about building brand equity. Branded entertainment initiatives are on the rise, responding to consumer aversion to traditional advertising. For example, Hasbro's recent foray into developing motion picture franchises that showcase its Transformers and GI Joe toy lines has been described as "the payoff of a strategy that the toy company has been cultivating for nearly a decade: infusing movie-friendly story lines into its popular playthings and teaching Hollywood that these stories can be translated to cinema screens."[128]

Beyond the international franchising of reality television formats, companies like Sesame Street also license localizable and customizable formats globally, while selectively recycling successful adaptations as part of the overall brand package. Sesame Street International not only works with non-U.S. licensees to adapt the Sesame Street format, but also to create customized Muppets and neighborhood sets that respond to local franchisee needs. In turn, popular localized Muppet creations have been recycled by Sesame Street in various capacities, appearing in a variety of U.S. and international Sesame Street products, including books, toys, videos, and public appearances, as well as being utilized as part of the Sesame Street Workshop's annual benefit gala. For example, the characters on Nac, Griotte, Yoyo, and Olive, residents of France's *Rue Sesame* and Hu Hu Zhu and Xiao Meizi from China's *Zhima Jie* appear in the book *Sesame Street First Look & Find: Hide & Seek, Near & Far* (1998), which features popular American muppets Grover and Elmo traveling around the globe.

In 2009, the Disney Corporation launched the D23 website, billed as the "official Disney fan club" hub. Clearly an attempt to orchestrate a brand community that brings together the company's many fans, the site offers multiple shopping opportunities, many of which allow consumers to customize their purchases by adding names, dates, and places to branded T-shirts and coffee mugs. More importantly, D23 offers members exclusive access to Disney historical factoids and production information, providing the kinds of additive comprehension opportunities that reward brand loyalists, as well as an array of interactive games and social networking tools that enhance the brand experience and foster a sense of "we-ness" among participants. Similar initiatives can be found on American Greetings' Strawberry Shortcake and Care Bears websites, which also play up the fact that they are providing safe virtual spaces for kids to interact, a message directed at parents concerned both about child safety and overt commercialism.

In this regard, these sites function much like LRI's LRSC, which in addition to promoting a wide range of activities indirectly linked to Lone Ranger products, was also reassuringly positioned as offsetting sponsor commercial impulses and teaching children to thrive in spite of modernity's mechanized dangers. Of course, the LRSC was born under very different economic and cultural conditions. American Greetings' website encourages virtual play that brings retail opportunities into the home via the computer, whereas the LRSC was partly intended to help children to escape the confines of the home and traverse dangerous commercial spaces.

LRI's market-by-market approach in extending the Lone Ranger brand in the late 1930s also seemingly sets it apart from contemporary media franchising endeavors. In the current era there does not appear to be a single customizable media format sold exclusively at the local level. Yet LRI's influence can still be felt, especially when it comes to incorporating local communities into a national brand community and tailoring the extra-textual materials surrounding a standardized media property to local sensibilities. Take, for example, the animated children's series *Arthur* (1994–), produced by the Cookie Jar Group and based on Marc Brown's books about an anthropomorphized aardvark and his friends. In addition to two self-contained stories, each episode also includes a segment called "And Now a Word from Us Kids," in which children from a wide variety of locales across the United States discuss their interpretation of the story and display original artwork based on the series and its characters. The 2003 spinoff series, *Postcards from Buster* (2003–2007, 2012–), took the localization strategy even further by having the animated rabbit (and Arthur's best friend) "visit" with real children as part of his adventures. Stories were devised based on letters sent to the producers from actual children, who were also featured in the episodes, viewed in live action from the viewpoint of Buster's camcorder. Episodes often focused on the diversity of children's experiences across regional, urban/rural, ethnic, class, and family lines (a 2005 episode where Buster visits Hinesburg, Vermont, to learn about how maple syrup is produced courted controversy because he interacted with children with same-sex parents), while also reminding the broader audience that all of these diverse constituencies share a deep investment in the Arthur brand.

Similarly, while most of Marvel's licenses are with national and international manufacturers and media firms, the company still licenses public appearances locally through its Marvel Public Appearances Program, which provides costumed performers for a wide range of venues, from schools to department stores, and for a wide range of activities, from promoting physical fitness and antibullying in schools to motivational entertainment for corporate retreats. Public appearances can be tailored to local needs and provide interactive opportunities to engage popular icons.

Marvel's Public Appearances Program also evidences the ways that brand communities are still courted and cultivated at local levels. While most brand community activity now takes place online, many digital hubs still offer ways to localize brand experiences through structured face-to-face community activities, which, in turn, expand community membership by introducing new consumers to the property in more intimate venues. As such, the *Dora the Explorer* website offers parents suggestions as well as free downloadable materials for hosting Dora-themed birthday parties and other activities. Though activities and dissemination methods change over time, it isn't a far leap from the Lone Ranger Safety Club to Dora's efforts at building lifestyle brands that deepen a brand community's connection to a given property. Importantly, though the Internet might provide fans of these properties with the ability to communicate with one another across space, much of this dialogue continues to be about localized brand experiences.

CHAPTER 4

The Lone Ranger and the Law: The Construction of Corporate Authorship

Introduction

In his 2004 book, *Free Culture: The Nature and Future of Creativity*, Lawrence Lessig recounts with great dismay the Supreme Court's failure to overturn the 1998 Sonny Bono Copyright Extension Act, a law granting copyright holders an additional twenty years before their works fall into the public domain. Lessig was lead counsel in the case, *Eldred v. Ashcroft*. He concludes that in ignoring the "rent seeking" motivations of corporate owners and by accepting their moralizing hyperbole, the Supreme Court revealed its own conservative cultural biases. Dr. Seuss Enterprises, for example, argued that its continued control over creations like the Cat in the Hat would prevent use of these characters to "glorify drugs or to create pornography" or otherwise debase their iconic images.[1]

Lessig's observations echo the work of other legal scholars, who have argued that corporations repeatedly seek to exploit legal ambiguities in order to lobby for narrower interpretations of copyright and trademark law. This, in turn, allows them to severely limit and tightly control all forms of creative expression involving their holdings.[2] Where the field of legal studies has largely tended to analyze abuses of intellectual property law as examples of misinterpretation and misappropriation of legal doctrine,[3] some critical cultural legal scholars note how intellectual property law often conflates romanticized notions of origination and inspiration with distribution and reproduction rights, fetishizing the former to justify control over the latter.[4] Several of these scholars have also noted that the courts increasingly attribute such authorial qualities to corporate entities. Accordingly, Dr. Seuss Enterprises not only claimed the rights of long-dead authors as their own in *Eldred v. Ashcroft*, but also positioned itself as possessing an authorial pedigree deserving of continued protection, since it alone understood the work's "true/intended" meanings.

And yet Dr. Seuss Enterprises' argument in favor of extending copyright terms did not hinge on either its creative labor in originating the properties it controlled or the reputation it had vested in the works, but rather on its managerial acumen in safeguarding and maintaining the reputations of these beloved fictional characters. In other words, corporate authorship was equated with cultural stewardship. After all, the actual creator of the Cat in the Hat, Theodor Geisel, had died in 1991, and no member of Dr. Seuss Enterprises actually performed any creative work based on the characters Geisel originated. Instead, the authority vested in Dr. Seuss Enterprises is directly correlated with the inspiration it supposedly draws from Geisel's vision and its dedication to ensuring that others continue to uphold that vision. To this effect, Audrey S. Geisel, Geisel's widow and also president of Dr. Seuss Enterprises, has repeatedly asserted her intimate understanding of her late husband's creations as justification for the company's litigiousness.[5]

To understand why the Supreme Court would validate this interpretation of authorship, it is essential to take corporate rhetoric seriously—as more than just disingenuous posturing designed to conceal abuses of power and justify corporate greed. While it is appealingly simple to dismiss corporate claims to safeguarding iconic properties like Mickey Mouse, Superman, and Bugs Bunny against immoral scoundrels lurking in the public domain as ideological mystifications designed to maintain their legal control and economic interests, this would underestimate the discursive labor invested by corporations in establishing cultural stewardship as central to their authorial rights. To scholars like Jane Gaines, Peter Jaszi, Rosemary Coombe, and Siva Vaidhyanathan, the legal arena is a cultural battleground upon which ideas about authorship and ownership are not only debated, but also given meaning through discourse.[6] As Vaidhyanathan eloquently summarizes, "An 'author' does not precede a 'work' . . . but comes into being only as it functions in a legal and cultural environment."[7] In other words, "an author" does not create "a work," but rather is created through said work.

It is imperative that scholars investigate how corporate owners have historically engaged the courts in discursive battles over what constitutes authorship's functions when it comes to intellectual property (IP). On the surface, the Lone Ranger and the Cat in the Hat share little in common. Yet Dr. Seuss Enterprises' recent success in defending its rights owes much to LRI's courtroom tactics in the late 1930s and early 1940s. In this chapter, I analyze the construction of the Lone Ranger's corporate authorship during those years and its continued significance for understanding how contemporary copyright and trademark laws recognize creative authority as vested in corporate institutions. LRI fought several legal battles during this period that reveal how a corporate entity both articulated and had authorship conferred upon it through particular discursive and juridical practices.

LRI sought to link its authorial rights with its managerial role as a cultural intermediary, simultaneously promising to deliver consumers to corporations and to protect consumers from corporate exploitation. Concerns over commercial exploitation are especially acute when children are imagined as the primary audiences for cultural commodities. Nicholas Sammond has argued that children's media producers are often attuned to prevailing discourses on child rearing and seek to position their products in relation to dominant social ideals.[8] Throughout the 1930s, fears over consumer backlash led many corporations to welcome LRI's oversight because it provided assurances that sponsored properties like the Lone Ranger served important civic as well as sales functions. LRI positioned itself as mediating between producers and consumers, particularly child consumers, explaining to both the appropriate ways of understanding and aligning the Lone Ranger's economic and cultural values.

Instead of treating LRI's authority as a given, I position the corporation as one of several stakeholders invested in exploiting the Lone Ranger property, each seeking legal recognition of its rights to claim ownership over the Masked Man's various representational and textual iterations.

According to Thomas Donaldson and Lee Preston, the stakeholder model as applied to corporations recognizes that "*all* persons or groups with legitimate interests participating in an enterprise do so to obtain benefits and that there is no prima facie priority of one set of interests or benefits over another." Though Donaldson and Preston are describing stakeholders in a corporation, the same logic might easily be applied to stakeholders in franchisable IP. Since the Lone Ranger promised "value added" to every product (and production) bearing his name and image, the property was consistently the object of multiple, sometimes contested, investments from a dispersed set of stakeholders, some sanctioned and some unsanctioned.[9]

Through a discourse analysis of two cases, I will demonstrate how the courts eventually conferred authorial status upon LRI via its assertion of its managerial acumen. In the first case, *Buck Jones v. Republic Productions* (1938), LRI faced accusations that it had based the masked rider's appearance on B-actor Jones's established personality, thus profiting from his reputation. In the second case, *The Lone Ranger Incorporated v. Cox Circus* (1942), LRI sought to prevent Lee Powell from performing as the Lone Ranger in a traveling circus without its permission or managerial oversight. In both instances, LRI's corporate authorial moniker would prove essential to its victories.

LRI strategically invoked management as authorial imprimatur precisely because it sought to suppress its own creative labor—as well as that of others—to maintain the illusion that the Lone Ranger had a mythic rather than scripted existence. In manufacturing a mythic hero over whom it still maintained ownership rights, LRI now sought to redefine the authorial qualities of origination and originality typically associated with IP law. By enjoining corporate authority with cultural stewardship, it also positioned the corporation as an inspired vessel through which its branded muse spoke.

While LRI was far from unique in using the courts during this period to shore up its exclusive IP rights, the legal battles it fought were representative of how corporations constructed—and continue to construct—alternate definitions of "authorship" that elevate notions of stewardship and managerial acumen over creativity and origination. In so doing, LRI would play a significant role in reconceptualizing legal interpretations of copyright and trademark. This is especially true of the latter, as LRI's successful trademark infringement suit against Cox Circus predated—and thus would serve as a model for—the 1946 Lanham Trademark Revision, which would recognize consumer association of particular images, icons, and logos with their corporate auteurs through the ascription of secondary meaning.

Following a brief elaboration on the historical use of copyright and trademark laws during the first decades of the twentieth century to confer and deny ownership rights over entertainment properties, I then lay out my argument for how corporate authorship functions within institutional and juridical settings. In analyzing the two Lone Ranger cases mentioned above, I argue for their significance in shifting legal rhetoric toward a nonromantic conceptualization of authorship rooted in management as stewardship. In the conclusion to this chapter, I outline the broader significance of these early twentieth-century court battles to the contemporary legal and cultural landscape in which IP rights are deliberated.

A Primer on Copyright Law and Its Early History

Copyright law provides artists and inventors with exclusive but limited-term rights to exploit their creations commercially, encouraging the "progress of science and the useful arts" by securing rights and benefits for innovators.[10] This Romantic notion of authorship, one rooted in originality and individual creativity, has been a standard of legal evaluation for intellectual property law in the West since the eighteenth century.[11] But some scholars have successfully denaturalized the correlation.

In his seminal essay "What Is an Author?" Michel Foucault argues that authorship initially emerged as a legal category so that the state could hold individuals accountable for their works, especially if those works were perceived as threatening of state authority.[12] Martha Woodmansee notes that German writers who sought legal protections for their works against unauthorized copying would cultivate and promote an authorial aura that assigned value to the individual creative genius.[13] And Mark Rose asserts that the 1710 Statute of Anne, generally regarded as the first copyright doctrine ever adopted, was primarily set in motion by London-based publishers and booksellers—not authors—seeking to prevent emerging regional publishing entities from crowding the market.[14] As Jaszi summarizes, "Distributors have reaped most of the benefits of copyright's cultivation of Romantic 'authorship.'"[15]

Dating back to 1884, the courts have entertained two competing ideas about ownership and its relation to authorship. On the one hand, authorial originality is a claim to ownership in the work, meaning that if a product bears the imprint of its author's personality, the law must recognize the work as originating with that person. On the other hand, the product can also contain zero degrees of authorial personality and still be proprietarily owned, according to copyright. Jane Gaines has argued that these dual meanings have actually contributed to the displacement of the author by the corporation, which needs not imbue products with personality to claim authorship over them.[16] Similarly, Matt Stahl has argued that the law regularly confers authorship on nonhuman corporate entities, equating economic ownership de facto with authorship rights.[17]

In 1909, Congress revised copyright law to distinguish between the rights of employers and work-for-hire employees, assigning authorship to the former even though the employees performed most of the creative labor. As Stahl has summarized, "Work for hire thus creates authors out of employers who may not be creative in any conventionally recognizable way, in fact who may not even be people but firms."[18] As Jaszi argues: "If the essence of 'authorship' is inspiration, then it is the employer's contribution as the 'motivating factor' behind that work that matters, rather than the mere drudgery of the 'employee.'"[19] Citing the verdict in the 1972 case of *Picture Music, Inc. v. Bourne, Inc.*, Jaszi notes that work-for-hire doctrine casts the employer "as the visionary, and the employee as a mere mechanic following orders."[20] In that case, Anne Ronnell, who in 1933 had been hired by the Walt Disney Corporation to rearrange the lyrics and chords to the Irving Berlin song, "Who's Afraid of the Big Bad Wolf?" for Disney's animated short *Three Little Pigs*, was denied joint-author status in the song.

In part, this slippage is made possible by the absence of "moral rights" within U.S. copyright law, which guarantees authors the rights to preserve the integrity of their work even if they have assigned ownership rights to a third party.[21] Without this safeguard, creative labor hired under work-for-hire contracts in the United States must abdicate creative as well as economic control over how its work is ultimately used.

When it comes to character brands, legal debates over authorship and ownership are not new. Early efforts at licensing comic strip characters often pitted their creators against the publishing syndicates that exploited their labor and claimed ownership over the strips as well as against the horde of unlicensed merchandise in circulation that bore images of their creations. Richard Outcault's experiences with his highly popular comic strip *Hogan's Alley* and its star character, the Yellow Kid, epitomized these struggles. Created in 1900, "the Yellow Kid's meaning and reception often slipped from his creator's control . . . unauthorized Yellow Kid products, including songbooks, buttons, chewing gum, chocolate figurines, cigars, and ladies' fans" abounded.[22] Additionally, Hearst Publishing, Outcault's employer, often sought to exploit the Yellow Kid's image for newspaper sales without compensating Outcault, prompting the cartoonist to add a warning, which read, "Do Not Be Deceived. None Genuine Without This Signature."[23]

Throughout the Depression, creators often sold the rights to their creations to their corporate benefactors in exchange for a steady paycheck. On May 22, 1934, Fran Striker, the man fans largely recognize as the Lone Ranger's originator, transferred all of his rights to *The Lone Ranger* scripts he had already written as well as those he would write in perpetuity to LRI, along with "any profit, benefit, or advantage that might arise from printing, publishing, vending and broadcasting" them.[24] While Striker would lose out on the millions of dollars the Lone Ranger would earn LRI, in signing away his rights, Striker went from being paid four dollars for every script he sold to earning one hundred dollars per week in exchange for his services.[25] Similarly, Jerry Siegel and Joe Shuster sold their rights to Superman to DC Comics (then National Periodical Publications) in 1938 in exchange for a guaranteed ten-year contract and a one-time $130 payout.[26] Seeing the millions of dollars Superman earned DC Comics, Siegel and Shuster first attempted to reclaim their rights to the character in 1947 and made several failed attempts to do so throughout their lifetimes.[27] Their estates are still seeking to reclaim the rights to Superman.[28]

Harold Gray, creator of *Little Orphan Annie*, also signed over the rights to his creation to the Chicago Tribune Syndicate in exchange for a guaranteed salary and a gentleman's agreement that Gray would be hired to do all artwork related to the character's use in advertising and merchandising as well as share in any profits from the property's exploitation in other media. As part of the Tribune Syndicate's expansion into radio in the mid-to-late 1920s with station WGN, it converted many of its popular print features into programming, including Gray's Orphan Annie. The series' popularity attracted sponsorship from Ovaltine, which paid the Tribune syndicate a royalty for the rights to use the character. When Gray (1931) approached his boss, J. M. Patterson, looking for compensation, stating "the *letter* of my contract . . . gives the radio rights to the Tribune by implication. But, as we both know, the *spirit* of that contract when signed three years ago, was that the syndicate was to pay me fifty percent," Patterson (1931) responded that Gray had no legal claim to the property and that the Tribune "would rather have it settled according to law" than debate Gray's moral entitlements.[29]

Gray's experience seems to confirm assertions that corporations have displaced creators as owners for properties upon which they have seemingly offered no originating labor. At the same time, corporate owners have historically employed copyright violation claims as a means of preventing unauthorized adaptations of their properties. Infamously, in 1972 the Disney Corporation won its case to prevent the underground countercultural comic book *The Air Pirates* from utilizing its stable of cartoon creations, including Mickey Mouse, in a series of anticapitalist parodies.[30] Rejecting *The Air Pirates*' fair use defense on the grounds that the comic book both copied too much material and posed a genuine threat to Disney's market standing (a dubious claim considering the comic book's limited circulation), the court found that "the principal appeal of each of [Walt Disney's] works to the primary audience of children for which they were intended lies with the character and nothing more."[31] In recognizing Mickey Mouse as "the story being told," the court also recognized the character's corporate owner as its only rightful storyteller, assigning the iconic mouse proprietary status that denied the public full access to the range of possible cultural meanings that might circulate about it and *The Air Pirates* the right to find (or, more accurately, to circulate) "undesirable" meaning in the character.

Nevertheless, I argue that the articulation and conferral of authorship through such legal proceedings cannot simply be understood as resulting from a complicit or compromised legal system reinforcing society's capitalist economic base. Instead, as I will demonstrate by analyzing deposition transcripts and judicial opinions for the Lone Ranger legal cases, these court battles have generated what Paul du Gay and Michael Pryke term "a discourse of the economy . . . the elaboration of a language for conceiving of and hence constructing an object in a certain way so that the object can then be deliberated about and acted upon."[32] The legal system constitutes a site where the cultural logics of capitalism and creativity are discursively interwoven and where economic rights are often determined based on cultural and ideological assumptions about authorial rights and responsibilities. In other words, corporations must continually make an argument for their authorial ownership rights under the law that situates their underlying profit motives within shared (and shifting) social and cultural value systems.

A Primer on Trademark Law and Its Early History

While copyright laws are most obviously invested in discursive battles over authorship, trademark laws have also played a significant if less overt role in legitimating the rights of corporate authors. Trademark legislation is intended to protect consumers against confusion and deception created through the use of similar marks by competing businesses, and as such, is designed to promote competition by facilitating comparison shopping. It is also intended to preserve the "goodwill" that trademark owners have accrued from consumers by preventing a competing entity from using the same mark to perpetuate a fraud on the public. Historically, there have been considerable struggles over defining what categories of business are in competition with one another.

For example, in 1923, William Donahey, creator of *The Teenie Weenies* comic strip, lost his battle against the Oconomowoc Canning Company when the State Supreme Court of Wisconsin ruled that there was little chance that consumers would be confused, even though the canned goods company had used the Teenie Weenie name and approximate character likenesses to promote its new line of peas.[33] Similarly, Percy Crosby, creator of the Skippy comic strip character, was unsuccessful in retaining his rights to the name "Skippy" in nonpaper goods, thus allowing Joseph Rosefield to appropriate the name for his peanut butter in 1933.[34] Trademark law at the time had no mechanism for distinguishing between a product and its recognizable attributes or for recognizing how consumers might associate different products that carried similar attributes.

In contemporary trademark law, secondary meanings become attached to suggestive and descriptive properties when owners demonstrate that the public has come to associate the brand name with a particular producer rather than its underlying products (e.g., that the brand name "Coca-Cola" is associated with the Coca-Cola Company, not just the soft drink produced by it). In practice, this would lead to the popular acceptance among licensors and licensees that brands maintain their "goodwill" with consumers across product lines. Secondary meaning would have considerable implications for IP holders, as it would confer greater value upon the corporate brand than upon the products it endorsed. The test of secondary meaning comes from only the mere possibility of consumer confusion. The names and physical characteristics of licensed characters are also protected through secondary meaning. It was only in the 1930s that legislators undertook a concerted effort to modernize trademark law, with the initial draft of the Lanham Trademark Act—still the basis for all modern-day intellectual property law—first introduced before Congress in 1938. The act would only pass into law in 1946. Gaines has asserted that it is this revision of trademark law that allows merchandise licensing and other cross-platform media brand adaptations to thrive.[35]

Though the recognition of secondary meaning certainly made brand extension practices easier, many corporate IP owners were already hard at work extending their holdings across media and merchandising terrains long before the revamped trademark laws. By the end of the 1930s, characters like the Lone Ranger, Little Orphan Annie, Dick Tracy, Popeye, and Superman had already been successfully licensed into adjacent media and as consumer goods. Before secondary meaning became the standard for assigning ownership over names and logos used in noncompeting markets, actor Charlie Chaplin had successfully applied trademark law as an authorship standard in 1928 when he won his case against an imitator found guilty of perpetrating a public deception by copying Chaplin's on-screen costume and mannerisms.[36] Similarly, in 1939, the district court of Massachusetts found in favor of Olive Higgins Prouty, author of the 1920 novel *Stella Dallas*, when NBC created a series of unauthorized radio skits featuring a character by the same name.[37] The court found that NBC not only perpetuated a deception on the public by suggesting that the radio play and the novel emanated from the same source, but in so doing, they also injured both the reputation of the work and of its author, an argument seemingly more in line with copyright and, more to the point, the types of moral rights that U.S. copyright doesn't actually recognize.

On the surface, however, trademark battles appear to have little to do with authorship, corporate or otherwise. After all, trademark law is designed to protect the consumer against product confusion, whereas copyright law protects authors against illegal copying. Yet Michael Todd Helfand argues that there has long been a "convergence of copyright and trademark" in the legal arena.[38] For example, Helfand (1992) points out that when Jeff Fisher, creator of the *Mutt and Jeff* comic strip, took his former distributor, the Star Company, to court in 1921 for trademark violation—the company had continued to distribute *Mutt and Jeff* comics drawn by a different artist after Fisher had left its employ despite Fisher's having trademarked the title of his strip—the New York court of appeals applied a copyright justification in supporting the cartoonist's trademark violation claims. Though the court recognized the trademark argument that an inferior imitation would sully the comic strip's market value, it also reasoned that Star's actions constituted "an unfair appropriation of [Fisher's] skill and the celebrity acquired by him in originating, producing and maintaining the characters and figures so as to continue the demand for further cartoons."[39] Hence, Fisher's authorial reputation and his right to profit from his creative labor were also recognized. Rosemary Coombe has similarly demonstrated how judicial recognition that "through investment, labor, and strategic dissemination, the holder of a trademark creates a set of unique meanings in the minds of consumers and that this value is created solely by the owner's efforts" and effectively confers upon trademark owners "quasi-author" status.[40]

Of course, as Donahey and Crosby's experiences suggest, far from being assured, legal recognition of an author's trademark largely depended on whether or not the court assumed that consumers would recognize a property's ownership source. Or, as David B. Feldman argues, secondary meaning for trademarked characters comes into effect only once the public begins to associate the property's name, logo, or image with its corporate author, "who is analogous to the character's manufacturer . . . almost everyone [already] knows that 'Mickey Mouse' is a Disney character."[41]

LRI: Corporate Auteur

The Lone Ranger had many authors, or, at least, many people contributed to the Lone Ranger character and story world, and many more wrote, drew, performed, and directed the various adventures and products that bore the brand name. Yet the man most often credited as the Lone Ranger's creator, George W. Trendle, president of LRI, never wrote or drew a single one of these. Still, Trendle insisted on distinguishing his role as creator from the development work done by others. Admonishing LRI partner and attorney Raymond Meurer for claiming to have helped create the Lone Ranger and Green Hornet properties, Trendle asserted, "I do get irritated when the writers infer that the creation of the subjects mentioned was not entirely my own, and I am kidded about it on occasions. My reply has always been that I was the sole creator of all those shows, but that the development of them, after their creation was a three-cornered deal . . . if you can stick to the use of the word 'development' rather than 'create,' it would please [me] very much."[42] The distinction Trendle made between creation and development placed him apart from those hired to toil on the property. Yet his authority would be based on his managerial rather than his inspirational role in overseeing how the Lone Ranger was developed.

While to this day some Lone Ranger fans debate whether or not Fran Striker, *The Lone Ranger*'s head writer on radio and author of most of the Lone Ranger novelizations and comic strips, originated the hero, Striker usually credited Trendle with the character's creation and described himself as merely an employee realizing his boss's vision, though sometimes such distinctions were made under duress. As Striker would later explain at Trendle's behest to Gil Fatos, executive producer of *To Tell The Truth*, a game show upon which Striker appeared in 1960 claiming to have created the Lone Ranger, "I was under the impression that this dramatic show was my own creation . . . Mr. Trendle feels that this claim is not justified. Apparently, and I have no reason to doubt this, Mr. Trendle had the character and the format of the program well established before he asked [WXYZ dramatic department director] Mr. Jewell to find [someone to write] the scripts."[43]

Despite these PR hiccups, the confusion expressed by the likes of Striker and Meurer actually served LRI's corporate agenda, since it encouraged innovation, but also uncertainty as to who had inevitably first proposed which version of the Lone Ranger character. What is clear from analyzing the back-and-forth correspondence between James Jewell, who was responsible for overseeing production, and Striker—letters that laid out the basic attributes of the Lone Ranger character and radio series—is that their ideas were always subject to evaluation and revision from multiple parties within the KTBC operation, and that Jewell and Striker saw themselves as adapting ideas proposed by others and melding them with their own into what would eventually become the Lone Ranger.

Jewell, always acting as a proxy for "the bosses," would instruct Striker on how to adjust *The Lone Ranger* scripts to conform to the wishes of upper management. This is evidenced in a letter written by Jewell to Striker a mere ten days before the Lone Ranger's radio debut, which states, "I wish you would also notice on the attached script that I have struck out all the reference to killing by the Lone Ranger and also the fact that I have taken the Jesse James aspect out (I realize this is good theatre, but the bosses want the Lone Ranger more of a hero for the children to pattern after) . . . I realize they have changed the character you have created, but only in a minor way and I am hoping that it won't be difficult to conform with the wishes of my twenty bosses."[44]

Though Jewell acknowledges Striker as the Lone Ranger's creator, Striker's value—as well as the value of his creations—is defined in relation to his ability to translate KTBC' programming needs and, as such, by his openness to revision by management. Ultimately, LRI framed Trendle's decision-making function as the most important contribution to the Lone Ranger's success, valuing his "censorial powers" above the creative work performed by the likes of Striker. In a 1943 article in the *Detroit Times*, Meurer explained how "the first script had to be written about fifteen times before it was acceptable to Mr. Trendle. . . . Whenever Striker gets off his beam, Mr. Trendle checks him on it." It is precisely this managerial oversight that led Meurer to conclude, "The real creator of the Lone Ranger was George W. Trendle."[45]

Of course, the search for origination in analyzing cultural commodities can be folly because most productions are not created in isolation; they rely on both a collaborative labor force and a division of labor that assigns different creative tasks to various occupational communities. The Lone Ranger's true origins are no different, and as explained by Striker's son, Robert H. Striker, following his father's death in 1961, "Correspondence dating back to 1932 indicates rather strongly that the Lone Ranger was not *created* but *evolved*."[46] In some ways, the Lone Ranger's origins are best understood as corporate. As outlined in Chapter 2, KTBC initially conceived the Lone Ranger's appearance, characterization, and actions as an affordable response to the national networks' reliance on star power to attract sponsors for its fledgling Michigan Radio Network.

LRI's efforts to elevate Trendle's managerial role above the creative labor involved in generating Lone Ranger productions is on par with how the discourse of corporate authorship works to establish a company's proprietary authority over an otherwise "authorless" cultural icon like the Masked Man.

It may seem as though the work culture at LRI actively discouraged creativity and innovation. Certainly, the work-for-hire contract encouraged a fast turnover of materials, since writers were paid based on the quantity of approved scripts they delivered, not necessarily their originality. Moreover, the script approval process provided little incentive to introduce creative flourishes that might be rejected and require rewriting, delaying payment for work rendered. Furthermore, the company's efforts at suppressing and belittling the creative labor that went into producing the Lone Ranger left many employees toiling anonymously and offered few opportunities for recognition. These practices, quite common in mass cultural production throughout the 1930s and 1940s, from comic book publishing to B-movie production, are often seen as constraining the true creative potential of these media forms since they encouraged "repetitive, formulaic work" and constrained artistic license.[47]

And yet it would be a mistake to see this work environment as entirely stifling of creativity. After all, for the Lone Ranger, as well as for hundreds of other early twentieth-century character brands from Dick Tracy to Superman, there had to be enough creative variation to sustain their level of popularity both with consumers and with other licensees.

Hence, it is essential to rethink how such production cultures valued and rewarded certain forms of creative practice. Though Trendle took Striker to task whenever mention was made of his role in creating the Lone Ranger, Striker was regularly rewarded by the company for his skills at varying Lone Ranger adventures in ways that still ensured their formulaic consistency. Striker developed a system for mass-producing Lone Ranger plots that consisted of methodically varying recurring character types (i.e., rancher, banker, railroad operator) problems (kidnapping, theft, harassment), how the Lone Ranger learns of the problem (in town, while investigating another crime, by stumbling upon it by chance), and how the Lone Ranger overcomes the problem (sets a trap, outraces the villain, relies on his marksmanship skills).[48] Each variation was designed to showcase the Lone Ranger's most marketable attributes as essential to the conflict's turning point or resolution.

It was in recognition of his formula-management innovations—not for his creative origination of the character—that Striker was offered numerous opportunities to either write or supervise the writing of Lone Ranger adventures as they extended beyond radio. Striker was Trendle's choice as consultant on the first Republic film serial. Starting in 1938, Striker wrote the *Lone Ranger* comic strip, and he also wrote a series of novels featuring the masked cowboy dating back to 1935. He was also asked by Trendle to review and give notes on the scripts written for the *Lone Ranger* television series in the late 1940s/early 1950s. By 1940, Striker's annual income, cobbled together from these myriad assignments, was $10,000.[49]

Corporate authorship is a term most often evoked to convey the cultivation of an aesthetic, generic, or thematic "house style" associated with a particular organization that can be found across a wide array of texts and products distributed under its name.[50] For example, in the 1940s, MGM's extravagant musicals became the studio's signature and helped establish and differentiate its brand identity from those of other Hollywood film producers.[51] My purpose here, however, is to conceptualize corporate authorship as a discourse that confers creative authority upon and instills trust in particular organizations to manage culturally iconic properties. Corporate creative authority is vested in the ability to convincingly speak on behalf of the brand and to translate its popular attributes into appropriate production and consumption outlets; to act as cultural intermediaries between creative laborers and consumers, offering trusted advice and guidance, as well as doctrine, on how best to interpret brand attributes and meanings.

For example, in 1943, LRI assembled a writer's guide to be used by all creative personnel working on Lone Ranger stories across various media. Rather than use an adversarial tone and police freelance labor, the guide positioned LRI as a bastion of knowledge about the Masked Man and his adoring fans. The guide casually introduces the relationship between creative labor and management, beginning, "So you want to write a Lone Ranger story? That's fine, and to help you do a really good job of it, we are going to acquaint you with some interesting things to bear in mind."[52] The guide encouraged writers to draw inspiration from the popular attributes the property already possessed and to trust in LRI's understanding of what audiences liked about the character. "We have found that many young writers, when first attempting to write this show, immediately want to change the Lone Ranger, make him different than he is. Don't do that. The Lone Ranger has been a top favorite of the American radio audience for more than ten years, so people must like him as he is."[53]

Though the guide does go on to provide instructions on how to tell "proper" Lone Ranger stories, including descriptions of the period, the recurring characters, and their types of weaponry and admonishments against using "phony heroics" and writing from a "juvenile viewpoint," ultimately its value is less prescriptive than it is rhetorical. LRI needed a way to manage creativity without alienating its labor force. The guide established a commonsense framework for creative labor to adhere to, in which LRI's authority is derived from its successful stewardship of a property whose qualities are both inherent and inspirational, but which can fall victim to misinterpretations and misappropriations by authors who put their own creative impulses ahead of the interests of the brand and its devotees. Or, as the guide concludes, "The Lone Ranger has been recognized as Americana, a literary legend. Approach it with that viewpoint and you will probably do a good job."[54]

Ideally, property owners want licensees and workers-for-hire to see themselves as externalizing, rather than creating, brand meanings through their products—meanings understood as already inherent to the property. In so doing, they try to convince stakeholders to draw their inspiration from the attributes that a property already possesses, rather than trying to modify it to suit the needs of their particular product lines.

Take, for example, the following exchange between Hank Ketcham, creator of Dennis the Menace, and the Dancer-Fitzgerald-Sample Advertising Agency (DFS) regarding several 1968 radio commercial spots for A&W Restaurants that featured Dennis as their spokesman. Writing to DFS advertising executive Sandy McGowan, Ketcham attempted to explain how licensee A&W could best use the character: "My main objection is that DENNIS is completely out of his element. He does not have such a vocabulary and he is not a little pitchman. He's merely the dirty-faced kid next door who couldn't care less about saving nickels or even where he gets his next root beer. True, we've established that he does know about A&W and the fact that they have goodies for sale. But that's all. He might pitch his parents, or poor Mr. Wilson . . . but not the 'public.'"[55] Ketcham sought to minimize the risk of overcommercialization by encouraging Dennis the Menace licensees to adapt their sales strategies to suit the property's existing personality traits, including verbiage and demeanor, instead of merely using Dennis's recognizable attributes to sell their products.

What is striking about Ketcham's intervention is that he does not evoke his own authorial identity in expressing his displeasure with how the property is being used. Instead, he refers to his creation in the third person, while positioning himself as merely possessing the strongest understanding of Dennis's psyche. Ketcham treats Dennis as if he were an actual person, albeit one who requires an intermediary to speak on his behalf. In other words, Ketcham's authority is derived from his interpretive rather than his creative abilities.

Corporations often anthropomorphize character brands into popular heroes who essentially sell themselves. Consider LRI's 1951 full-page advertisement in *Variety* (see Figure 4.1), in which the licensor aggregates over fifty separate Lone Ranger media and merchandise licenses onto one page and recycles statistics on the Masked Man's successes in various media, all in an attempt to attract new licensees into the fold.

Yet even as the ad displays multiple points of consumer contact with the Lone Ranger and implies that these disparate sites can be made to work together to indirectly promote a new license, LRI carefully obfuscates any direct labor performed by these licensees in shaping the iconic property. Instead, the ad clearly articulates that all these licensees have chosen to follow "the leader," rather than to pave his path. While LRI certainly privileges particular *Lone Ranger* texts (radio and television—this is an ad for *Variety*, after all) as indicators of the property's success, the ad also refers to the Masked Man as "the oldest and best western *character* [italics added]," a descriptor that transcends any of its production sites and imbues the property with characteristics—a long history of leadership—that transform the Lone Ranger into a powerful sales agent capable of endorsing any object, rather than merely a helpful tool for promoting a particular product.

The very structure of the LRI ad actually models several of the lessons licensors typically seek to teach clients about using an entertainment property. Chief among these lessons are the value of promoting the brand over the products associated with it and the importance of never directly using the property to sell any particular item other than its own recognizable personality. While the ad certainly provides an extensive list of licensed Lone Ranger products in circulation, it offers almost no information about these items other than that their manufacturers have chosen to tie in with the masked cowboy character. Instead of showing potential

Figure 4.1. LRI Lone Ranger ad in *Variety*, ca. 1951. Author's collection.

licensees what these various products look like, the ad uses one uniform image of the Lone Ranger riding Silver to represent all of them, suggesting that they are all variations on a common theme. Moreover, the Lone Ranger never directly endorses any of these products. Instead, all these licensees collectively affirm the Lone Ranger's value while the property hovers above them (or, in this case, beside them) as a consumer advocate of sorts, choosing only to associate with particular products and sponsors that endorse his mission and, through the power of his personality, inspiring consumers to do the same.

In the ad, LRI encourages potential clients to "write today for information on joining in with the leader," positioning itself as an intermediary between the Lone Ranger and his future followers but otherwise obscuring its own labor. LRI is merely there to offer information on how to become a Lone Ranger devotee.

Similarly, in February 1975, the Licensing Corporation of America (LCA) took out an ad in the toy industry trade magazine *Playthings* to promote its DC Comics superhero properties to potential licensees (see Figure 4.2). In the ad, LCA made use of existing client Mego International Toys' success at merchandising superhero action figures. The ad featured seven twelve-inch action figures created by Mego along with copy that read, "When Super Heroes Action Figures were introduced in 1972, they skyrocketed into the Top Ten Selling Toys. They've been there ever since. Their success enabled Mego International to expand into several new Super Heroes product lines." Rhetorically, the ad positions DC's stable of characters, not Mego's designers, manufacturers, or marketing team, as driving toy sales.

While Mego's work is obfuscated in favor of promoting the power of the superhero as sales agent, the ad does position LCA as performing an important, if also vague, function in helping potential licensees reap the rewards for investing in these properties. In inviting inquiries about its other licensable properties, LCA assures potential licensees that "we can help make you a hero too."

Corporate marketing finds its corollary in the legal arena. Helfand asserts that the courts also "attribute human traits to inanimate characters, often treating them as having their own reputational interest capable of being impugned by unauthorized, especially disparaging uses."[56] In *DC Comics, Inc. v. Unlimited Monkey Business* (1984), the district court of Georgia found that the defendant had sullied the reputations of the superheroes it had borrowed without permission, instead of the reputation of their corporate benefactor.[57] Similarly, in *Walt Disney Co. v. Powell* (1988), a case fought over the sale of unauthorized T-shirt decals, the U.S. Court of Appeals declared, "Defendant's free ride on the *ingenuity, skillful promotion, and resulting public acceptance* [emphasis added] which Disney has rightfully gained *from these charming mouse characters* must come to an end."[58] Where Helfand notes how the verdict suggests that Disney's mouse characters seemingly possess an innate charm, the above quotation also points to the type of labor Disney has performed in earning the right to profit from Mickey's reputation: its "skillful promotion" has contributed to Mickey's "public acceptance."

Corporations are not required to demonstrate creative ability in order to claim creative authority or have it conferred upon them; it suffices that

Figure 4.2. Licensing Corporation of America ad in *Playthings*, February 1975.

they are entities capable of ensuring a consistent level of quality and value for the material productions they authorize. Corporations demonstrate their authorial function through their managerial acumen: their ability to coordinate between creative labor and the cultural artifacts they are assigned to represent, to generate a work environment in which innovation and continuity are in balance, and to anticipate consumer expectations from materials stamped with their imprint. When the courts have conferred authorial status on corporate entities, it has often been in response to these parameters. LRI's efforts in the late 1930s and early 1940s to link its IP rights to its corporate authorial role as brand steward and manager are exemplary of how property owners have sought to reconfigure copyright and trademark laws, and as such, provide important insights into how corporate authorship operates within legal and cultural contexts.

Through its legal battles in the late 1930s, LRI became aligned with functions normally attributed to authorial practice. Even as LRI would attempt to keep the Lone Ranger's origins a mystery, the corporation also sought to demonstrate that the Lone Ranger, to quote Gaines, was "indelibly etched with the sign of its author."[59] The courts would eventually validate LRI's managerial role as imbuing the corporation with a recognizable authorial imprint.

Buck Jones v. Republic Productions

From the mid-1930s to the mid-1950s, LRI encountered unexpected challenges to its corporate authority and exclusive rights to exploit the Lone Ranger property. It engaged in several court battles defending its sole authority over the iconic hero.[60] It was not alone in having to define and defend its IP rights, as a few examples show: in 1939, Detective Comics, Inc. won its copyright suit against Fox Features Syndicate, requiring the latter to cease publishing its *Wonderman* comic book, which was deemed to be an unauthorized derivative of Superman; starting in 1941, Fawcett Publications had to fend off rival National Comics Publications' (formerly Detective Comics Inc.) multiple suits (1948, 1951) that its Captain Marvel character was a derivative of Superman (Fawcett would eventually lose despite much evidence that the characters were distinct from one another); and in what might have been a precursor to the case described below, in 1932, Fleischer Studios successfully defended its origination claims to the Betty Boop character against actress Helen Kane, who claimed the character's likeness and singing style were based on her own (the court found that Kane's look and sound were derivatives of Clara Bow's and Baby Esther's and that therefore she had no claim to being the inspiration for Betty Boop).[61] But what is of interest is the particular way that LRI argued for its authorial rights by asserting its managerial acumen without making any overt origination claims over the Lone Ranger.

On June 22, 1937, LRI entered into a production deal with Republic Pictures to produce a fifteen-part film serial based on the Lone Ranger radio personality. Released in early 1938, the first installment quickly became a box office phenomenon.[62] *The Lone Ranger* film serial's success also brought with it a tidal wave of legal troubles.

In July 1938, Buck Jones, a professional cowboy and part-time movie actor, filed suit against Republic, claiming that *The Lone Ranger* serial had stolen its representation of the lead hero from his own established personality and was thus profiting from Jones's reputation. In his accusation, Jones pointed out that he had starred in more than two dozen Western film serials (several for Republic), often playing a heroic role similar to that of the Lone Ranger, and that he too rode a white horse named Silver. In turn, Republic filed suit against LRI since the terms of their contract required the licensor to defend against any legal claims made on the properties it licensed.

At stake for Jones was his ability to control his star image by securing certain identifiable attributes as uniquely his own and preventing others from using those attributes without permission or compensation. Jones's suit against Republic and LRI actually asserted that the two companies had infringed on his right of publicity. This grants individuals the right to commercially exploit their own name and likeness and defend against unauthorized use of their name and likeness by others. At stake for LRI was its ability to extend the Lone Ranger radio property into visual media without risking accusations that the corporation was appropriating the established image of existing performers, which carried with it significant negative economic consequences. Though *The Lone Ranger* had been on the radio since 1933, and had been heard on the West Coast over the Don Lee Network since 1937, Jones sued over the visual representation of the character. As Gaines points out, copyright law has typically reinforced the hegemony of the image. (Sounding like someone else is not a copyright infringement.[63]) If film studios and newspaper syndicates feared constant lawsuits when partnering with LRI to produce and disseminate Lone Ranger adventures, the Masked Man's value as a licensable commodity would be greatly diminished regardless of its radio popularity. Also at stake was LRI's ability to demonstrate authorial control over a property that it did not "author" in any traditional sense of the word, and whose attribution and origination had, for the purposes of marketing, been left strategically vague. If LRI failed to establish its authorial mark, it risked every potential cowboy hero and his creator claiming to be the inspiration for the Lone Ranger. In denying Jones's assertion that his likeness was the basis for the Lone Ranger character appearing in Republic's film serial, LRI instead took the tack of demonstrating to the court its ownership rights to the property in accordance with copyright regulations.

The courts have historically recognized characters as possessing three distinct and dissimilar parts, each of which may be the basis for copyright claims: the character's name, its physical attributes, and its "characterization" or personality traits. Though Buck Jones and the Lone Ranger did not share the same stage name, Jones claimed that his preexisting persona inspired the Lone Ranger's visual rendering in the film serial. Hence, LRI could not simply claim that the Lone Ranger's name was unique. It also needed to demonstrate sole responsibility for delineating the Masked Man's distinctly identifiable characterization.

LRI thus found itself needing to prove that Buck Jones had not inspired the character's physical appearance, and that the basis for how the Lone Ranger should act and, more importantly, look originally emanated from LRI. The corporation faced a double bind: how could it claim origination over an intangible idea that had very few visible signifiers? Even in their depositions, company employees claimed that the Lone Ranger's physical description had been kept purposely vague in order to keep the hero mysterious. As Striker explained in his deposition, "The character has always been more or less idealistic, with enough latitude so that the children listening to the shows and making a heroic figure of the Lone Ranger could use their own judgment in working out the details of his face."[64] Beyond this, how could the corporation claim authorship over a property whose economic value largely depended on its iconic, and hence authorless, status? Though copyright law merely required LRI to demonstrate origination in order to be granted ownership over the property, the corporation was reluctant to reveal its role in creating the Lone Ranger.

At the hearing, George Trendle, Fran Striker, WXYZ station manager Harold True, and sales promotion and advertising manager Charles C. Hicks all testified as to the inspirations for the Lone Ranger. Consistently, each witness recounted the amorphous way that the character and his supporting cast had evolved out of a series of group meetings, back-and-forth correspondence, and trial and error. For instance, the following is an excerpt from True's testimony (April 4, 1939) about Silver's origins:

> True: Naturally we wanted to make him as romantic as possible, so, the first thing that came in my mind was that he should be riding a super horse, a horse that would be easily discernible, as far as radio purposes

were concerned, in the night, as well as in the day. Therefore, he must either be a white horse, or a silver horse. Then the name of Silver, in connection with the idea of light, moonlight glistening on the horse, that gave us the idea of Silver.

Lawyer: Who suggested the name Silver for the horse?

True: Well, as I recall it, it sort of grew in there.

Lawyer: Someone must have originally suggested it though?

True: The name Silver came out in describing the appearance of this horse.

Lawyer: You do not know whether you personally suggested the name Silver?

True: No, I could not say.

Lawyer: And you do not know who did?

True: No. I recall Mr. Campbell [the sales manager] mentioning the word.

Lawyer: Then you do not know what prompted the person to suggest the name Silver, except as you yourself were prompted to suggest names from the ideas that you had in your own mind?

True: That is right.[65]

All of this had the desired effect of rendering the character's authorship both collective and unknowable. While testimony and evidence given in *Buck Jones v. Republic* made it impossible to identify any one individual as the Lone Ranger's originator, it did repeatedly help in establishing LRI's corporate environment as the ultimate inspirational source for the property, complementing Jaszi's assertion that work-for-hire legislation transferred authorial status to employers by recognizing managerial oversight as integral to creative output.[66] LRI also furnished as evidence dozens of back-and-forth letters between Striker, Jewell, and other members of KTBC that further muddied the possibilities of attributing the Lone Ranger's origins to any one person.

Regardless of the company's opaque workflow, Jones's accusation claimed that LRI's inspiration for the Lone Ranger had come from his already established persona. As argued in the previous section, corporate authority often resides in its ability to act as an inspired vessel through which a branded muse speaks and which in turn confers upon the corporation the ability to interpret its popular attributes. Thus, LRI had to demonstrate that though inspired to represent the Lone Ranger, it did not look to Jones as a muse in this endeavor. Acknowledging that all inspiration has roots in some form of imitation, the defendants repeatedly drew connections between the Lone Ranger and character types, as well as fictional figures long in the public domain.

Repeatedly, Jones's attorney raised the question of whether any of the defendants had ever heard of or seen Buck Jones, live or in films. Trendle and the other witnesses all claimed to be unfamiliar with Buck Jones (a dubious claim considering that Trendle had managed a chain of movie theaters throughout the 1920s) and instead asserted that an amalgam of personality traits and qualities possessed by existing heroic archetypes inspired the Lone Ranger's appearance and characterization. True testified that "of course, I think that any time we . . . try to create a character . . . we are all somewhat prone to imitation . . . my ideal of this man was a portrayal like the character of Robin Hood by Doug Fairbanks."[67] Similarly, Striker would admit, "it is the custom of writers to always visualize someone or a group of people in creating a character. In this case, I visualized a man such as Robin Hood might have been."[68]

The oft-repeated comparison of the Lone Ranger to a Robin Hood type was a calculated choice of inspirations. Though the characters shared little in common (other than both being "heroes," broadly conceived), Robin Hood had slipped into the public domain and could be copied by anyone without permission or risk of a lawsuit. Still, almost all the defendants took the further step of testifying that a Robin Hood "type" inspired the Lone Ranger, further distancing the property from any direct attribution. In this manner, when True admitted that Douglas Fairbanks's portrayal of Robin Hood had inspired his own contributions to the Lone Ranger, he essentially was confessing only to imitating a characterization of a type, twice removed. Or, as Trendle described the inspiration: "[I] eventually evolved the thought for a serial more or less based on that type of story, but something somewhat different."[69]

When defendants mentioned living persons, such as Fairbanks or Tom Mix, they quickly pointed out that they had been inspired by either a character they had portrayed or a character value they possessed, not the actual physical appearance of these performers. Striker also admitted to drawing inspiration from Fairbanks, but was careful to qualify that it was "not from the appearance, but from the virile activity that he portrayed in a picture from a story I read in the *Argosy* magazine, one of the Zorro series."[70] Denying any knowledge of Buck Jones, Trendle instead invoked Tom Mix, another cowboy star, as an inspirational source. "We discussed Tom Mix during that discussion, as I recall it, as the type of character we thought the Lone Ranger ought to be, that is, a great big strong, hard-hitting, fast-riding cowboy type."[71] Generalized characteristics found in particular performances—such as being virile, active, or hard-hitting—are not covered by copyright.

Meanwhile, the witnesses' admission that the Lone Ranger character possessed qualities that bore resemblance to those found in other heroic performances worked to position the Lone Ranger as existing alongside these other great heroes, rather than merely being a derivative of them. Though writers, artists, and performers might be accused of copying one another's works, corporate authors demonstrated their managerial acumen by positioning a given property in relation to other cultural commodities through selective and interpretive marketing strategies.

While LRI was vague about the Lone Ranger's origination, it adamantly stressed the labor it put into the property's promotion and exploitation as evidence of its authorial imprint. Sales promotion and advertising manager Hicks gave the most detailed testimony, speaking at length about his job of preparing promotional giveaways to gauge the size of the radio audience for potential sponsors. On the surface, Hicks's testimony offered tangible evidence that visual representations of the Lone Ranger predated the Republic serial. Yet Hicks's elaboration on LRI's use of these marketing materials also articulated how the corporation understood its authorial position vis-à-vis the property. Hicks essentially positioned the company as spreading the Lone Ranger gospel. For example, Hicks described in detail the results of an early public appearance of an actor in a Lone Ranger costume:

> I used [the picture] to show the popularity of the radio program, because of the fact that so many children came particularly to Belle Isle to see the Lone Ranger, proof of which was when all that crowd of 72,000 kids broke ranks and it took the police two hours to keep re-forming, and finally only the Lone Ranger himself could get those kids back on the grand-stands to allow the parade to proceed, which made good publicity in the popularity of the Lone Ranger.[72]

While opposing counsel repeatedly objected to the relevance of Hicks's testimony, it is clear that it served an important function in articulating LRI's authorial relationship with the property. Hicks's testimony furthered the Lone Ranger's legend, all the while foregrounding the company's role in furthering it as a mark of personality and proof of authorship. Within legal discourse concerning the relationship between authorship and ownership, Gaines argues, "The notion of artistic conception rewrites the process of origination to make the artistic act interchangeable with the only means through which we can know it: the thing produced."[73] In other words, the object produced becomes proof of the authoring act. Hicks's testimony inverts Gaines's assertion, producing the Lone Ranger through an enunciation of LRI's artistic act, namely, its responsible marketing practices, which served as proof of the corporation's stewardship over the property.

Ted Striphas makes a similar point regarding the New York District Court of New York's decision over the origins of the term "Muggles" in *Scholastic, Inc., J. K. Rowling, and Time Warner Entertainment Company, L. P. v. Nancy Stouffer*. Although Nancy Stouffer's use of the term Muggles had preceded Rowling's into publication, the court recognized the work done by Rowling, her publishers, and Warner in popularizing the term as key to their continued authority over it.[74] Similarly, while LRI's origination of the Lone Ranger remained murky, the company connected its authorship claims to its role in making the Lone Ranger a strong mark. In particular, LRI submitted as proof of its authorial function its promotional work advocating the Lone Ranger's positive ability to inspire children to respect authority, thus staking its own corporate authority on its role as cultural intermediary.

In essence, LRI claimed a variation of moral rights to the property by demonstrating how its corporate reputation emerged through its managing the Lone Ranger's reputation. While officially there is no recognition of moral rights in U.S. copyright law, LRI's efforts reveal how corporations often justify their economic rights on the basis of their reputation-management skills as much as their financial investment in a property.

The court eventually found in Republic's favor, and Jones withdrew his complaint. Though not well cited in either legal decisions or law reviews,[75] *Buck Jones v. Republic* nonetheless offers important insights into how corporations discursively construct their legal ownership rights over IP in ways that eschew Romantic ideologies of authorship. Indeed, the case's lack of citation might suggest how much managerial authority has become commonsensical in legal discourses on authorship. Certainly, the case was extremely important for LRI's continued ability to maintain ownership over a popular icon for which it claimed only a tenuous origination.

LRI's victory, however, would be short-lived, as it soon faced challenges to its rights to control the Lone Ranger's exploitation across media and merchandising outlets. As with the Buck Jones case, the court's decision in *The Lone Ranger, Inc. v. Cox Circus* would hinge on LRI's track record in managing the interactions between the Lone Ranger and imagined child consumers.

The Lone Ranger, Inc. v. Cox Circus

Perhaps the most significant court battle LRI took part in was against Cox Circus and actor Lee Powell in 1942. LRI sued Cox over Powell's performance as the Lone Ranger in their traveling circus, which Cox promoted as an appearance by "the original 'Lone Ranger'" or "'the Lone Ranger' in person."[76] Powell had in fact appeared as the Lone Ranger in the first Republic movie serial, which Cox mentioned in the ads, though in small type.[77] LRI claimed that Powell's performance infringed on its trademark by perpetuating a deception on the public and by seeking to profit from the goodwill LRI had established with the Lone Ranger property on radio and elsewhere. Cox and Powell contended that since they made no claim to be impersonating the Lone Ranger from the radio, they had the right to publicize Powell's appearance as the Lone Ranger in the films. At stake for Powell was the actor's ability to claim ownership over his performance, which, if granted, would have had lasting repercussions for corporate control over IP by essentially recognizing the moral rights of individual creators to their particular contributions. At stake for LRI was its ability to claim ownership of a brand name and image across seemingly noncompetitive markets, which was essential to its efforts at licensing the Lone Ranger for third-party media and merchandising opportunities.

Whereas LRI had countered Jones's accusations with a copyright defense, the company went on the offensive against Powell and Cox Circus with a claim of trademark violation. Why would LRI choose to argue trademark over copyright infringement in this case, given that the corporation had already successfully established its authorial rights to the property under copyright law? In part, Powell's assertion that he was continuing his role as the Lone Ranger on film, and not from the radio adventures, drove LRI's choice of actions. Copyright law only protects fictional characters when they are integral parts of preexisting works. Since Powell was neither re-creating an existing Lone Ranger story through his performance, nor was he basing his characterization on the Lone Ranger's radio adventures, LRI's copyright remained unperturbed.

In fact, the lower courts originally sided with Powell against LRI, drawing a distinction between the radio program and the films as entirely different and, thereby, noncompetitive products that would not confuse the public. This decision was in line with other rulings of the day, which upheld rigid distinctions between the very markets that character brands had been designed to bridge. As such, when the court of appeals overturned the lower court's verdict, it issued a landmark decision that preceded, but also paved the way for, interpreting secondary meanings in modern-day trademark law. Though LRI was not the first entertainment property owner to successfully pursue a trademark defense, it was the first to have the courts recognize the various indicia, or distinctive marks, associated with a character as also protected by trademark.

Hence, the court of appeals not only found the Lone Ranger to be a sufficiently recognizable mark that extended beyond any one particular product (in this case, a radio series), but it also found that the supporting characters of Tonto and Silver, as well as the Lone Ranger's mask and use of silver bullets, were also independently covered by LRI's trademark. What this meant for Powell and Cox was that they could not simply change the character's name but continue to use the same costume and props in their act. The significance for IP extension was far more significant since it allowed property owners to separately license component parts like Batman's utility belt, Donald Duck's sailor outfit, or Superman's crested "S" insignia without the actual character's presence, effectively opening up many new avenues for merchandising now protected under trademark.[78] Dr. Seuss Enterprises would later directly benefit from the court's decision in *The Lone Ranger, Inc. v. Cox Circus*, when in 1997 it successfully prevented distribution of the book *The Cat NOT in the Hat! A Parody by Dr. Juice*, a satirical retelling of the O. J. Simpson murder case written and illustrated in the style of Dr. Seuss. Dr. Seuss Enterprises was able to get an injunction against Penguin Publishing because the image on the back cover of the book was of a hat reminiscent of the famous accoutrement worn by Seuss's Cat in the Hat. The court found that the hat was enough of an indexical signifier to stand in for the trademarked character.[79] LRI's victory against Powell and Cox Circus would also help pave the way for Congress and the courts to redefine trademark law and extend the definitional boundaries of what constituted like markets, in essence recognizing brand communities as markets built around IP rather than individuated products.

The court of appeals sided with LRI, proclaiming both plaintiff and defendant to be in the same business, the "business of furnishing entertainment."[80] Moreover, the court acknowledged that "the specific and distinctive characteristics" of *The Lone Ranger* broadcast "have a peculiar monetary value" that entitled LRI protection against unauthorized uses of "the name or the character of the program which have been identified to the general public."[81] In recognizing that the Lone Ranger's value was intrinsically tied to the public's perception of it beyond the radio program, the court of appeals also justified LRI's ownership rights on the basis of its brand management skills.

Significantly, the court invoked children in its decision, recognizing the tenuous relationship between the Lone Ranger's profitable personality and its unmanaged representation. The ruling asserted that Cox's publicity would confuse children, imagined as less discerning than adult consumers and therefore more apt to believe that the actual Lone Ranger had come to town:

> Newspaper advertisements are addressed particularly to children and stress that "the Lone Ranger" is appearing in person. In all, the effect of the advertisement is to create the impression that the original "Lone Ranger," made famous by the radio programs, is appearing with the circus; a result more easily achieved because the public interested is composed very largely of children. . . . The inevitable effect of this infringement . . . is to destroy the element of mystery surrounding the character . . . and show him to be a very commonplace person in whom the young people have no further interest, once he has been seen.[82]

It is essential to note that the court did not link its concern about deceiving children to the Lone Ranger's appearance in public, but rather to his unsupervised appearance. As LRI's employees noted in the Buck Jones case, when properly managed, the Lone Ranger's public appearances could have a positive impact on children. And, in fact, the Lone Ranger not only made multiple sanctioned public appearances throughout the late 1930s and early 1940s, but LRI would also lease the character to several circuses across the United States and Canada during this same period, though under fairly detailed and rigid contract stipulations. Thus, it can be inferred that the court recognized LRI's corporate oversight of the Lone Ranger as essential to the character's continued cultural value for children.

In recognizing LRI's ability to protect the public against the unregulated power of the Lone Ranger's personality, the court conferred authorship status upon the corporation by articulating this managerial function as the distinct mark it left on the brand. LRI's managerial discourse worked to eschew concerns over the Lone Ranger's marketability with children, just as long as LRI held creative authority over the brand. To some extent, this is a complication of Gaines's claim that IP licensing is merely a "parasitic industry" taking advantage of the inversion of trademark law's initial intent.[83] Where Gaines saw the Lanham Act as privileging IP owner rights to profit over those of the consumer's right to informed choice, the appellate court's decision in LRI's favor essentially articulates the corporation's function as ensuring that consumers are protected against misrepresentations of a property's core values through unauthorized and unsupervised usages. While it is not my claim that corporate IP owners truly have the consumer's best interests at heart, it is important to clarify how corporate authorship has come to be understood as more than simply a claim to economic ownership.

The court battles that LRI took part in reveal how economic and legal conceptualizations of ownership are shaped by cultural definitions of management and authorship, in this case management *as* authorship, rather than the other way around. Much like in the Buck Jones case, the court's decision—as well as LRI's assertion of its rights to oversee how the Lone Ranger was interpreted across markets—demonstrates how the essence of moral rights is infused into corporate managerial claims. The Lone Ranger's reputation was ultimately determined to be sutured to the reputation of its corporate author (even as Powell's moral rights to his performance as the Masked Man were categorically denied). In stating, "Powell is not 'the Lone Ranger' at all" and decrying him to be merely a "moving picture actor who took the part of 'the Lone Ranger,'" the ruling recognized the property as synonymous with its corporate owner, whose reputation ensured the integrity of the Lone Ranger brand across markets. "There can be no question, we think, but that 'the Lone Ranger' should be considered as a trade name under which plaintiff's radio programs are broadcast, and that defendants infringed plaintiff's rights therein when they advertised Powell as the 'Original Lone Ranger.'"[84]

LRI's trademark claims would come to rest on the assertion that the Lone Ranger's secondary meanings could be attributed to the property's manager, which assured a coherence of meaning and an alignment of economic and social values across the various markets. Importantly, in the 1958 *Wyatt Earp Enterprises v. Sackman, Inc.* case, the court would apply a similar standard of managerial oversight in interpreting secondary meanings' associative connotations. The case rested on whether or not Sackman had the right to manufacture a Wyatt Earp playsuit without permission from the television production company then producing the series. Sackman argued that Wyatt Earp was an actual historical figure that could inspire any number of noncompeting productions, while Wyatt Earp Enterprises argued that Sackman was perpetuating a fraud against the public by profiting from the goodwill garnered by the television production. The court found in favor of the plaintiff, identifying Wyatt Earp Enterprises as the source of the public's current association with the character—though not the character's originator—and asking the pertinent rhetorical question, "What are the features by which [the public] distinguishes that source?"[85] The court's answer pointed to Wyatt Earp Enterprises' licensing practices as the means by which the public identified it as the source of meaning for the property.

Perhaps the most infamous invocation of *The Lone Ranger, Inc. v. Cox Circus* was in *Columbia Broadcasting System, Inc. v. DeCosta*, in which the U.S. Court of Customs and Patent Appeals essentially gave CBS permission to steal another person's intellectual property on the grounds that they had simply done a better job of promoting it and therefore had become associated with it in the public's eye.[86] For nearly a decade, Victor DeCosta, a mechanic from Rhode Island, had made multiple unpaid public appearances at rodeos and parades as his alter ego, a mustached cowboy named Paladin. He would volunteer his services by distributing business cards that read, "Have Gun Will Travel." When CBS aired a television series by the same name featuring a character named Paladin, who dressed almost identically to DeCosta's creation and used the same calling card, DeCosta sued for unfair competition. Though the initial decision issued was in his favor, the court of appeals reversed the decision, using DeCosta's own invocation of *The Lone Ranger, Inc. v. Cox Circus* against him:

> The plaintiff quotes the Lone Ranger case as involving "the element of fraudulent attempt of someone to 'reap where he has not sown' and to appropriate to himself 'the harvest of those who have sown.'" But the opinion makes it clear that the "harvest" is the goodwill generated by long establishment of the Lone Ranger in the public eye, and the element of fraud is quite as important as the element of appropriation . . . appropriation not of the creation but of the value attached to it by public association (the so-called "secondary meaning"), by misleading the public into thinking that the defendant's offering is the product of the plaintiff's established skill.[87]

Though DeCosta was recognized as Paladin's originator, the ruling privileged the managerial labor that CBS had performed in popularizing the character as the true source of its value. As William T. Jaeger summarizes, "A character's goodwill is based upon how well-known and popular he is. . . . Advertising and promotional activities play a large role in determining the amount of such goodwill. . . . [CBS] transformed the general deal of a western gunman for hire with a specific name and appearance into a commercially valuable character attractive to the public."[88]

The courts would also come to recognize LRI's corporate authorial role in managing the Lone Ranger's reputation across entertainment platforms and ensuring the property's goodwill among consumers, even though it did not "author" every Lone Ranger iteration in the traditional sense of the word. Instead, the corporation was recognized as "authoring" the secondary meanings that became associated with its particular IP holdings through its managerial acumen.

Conclusion

LRI's legal battles played an important role in both protecting the company's assets and defining its public identity as the Lone Ranger's steward and consumer guardian. The company staked its reputation on its managerial skill, which it employed in aligning the Masked Man's popularity with profitable and normative social values, all the while claiming to speak on behalf of both its corporate muse and the average consumer. While LRI was no more litigious during this period than other character brand owners—Disney took part in no less than ten court battles between 1939 and 1947; Detective Comics was involved in four such disputes—the company was instrumental in rhetorically constructing a corporate authorial persona for itself that participated in the juridical reimagining of how copyright and trademark laws operated.

Though intellectual property law and authorial identities are mutually constitutive cultural and ideological constructs, I do not see a singular vision or version of authorship necessarily evoked through juridical processes. Romantic notions of authorship compete with corporate interpretations, which advocate for rewarding stewardship over origination as the basis for IP rights.

In recognizing the law as a site for discursive struggle, not only over which entities get to claim authorship, but also over which definitions of authorship should prevail, legal scholars can further demystify legal proceedings and devise new tactics for challenging corporate hegemony. Lessig (2004) concedes that he erred in assuming that the Supreme Court did not require a cultural argument in favor of releasing popular characters into the public domain. But I would suggest that the greater error lies in assuming that the Supreme Court misunderstood copyright's intentions or mistook corporations like Disney and Dr. Seuss Enterprises for creative geniuses entitled to authorial privilege. If a cultural argument is to be made for loosening and lessening corporate control over American cultural icons, it must be able to confront corporate managerial rhetoric head-on in order to shift authorial discourses in another direction. In pressing the courts to recognize the different cultural definitions of authorship at play in corporate versus creator usages of the term, a more direct and nuanced rebuttal to claims of stewardship might be made, which challenges the relationship between economic value and social values that corporate owners have successfully sutured together.

The Lone Ranger legal battles also highlight that we must look to the ways legal arguments have shaped larger cultural discussion about authorship, ownership, and free circulation of popular culture. In this regard, I build on Coombe's assertion that the law's cultural power rests in its "interpretive life . . . found in rumors and myths about rights and obligations . . . in disputes rarely addressed at trial on their legal merits."[89]

Coombe believes that legal debates about authorship permeate cultural forums well beyond juridical boundaries. One can certainly see how articulations of corporate authorship play into fan debates over whether or not the Siegel and Shuster estates should regain their rights to Superman, with many fans expressing concern that the quality of the character's representations would inevitably suffer without institutional resources and managerial acumen. A sampling from a 2010 online discussion of the latest legal intrigues produced statements like: "It would be absolutely tragic if DC were to lose Superman. Look, no one is denying that the Siegel & Schuster got epically screwed. That being said, the only reason the Superman character is what it is today (and worth all that money) is because of DC's work shepherding him over the past 70 years," and "Superman didn't become the major property he is today because of [Siegel and Shuster]. He became this property because DC used and marketed him in this way."[90] Not only do these fan postings seemingly reproduce and legitimate corporate authorial discourses, but they also offer glimpses as to how legal debates intersect with cultural evaluations of IP rights among consumers.

Unsurprisingly, given the goodwill that consumers often express toward corporate stewards, LRI wore its litigiousness like a badge of honor, going so far as to equate its legal counsel Meurer's efforts to quash infringements with the heroic actions of the Lone Ranger himself. The publicity materials LRI circulated to its clients in celebration of the Lone

Figure 4.3. This 1970s ad was widely disseminated by the Wrather Corporation, demonstrating the continued pride LRI took in its litigiousness as well as the anxiety that unauthorized Lone Ranger merchandise generated. Note how the Lone Ranger does the talking on Wrather's behalf. Author's collection.

Ranger's twentieth anniversary describe Meurer as tirelessly traveling to every part of the country to "put down imposters, block infringements and guard against misrepresentation in publicity or advertising" in order to protect the American values the Lone Ranger embodied.[91] Thus, LRI not only actively sought recognition of its authority through legal action, it also sought to articulate its authority by actively promoting this work as essential to its property rights (see Figure 4.3).

Similarly, Dr. Seuss Enterprises, which has repeatedly positioned itself as steward of Theodor Geisel's creations and guardian of public sentiment toward Geisel's many characters, has not shied away from its litigious reputation, but rather publicly embraces it. In the injunction filed to keep *The Cat NOT in the Hat! A Parody by Dr. Juice* from being distributed, Audrey S. Geisel argued forcefully that her late husband would not have supported his characters' association with a murderer; and as upholders of Seuss's legacy, neither would the Cat in the Hat's corporate benefactor.[92] Such sentiments can also be found on the Dr. Seuss website, which explains, "The primary focus of Dr. Seuss Enterprises, L.P. is to protect the integrity of the Dr. Seuss books while expanding beyond books into ancillary areas. This effort is a strategic part of the overall mission to nurture and safeguard the relationship consumers have with Dr. Seuss characters. Theodor Seuss Geisel (Dr. Seuss) said he never wanted to license his characters to anyone who would 'round out the edges.' That is one of the guiding philosophies of Dr. Seuss Enterprises."[93] By proclaiming itself intermediary between the public and the long-dead creator, Dr. Seuss Enterprises couches its legal authority over the Dr. Seuss brand in cultural terms designed to affirm consumer and juridical faith in its cultural stewardship.

CHAPTER 5

Containing the Ranger: Postwar Cultural (Re)Branding and the Industrial Logics of Containment

Introduction

On February 12, 1950, Harry Poppe, associate producer for Apex Film's recently launched *Lone Ranger* television series, sent LRI president George W. Trendle a batch of publicity stills taken to promote the series in newspapers across the United States. Among the photos was one of actor Clayton Moore, dressed in full Lone Ranger regalia, enjoying a slice of cake between takes on the set. Indeed, the Lone Ranger had much to celebrate. During the post–World War II era (1946–1954), the Lone Ranger's popularity among consumers and licensees was at its height. While its precise market share is hard to gauge, the property's ubiquitous cross-media and merchandising presence suggest that LRI was at the top of its game in extending the Lone Ranger's market presence.

By 1953, the twentieth anniversary of the radio series debut, *The Lone Ranger* was being heard over 221 radio stations on the ABC Radio network by an estimated audience of twelve million each week.[1] The *Lone Ranger* comic strip appeared worldwide in 177 daily newspapers and 119 Sunday newspapers, by far the most for any Western hero. Comic strip readership was estimated at 71 million people per week.[2] Three separate Lone Ranger comic books sold more than two million copies each month, and fifteen Lone Ranger novels were available in bookstores. Decca Records had recorded eight original Lone Ranger adventures, listed among the top fifteen best-selling children's records of the early 1950s.[3] Under General Mills' sponsorship since 1941, the Masked Man served as the face of Cheerios, Kix, Trix, and Wheaties cereals.[4] The Lone Ranger Safety Club was still going strong in the early 1950s with an estimated membership of four million children.[5] And *The Lone Ranger* television series debuted in 1949, the only ABC TV series to crack Nielsen's top fifteen that year.[6] In turn, television generated a new licensing and merchandising boom. In 1953, LRI earned $2.5 million in revenue from merchandising alone.[7]

While the Lone Ranger's popularity appeared to be a natural outgrowth of the Masked Man's textual and extra-textual exploits dating back to the 1930s, its postwar success was actually predicated on significant changes in both marketing and managing the property. LRI engaged in what Douglas Holt has termed "cultural branding" and adjusted the Lone Ranger's formula by embracing the ethos of patriotic consumption and cultural containment that defined the era.[8] As corporate and government interests began promoting an American identity that was inherently linked with consumerism, the Lone Ranger's marketing shifted, from giving civic lessons about traffic safety to equating consumption with the American Heritage. Thus the property became not merely a sales agent for particular corporate sponsors but for Americanism in general. The Lone Ranger's omnipresence in the postwar era caused one anonymous author to comment that "the 'Masked Man of justice' had become, as his creators put it, 'an American institution.'"[9]

With so much to celebrate, it must have seemed strange when Trendle immediately rejected the good-humored publicity photo of the Masked Man indulging his sweet tooth, bluntly telling Poppe, "It might be good General Mills publicity but it is not the type of material we wish to use for newspaper copy."[10] Instead, Trendle insisted that all publicity shots show the Lone Ranger in "action"—though clearly not the act of consuming food.[11] Presumably the photograph was destroyed, since no copies of it have ever circulated. But Trendle's humorless rebuke is significant, epitomizing LRI's typical—and tactical—response to postwar anxieties over ownership and control of the property. Trendle's tepid reaction to the photo certainly betrayed his concern over national sponsor General Mills' growing association with the Lone Ranger in the eyes of consumers. It also represented a tactical attempt to fortify LRI's managerial authority in the wake of media industry changes that, while lucrative, lessened the licensor's direct control over the property and potentially strengthened the grasp of its licensees. Yet it would be shortsighted to see Trendle's reaction as merely nervous micromanagement brought on by a shifting production context. In actuality, LRI openly endorsed containment as a proactive tactic intended not only to push back against aggressive licensees, but also to better align the Lone Ranger's economic and cultural value with the postwar social climate, echoing both U.S. foreign and domestic containment policies.

Broadly, "containment" is a concept associated with President Harry Truman's (1945–1953) Cold War foreign policy initiatives intended to prevent the spread of Soviet-backed Communist regimes in Asia and Eastern Europe through the provision of economic, military, and political aid to emerging nation-states choosing to embrace democratic rather than socialist principles.[12] Containing Communism abroad became conflated with suppressing social unrest at home through what have subsequently been labeled domestic containment practices, which rendered suspect anything that fell outside the "norm" of white, suburban, middle-class values.[13]

Historians often describe the postwar years in America as a period of economic prosperity vying with cultural conformity.[14] Any group perceived to question the status quo risked being labeled a threat to national security and the social order. Suburbia emerged as an imagined safe haven against the imminent dangers posed by groups either demanding a greater slice of the pie or refusing to embrace cultural norms—a safe haven repeatedly besieged by threat of infiltration or collapse and in need of constant refortification. In this sense, containment refers to the ways social policy during the postwar period was driven by fears that the American Heritage could not be sustained without vigilant enforcement of traditional norms and values.

If prosperity and conformity went hand-in-hand, LRI argued that the key to the Lone Ranger's economic vitality—as well as that of its licensees—was coherence across franchise outposts. Where local customization and flexibility had previously been integral to extending the Masked Man's reach, LRI now imposed a series of rules on all Lone Ranger productions. The licensor also became increasingly vigilant about monitoring the compatibility of the Masked Man's brand image across media platforms.

While media representations have always served as a battleground over teaching normative American values, in the postwar era the media industries faced accusations of covertly spreading Communist ideology. Children's media came under particularly harsh scrutiny from regulators and cultural critics for potentially contributing to the rise of juvenile delinquency. Not surprisingly, IP owners like LRI used their intractable managerial ability to reel in licensees whose visions deviated even slightly from perceived social norms, while also vigorously promoting their own allegiance to teaching the virtues of American capitalism and patriotism. The formulaic rigidity LRI imposed on licensees was intended not only to fend off potential accusations that the property promoted the wrong values, but also to demonstrate to its clients how to contain and productively repurpose tensions that threatened the postwar economic stability. LRI's marketing materials gave special attention to the Masked Man's ability to offset concerns over racial discrimination and juvenile delinquency. It did so by integrating both groups into the emerging "Consumers' Republic," defined by Lizabeth Cohen as "an economy, culture and politics built around the promises of mass consumption, both in terms of material life and the more idealistic goals of greater freedom, democracy and equality."[15]

Lone Ranger stories not only took on greater patriotic significance, but also expressed a far more expansive mythology emphasizing the Masked Man's origin, motivations, and relationships. Paradoxically, containment tactics intended to shield character brands against industrial and cultural pressures also produced a series of postwar storytelling and brand extension innovations that bear a remarkable similarity to contemporary world-building practices celebrated by media scholar Henry Jenkins for their ability to deepen consumer investment in popular story worlds.[16] Where Lone Ranger paratextual materials in the 1930s had integrated the Masked Man into local communities and deepened consumer investment in the Lone Ranger–brand lifestyle, postwar extra-textual efforts often sought to reimmerse consumer desires within the text itself.

This was certainly the case with the 1948 Frontier Town initiative with which this chapter culminates. The Frontier Town campaign exemplifies how containment as both cultural and business ethos shaped brand management tactics during this period. Co-created by LRI and General Mills, Frontier Town was an elaborate year-long experiment in immersive and integrated marketing that granted radio listeners entry into the Masked Man's story world by collecting maps and set pieces available on the backs of Cheerios boxes. In some ways, Frontier Town resembles contemporary media franchise expansion endeavors that encourage fans to inhabit and map the boundaries of branded universes. Yet the Frontier Town initiative was also a tactical response to the postwar white flight to the suburbs, responding to emerging tensions brought on by business and social changes and literally containing them within the Lone Ranger's textual exploits. Frontier Town thus captures a paradoxical aspect of character brand management in the 1950s: despite what may appear to be restrictive measures employed by IP owners like LRI, postwar containment tactics actually produced vibrant creative work that would subtly influence contemporary transmedia storytelling efforts. In this chapter's conclusion, I also return to the question of containment's lasting legacy on brand management.

Cultural Rebranding and the Postwar Consumers' Republic

In his book *How Brands Become Icons: The Principles of Cultural Branding*, Douglas Holt (2005) argues that successful brands play out identity myths that resolve societal contradictions through consumer engagement. Brand managers must, therefore, be constantly attuned to the ways their properties can offer fantasy solutions to ever-changing cultural anxieties. For example, Holt analyzes how the successful 1970s "Hilltop" Coca-Cola ad campaign tapped into existing anxieties over race relations at home and mounting global tensions abroad by offering up an image of world harmony built around and through Coke's product. The commercial features a multiracial, multiaccented group of people joining hands around a pastoral hill in the Italian countryside and singing a folksy jingle about wanting to teach the world to sing and also wanting to buy it a Coke. Holt also asserts that when cultural disruptions upset the previous myths that brands had tapped into, these iconic properties must "reinvent their myth, or they fade in relevance."[17]

In post–World War II America, many popular icons from the 1930s were reenvisioned to meet a cultural climate now embracing consumerism and fearful of changes that might upset the status quo. The U.S. entrance into World War II in December 1941 put on hold the competing visions of consumer citizenship between big business and big government that had dominated the Depression years. New energies were directed toward munitions manufacturing and other essential military needs. The U.S. government asked advertising agencies and manufacturers to help promote mobilization, war bond sales, rationing, and other public safety information. In exchange, ad agencies and their corporate clients received government contracts, tax breaks, and public goodwill.

Marketers stressed the educational value of popular characters in selling the war and appropriate modes of wartime citizenship. As an article in *Collier's* explained, "Who won social acceptance for our new-style doughboys? The USO, the Red Cross, the YMCA? No, Joe Palooka's ma. And who sold the kids of America on pitching in to help war-working mothers with the housework? Little Orphan Annie, that's who. The minute Annie organized her Junior Commandos, millions of little nippers uttered hoarse cries and sprang to their brooms."[18]

LRI's marketing boasted that the Lone Ranger's inspirational virtue could be shown through "the fact that during the African campaign of World War II, the soldiers chose the expression, 'Hi Yo Silver!' as a battle cry. It seemed to inspire them to action on behalf of justice—to embody in three short words the whole American Heritage for which they were fighting."[19] The Lone Ranger also made multiple public appearances in support of the troops, while comic book pages and comic strip panels were devoted to encouraging children to invest in war bonds.

In 1941, LRI temporarily suspended the Lone Ranger Safety Club and replaced it with the Lone Ranger National Defenders club, which for the first time explicitly addressed children as members of a national organization, eschewing the local approach that had been central to marketing the LRSC. The mission of the new club shifted from practicing good traffic safety etiquette to "defend[ing] our nation against defamers, propagandists, traitors and spies by reporting suspicious activities to proper authorities"—in essence, to weed out people who did not conform to prescribed social beliefs about the war, although the club tried to couch these tattling activities as both an American duty and "loads of fun."[20] While some aspects of the LRSC's more mundane mission remained intact, the value ascribed to traffic safety shifted from setting a good example for younger children to preventing the enemy from gaining the upper hand. As a sample letter sent to a newly minted National Defender explained: "With this letter is your Victory Pledge Certificate. Sign it and put it up in your room where it will remind you every day to help Uncle Sam by following its ten rules. Five of them give you ways you can take part in the war effort. The other five are safety rules, which are now more important than ever, because every accident we have in America helps our country's enemies."[21]

Most important, however, were the overt connections now made between club activities, patriotism, and consumerism. Where previous insider information about the Lone Ranger's ensemble indirectly corresponded to merchandisable accoutrements, the National Defenders directly tied together investment in the Lone Ranger's mythos with acquisition of Lone Ranger merchandise. It openly advocated for members to consume Kix cereal as a means of "safeguard[ing] health as one of the nation's vital defenses" and, moreover, to send in proofs-of-purchase in exchange for items essential to the club mission. The club's "secret portfolio" manual made privy to members "the strange story of the silver bullets"—analogous to LRSC's sharing the tale of how the Lone Ranger captured Silver—immediately followed by instructions on how to be appointed a Silver Bullet Defender by sending in a Kix box top, a dime, and a coupon telling the Lone Ranger that "you're willing to do your part in this thrilling job of protecting our nation from the 'enemies within'!"[22] (see Figure 5.1).

The manual also included a two-page spread dedicated to cataloging essential National Defender equipment, including an emergency first aid kit and warning siren, as well as Lone Ranger hats, vests, belts, and other items of questionable wartime necessity, any of which could be obtained by sending in one of twelve coupons that came with the guide along with a Kix box top and anywhere from a dime to a quarter. The coupons were on the same page as the creed that members were expected to sign, promising to abide by the Lone Ranger's instructions. The catalog also listed Kix cereal as the most important piece of equipment National Defenders should have on hand. While this direct marketing might seem out of line with wartime rhetoric that otherwise stressed constraint and delayed gratification, it should be noted that the coupon system General Mills and LRI employed mimicked established wartime rationing practices of issuing coupon booklets to limit household purchases of essential items and that, moreover, many of the items included in the National Defenders equipment catalog were in fact much cheaper to acquire via club membership than at local department stores. Thus, while underhanded and opportunistic, the National Defenders club encouraged both consumption and constraint as patriotic. In so doing, it acted as a bridge between the prewar Lone Ranger and his postwar iteration.

The economic turnaround generated by the war, and corporate success in selling patriotism, erased much of the consumer distrust that had shrouded businesses during the Depression. American corporations found themselves key players in setting the postwar consumer agenda. In the postwar era, consumption was not only marketed as a reward for years of economic hardship, sacrifice, and bloodshed, it was also presented as inherently patriotic. As Lizabeth Cohen argues, "Mass consumption did not only deliver wonderful things for purchase . . . it also dictated the most central dimensions of postwar society, including the political economy (the way public policy and the mass consumption economy mutually reinforced each other), as well as the political culture (how political practice and American values, attitudes, and behaviors tied to mass consumption became intertwined)."[23]

In the postwar Consumers' Republic, economic growth and demo-

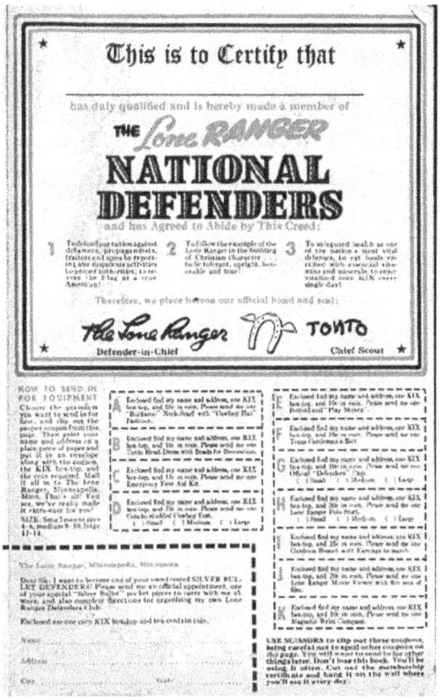

Figure 5.1. The Lone Ranger National Defenders Secret Portfolio, ca. 1941. Note the use of coupons and the direct links between patriotism, rationing, and consumerism.

cratic freedom became synonymous. In a 1956 speech, President Eisenhower advocated the potential for "people's' capitalism" to erase class lines.[24] Key debates in the political arena no longer questioned the distribution of wealth and the influence of big business, but instead centered on determining which policies would bring about greater purchasing power for all Americans. Yet, as Will Herberg asserts, the moral righteousness of consumer capitalism still needed foregrounding: "Americans cannot go on making money or achieving worldly success simply on its own merits; such 'materialistic' things must, in the American mind, be justified in 'higher' terms, in terms of 'service' or 'stewardship' or 'general welfare.'"[25] The Advertising Council pushed big business to adopt a "corporate idiom of public service."[26] The corporation became the public face of postwar society, offering liberal concessions such as health and retirement benefits to their employees in exchange for their unquestioning cooperation in building the postwar economy. In so doing, corporate interests were interpreted as mere neutral agents of progress and democracy.[27]

Popular culture was seen as a strategic means of conveying the inherent moral righteousness of materialism. The formulas of many licensed properties were reshuffled to better reflect the patriotic corporate ethos of their sponsors. For example, it was only in 1951 that Superman became a champion for "Truth, Justice and the American Way." As late as 1948, Superman fought "in the interests of truth, tolerance and justice." "The American Way" was a popular Cold War expression that was often used to distinguish between the quality of life available to Americans versus their Communist counterparts. Herberg defined the phrase "the American Way of Life" as "compounded almost equally of democracy and free enterprise."[28] Though the phrase had been used sporadically on radio during the war years, the 1951 television series made it the centerpiece of the opening credits. Sponsored by Kellogg's cereal, *The Adventures of Superman* transformed the hero into an advocate for an American lifestyle commensurate with corporate values (actor George Reeves appeared as the always-suited Clark Kent for nearly three-quarters of every episode) and unabashed consumerism (commercials regularly featured Clark dashing off to replenish empty boxes of Kellogg's Corn Flakes with the same enthusiasm as the Man of Steel captured villains). Similarly, in the postwar era, working class fictional families like the Goldbergs and *Blondie*'s Bumsteads entered the middle class, while the rags-to-riches fable that undergirded Little Orphan Annie's formula fell into disfavor, replaced by the mildly rebellious antics of Hank Ketcham's Dennis the Menace and Charles Schulz's Peanuts gang.

Where the Depression-era Lone Ranger was often positioned as counterbalancing sponsored commercial impulses through his benign civic advocacy under the auspices of the LRSC, the postwar Lone Ranger was an advocate for consumerism and a staunch defender of American enterprise. The Consumers' Republic that the Lone Ranger championed promoted new consumer goods as rooted in an American Heritage of free enterprise, and the conflation of citizenship and consumption. In a 1953 PR document titled "Subject: Lone Ranger Anniversary Story," issued in celebration of the Masked Man's twentieth year in existence, LRI simultaneously positioned its hero within and outside of history. The document began:

> In January, 1933, Franklin D. Roosevelt became President. In Germany, a man named Hitler was made chancellor. That month saw the beginning of the New Deal in America, and the beginning of upheaval in Europe. That was the month in which the words, "Hi Yo Silver," were first heard by radio listeners. . . . The New Deal, the Fair Deal, war and peace have come and gone. Great men have risen for their hour of glory—only to be forgotten. Fiends who seemed invincible have been stomped into the dust. During the past two decades the world has changed. But the Lone Ranger still rides the airways three times every week.[29]

The Lone Ranger's popularity was promoted as both reflecting and transcending historical events and figures. Notably, the Lone Ranger's primary competitors in this narrative are FDR and Hitler, two people whom American corporations had positioned themselves against. The message was simple. Like corporate America, the Lone Ranger had survived the dual threats of government regulation and consumer rationing and, while those "anomalous" events passed, "forgotten" into history, the Lone Ranger's popularity remained intact. By evoking continuity between the past and the present, the Lone Ranger's rightful place in America seemed as inevitable as the American Heritage that had produced him and for which he fought.

As early as 1944, *The Lone Ranger* radio series began devoting each Monday episode to the Lone Ranger participating in a real historical event or riding to the rescue of a real historical figure. Over a seven-month stretch in 1944, the Lone Ranger and Tonto met up with the likes of Buffalo Bill, Bat Masterson, Ulysses S. Grant, Calamity Jane, Annie Oakley, Teddy Roosevelt, Billy the Kid, and Kit Carson. In almost all of these episodes, the Lone Ranger is depicted as being instrumental to a famous historical event featuring these individuals, either being present at the event itself or inspiring the real-life person in a way that indirectly contributes to their later greatness. The Lone Ranger not only assists Teddy Roosevelt and his Rough Riders in hunting down Butch Cavendish, but his admiration for Annie Oakley's marksmanship leads him to recommend that Buffalo Bill hire her for his traveling Western show.[30]

In 1951, LRI began writing letters to various corporations that traced their origins back to the Old West, requesting early histories that could be incorporated into *The Lone Ranger* adventures. As the licensor explained, "We have been giving considerable thought toward story treatment of pioneer industries who, as a result of initiative and under our free enterprise system, were greatly responsible for the building of the Southwest in the years immediately following the Civil War. . . . We would like to make use of such history with a series of Lone Ranger stories . . . as our effort toward showing Democracy in action, and the part played by industry in the building of this great territory."[31] On radio, often by "special request" from President Lincoln, the Lone Ranger worked with the likes of the Western Union Telegraph and Union Pacific Railroad companies, helping them to join the nation together.[32] This was a very different type of fight than the one undertaken by his 1930s counterpart, who protected small towns from schemers and gangs. By the early 1950s, the imperative that the Lone Ranger "must work and fight to promote the development of the West" and not merely to rescue individuals was worked into the "Lone Ranger Rules" that LRI prepared for its licensees.

The overarching messages sold by the postwar Lone Ranger were that free enterprise had made America great and that the benevolent power of contemporary American corporations had direct historical linkages with the pioneering spirit that had built the country. In fact, *The Lone Ranger: Standards and Background*, a guide assembled for third-party media producers, explicitly linked the pioneering spirit of the American West with postwar consumerist goals: "The Lone Ranger has contributed to Americana by showing as accurately as possible how hardships were overcome by the courage and determination of the pioneers . . . without benefit of government assistance . . . how these pioneers toiled and suffered to improve their nation that life might be better for their descendants . . . the Lone Ranger programs show that young people of America today owe much to their ancestors and to pay this debt, they must make the most of opportunities and in turn, pass on to their descendants an even greater country."[33]

LRI credited the Lone Ranger's tremendous success with its "message" of "Patriotism—Tolerance—Fairness and a Sympathetic Understanding of fellow men and their rights and privileges."[34] LRI equated these qualities with distinctly corporate visions of America. Under "Patriotism," the document explained, "the Lone Ranger is motivated by love of country—a desire to help those who are building the West. . . . Patriotism means service to a community; voting; aiding in community projects and the development of schools and churches." Love of country is equated with economic expansion, "the building of the West," while service and voting are rooted in local politics and communal living, just as they had been positioned by American corporations during the Depression. Under "Fairness," the document stated, "the Lone Ranger advocates the American Tradition, which gives each man the right to choose his work and to profit in proportion to his effort; and to retain for himself a fair proportion of his profits. The Lone Ranger also advocates the right to possess and hold worldly goods."[35]

While clearly there is a certain amount of anti-Communist rhetoric at play here (after all, as the "Communist leanings" of the entertainment industries came under scrutiny, it became even more important for cultural producers to declare emphatically their allegiances to God and Country. Mere mention of one's name in anti-Communist publications such as *Red Channels* could—and did—spell the end of one's career in entertainment),[36] LRI's idealistic rhetoric was also perfectly attuned to changes in the cultural valuation of the independent professional in the workplace and the accompanying valorization of the company man. While labor and ownership had been at war with one another prior to World War II, they could now be reconciled through their shared admiration for the values the Lone Ranger stood for. Significantly, throughout the late 1940s and the 1950s, the Lone Ranger made multiple visits to General Mills factories to boost morale and was touted by his sponsor as the ultimate company man, serving as a powerful sales agent for its products and ensuring a better quality of life for its employees.

As a *Saturday Evening Post* ad from November 1949, featuring the Masked Man riding alongside a General Mills company car, summarized, "But this handsome horseman is more than an entertainer. Like his friend [in the car]—William H. Barry, one of our 723 grocery products salesmen—he's a 'crack salesman' of General Mills products. And like all crack salesmen, the Lone Ranger creates better jobs—for a lot of people" (see Figure 5.2).[37]

Figure 5.2. "How the Lone Ranger rounds up jobs," General Mills ad, *Saturday Evening Post*, November 1949. Author's collection.

In the 1930s, sponsor Gordon Bakery had admonished grocers who failed to recognize the Lone Ranger's sales appeal as "asleep at the wheel," and LRI had sought to teach salesmen how to draw inspiration from the Masked Man's merchandisable attributes in hawking to retailers.[38] Now General Mills conflated the Lone Ranger's heroics in defending the Old West with its sales staff's work in bolstering the postwar economy. To be a loyal mid-level employee was pitched as the ultimate act of patriotism and heroism: "Modern corporate capitalism had transformed a nation of entrepreneurs—Self-Made Men—into a nation of hired employees."[39]

Efforts to promote the Consumers' Republic also gestured at its unraveling, as the overdetermined efforts to defend the American Heritage repeatedly hinted that many did not share these beliefs. The demands for equal opportunities made by groups that continued to be marginalized in the postwar economy made visible America's continued bigotries and the potential failure of the free market system to correct these injustices. Also, rebelliousness in the emergent youth culture inspired fear that American children were suffering from lethargy and other psychological ailments that impeded their ability to become ideal consumers. Thus, the American Heritage was often presented as a utopian ideal on the verge of collapse. In a scripted Lone Ranger promotional radio interview aimed at parents, the character explained, "The builders of America had none of the benefits and privileges of the people who are living today. . . . Yet, those pioneers did great things. . . . We want the young people to realize that we owe all that we have to the pioneers. We can pay our debt to those early settlers by making the most of today's opportunity."[40]

In this manner, LRI sought to position the Lone Ranger as capable of containing cultural tensions that threatened the postwar status quo—specifically, racial tensions and disaffected youth.

Containing Race and Curing Juvenile Delinquency

In the postwar era, there was a growing recognition that racial minorities, especially African Americans, remained a largely untapped market. Many African Americans were happy for this recognition, seen as an important step toward achieving equality and acceptance. Having served their country during World War II, many minorities returned home anxious to partake in the consumer fantasy that had been promised to all Americans. At the same time, a 1944 Supreme Court decision overturned the whites-only primary laws in the South, and the black vote became increasingly important to northern Democrats.

Still, Lizabeth Cohen has argued that African Americans faced a paradoxical dilemma. On the one hand, public trust in the fairness of the private market often was not justified. Discriminatory policies continued, as the private institutions responsible for realizing the government's commitment to war veterans through the GI Bill often systematically denied and misdirected African American veterans when it came to qualifying for school or home ownership loans. On the other hand, the new conflation of citizenship with consumption presented African Americans new opportunities to fight discrimination publicly by challenging their exclusion from public sites of consumption and leisure, culminating in the sit-in protests of the 1950s.[41] Early civil rights boycott campaigns linked this consumer power to demands for economic, political, and representational change. Minority advocacy groups such as the NAACP targeted television as an important site of consumer resistance through boycotts of sponsors whose programs misrepresented the black experience. In 1950–1952, the NAACP launched a fairly vocal attack against the Blatz Beer–sponsored *Amos 'n' Andy* television program.[42]

LRI responded to this emerging minority consumer power by enthusiastically recounting the Lone Ranger's 1951 public appearance at the Miami Orange Bowl, where the hero crossed the color line to shake hands with African American children, explaining, "The likelihood of audience segregation had completely escaped [the Lone Ranger and its licensor's] thinking."[43] The company also showed renewed recognition of Tonto's Native American status. Though the Lone Ranger's sidekick had been around since 1933, the character was unabashedly described on radio as a "half-breed" until 1950.[44] In 1952, however, the *Lone Ranger Standards and Background* packet began acknowledging, for the first time in twenty years, that Tonto was more than just the Lone Ranger's companion; he was also his friend.[45]

Significantly, Tonto's representation in the postwar period was a marked departure from what it had been in the 1930s, where his sidekick status often left him clueless as to the Lone Ranger's plans even as he blindly carried out the Masked Man's instructions. Even the character's origin story shifted from the prewar to postwar periods. On December 7, 1938, the radio series told the story of the Lone Ranger and Tonto's first encounter. In it, the Lone Ranger rescues Tonto from an explosion in a gold mine and clears Tonto's name when he is falsely implicated in setting off the dynamite.[46] Though never overtly stated, the story implies that Tonto chose to follow the Lone Ranger out of gratitude. In the late 1940s, the story of Tonto and the Lone Ranger's initial meeting would change dramatically. On the very first episode of the television series, Tonto is introduced saving the life of a Texas Ranger ambushed by the Butch Cavendish gang. The unidentified survivor dawns a mask and becomes the Lone Ranger.[47] Though Butch Cavendish had been introduced on radio as the Lone Ranger's arch nemesis in 1941, Tonto's involvement in the tale would emerge only several years afterward. In placing the Lone Ranger in Tonto's debt, the new origin story tacitly acknowledged the historical roles played by minorities in facilitating Anglo survival and success in America (even as it ignored the harsh cruelties and lasting implications of real institutions like slavery). Tonto was also shown to be somewhat more independent in the postwar era. This was perhaps most apparent in Tonto's solo comic book series published by Dell starting in 1951 and lasting thirty-one issues, which expanded upon the character's ongoing relationships with various Native American tribes, suggesting that he was often off performing solo acts of heroism when not at the Masked Man's side. Occasionally dealing quite overtly with issues of prejudice—though just as likely to present Native Americans as reactionary and violent—the comic book spinoff seems designed to appeal simultaneously to minority readers and white, middle-class boys through its depiction of a nonwhite hero encountering "exotic" (i.e., Native American) cultures.

Recognition of minority consumers, however, did not necessarily yield greater understanding of minority struggles. Tellingly, in its list of "Lone Ranger Don'ts," LRI acknowledged the impact that minority protests had on the Lone Ranger's representational strategies, while failing to connect minority consumer demands with their efforts to gain recognition of their rights as American citizens. Rule #8 stated: "Because of minority groups who have complained, there should be no unfavorable characters who are unmistakably Negro, Mexican, English, Italian, Polish, etc. In short, all bad characters must be American."[48] Not only was LRI's solution to avoid controversy at all costs by literally whitewashing the Lone Ranger's adventures, but it also categorically erased people of color from American history in the process, conflating Americans with whites and minorities with foreigners, who were perhaps deserving of tolerance as valuable (or dangerous) consumers but not as citizens. LRI was not alone in adopting the tactic of erasing nonwhites from the American representational spectrum in order to avoid possible controversy. The 1955 Comic Book Code also forbade depicting minority groups as villains.[49]

In advocating tolerance as economically prudent, LRI made sure its Lone Ranger formula dissuaded any actions that might upset the status quo. While the Lone Ranger's greatness is established by means of his willingness to accept Tonto as a friend, Tonto's greatest qualities lay in his deference to the Masked Man and his willingness to put his stereotypically racialized attributes to work in defense of the American Heritage, rather than to upend it. As the description of Tonto's habits included in Appendix B of the 1952 television production contract stipulated, "When the Lone Ranger removes his mask for any purpose, [Tonto] makes a point of looking the other way." Moreover, when killing was absolutely necessary to the plot, this was Tonto's job, "and then somewhat secretly and without the Lone Ranger's permission."[50] The Consumers' Republic might have promised opportunity for all, but this was premised on whites tolerating the economically useful (but otherwise dubious) racialized "qualities" minorities possessed. Minorities, in turn, were expected to show deference to an American Heritage that they were apparently not fully a part of.

Meanwhile, Tonto's usefulness—derived entirely from stereotypes of Native American savagery and loyalty—allowed the Lone Ranger to remain morally righteous, even as he violently engaged unscrupulous criminals. In this manner, the Lone Ranger formula could flirt with undermining the strict code of conduct and respect for law and order that containment culture demanded without ever having these transgressions smudge the Masked Man's reputation. Tonto's willingness to break the rules so that the Lone Ranger did not have to both affirmed the sanctity of white, middle-class values and explained minority failures to attain them. At the same time, Tonto's occasional failure to repress his base savagery offered a respite from the stifling conformity demanded of white Americans, who, like the Lone Ranger, could reap the vicarious exotic rewards of associating with minorities without having to acknowledge that whites' success was partly predicated on forcing marginalized groups to do the "dirty work." While the postwar Tonto was no less stereotypically depicted than his prewar variation, his second-class status now seemed to derive less from subservience or lack of value, but instead from his occasional inability to fall in line. Thus, LRI's formula deflected minority consumer demands while appeasing white, middle-class fantasies.

Fears of juvenile delinquency in the 1950s also had a direct impact on how popular character brand formulas were restructured to steer children back onto the proper course and embrace American values. Many critics pointed to comic books and other forms of popular culture as corrupting American youth, contributing to juvenile delinquency, and possibly leading to increased Communist sympathy, criminality, and even homosexuality.[51] On April 22, 1954, one day before the Army-McCarthy hearings commenced, the Senate Subcommittee to Investigate Juvenile Delinquency began its investigation of the entertainment industries. The subcommittee's most vocal member, Senator Estes Kefauver, argued, "Not even the Communist conspiracy could devise a more effective way to demoralize, disrupt, confuse and destroy our future citizens than apathy on the part of adult Americans to the scourge known as juvenile delinquency."[52]

Faced with the threat of regulation, the comic book industry created the Comics Magazine Association of America (CMAA), whose function was to enforce a code of standards that would reverse the negative public opinion that comic books had received. Within two years, eighteen publishers went out of business and nearly 350 titles were canceled, including all horror and crime comics.[53] Though the comic book industry's postwar business model seemed by design to stymie creative innovation, quite the opposite would prove to be true. Indeed, the postwar period was a tremendously innovative era for character brands. Efforts to limit controversy led many IP owners to focus inward on developing elaborate story worlds and mythologies that were largely detached from real-world events.

Whereas Superman had fought racketeers and spousal abuse in the late 1930s, his villains now became both more fantastical and uncomplicated in their quest for mayhem, and the Man of Steel's exploits largely went toward elaborating a "self-sustaining fantasy world" that eschewed social relevance entirely.[54] Moreover, eschewing the oneiric temporality that Umberto Eco claims governed early Superman adventures (i.e., that they took place in nonsequential order that allowed the character never to age),[55] DC Comics developed an elaborate mythology for the Man of Steel that vastly expanded his supporting cast, family ties, and rogues' gallery of villains and explained how numerous forms of colored Kryptonite affected his powers. Superman's teenage years were covered in *Adventure Comics*, which focused on his exploits as Superboy while growing up in Smallville, and the future history of the DC Universe was also explored through Superboy's adventures with the Legion of Superheroes. All these books existed as part of an expansive Superman continuity, with Superboy stories providing motivation for the Man of Steel's future rivalry with Lex Luthor and Superboy's teenage crush, Lana Lang, showing up in adult form in the pages of Superman comic books.[56]

In addition to filling in temporal gaps, comic book publishers actively pursued world-building initiatives, with the world of Krypton, the bottle city of Kandor, Smallville, and Metropolis all taking on important narrative functions, fleshing out social rituals, kinship bonds, and other textural elements that linked the Superman family of comics together. Expanding the temporal and spatial parameters of these heroes' fictional worlds enabled their creators to retreat from controversial topics without seeming to restrict—but, more accurately, without needing to reveal—the narrative boundaries erected around these popular icons.

Some IP owners also experimented with what Henry Jenkins calls the transmedia principle of "multiplicity," or the provision of "alternative versions of the characters or parallel universe versions of the stories—as an alternative set of rewards for our mastery over the source material."[57] In particular, DC Comics invested in telling "imaginary tales" primarily featuring Superman and Batman in stories officially marked as not part of continuity, but wholly reliant on reader knowledge of existing continuity for their twists. In such imaginary stories, readers could find out what would happen if Superman ever married Lois Lane and raised a family or if the Kent family had adopted Bruce Wayne after his parents' murder.[58]

Another trend pursued by comic book publishers seeking to expand readership and extend reader experiences was to spin off supporting cast members into their own comic books. For instance, the 1950s Lone Ranger comic books published by Dell greatly expanded the roles of the Masked Man's supporting cast by featuring Tonto and Silver in their own books, which told of their solo exploits.[59] Superman's pal Jimmy Olsen and gal Friday Lois Lane also each got their own titles during this period.[60] These titles were aimed at diversifying (as well as segregating) readership to include younger, racially stratified and female consumers. Both examples also correlate with Jenkins's definition of "subjectivity," in which stories "show us the experiences and perspectives of secondary characters."[61]

While LRI endorsed textual strategies that expanded the Lone Ranger's story world as a way of distancing the hero from any possible allegorical whiff of controversy—for example, the introduction of Butch Cavendish as the Masked Man's arch nemesis gave the Lone Ranger a backstory that motivated his pursuit of justice rather than a nonspecific need to right wrongs—it was LRI's rethinking of the Lone Ranger's role in protecting children that most clearly repositioned the postwar Masked Man as a deterrent against maladjusted youth. In LRI's postwar approach, children were no longer imagined as needing protection from threats of consumer exploitation, but instead from social illnesses that took away from their healthful desire to consume. LRI circulated press materials resulting in dozens of newspaper articles emphasizing the Lone Ranger's "miraculous" ability to cure young children of psychological afflictions and transform them back into "healthy" consumers. In one celebrated case, the Lone Ranger visited a hospital and convinced a child to eat solid foods for the first time in three years by furnishing him with a set of Lone Ranger dishes. LRI conflated the circulation of consumer goods with curing social ills—ills defined as having a negative impact on consumption itself. According to the story, the Lone Ranger had transformed the child from sickly to healthy, nonconsumer to consumer. LRI called it "psychosomatic medicine" (see Figure 5.3).[62]

Still, the very acknowledgment that American youth suffered from

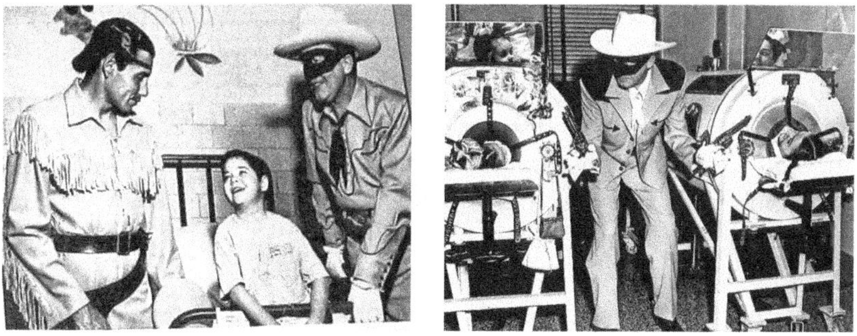

Figure 5.3. The Lone Ranger and Tonto made multiple appearances at local children's hospitals throughout the 1950s, claiming to offer "psychosomatic medicine" in the forms of branded merchandise.

psychological afflictions was a radical departure from the 1930s Safety Club rhetoric that encouraged youth to mobilize and prevent traffic accidents. While both instances suggest the need to protect children, the Safety Club depicted youth as self-reliant, active, and self-mobilizing, while the postwar Lone Ranger cured children suffering from "imaginary" illnesses that either prevented them from participating fully in the Consumers' Republic or caused them to deviate from the norms imposed upon them for their own protection.

Containment as Industrial Discourse

LRI embraced containment not only in its cultural rebranding of the Lone Ranger, but also to fortify its authority in the face of industrial changes that threatened to undermine its control over the property. John Caldwell suggests that media industry turf-marking is at its most pronounced at moments when occupational identities are in flux and power structures are threatened.[63] As such, LRI's insistence that all Lone Ranger licensees follow a codified set of rules in adapting the property and, moreover, that the property owner, not the consumer, was the ultimate arbiter of the Lone Ranger's meanings, must in part be read as an anxious expression of LRI's diminishing status. Nonetheless, LRI also redefined the very role that licensing agents performed in extending IP rights. Whereas LRI had positioned itself in the 1930s as facilitating localized Lone Ranger merchandising campaigns and coordinating communication between various licensees, in postwar America, LRI's primary function shifted to policing licensee interpretations in order to ensure a uniform depiction. Simply put, maintaining brand coherence replaced promoting brand elasticity and malleability as LRI's primary occupational function. In turn, this goal shaped the occupational disposition the licensor adopted as well as the managerial tactics it pursued.

Beginning in the early 1940s, LRI abandoned its market-by-market franchising efforts and embraced both national sponsorship by General Mills in 1941 and, shortly thereafter, national distribution on the NBC Blue radio network. LRI's decision to forgo its market-by-market, sponsor-by-sponsor expansion practices had a lot to do with its desire to streamline sales and reduce redundancies in its marketing practices. Or, as Dick Osgood explains in his history of station WXYZ, what LRI sought in sponsor General Mills was a way to "simplify the whole set-up by having a single sponsor in all major markets coast to coast."[64]

The first contract signed between LRI and General Mills on March 3, 1941, gave the sponsor full rights to merchandise the series in thirty-seven U.S. states.[65] The American Bakeries Company, makers of Merita Bread, sponsored the radio series in eight southeastern states and continued to do so through the mid-1950s. In May 1947, General Mills signed a seven-year extension agreeing to pay LRI $6,607.11 per week ($343,569.72 per year) in exchange for three thirty-minute episodes and commercial exploitation rights to the radio version of the character.[66]

Though LRI was required to supply advance synopses of every *Lone Ranger* episode to General Mills' advertising agency, Blackett, Sample & Hummert (BSH), for approval, the series' formulaic plotting rarely met with objections, and Trendle's direct oversight of the radio production allowed LRI to continue to control the property. This situation would change when television emerged as the primary medium for sponsored productions in the early 1950s.

After the war, radio audiences radically declined, dropping from 4.4 hours of listening per day in 1948 to 2.2 hours in 1956.[67] This decline correlated with the increased investment by networks in television during these years. These transition years saw many of radio's most popular programs coexist in various capacities on both radio and television, while their sponsors and advertising agencies made similar leaps. Many early television series were adapted directly from network radio, often by simulcasting the same series over both media. Simulcasting ranged across genres, from comedy-variety (*Jack Benny*) to sitcoms (*The Goldbergs*) to action-adventure series (*Dick Tracy*).[68] *The Lone Ranger* was never simulcast, but the radio and television series did coexist. This doubling strategy sustained early network and sponsor investments in television by lessening the risks involved in diverting commercial resources to an untested, and by no means omnipresent, medium. Eventually, the popularity of the audiovisual content led to the elimination of fictional radio programming entirely, as it was replaced by musical formats and disk jockeys by the mid-1950s.

The Lone Ranger television series debuted on September 15, 1949. Though not the first Western to appear on TV, it was among the first radio programs to be adapted for television and the first Western to offer original content shot exclusively for network television. William Boyd Productions' *Hopalong Cassidy* debuted several months before *The Lone Ranger*, but unlike the Masked Man, Hoppy was syndicated to independent and local TV stations.[69] The TV series consisted of edited-together segments of Hopalong Cassidy films. In many ways, Boyd's marketing strategies in the 1950s emulated LRI's from the 1930s as *Hopalong Cassidy* was sold market-by-market to local and regional sponsors, with the TV series generating merchandising frenzies.

The Lone Ranger ran for eight seasons and 180 episodes, until September 12, 1957. At first, General Mills agreed to pay $10,000 per episode toward the production costs and an additional $2,000 per week to LRI.[70] By 1952, the production budget had risen to $16,800 per episode.[71] Throughout most of its run, the series was scheduled on ABC from 7:30 to 8:00 p.m. on Thursday evenings, often programmed against the nightly news on both CBS and NBC.[72] By 1953, the series was broadcast on ninety stations coast to coast.[73] *The Lone Ranger* was the biggest hit ABC TV had in its early years, averaging five million viewers per week. It was the only ABC show to make it into the top fifteen in 1950–1951, the year Nielsen started calculating national television ratings. *The Lone Ranger* finished seventh overall with a 41.2 rating.[74] The six programs ahead of it were live comedy-variety programs (*Texaco Star Theatre*; *Your Show of Shows*; *The Colgate Comedy Hour*), live anthology dramas (*Fireside Theatre*; *Philco TV Playhouse*), and a live sporting events series (*Gillette Cavalcade of Sports*), making the Lone Ranger the top-rated telefilm series on TV.[75] While its ratings would decline every year after that (it finished eighteenth in 1951–1952 and twenty-eighth in 1952–1953), *The Lone Ranger* remained the only ABC series to crack Nielsen's top thirty shows.[76] It also was the highest nationally rated Western TV series during those initial years, outperforming both *Hopalong Cassidy*, which came in ninth in 1950–1951 and twenty-eighth in 1951–1952, and *The Roy Rogers Show*, which debuted at number twenty-seven in 1951–1952.[77]

While the television series was popular, the commercial sustainability of the medium was still unclear. Given television's limited reach during the 1948–1952 freeze years, when the FCC placed a temporary moratorium on issuing television broadcast licenses, and many communities remained without access to the major network channels (or any at all), advertisers still preferred radio's larger national reach.[78] In particular, ABC had only nineteen affiliate stations (including five owned and operated stations) across the United States, well behind NBC's sixty-three and CBS's thirty.[79] Thus, neither licensor nor sponsor was overly confident about the new medium's potential. While the television contract LRI signed with General Mills was exclusive of its radio deal, it stipulated that neither party could cancel *The Lone Ranger* radio program for the first two years of the television contract. If General Mills entered into an arrangement for a third year of telecasts, the radio program would also become noncancelable for that third year.[80] But whereas General Mills sought to protect its investment in the radio series, LRI was far more concerned with ensuring the continued popularity of the Lone Ranger brand.

Trendle had originally wanted Brace Beemer, the radio voice of the character, as well as the performer appearing as the Lone Ranger at the majority of the property's licensed public appearances, to be the television hero as well, in order to maintain continuity across production lines. Trendle confessed to his Hollywood liaison Freddie Fralick, "Everybody I meet seems to think we are making a mistake by putting it in television, on the theory that people will be disappointed and the Lone Ranger will not look like what they thought he did, when they think of him as a radio character, so it becomes increasingly important that we have the right cast."[81] General Mills rejected casting Beemer, however, because it considered the radio series to be "the backbone of [its] radio operation . . . and we don't relish anything being done which could harm it in the slightest. We realize full well that the Lone Ranger radio show is a paying proposition for General Mills, whereas the television show is pretty much an experimental operation and we don't think it is good business to jeopardize a solid operation such as the radio show for an adventure into television. We feel that putting a substitute in the radio show may hurt that operation."[82]

While commercial television in its early days made both General Mills and LRI nervous, the licensor's concerns were exacerbated by its loss of direct control over the production of the Masked Man's representation. Though they existed as separate entities, LRI, KTBC, and WXYZ all operated out of the same Detroit office, allowing the property owner to oversee daily production and broadcast of the Lone Ranger product. The relatively small scale of the radio production placed ultimate control over the radio product in Trendle's hands, even after General Mills took over as national sponsor.[83] As Hollywood became the production hub for telefilm, however, LRI found itself geographically removed and reliant on proxies to oversee how the Lone Ranger was adapted. The decline of fictional radio programming further distanced LRI from exercising direct control over the Lone Ranger production, eventually eliminating the radio series. LRI's concerns were further exacerbated by General Mills' choice of Jack Chertok to produce the television series. Chertok had a previous relationship with General Mills, having filmed its 1946 annual report, *Operation '46*. LRI worried that General Mills had Chertok's ear and that BSH would encroach on the production process and attempt to reshape the Masked Man to suit its sponsor's specific needs. Thus, in a letter to Fralick informing him of a BSH upcoming visit to *The Lone Ranger* television set, Trendle warned his West Coast representative to be prudent and selective in offering up information on the production: "My main objection in talking too much to those fellows, is that I am of the opinion they might try to take over and tell us what to do."[84]

Trendle's concerns were not necessarily misplaced. The licensor fumed over an early draft of a 1952 puff piece prepared by BSH announcing new episodes of the TV show, which attributed too much of the series' success to its sponsor, General Mills. Trendle quickly took red pen to paper and excised the following paragraphs entirely from the press release:

> When we of the Lone Ranger Corporation, learned that General Mills had decided to send their masked, two-gun super-salesman riding Silver on the television airwaves, we knew that new trails would have to be blazed across the field of entertainment. . . .
>
> We share with General Mills a feeling of pride in what has been accomplished. From the start, the Lone Ranger on television has been one of the world's most popular features. General Mills has never been an organization to rest on past laurels. We of the Lone Ranger, are trying to emulate the example of the Mills. A new series of Lone Ranger films is now in production. In these, we are incorporating what we have learned from experience and further research.[85]

The revised document glorified LRI's oversight of the production and its concern for presenting the most "realistic" and technologically advanced series possible. Citing its obligation to loyal *Lone Ranger* radio listeners not to disappoint in the visual interpretation of the mental pictures they had formed from the radio show, LRI described its intense efforts to bring "the real thing" to the screen.[86]

LRI's concerns over losing control of the Lone Ranger property were also in part influenced by the licensor's prior dealings with Hollywood. LRI had ended up contractually ceding creative authority to Republic during negotiations over the two film serials it produced in 1938 and 1939 and felt burned by the outcomes. For both serials, LRI had granted Republic the right to use its "dramatic [radio] serial and the episodes thereof, including without any limitation thereto, each of the characters . . . language, plot, theme, action, titles, and/or dialogue, continuity, scenario," but had neither required that these elements be used, nor prevented Republic from making changes to the Lone Ranger's established formula. In fact, quite the opposite, LRI permitted Republic to "change, transpose . . . to interpolate in, add to, or subtract from the work" as it saw fit. So long as Republic agreed to "reasonably conform to the type of story and its characterization" of LRI's radio serial, the contract it signed also granted the film studio final right of approval over the script.[87] Fran Striker was sent to Hollywood to consult on the first serial, but had no direct creative input.

To Trendle's great dismay, the first film serial had engaged the audience in a guessing game as to the Lone Ranger's secret identity, unmasking him as actor Lee Powell in the final installment. The second serial had the Lone Ranger unmask himself to the audience at the end of the first episode, though his identity was kept secret to the other characters in the film. Of course, on radio, the Lone Ranger habitually removed his mask to don a disguise, but listeners were never privy to a description of his unmasked face. Though LRI tried to block both unmasking instances, it was contractually bound to let Republic's versions stand.

In seeking to prevent these types of formula deviations from recurring in the postwar era, LRI embraced a managerial tack that valorized brand coherence as essential to the Lone Ranger's continued cross-media success. LRI emphasized the importance of maintaining continuity across Lone Ranger franchise outposts. Arguing that Lone Ranger fans were paying attention to both the radio and television series, Trendle explained to Chertok in a letter critiquing an early episode of the television series, "I think the directors are forgetting all about the fact that there must be some comparison made between the television Ranger and the AM [radio] Ranger and we cannot afford to ignore it."[88]

Perhaps no issue concerned Trendle more than having the television

Lone Ranger live up to the imaginations of radio listeners. Once Brace Beemer was no longer an option for starring in the series, Trendle turned his attention to monitoring how closely Clayton Moore sounded like his radio counterpart: "I am definitely worried about our Lone Ranger. I am willing to go along with you on the thought the fellow is good looking, he wears a mask and he does his work well, but . . . the matter of voice is the most important of all. I would like to have you work with Mr. Moore so that he gets that easy, slow-moving, slightly nasal, languid type of voice that Mr. Beemer uses . . . unless this fellow does the same thing, he will not be the Lone Ranger."[89] Trendle repeatedly offered to send Chertok voice recordings of Beemer in order to help Moore to mimic his voice. Trendle's concern was that audiences would recognize the differences, which would alert them to the fictional construction of the mythical hero. He wrote Chertok, "His voice is beginning to pick up a little too much speed, while Mr. Beemer's is fairly slow. I want to hit a happy medium but not have the voices so far apart that it creates comment. I think you know what I mean."[90]

Trendle's concerns over the two Lone Rangers sounding alike certainly betrayed his radio roots, wherein linguistic markers were essential to an audience's ability to distinguish between characters.[91] But his insistence on vocal verisimilitude across media platforms is not altogether dissimilar from contemporary casting decisions for live-action versions of cartoon and comic book characters like Superman or Professor X of the X-Men, where looking the part plays an important function in appeasing the existing fan base's expectations.[92] Though LRI had promoted the existence of a cross-media Lone Ranger brand community since the late 1930s, the licensor now proclaimed itself guardian of that community's expectations. Empowered by its argument that Lone Ranger fans would become confused and disgruntled if the formula were not consistently applied across licensed productions, LRI sought to enforce coherence and contain deviations through both contractual and managerial tactics.

LRI repeatedly argued that Chertok's scripts and stories should follow the basic plot structure of the radio program. LRI raised objections to the insertion of romantic plots into the TV episodes; to the Lone Ranger's use of improper English (but also Tonto's occasional use of too proper English); to depictions of murder, kidnapping, or drinking; and to plots that featured the Lone Ranger in disguise or in improbable situations that should logically (but because of plot contrivance did not) lead to his unmasking. LRI insisted all these elements were contrary to the successful formula strictly adhered to on the radio.[93] Trendle complained to Chertok, "We have sent 300 plots to California and we cannot understand why out of these 300 there cannot be 52 adapted to visual production by the insertion of visual business and visual gimmicks without complete distortion."[94] In his zeal for continuity, Trendle had Striker review scripts so that they would "aline [*sic*] . . . as closely as possible to the radio stories" and compare plot points with both the radio scripts and Lone Ranger novels he had written.[95]

As is evident by the tone of many of Trendle's letters, the licensor's objections regularly were met with incredulity, and his authority was habitually challenged. Chertok often treated Trendle's notes as little more than an inconvenient intrusion on the production process, rather than as valued contributions to maintaining the Lone Ranger's mythos. Responding to yet another series of script change demands, this time objecting to a scene in which the Lone Ranger is cornered and forced to drop his guns, Chertok quipped, "You must realize that if you continue to eliminate the few methods we now have of creating jeopardy for the Lone Ranger he will soon be in no jeopardy at all."[96]

Despite Chertok's bristling, LRI did hold a significant trump card. In exchange for agreeing to let Chertok's Apex Film produce *The Lone Ranger* television series, LRI had insisted on being put in charge of money transfers from General Mills to Apex. Additionally, the 1949 television contract had stipulated that LRI was to have all final approvals over script, casting, and other production decisions, while General Mills would have "no voice in the production of the 'programs.'"[97] Thus, LRI gained some leverage over the production by overseeing its budget and occasionally threatening to withhold payment installations until Apex made the script changes it demanded. Chertok's earnings came from the overhead he collected on each $10,000 episode he produced, with the added possibility of earning extra income by bringing episodes in under budget. Trendle regularly insisted upon changes and reshoots that ate into Chertok's profits.[98]

Chertok's resistance to Trendle does, however, point to challenges that corporate authors sometimes face in managing investment in their IP as well as in selling stakeholders on their self-designated roles as brand stewards. The authority that corporate authors claim is contingent upon their professed ability to translate a property's value across product lines and shifting production conventions. The transition from radio to television called attention to Trendle's unfamiliarity with the medium, which in turn undermined his ability to speak convincingly on behalf of the property and its existing brand community and opened the door for creative pushback. LRI's rhetorical posturing during the postwar period, however, was also far more dictatorial and rule-oriented than the collaborative and advisory roles it had previously assumed, suggesting that to some degree, the adversarial back-and-forth between Trendle and Chertok was more indicative of a shift in managerial style inspired by notions of containment than a significant change to the real authority LRI exercised.

Embracing containment as a managerial ethos that guaranteed the property's continued vitality, LRI proudly promoted its efforts to prevent any negative publicity from sullying the property: "The Lone Ranger could be a vital factor in the teaching of Americanism. It was something that must be preserved, protected against cheap imitation and carefully guarded at all times. Moreover, there must never be the slightest degree of unfavorable publicity about the program or any individual connected with it that might disillusion the millions of boys and girls who idolized the masked hero."[99]

All of LRI's efforts to contain postwar challenges to its managerial authority, as well as its efforts to align the Lone Ranger property with discourses of domestic containment, coalesced in the 1948 Frontier Town campaign. Timed to coincide with the fifteenth anniversary of the Lone Ranger's radio debut, the elaborate yearlong promotion would prove to be one of the most successful in Lone Ranger history and would serve as a historical antecedent to contemporary story worlds that fans can explore and creatively inhabit.

Frontier Town

At its most basic, the Frontier Town promotion involved collecting four separate map quadrants along with seventy-one different cardboard set pieces made available on the backs of nine different Cheerios boxes. When combined and assembled, they displayed a three-dimensional replica of the Western setting where the majority of *The Lone Ranger*'s radio adventures took place in 1948. Frontier Town allowed listeners to explore the boundaries and contours of the Masked Man's narrative geography, adding a spatial dimension that enriched knowledge about the Lone Ranger's exploits. Now, when the sheriff summoned the Masked Man to the jail to alert him that there was trouble at the general store, listeners could literally map the distance between these locations and assess whether or not their hero could arrive in time to save the day. Instructions emphasized the need for children to first *build* the replica so they could "trace practically every step . . . almost 'be right there with [the Lone Ranger and

Figure 5.4. Ad for Frontier Town, ca. 1948. Author's collection.

Tonto]' on their dangerous and exciting adventures," promoting a sense of investment in the story through their participation in assembling the very town the Masked Man had sworn to protect (see Figure 5.4).

A precursor to contemporary media franchise world-building initiatives like HBO's interactive online maps and genealogies for *Game of Thrones* (2010–), in which a complex sociopolitical geography serves as a vital storytelling resource for fans to explore, Frontier Town made the Lone Ranger's world habitable, encouraging children either to ride along with the Masked Man on his adventures or to set up their own homestead. In this way, they could create their own Lone Ranger stories set within a story world they could now readily reach out and touch. Unlike any other promotion at the time, Frontier Town seemingly offered consumers what Jason Mittell calls "drillability," or "the ability to dig deeper into a story to understand its complexity,"[100] as well as what Jenkins labels "world-building" opportunities to map and master as much as they can about a fictional universe.[101] While the backs of each map quadrant offered play scenarios for children to act out, these games provided only a broad premise, leaving the rest to be filled in by player imaginations. For example, "The Race for Life" instructs that the game begins at Rimrock Bridge and ends at the Old Spanish Fort, and gives as its premise, "While camping near Rimrock Bridge, the Lone Ranger overhears a band of bad men plotting to ride to the Old Spanish Fort to give the commanding officer there false information about an attack by Comanche Indians." Should the Masked Man find a shortcut to the fort? Set up an ambush? Warn the Comanche tribe? Opt for a beer at the saloon instead? These options are left up to the players to determine. The game prompt merely provides an excuse to investigate the narrative possibilities through creative use of the map.

Frontier Town functioned as a very different type of extra-textual promotion than the 1930s LRSC or *How the Lone Ranger Captured Silver* giveaway. Though all three offered the Lone Ranger enthusiast opportunities for additive comprehension, the latter two were designed to generate localized cross-promotional brand synergies and highlight the communities where retailers and sponsors did business. In contrast, Frontier Town is an immersive paratext that draws consumers back into the Lone Ranger text, enhancing the ways listeners engage with the radio narrative and encouraging play that explores the Masked Man's fictional geography.

Frontier Town also necessitated significant changes to both *The Lone Ranger* radio series and merchandising formulas. Prior to General Mills becoming the radio series' national sponsor and moving the series to ABC, almost all of *The Lone Ranger* radio adventures throughout the 1930s had been episodic. LRI's preference for episodic stories was largely dictated by its need to take on new listeners with minimal confusion. Moreover, *The Lone Ranger*'s episodic structure allowed LRI to differentiate its product from other children's programs, which were constantly coming under fire for their cliff-hanger endings. A lack of serialization was integral to LRI's marketing the Lone Ranger as wholesome commercial fare.

In the postwar era, with both national sponsorship and distribution in place, *Lone Ranger* radio adventures became increasingly serialized, allowing General Mills to engage in longer marketing campaigns and LRI to tell sweeping stories that more effectively captured the character's newfound mission of defending the American Heritage. For example, in 1947, the Lone Ranger was tasked with tracking down a spy brandishing a stolen ring in the shape of a silver bullet, which contained a miniature atomic bomb. Once the Lone Ranger recovered the powerful device, he turned it over to American scientists to continue safely harvesting its energy.[102] The story both extolled the ingenuity of American industrialists seeking to exploit atomic power and deflected concerns over the bomb falling into enemy hands. The six-episode story arc coincided with one of the most heavily marketed Lone Ranger giveaway campaigns of its day, wherein listeners could acquire a replica of the ring in exchange for a Kix cereal box cover. Nearly six million such rings were eventually distributed.

These sustained story lines facilitated lengthier giveaway campaigns, which likely helped justify the costs of bulk premium production by giving them a (relatively) longer shelf life. While the atomic bullet ring serves as a perfect example of the types of extractable narrative elements that children's radio offered listeners, postwar immersive storytelling practices best exemplify the intersections of cultural and industrial containment discourses designed to manage changing production and consumption contexts. Chris Anderson refers to *Disneyland* as an "inhabitable text" that drew 1950s TV viewers into a branded world and encouraged exploration as essential to moving the Disney experience from the movie screen into the theme park.[103] Frontier Town also tied the Lone Ranger to a fairly finite space for nearly a year, while the various maps and models needed to construct the setting took several months to acquire, since General Mills timed the release of different components to coincide with specific narrative cues and a drawn-out advertising campaign. This encouraged a very different type of temporal and tactile investment in the Lone Ranger narrative than the LRSC's emphasis on living a Lone Ranger–inspired healthy and safe lifestyle.

General Mills now sought to tie its marketing campaign directly to the Lone Ranger's exciting work of building up the West. Whereas earlier Lone Ranger radio promotions had often served to deflect criticism over commercialism and to demonstrate a sponsor's civic-mindedness, postwar era tie-ins like Frontier Town allowed General Mills to associate itself directly with the corporate-capitalist American Heritage that the Lone Ranger fought to preserve. Tellingly, many of the Frontier Town stories revolved around the Lone Ranger helping companies like Wells Fargo and Union Pacific safely set up shop and connect the town to the rest of the nation. These same businesses were also prominently featured on the map. Thus, Frontier Town told the story of the American Heritage through the roles played by free enterprise in building it, letting consumers carry on that tradition by purchasing products that allowed them to literally build a replica of the Frontier Town that American corporations—with the help of the Lone Ranger—had helped make great.

Significantly, the Frontier Town campaign necessitated changes to the cereal box itself. Instead of exchanging proofs of purchase for premiums, Frontier Town transformed the Cheerios package into a premium, directly correlating the product with the "healthy" pursuit of popular entertainment. It was no longer necessary to bribe children into eating healthily in exchange for toys, as had been the mantra of breakfast food companies in the early twentieth century, nor was it still necessary for children to convince their parents to buy certain brands by pointing to the civic virtues taught through giveaway items. Rather, Frontier Town and other cardboard-container giveaways integrated the Cheerios brand into lived experiences of its clientele well beyond its vitamin-enriched appeal.

The Frontier Town campaign also benefited LRI and General Mills in that they productively—if also only temporarily—alleviated both licensor and sponsor anxieties over uncertainties about the untested promise of television. As previously noted, television's limited reach during the late 1940s and early 1950s, coupled with its relative expense compared to radio production, initially offset much of the potential that sponsors and ad agencies saw in it. In 1948, General Mills paid $10,000 per episode for the first season of *Lone Ranger* television, which ran on ABC TV's eighteen affiliate stations as well as on a host of independent channels in nonaffiliated markets, as compared with $6,607 per week for three 30-minute radio episodes heard over 221 stations.[104] While $10,000 per filmed episode was cheap compared to the production costs for live television (the average cost per episode of the *Milton Berle Show* was $25,000),[105] *The Lone Ranger*'s TV budget was considered high by both Trendle and General Mills when compared to the adaptation of other radio properties like *The Goldbergs*, which operated on a budget of $3,500 per episode.[106] Beyond high costs and limited distribution, early television production quality was also considered substandard, contributing to Trendle's assessment that viewers would inevitably be disappointed because the Masked Man's TV adventures would be on a far smaller scale than those told on the radio program. After all, the radio series' award-winning sound and Foley engineering allowed it to simulate grand cavalry attacks and sweeping chase sequences across vast swaths of terrain. Nevertheless, the emergence of independent and network-owned-and-operated TV stations in major U.S. markets throughout the 1940s was seen by both licensor and sponsor as a potential threat to *The Lone Ranger*'s existing listenership as well as an opportunity to expand the property's consumer base.[107]

Both companies regarded television as an experiment, and as such, both also sought to mitigate risk by simultaneously fortifying their investment in *The Lone Ranger* radio series. It is not coincidental that the Frontier Town campaign was initiated at the same time as LRI and General Mills were in preproduction for the television series. Frontier Town offered a visual alternative to TV that could hopefully offset listener defection in markets where television was already available. It also served as a means of preparing listeners for the eventual arrival of *The Lone Ranger* television series in their market. Though the map allowed children to "see" the terrain upon which the Lone Ranger's adventures took place, it also limited their imaginations as to the scope of the territory the Masked Man covered: the town and its immediate surroundings. In this manner, it presaged the limited topography that the television Lone Ranger would traverse. Due to its limited budget, most of the action on the television series would take place within the vicinity of nameless frontier towns that were easily assembled on studio back lots.

At the same time, Frontier Town served LRI's interests by refocusing attention on *The Lone Ranger* radio text. General Mills' investment in the property had proven both profitable and precarious for the licensor, generating concerns over the amount of creative control the sponsor could exercise over the property as well as the degree of consumer identification of the Lone Ranger as a General Mills employee. Since LRI still produced the radio series and excised a fair amount of control over its content, Frontier Town provided an opportunity for it to establish the radio narrative as central to General Mills' promotional endeavors for the property.

LRI also utilized the fanfare and publicity surrounding the Frontier Town campaign to extend other facets of its Lone Ranger licensing business. The yearlong Frontier Town promotion culminated with the celebration of the Lone Ranger's fifteenth anniversary, which took place on June 30, 1948, in Cheyenne, Wyoming. On that date, Cheyenne officially changed its name to the Lone Ranger Frontier Town and elected the Masked Man mayor for the day, yet another example of how the Lone Ranger formula was reconfigured to emphasize the character's status as a paragon of the existing social order.[108] The choice of Cheyenne as the modern-day incarnation of Frontier Town allowed LRI and General Mills to masterfully link the Lone Ranger's historical fiction to a contemporary "reality" far removed from the property's decidedly urban origins in Detroit. Cheyenne's relatively small population and remoteness made it a modern city that resembled the highly touted frontier.

The anniversary celebration was timed to coincide with Cheyenne's annual Frontier Days festivities, which included the largest outdoor rodeo show in the United States. While General Mills and ABC profited from *The Lone Ranger* radio series, LRI earned considerable money from Lone Ranger public appearances. For example, a two-day appearance at the Miami Orange Bowl in 1951 netted the licensor $4,500, for which all they supplied was actor Brace Beemer in costume. The venue was responsible for finding Beemer a horse, hiring the supporting cast, and covering the actor's expenses.[109] The Masked Man appeared with dozens of circuses and rodeos throughout the 1950s, and with each licensed pit stop, LRI would also rally local retailers and media outlets to participate in orchestrating merchandising frenzies. Thus, the Frontier Town campaign offered LRI an outlet for reconnecting the Lone Ranger brand with the local markets it had shelved in embracing national sponsorship and distribution, even as it allowed General Mills and ABC to write themselves into an American national heritage simultaneously founded on economic expansion and the preservation of small-town values.

By the late 1940s, the Lone Ranger was already a national icon, and its various licensees imagined themselves as serving a national market (or, perhaps more accurately, they imagined the market for their goods as national). Yet the Frontier Town promotion was able to transform a national consumer base into local inhabitants of this fictional locale, which in turn was presented as a microcosm for the formation of contemporary American social values. Ironically, as American national identity became increasingly represented in the postwar years through images of small-town Americana (as evidenced in the works of Norman Rockwell and TV series like *The Andy Griffith Show*), depictions of the diversity of local experiences actually receded, replaced by an idealized homogenous vision of small-town life. It is with this maneuver that Frontier Town's immersive function aligned most closely with domestic containment discourses that sought to safeguard the Consumers' Republic by confining it within gated communities.

With record numbers of white, middle-class Americans escaping the "dangers" of living in cramped and overcrowded urban areas in the decade immediately following the end of World War II by moving to fenced-in yet spacious suburban enclaves,[110] it is perhaps not that shocking that Frontier Town also relocated listeners to a remote territory guarded by a champion sworn to protect the American Heritage. After all, as Sean Griffin has noted, the move to suburbia was often promoted through imagery and rhetoric associating it with a return to the wide-open expanses of the western frontier (but with all the conveniences of modern living).[111] Meanwhile, though the Frontier Town map did include Native American encampments surrounding the town, and the radio stories depicted the relationship between Native American tribes and Frontier Town inhabitants as cordial, profitable, and even symbiotic (tensions were the result of misunderstandings brought about by villainous opportunists, not social inequalities), the map also helped to accentuate the segregation of spaces between these two communities, with only the Lone Ranger capable of successfully walking in both worlds—and allowing suburban listeners to safely follow along.

In postwar America, tensions were brewing within suburban homes over parental desires to protect children against the dangers of the outside world without denying them opportunities for play and exploration. These "dangers" were variously identified as "urban" problems related to gangs and racial minorities, juvenile delinquency, sexual predators, or just kids' natural proclivity to get into trouble and hurt themselves. As Griffin succinctly puts it, "Adults' concern over children in this new space attempted to close off children's freedom even as they professed to endorse it."[112] Griffin points to the ways that television heroes like Davy Crockett were marketed to parents as offering their children vicarious, clean adventuring opportunities that could be acted out in the safety of their backyards through the purchase of a coonskin cap or other licensed merchandise.[113] Though I make no claims about how actual children (or adults) used the Frontier Town maps, their intended value was fairly transparent: to encourage fantasy play that transpired under the watchful eyes of concerned parents.

While LRI had always encouraged Lone Ranger play as a means of both promoting the property's popularity and articulating how licensees might exploit its merchandisable attributes, publicity had typically focused on how the radio program and other storytelling outlets inspired play scenarios that expanded into the real world. For instance, on October 15, 1939, LRI supplied the *Detroit Times* with a puff piece about children inventing Lone Ranger games during recess.[114] Frontier Town encouraged not only a much more textually engaged type of Lone Ranger play, but also the kind that displaced actual outdoor adventuring with simulation of the Masked Man's exploration of the frontier from the comfort of one's living room—a celebrated point emphasized in advertisements for the promotion.

Even without ad copy actively identifying the living room as the ideal play site for the game, the actual spaces children could interact with the Frontier Town map were likely limited by its fragile and unruly cardboard design that could easily be blown away outdoors, assuming children could even figure out how to transport a map that took up fifteen square feet of floor space (see Figure 5.5). Still, what children lost in physical mobility was supposedly made up for by the Lone Ranger's ability to activate temporal imaginations that converted suburban enclaves into the very frontier that Americans were now tasked with protecting. The level of detail offered by the Frontier Town map transformed a finite space into a robust playground-of-the-mind that could provide infinite opportunities for exploration.

Figure 5.5. When fully assembled, the Frontier Town map took up nearly fifteen square feet of floor space.

Conclusion

Throughout this chapter, I have argued that LRI's postwar embrace of containment as a managerial discourse was a tactical response to a changing business and cultural context that, while at times intransigent, was also productive in redefining the Lone Ranger's value as a cultural commodity. It also reestablished LRI's role in protecting that value. Indeed, the Lone Ranger was an incredibly successful merchandising phenomenon throughout the late 1940s and the 1950s, culminating in Trendle's selling the property rights, along with all of its existing licenses, to the Jack Wrather Corporation in 1954 for a then-record $3 million (that's $24.4 million in 2010 dollars according to the Consumer Price Index converter).[115]

Trendle's decision to sell the Lone Ranger at the height of its earning power was in part motivated by his increasing realization that the authority and autonomy he demanded were becoming increasingly untenable. As uncertainties about television dissipated, General Mills shifted its marketing resources away from radio. The last bastion of direct production oversight that Trendle maintained went off the air in 1955. Already at a geographic disadvantage by being headquartered in Detroit, Trendle might have seen the writing on the wall, choosing to go out on his own terms rather than sacrificing more of his authority and autonomy over the Lone Ranger property than he already had to Chertok, Apex, and General Mills.

By the end of the 1950s, many of the branding strategies and licensing practices LRI had helped shepherd were beginning to be handled in-house by the networks and film studios. ABC launched its own character-licensing division in 1957 to merchandise *Maverick* toys and clothing.[116] The emerging power players in the licensing field, companies like the Licensing Corporation of America, were for the most part subsidiaries working for corporate content owners, instead of independent entities working alongside them. In 1965, the Licensing Corporation of America became a subdivision of Warner Communications Inc.

Though LRI's rigid postwar managerial tactics were motivated by the sociohistorical context in which the company operated, its struggles to codify how a dispersed creative labor force should approach an established character brand and what ought to be the preferred relationship between franchise outposts and the properties they collectively promote, continue to resonate within the contemporary media environment. Managerial guidance remains paramount as IP increasingly serves as a content resource for conglomerates seeking convergent platform distribution opportunities. Jeff Gomez, cofounder of Starlight Runner Entertainment, describes the company's role as creating "mega-bibles and mythologies" designed to "teach the studio, other divisions of its parent company and its [licensees] how to bring these characters to life in a way that's true to the original platform."[117]

At the 2011 Transmedia Hollywood Symposium, I participated on a panel with Steven DeKnight (executive producer of *Spartacus*), Jeph Loeb (executive vice president/head of TV, Marvel Entertainment), Craig Relyea (SVP, Global Marketing, Disney Interactive), and Matt Wolf (founder of Double 2.0, ARG), who all rhapsodically endorsed the need for greater centralized control over how content is distributed across media platforms. While Wolf acknowledged that it is virtually impossible for one person to provide all aspects of creative development, he nonetheless argued that consumers would quickly recognize materials not subjected to creative oversight as inauthentic. Interestingly, without a central creative vision, panelists saw the transmedia franchise as at risk of being hijacked by both overinvested fans and competing divisions within and across media corporations. Loeb jokingly argued that too little supervision would result in even more undesirable Kirk/Spock slash/fiction, a statement that betrays not only anxiety over what audiences really want, but also the lingering cultural containment logics that characterize efforts to manage fan creativity. He also bemoaned the fate of the NBC series *Heroes*, which he claimed fell victim to too many executives trying to steer the franchise in different directions, resulting in its eventual capsizing.

DeKnight and Loeb both pointed to George Lucas's insistence on brand coherence across *Star Wars* franchise outposts as ideal.[118]

Contemporary managerial discourses continue to promote the importance of brand coherence in generating a consistency of experience among consumers. Derek Johnson argues, citing Janet Wasko and David Aaker, that "successful leveraging of a brand depends upon its cohesiveness as a carefully controlled set of texts" and points to Marvel's efforts to achieve character coherence across media platforms by revising Wolverine's comic book appearance to better conform with Hugh Jackman's depiction of the character on-screen in the X-Men franchise.[119] Marketing guru Aaker advocates for coherence among corporate, product, and subbrands as essential for maintaining a brand's core identity.[120] As such, it is important to recognize how LRI not only sought to achieve brand coherence between the Lone Ranger and its various licensed sub-brands, but also sought to link its corporate identity to the property it managed. LRI sought to embody the values it claimed made the Lone Ranger popular.

Yet the approach brand managers now take with creative personnel tends to be far less punitive than LRI's dealings with its various licensees. Instead, Aaker suggests that today's chief marketing officers need to redefine their current roles in order to come across as "facilitator, consultant, or service provider—not a central consolidator and decision maker (at least, in the absence of crisis)."[121] In some ways, this harkens back to LRI's approach to franchising the Lone Ranger in the late 1930s and, ironically, marks the property's postwar success and LRI's centralization efforts as driven by crisis, not consensus.

And yet, despite LRI's managerial appeals for maintaining the status quo, it is quite evident that the Lone Ranger formula underwent significant revision throughout the postwar period, both in terms of elaborating on the Masked Man's backstory and expanding his story world, and also in terms of marketing the property's ability to teach children to appreciate the American Heritage and link those sentiments to promoting and preserving the emerging Consumers' Republic. What this implies is that LRI's containment tactics were intended less to prevent changes to the Lone Ranger formula, which would have caused brand extension to stagnate, than to control how changes were integrated and by whom.

CHAPTER 6

Managing a Legend: The Troubled Career of the Lone Ranger as Heritage Brand

Introduction

The August 1973 cover of *Esquire* magazine (see Figure 6.1) features *Kung Fu*'s (1972–1975) David Carradine delivering a decisive martial arts–style kick to the behind of an unwitting Lone Ranger. The headline, worded in a caricaturized Asian manner, reads, "Ah, so! A new American hero at last!"[1]

At first glance, the implication seems clear: in an era dominated by internal unrest over the Vietnam War and Watergate, the Lone Ranger's popularity as a symbol for the American Heritage was on the decline, even if the Masked Man wasn't yet fully aware of his growing irrelevance. The notion that the Lone Ranger was somehow out of touch with the American cultural zeitgeist had actually been dogging the property since the mid-1960s, as evidenced by a 1965 *Berry's World* editorial cartoon (see Figure 6.2) depicting a middle-aged businessman admonishing a shaggy-haired teen for listening to a transistor radio in public with the exclamation, "If I were the Lone Ranger, I'd shoot that transistor right out of your hand!"[2]

The cartoon's layered humor addressed an older generation's befuddlement at changing youth culture attitudes, but also depicted a Lone Ranger whose straightlaced virtues did not speak to a new generation. This assessment would certainly seem to jibe with the steady decline in popularity of the Western genre as a whole and with the ensuing colossal failure of the motion picture *Legend of the Lone Ranger* (*LLR*) (1981), still considered one of the biggest box office busts of all time. Instead of declaring the Lone Ranger's eventual box office failure a proof-positive sign of the Masked Man's long declining popularity, however, I argue that the motion picture's failure was directly correlated with unsuccessful managerial attempts to reconfigure the property for a new generation of consumers while still maintaining its nostalgic appeal as a heritage brand.

Since the late 1990s, market research experts have begun to champion the emergence of heritage brands and retro branding strategies, which purposely call upon a brand's reputation and longevity in the marketplace to distinguish it from the unproven standing of its competitors. As Andy Nairn states, "In these uncertain times, reminding consumers of your heritage can be a powerful demonstration of your staying power and enduring reliability."[3] David Aaker suggests that in playing on contemporary social anxieties, heritage brands "elicit emotional responses from consumers based on . . . an idealized childhood that they would have liked to have had."[4]

Character brands like Mickey Mouse are often promoted as offering gateways for parents to reexperience their own childhoods—or the childhoods they imagined others had—alongside their kids. As Brooks Barnes reports, "Licensing experts say they perceive a subtle psychological game at play, an attempt to hit the nostalgia button on a generation of young parents just as they start to feel their first twinges of middle age."[5] Meanwhile, Allison Hugley, senior vice president and director of insight and research for the marketing consultancy firm MS&L, suggests that "all of

Figure 6.1. *Esquire* magazine cover, February 1973. Author's collection.

Figure 6.2. *Berry's World, Fort Worth Press*, July 29, 1965. Author's collection.

these entertainment properties we grew up with and have as a source of comfort are experiences we can now share with kids. That connection and shared experience is part of what's driving this trend."[6]

While supposedly empowering parents, the goal of children's heritage brands is ultimately to gain a foothold among younger consumers by transcending this nostalgic evocation and establishing the brands' contemporary relevance. For brand managers, heritage brands offer opportunities to reach a younger generation of consumers through their parents, transforming a brand's "life cycle" into a "life circle."[7] Heritage brands must evoke their past without seeming stuck in it. They must also reinvent themselves with each new generation of consumers without becoming unrecognizable to past brand loyalists—in other words, without altering their brand essence. Barnes suggests that the trick is to "keep the core attributes of the character the same, but update the world in which they live."[8] When successful, heritage brands can act as bridges between different generations of consumers, though each group appreciates the brand at a different level. When unsuccessful, heritage brands can come across as either out of touch with contemporary consumer desires or as rejecting past appreciation of the property.

Potential complications arise when existing brand-community nostalgia fails to align with retro branding initiatives. Heritage brands can become sites of struggle between brand loyalists and corporate owners, especially when the latter seek to rejuvenate the brand. This captures one of the central tensions surrounding heritage brands: brand loyalists are their strongest resource in maintaining market presence, but they are also the most resistant to any significant attempts to update the brand. This fan base is both valued and feared by IP owners for its loyalty. But when fans' nostalgic reverence cannot assist in bridging the generational gap or perhaps even proves an impediment to gaining new market access, industry lore dictates that brand managers must be willing to risk the backlash and pursue more lucrative markets: "If the heritage brand's strength continues to provide both current customers and future consumers with reason and desire for the product, its heritage continues to be a key asset of its overall brand equity. If, however, the heritage brand maintains its appeal only to its current (and past) consumers, its heritage has shifted from being a benefit to a liability."[9]

Despite these risks, heritage brands have long been regarded by the entertainment industry as stabilizers, especially at moments of cultural or industrial flux. Given that, I situate the deployment of heritage brands within the institutional and cultural contexts of 1960s and 1970s television and early 1980s motion pictures. During this period, many 1930s pulp, radio, and comic strip heroes, ranging from Little Orphan Annie and Superman to Flash Gordon and Popeye, made comebacks, with varying degrees of success. By the mid-1960s, the Lone Ranger's heritage status was the primary source of the brand's continued equity but also a potential liability that threatened to cut off access to a new generation of consumers that perceived the Masked Man as old-fashioned. Certainly, the *Berry's World* cartoon and the *Esquire* cover capture the central tension governing the management of the Lone Ranger property throughout the 1960s and 1970s: namely, how to renew interest in the Lone Ranger among an emerging youth culture without sacrificing the established—if also nostalgic—appeal that the property already possessed with an aging "silent generation" born between 1925 and 1942, who constituted the Masked Man's original fan base.

These tensions encapsulate the predicament that the Jack Wrather Corporation (JWC) faced with the Lone Ranger throughout the 1970s. Though his patriotism and enthusiasm for American virtue likely seemed out of place in a decade rocked by race riots, political scandal, and an unpopular war, the property's appeal rested precisely on its ability to evoke memories of simpler times. Now the managerial efforts of JWC were dedicated to retooling its property for a new generation of consumers. While some of JWC's ideas were ahead of their time, others clearly misread the emerging consumer advocacy power of fan communities. This final miscue was most evident with *LLR*. I end the chapter with a case study exploring how tensions over balancing innovation and nostalgia shaped the production and marketing for *LLR*. I argue that the Lone Ranger's decline in popularity had less to do with stagnation than with an imbalanced approach to rebooting the iconic brand.

The Ranger and the Wrather Corporation

When the Jack Wrather Corporation acquired the Lone Ranger in 1954, the purchase included 178 live-action television episodes, 3,500 radio episodes, film production rights, comic book and comic strip rights, and other publication, syndication, and merchandising rights.[10] Given that JWC bought the Masked Man at the height of his popularity and managed the property all the way through the release of the disastrous *Legend of the Lone Ranger* motion picture, it might seem obvious that JWC either failed to anticipate the Lone Ranger's declining appeal or was somehow directly responsible for damaging his reputation. While the latter notion perhaps has some validity, as I will demonstrate in this section, much of JWC's oversight of the property was perfectly in line with other heritage brand revival efforts of the day. In fact, several of the initiatives it undertook to either maintain or reactivate interest in the property were even ahead of their day, suggesting that the entertainment industries' dominant discourses about heritage brands played some part in circumscribing the tactics it pursued.

A petroleum distributor that had slowly transformed itself into an entertainment and leisure conglomerate beginning in 1946, JWC presaged the diversification efforts of companies like Gulf & Western and Kinney in the mid-to-late 1960s with their respective acquisitions of Paramount and Warner Bros. studios.[11] Company president Jack Wrather first created Jack Wrather Productions, Inc. as a subdivision of the Wrather Petroleum Corporation in order to finance film productions shot on location in his native Texas, including *High Tide* (1947) and *Strike it Rich* (1948). By 1950, Wrather had relocated to Hollywood, and in addition to producing the anti-Communist motion picture *Guilty of Treason* (1950), he began to buy up network affiliate TV stations in Oklahoma, California, New York, and Pennsylvania, those in the latter two states through a 1953 merger with the Transcontinent Television Corporation, of which Wrather was the principal stockholder.[12] In 1955, when Disney found itself strapped for cash because of delays in opening its theme park, JWC stepped in and built the $10 million Disneyland Hotel, the first of several high-end luxury hotels the company would build or purchase, each strategically located adjacent to popular entertainment and leisure sites.[13] JWC combined these holdings with beach resort clubs along the California coast, and also purchased a controlling interest in Stephens Bros., Inc., the premiere pleasure craft manufacturer in the United States, leading *Businessweek* to retroactively anoint JWC a "minor star in the fallen galaxy of leisure-time conglomerates."[14] JWC also owned Muzak, which distributed piped-in background music for elevators, waiting rooms, and other locales, and in 1973, merged that holding with Teleprompter, Inc., which supplied electronic transcriptions for the television and film industries.[15]

What separated JWC from other emerging conglomerates was the company's strategic enactment of a plan to generate synergies across its various investments. Aside from the resort club/leisure boat manufacturing pairing, this is most evident in its acquisition of several high-profile intellectual properties in the mid-1950s. In addition to the Lone Ranger, in 1957 JWC also bought the rights to Sergeant Preston of the Yukon from

Figure 6.3. The Jack Wrather Corporation was an early example of what are known today as leisure and media conglomerates.

Trendle for $1.5 million and the rights to Lassie from Robert Maxwell for $3.25 million.[16] Even as all three properties were still engaged in active television production, with new episodes appearing weekly on ABC TV, the acquisition of their back catalogs also allowed JWC to fill important time slots on the local affiliate stations it owned with syndicated reruns. In 1955, JWC also purchased the Corriganville Ranch, where most of the outdoor shooting for *The Lone Ranger* series took place.[17] JWC renamed Corriganville the Lone Ranger Ranch, booked Clayton Moore and Jay Silverheels, who portrayed Tonto on the TV series, to make personal appearances (usually organized around their shooting schedule), and promoted the site as a family-friendly tourist attraction. JWC also bought the A. C. Gilbert toy company in 1961, with the express purpose of manufacturing toys based on its television holdings[18] (see Figure 6.3).

In 1969, it opened up six Lone Ranger–themed restaurant franchises in the Los Angeles area, complete with branded menu items like the Pronto Tonto hotdog on a stick.[19] The restaurant franchises also provided a new outlet for generating premium/giveaway licenses, which had by then declined in popularity on television. Though their relationship would later turn antagonistic, JWC paid Clayton Moore to make personal appearances each weekend at a different franchise.[20] The toy venture quickly went awry when A. C. Gilbert's manufacturing plants proved too antiquated to meet production demands for a $6 million order placed by Sears Roebuck,[21] and the restaurants tanked within a year due to poor franchise marketing,[22] suggesting that JWC's ambition in extending its IP reach was not always backed with the necessary planning or infrastructure.

Despite these failed ventures, the company continued to experiment with new ways to extend the reach of its IP holdings. In the late 1970s, JWC defined itself as a "resource development organization" that used its "creative and financial resources to create and acquire new properties which can be developed" and where "the measure of success is the increase in the property's *value* (defined broadly) resulting from the development process"—a process requiring "commitment and creativity."[23] Though its development efforts were open to some degree of risk-taking, its selection process was not. JWC sought out properties that could "be measured by the yardstick of stability and past performance, of being firmly established in the public consciousness," but which also possessed "hidden or undeveloped potentials for further expansion, development and growth beyond the current state" and, significantly, could generate a "breadth and depth of audience appeal."[24] Hence, JWC's property-acquisition and development strategy was perfectly attuned to the labor of managing established heritage brands while tapping into new markets that expanded its consumer base.

And there can be little doubt that JWC's managerial efforts with the Lone Ranger were initially very successful. In 1956, the *Los Angeles Times* entertainment journalist Hal Humphrey reported that in less than a year since JWC had acquired the property, the Lone Ranger's value had doubled to $6 million, with licensed merchandise grossing $15 million (JWC received a 5% royalty).[25] By 1958, JWC had syndicated Lone Ranger reruns to over 156 U.S. TV stations plus 31 more in Canada and 54 overseas stations, the latter aided by the company's 1958 joint venture with the British Incorporated Television Company, which functioned primarily to distribute JWC programming in the UK.[26] By 1960, *Lone Ranger* television episodes could be seen weekly on a then-record 292 stations across the United States and on five continents.[27]

Like many contemporary proprietors of heritage brands, JWC developed a retro-branding strategy that sought to capitalize on the Lone Ranger's nostalgic appeal while also updating the property in accordance with the latest production conventions. In purchasing the back catalog of radio and TV episodes from Trendle, Wrather clearly understood that reruns were a key component of the property's brand equity. Derek Kompare has effectively argued that throughout the 1960s and 1970s, the rerun would become central to television production, distribution, and programming practices, serving as "the perfect incarnation of stability in an often unpredictable programming game."[28]

While reruns offered the networks a known commodity ripe for continued exploitation, property owners took risks to stay ahead in a competitive syndication marketplace. Significantly, to increase interest in the eventual rebroadcasting of *Lone Ranger* episodes, JWC invested (or, more accurately, it convinced longtime series sponsor General Mills to invest) in shooting all thirty-nine episodes of the 1956–1957 season—also the final season of the series—in color, even though color television would not become a standard for programming until the mid-1960s. The company explained that this was done in anticipation of the day "when color TV will have the wide audience demand black and white TV now has."[29] Thus, JWC's approach to maintaining the Lone Ranger property in the public's eye was simultaneously backward- and forward-looking, anticipating future audience desires to see old episodes of the series but within new viewing contexts.

Meanwhile, even as JWC invested resources in building up the Lone Ranger's second-run syndication appeal, it also continued to explore new modes of television production that adjusted the property to changing industrial, cultural, and textual standards for cultivating a children's market. In anticipation of shifts from sponsor to network hegemony that would bring significant restructuring of series financing, JWC ceased production of the live-action television series in 1957. JWC followed the path of other 1950s live-action TV series whose sponsors had primarily targeted children, like *The Adventures of Superman* and *Dick Tracy*, and reconfigured the property as an animated series. Conforming to emerging programming logic, the *Lone Ranger* animated series ran on CBS from 1966 to 1969 on Saturday mornings, a time slot dedicated exclusively to children's fare.

Jason Mittell argues that animation was reconceived as a juvenile genre in the 1960s, with materials previously understood by the media-industry professionals as having a dual audience appeal now "exiled" to Saturday mornings.[30] The devaluation of the genre appeared to go hand-in-hand with the elevation of child consumers as a distinct group who could be targeted directly by advertisers, but who were not particularly discerning in their tastes and therefore required little in the way of "quality" programming. Whereas LRI had previously defined the Lone Ranger as appealing to both adults and children, and late afternoon scheduling had offered sponsors access to both these markets, the new emphasis on developing a programming block just for children necessitated that the Masked Man choose one audience over the other. Given the centrality of licensed products—most of which were designed for children—to the Lone Ranger business, the decision of what direction to pursue was likely not too difficult. Yet the decision to switch from live action to animation and migrate to Saturday mornings was also to some extent out of JWC's hands. Though no longer financed via General Mills' sponsorship, the two likely remained tethered in the eyes of network programmers. General Mills' long-standing sponsorship of the series categorized the Lone Ranger in the eyes of most network executives as a children's property, and where General Mills' advertising dollars went, the Lone Ranger was expected to follow.[31]

The animated series as a whole reworked the Lone Ranger formula so as to make it similar to revisionist Westerns and other fantastical series of its day. In the animated series, the Lone Ranger and Tonto battled monsters, robots, and other science fiction–based villains. Indeed, the series has been compared with CBS's popular live-action Western, *The Wild, Wild West* (1965–1969). While it is not uncommon for networks and studios to seize upon a popular concept and recycle it—a practice often derided by mass culture critics bemoaning how standardization and repetition stifle creativity—JWC's willingness to adjust the Lone Ranger formula to meet shifting industrial conceptualizations of audience and genre is nonetheless significant in demonstrating the pressures placed on heritage brands to stay relevant yet fit within new contexts. Still, JWC never completely abandoned the possibility of retooling the Lone Ranger as an adult and youth market property.

In the decade between original television productions, JWC had produced two feature-length Lone Ranger films, *The Lone Ranger* (1956, distributed by Warner Bros.) and *The Lone Ranger and the Lost City of Gold* (1958, distributed by United Artists). Where the syndicated live-action and later the animated series were both clearly directed—at least in part—at (changing) children's markets via their sponsorship arrangements, scheduling, and content, the feature films tackled more complex subject matter aimed at a young adult audience concerned with social change. In particular, the plot of *The Lone Ranger and the Lost City of Gold* dealt overtly with both racial prejudice and racial passing. Moreover, the production values on these films place them squarely within the emerging B-movie circuit that Eric Schaefer identifies as specifically catering to teenagers and college-aged filmgoers, who sought alternatives to the more conservative Hollywood prestige films of the day.[32] The first feature did respectably at the box office, ranking sixty-fifth out of 109 feature films released in 1956 and grossing $1.55 million.[33] The second feature was less financially successful, but this likely owed more to United Artists' diminished distribution network as compared to Warner's. Thus, it might be argued that from 1956 to 1969, JWC adopted a two-pronged approach to keeping the Lone Ranger property active: (1) catering to children and offering up family-friendly television content through reruns of the original TV series as well as an animated version of the Masked Man, while (2) targeting young adults who had grown up watching the TV series and were now ready for a more complex rendition of the Lone Ranger. The decision to keep Clayton Moore and Jay Silverheels in the roles of the Lone Ranger and Tonto rather than to recast the parts offered continuity between television and film that likely aided in mobilizing audience migration.

Film and television were by no means the only sites JWC pursued in attempting to keep the property relevant. Merchandising would prove to be an important arena for negotiating the Lone Ranger's heritage status. Perhaps the most innovative licensing and merchandising work was a line of eight-inch Lone Ranger action figures released by Gabriel Toys from 1974 to 1976. Despite JWC's efforts to develop a new Lone Ranger television series throughout the 1970s (see below), the property remained largely relegated to reruns. This was still a lucrative business, earning the company $400,000 in net profits in the first half of 1975 alone,[34] but JWC also understood that it needed to find a way to keep Lone Ranger adventures fresh, particularly for children. Jonathan Gray has argued that Star Wars toys provided outlets for children to act out stories with the characters through play, which sustained interest in the overall franchise in between film installments.[35] Predating *Star Wars* by nearly three years, *The Lone Ranger Rides Again* toy line expanded the character's story world at a time when no new Lone Ranger stories were in circulation.

Initially, it did so by emphasizing allied and adversarial relationships among Lone Ranger peripheral characters as the basis for play. Gabriel was one of the first companies to release villain dolls as part of its toy line. Though Butch Cavendish had existed as part of the Lone Ranger mythos since the early 1940s, no merchandised materials had ever been created featuring his likeness until 1975. In part, this was because child rearing experts from the 1930s to the 1950s believed that children sought to emulate their heroes and that therefore playing with villainous characters provided children with the wrong role models. These ideas began to erode in the 1960s, as play was reconceived as a space for children to be imaginative, rather than learn to be good citizens.[36] Moreover, as the cost of plastic molding decreased, toy manufacturers began embracing the idea of releasing expanded toy lines that prolonged the play experience. Mego Toys, which licensed the rights to DC's and Marvel's stables of heroes, followed suit in 1976.[37]

Gabriel not only manufactured a Butch Cavendish doll, but also created several new enemy and ally action figures for the Lone Ranger and Tonto to interact with. These included the stereotypically racialized Mexican bandit El Lobo and the Apache Indian Red Sleeves. Besides having a Danny Reid doll—the Lone Ranger's long-lost nephew (based on the character first introduced on radio in 1944)—the line also included the teenage Little Bear, described as "The Indian brother of the Lone Ranger's nephew, Danny Reid."[38] These kid brother dolls offered varying generational points of entry. Gabriel also manufactured horses for each of the major characters, either sold separately or together with their intended riders. Gabriel even released an American eagle named Taka, billed as Tonto's trusted (yet never before seen) companion (see Figure 6.4).

Aside from the seven characters and six animals, the Gabriel line took a page from Mattel's Barbie product extension strategy by releasing over two dozen outfits and adventure sets. Since it was (and in many ways, still is) uncommon for a line of toys targeting boys to include outfit changes, Gabriel worked to ensure that the ensembles were motivated by an accompanying narrative that stressed action and adventure. Each package included a comic strip on the back that provided a preamble for how the play scenario began, but left the rest up to the consumer to fill in as they saw fit (by now, variations of this participatory strategy had been a part of several Lone Ranger merchandising initiatives, dating back to the LRSC and Frontier Town). For example, the Red River Flood adventure set, which included a miniature plastic rendition of a wooden raft and a medical supply kit, starts the story off with the Masked Man and Tonto caught in a raging storm while on a mission to deliver a typhoid vaccine to Carson City. In order to cross the flooding river, they build a raft, but as soon as they set out, the vaccine is swept overboard. Thus, without the benefit of a TV series or motion picture to build upon (and, arguably, precisely because none existed), the Gabriel toy line effectively kept the Lone Ranger adventure going by handing over most of the storytelling reins to children, while also providing narrative motivation for an extensive line

Figure 6.4. In 1974, Gabriel Toys introduced new Lone Ranger sidekicks, animal companions, and villains, including the first Butch Cavendish doll, as well as a Danny Reid doll for younger Lone Ranger enthusiasts.

of props that otherwise bore no obvious connection to the property (see Figure 6.5).

Though no actual sales figures exist to confirm the toy line's success, the fact that Gabriel sustained the line for three years while staggering product releases, as well as rereleasing the core Lone Ranger characters three times in new packaging, suggests that it was quite popular. Moreover, JWC would later seek to incorporate several of the characters introduced by Gabriel into possible Lone Ranger television projects, suggesting at the very least that the company perceived these new additions as part of the Lone Ranger canon (see below).

By the mid-1970s, JWC also openly embraced the Lone Ranger's continuity as a marketable resource. The company began to see the property's value as residing in the storytelling possibilities that could be exploited by filling in previously uncharted gaps in its fictional history or by tracing the Lone Ranger story alongside actual historical events. In 1975, JWC signed a contract with Doubleday Publishing and hired Lester Heverling and David Howe to research and write a "fictional historical novel" tentatively titled, *The Life and Legend of the Lone Ranger*.[39] This idea was not

Figure 6.5. Gabriel's Lone Ranger Rides Again toy line included outfits and adventure sets that extended the play experience. Each adventure set featured a comic strip that introduced the scenario, but left it up to consumers to save the day.

entirely new, as the radio program in the mid-1940s had similarly tied the Lone Ranger's adventures to real historical events and figures. In typical heritage brand fashion, the novel was imagined as nostalgically evoking those earlier adventures by retracing the Masked Man and Tonto's first encounters with Butch Cavendish and the Black Arrow gang, while also reconfiguring the story's tone for a more somber era. The novel was imagined as expanding upon the character's origin by focusing on the Masked Man's childhood and early adult life, before he became the Lone Ranger. As such, it was very much imagined as a coming-of-age story that fleshed out the character's past as a means of both deepening consumer investment in the Lone Ranger mythos and evoking a sense of nostalgia from readers about their own childhood encounters with the property. At the same time, it was thought to offer a new take on the property by mining its fictional past.

JWC also positioned the Lone Ranger novel as part of an expansive paratextual network intended to open up new product opportunities for the Lone Ranger brand. As Stan Stunell, JWC vice president in charge of the Lone Ranger, Inc., explained, "The Heverling/Howe novel might adapt very well to [a made-for-television miniseries]," which would serve as "a vehicle to establish the Lone Ranger, Tonto, and the important secondary characters with a tremendous degree of impact, and would be in a perfect spring-board position for a full-blown continuing series."[40] Stunell further argued that the TV miniseries could be timed closely with the release of the novel to allow for effective cross-marketing, ensuring commitment from all parties: "The picture will help the book. The book will help the picture. There will be a consistency, and reinforcement in the marketplace."[41]

Ultimately, Stunell's plan never materialized. Partly this was because the draft of the novel that Heverling and Howe delivered to Doubleday was deemed unpublishable, coming in at over eight hundred pages.[42] More to the point, Stunell's vision required a considerable amount of horizontal cooperation in order to succeed. Having extricated itself in the late 1950s from producing *The Lone Ranger* television series, JWC possessed neither production nor distribution resources. While conglomerates like Warner Communications were by the late 1970s beginning to explore the synergistic possibilities of exploiting IP like Superman across multiple simultaneous production outlets (see next section), JWC was unable to capitalize on the success of existing IP extensions like the Gabriel toy line through a coordinated cross-media campaign. Thus, Stunell's vision simply did not match JWC's capabilities.

This would not prevent JWC, however, from trying to salvage plot elements from the Heverling and Howe manuscript as the basis for a future Lone Ranger TV series. Internal correspondence as well as solicited treatments for a potential TV series stressed both the potential value of mining the Lone Ranger's historical setting and the importance of humanizing the property by exploring in greater depth his life before he donned the mask. As William Kelley suggested in his 1976 treatment for a possible Lone Ranger television series:

> Legends are laudable, myths are marvelous . . . but the question television poses now and forever is . . . what's new? What's new about your forty year old legend? What's he got now that he didn't have then? We begin the answer with our pilot. In all the history of the Lone Ranger, his past has been suggested, but never delineated. . . . It will establish the Lone Ranger and Tonto as individuals, as men of their time, as real persons with whom we can identify and empathize. . . . also new is our emphasis upon American history. . . . We will endeavor to involve him, at least peripherally, in major historical events, with major historical figures, taking a care always to be as historically accurate insofar as possible.[43]

In 1970, the television networks began redefining their programming strategies. In search of younger and more urban viewers who brought in higher returns on advertising rates, the networks embraced "quality" programming that was broadly conceived as edgier and more socially relevant, and placed a greater emphasis on realism. Replacing most of the fantastical sitcoms now deemed popular only among less desirable demographics (i.e., older and rural viewers) with "grittier" fare like *All in the Family* and *The Mary Tyler Moore Show*, the networks also invested in producing hour-long historical dramas (*The Waltons* [1972–1981], *Little House on the Prairie* [1974–1983]) that evoked nostalgia for simpler times even as they grappled with contemporary social issues.[44] By the mid-1970s, all three networks began to showcase more action-oriented fare (*Charlie's Angels* [1976–1981], *The Six Million Dollar Man* [1974–1978]) that once again targeted dual audiences segmented by generation, but tended to favor melodrama over comedy and social realism over camp, grounding their adventure and sci-fi elements in real-world settings.

Stunell maintained a list of potential formats for a new Lone Ranger TV series that focused on the characters' prehistories. For example, a potential series called *The Reids* would be about the Lone Ranger and his brother as children "with flavor of 'The Waltons' . . . each episode would be a selected event in the boys' lives which will heighten the dramatic impact of our viewers' knowledge of what and who the boys are to become, and to provide answers to the question of why."[45] Other format concepts focused on the Reid brothers as teenagers working on a Texas ranch or as young adults just joining the Texas Rangers.[46]

It is worth noting that while it had been established in the late 1940s and early 1950s on radio (and later television) that the Lone Ranger's brother had been one of the Texas Rangers murdered by Butch Cavendish, none of the previous Lone Ranger iterations had ever revealed the Masked Man's real identity. Thus, Stunell's proposal to focus on the Reid brothers' early years not only would have further humanized the hero, but also would have had a tremendous amount of built-in angst and anticipation, since audiences did not actually know which brother was fated to die and which one would become a legendary hero (although notes for the proposed series seem to clearly designate "John Reid" as the future Lone Ranger and his older brother, "Dan Reid," as the eventual fallen ranger).[47]

Significantly, none of these proposed prequels would feature the Masked Man, suggesting that the company believed that the costumed version of the character might fail to resonate with viewers seeking greater realism in the portrayal of their heroes. In gesturing at what the Reid brothers would one day become, JWC could keep the character's iconic attributes in the public mind without ever showing them. Twenty-five years later, the creators of *Smallville* would make a similar determination when they touted the series' "no tights, no flight" policy as key to its successful reinterpretation of the Superman mythos.

Another possible series, based on Tonto's exploits in his late teens and early twenties, was described by Stunell as addressing racial tensions between Native Americans and white settlers.[48] In this manner, JWC attempted to infuse the property with both youthfulness and social relevance that tied in directly with its historicity. A teenage Tonto coming of age while dealing with racial tensions captured perfectly how the property's heritage status could be exploited: the series would simultaneously rejuvenate the character and associate it with social issues believed to be relevant to the much-desired youth market, while resolving those same racial tensions by nostalgically reminding viewers of Tonto's eventual lifelong friendship with the Lone Ranger.

In addition to repositioning the Lone Ranger historically and exploring the Lone Ranger's own fictional history, JWC pursued other means of renewing interest in the property that built upon its "strong recognition value."[49] In a move reminiscent of Marvel's efforts to have its properties coexist in a shared universe, Stunell proposed combining the Lone Ranger and Lassie worlds in a TV series that followed Danny Reid and Lassie as they set out in search of the Lone Ranger and Tonto.[50] Drawing on elements developed in the Gabriel toy line, Stunell's proposal also incorporated the young Native American Little Bear, who would join Danny and Lassie on their adventures, creating in essence a junior version of the Lone Ranger and Tonto partnership. Stunell further proposed that this child-friendly reworking of the Lone Ranger formula could generate several spin-off possibilities, including a parallel series featuring the Lone Ranger and Tonto, where the titular heroes would be only one step ahead of Danny, Little Bear, and Lassie.[51] Pairing the two series was also envisioned as a means of tackling the property's multigenerational appeal without alienating audiences who might otherwise find the concept too juvenile or too mature.

Clearly, then, rather than rest on its laurels, JWC was in many ways quite proactive in its efforts to manage the Lone Ranger property as a heritage brand that balanced nostalgia with renewal and offered something for multiple generations. Though in the first decade of the twenty-first century properties like Star Wars, Star Trek, Superman, and Battlestar Galactica would all mine their own fictional histories as a means of expanding their franchise outposts—and stoking viewer interest in seeing narrative gaps filled in—JWC's vision for extending the Lone Ranger was certainly out of step with the media landscape in the mid-1970s. Most executives did not presume that casual viewers were invested enough in a property's mythology to accept a series of interwoven prequels that gestured audiences backward to the syndicated 1950s TV series and forward to the eventual emergence of the popular hero. Moreover, though the networks certainly embraced spin-offs as a safe way of generating new content that built on preestablished successes, series like *All in the Family*, *The Jeffersons*, *Maude*, and *Good Times* all shared a loose spatial—not temporal—relation to one another.

Another possible reason why none of Stunell's proposed Lone Ranger prequels and reboots ever moved beyond the development stage is that JWC simply could not decide how best to update the property while still maintaining its core attributes. JWC's files were filled with possible Lone Ranger revival concepts that never got off the ground. While some ideas were simply not feasible given the company's position within the entertainment industry in the 1970s and might have been filed away awaiting a restructuring of sorts, the sheer accumulation of brand revival concepts also points to uncertainty within the organization over what ideas would resonate best with consumers and licensees. In this regard, the myriad Lone Ranger formats that Stunell assembled not only reveal the extent to which the company sought to reach a younger audience, but also collectively capture the industry's ongoing struggle throughout this period to understand and define the tastes and cultural sensibilities of the much-sought-after youth market.

Perhaps the licensor felt trapped by the Masked Man's prior success and was wary of veering too far away from the property's perceived brand essence. Certainly, some of Stunell's ideas greatly reduced many of the Lone Ranger's most recognizable attributes altogether. Without a clear sense of what emerging Lone Ranger fans might want from their hero, JWC might have favored a more conservative approach that emphasized playing up—rather than playing with—the Lone Ranger's iconic elements. These anxieties would rear their head again in developing the Lone Ranger motion picture (see below), and as I argue further in the next chapter, are a recurring aspect of many heritage brand reformulations.

By decade's end, JWC was literally sending out the Lone Ranger's resume in the hopes of drumming up business for the property. In a mock cover letter addressed to creative directors, the Lone Ranger proclaimed, "After years of bringing law and order to the West, I am available, on a freelance basis, to help bring orders to your clients."[52] In the absence of a new central text to entice licensees, however, JWC's clever attempts to call attention to the Masked Man's decorated career instead came across as a desperate search for work by an unemployed and possibly unemployable brand.

With a new television series failing to materialize, JWC turned its attention to developing a Lone Ranger motion picture in the mold of the emerging Hollywood blockbuster. Though this too would fail—and fail colossally—it was not because JWC was unwilling to adjust the property to prevailing industry norms and perceived cultural tastes. Rather, it failed because of the company's inability to achieve a balance between nostalgia and innovation that would appease the Lone Ranger's core fan base while still attracting new consumers. In the next section, I elaborate upon the industrial climate in Hollywood in the 1970s, a period that was ripe for heritage brand revivals, but also greatly constrained in retooling retro brands.

The Hollywood Blockbuster and Heritage Brands

The period from the mid-1960s through the early 1980s is considered a period of tremendous social unrest in America. In Hollywood, it was also a period of significant organizational restructuring of the American film industry. Heritage brands offered a nostalgic distraction from current social ills as well as a means of overlaying financial uncertainties by investing in presold properties with established reputations and existing markets. The film industry approached heritage brands with an eye toward rendering "disreputable" yet popular 1930s content from the comic strips (*Flash Gordon* [1980], *Little Orphan Annie* [1982], *Popeye* [1980]), comic books (*Superman* [1978]), and film serials (*Star Wars* [1977] is largely a pastiche of scenes from old sci-fi serials) respectable again by subjecting them to "high-concept" revitalizations that emphasized big budgets, spectacular effects, heavily marketed star casting and directing, and often, a PR blitz focused on the wonders of bringing cartoon and comic strip characters to life in both "realistic" and "spectacular" ways. This is perhaps best captured in the marketing campaign for *Superman: The Motion Picture*, which bluntly stated: "You will believe a man can fly," a reference to how the special effects used in the film made the flying sequences look effortless and believable even as they provided key moments of spectacle for filmgoers.[53] Though Warner Communications Inc. (WCI) spent millions on advance marketing, they avoided including any footage from the film in their TV spots or theatrical trailers, instead promising consumers the visceral sensation of flying alongside the Man of Steel. WCI's "low key" advertising corresponds nicely with Justin Wyatt's definition of high concept marketing, which seeks to reduce a campaign down to a few iconic images or slogans that capture the film's essence.

In typical high concept fashion, WCI packaged *Superman* as bringing together a popular icon with proven blockbuster box office draws: Mario Puzo, author of *The Godfather*, who was commissioned to write the screenplay; John Williams III, who had previously scored *Jaws* and *Star Wars*; Gene Hackman, fresh off his successful reprisal of Jimmie "Popeye" Doyle in *The French Connection 2* (1976); and Marlon Brando, who was paid $3.7 million and given a percentage of the box office gross in exchange for twelve days' worth of work portraying Superman's Kryptonian father, Jor-El. WCI initially also sought to cast a major star in the principal role of Clark Kent/Superman, offering the role to numerous Hollywood A-listers including Robert Redford, Paul Newman, and Burt Reynolds. DC Comics also approved a list of Superman possibles that included Al Pacino, James Caan, Steve McQueen, Clint Eastwood, Dustin Hoffman, and interestingly, Muhammad Ali.[54] A combination of scheduling and salary disagreements along with anxiety over diluting Superman's existing brand equity by grafting the character onto an existing star persona all contributed to the eventual decision to cast a fresh face in the role. Thus, what would become a casting trend for heritage brands adapted to the big screen in the late 1970s and early 1980s, where the principal role went to a relative unknown who "looked the part" while major stars populated key supporting roles (see the Lone Ranger, Flash Gordon, Annie), actually emerged in hindsight out of WCI's inability to land its top choices.

Thomas Schatz has argued that the film industry's investment in blockbusters—a type of film defined more by its large production, marketing budget, and merchandising potential than its success at the box office—began in the postwar era, in response to diminishing movie attendance blamed largely on the popularity of television and on suburban flight.[55] This led to an increased emphasis on generating event films that would lure people back into the theaters. Though early blockbusters like *Ben-Hur* (1959) and *The Sound of Music* (1965) remade successful films and popular genres with ramped-up production values, by the late 1960s the studios began to focus more intently on cultivating the youth market, leading to both a cycle of big-budget disaster films as well as the dawn of what Schatz refers to as the "Hollywood renaissance," wherein the studios briefly banked on the artistic and political credentials of an emerging set of young filmmakers, many of whom were film school–trained and conversant in the European art cinema movement as well as Hollywood's own history. The shifting conceptualization of the youth market throughout the 1970s from politically engaged and media-savvy to apolitical and juvenile contributed to Hollywood's gradual loss of faith in the art cinema movement. By decade's end the Hollywood art cinema wave would be eclipsed by the high concept logics of the New Hollywood.[56] Still, throughout the 1970s art cinema and blockbuster approaches to reviving heritage brands not only competed with one another but also often coexisted within the same production. In part, this attests to the uncertainty among Hollywood studios over how to exploit retro properties for contemporary audience sensibilities.

Heritage brand adaptations tended to follow John Cawelti's overlapping modes of genre revision. Many engaged in burlesque deconstruction, in which "elements of a conventional formula or style are situated in contexts so incongruous or exaggerated that they result in laughter."[57] Bringing grotesque and surreal characters to life from the worlds of Popeye or Dick Tracy offered an opportunity to comment—either comically or critically, sometimes both—on their unreality, in turn deconstructing both property and cinematic convention alike. Though such an approach risked demythologizing iconic properties, many such adaptations inevitably worked to reaffirm the mythic place these characters held in American society. Cawelti argues that in this mode, "a traditional genre and its myth are probed and shown to be unreal, but then the myth is at least partially affirmed as a reflection of authentic human aspirations and needs."[58] Accordingly, while Little Orphan Annie's comic strip adventures might be purposely depicted on film as the kind of stuff that could only happen in the funnies, the movie still champions her relentless positivity and entrepreneurial spirit as quintessentially American.

Other heritage brand adaptations engaged directly in the cultivation of nostalgia through stylistic and narrative cues that "recreate the aura of a past time," while working to draw parallels and juxtapositions between past and present by deploying "highly traditional generic content in a slightly different context, thereby giving us both a sense of contemporaneity and of pastness."[59] As such, a film like *Superman* (1978) purposely juxtaposed the Man of Steel's all-American values with the grittiness of a contemporary Metropolis landscape. Importantly, Cawelti states that several of these modes could often be found operating within the same text, suggesting that at their best they all worked together in helping a filmmaker to realize some "overriding artistic purpose."[60] Alternatively, it might be suggested that the weaving together of these modes presented less a coherent strategy for differentiation than the uncertainty of how best to strike the proper tonal balance in reviving heritage brands to achieve a cross-generational appeal.

Though the best way to revitalize heritage brands remained an open debate throughout the 1970s, as production budgets rose, heritage brands like Popeye, Flash Gordon, Superman, and the Lone Ranger nonetheless were recognized as offering the studios a proven presold commodity with an established audience that was likely to show up on opening weekend. As the studios shifted from a staggered- to a wide-release pattern for distribution, opening weekend box office returns became vital to a film's theatrical run, and presold properties offered greater opportunities to draw in audiences already familiar with the material.[61] As David A. Cook contends, *Superman* (1978) featured a "pre-sold title character [that] had been known to every generation of sentient Americans since 1938."[62] WCI's marketing reps similarly gloated that the property's prominence allowed them to develop a "low-key" advertising campaign:[63] "Millions of people have their own image of Superman, and we realized that all we'd have to tell them is that the movie is coming."[64]

Their longevity also meant that heritage properties had cataloged thousands of stories in various media formats, which not only provided source materials for the motion pictures, but also proved attractive for studios seeking to develop film franchises through sequels and spin-offs. As the film studios gradually became divisions within larger conglomerates throughout the 1960s, greater emphasis was placed on producing motion pictures that could be exploited across corporate holdings, generating merchandising and product tie-ins. Heritage brands not only offered the studios a degree of predictability based on their instant recognition among consumers, but also had established track records in attracting licensing tie-ins and merchandising opportunities.

As such, WCI also developed a highly integrated corporate strategy designed to generate synergy across its various divisions. Warner Books published a Superman quiz book, an original novel, a book about how the film was made, a Superman encyclopedia, a calendar, and a set of blueprints depicting Superman's Fortress of Solitude. DC Comics published an official comic book adaptation as well as a special rerelease of *Action Comics* #1, made available exclusively in supermarkets, further extending the property into new areas. WCI's music division released a soundtrack featuring John Williams's score. Echoing both current and past branded entertainment initiatives, WCI saw the film as creating demand for these myriad products, which in turn increased interest in the film across its various distribution windows, including Warner home video and Warner cable outlets like HBO, as well as generating anticipation for the sequel.

Associated with a bygone era, these properties also tapped into a nostalgic vibe that reverberated throughout many blockbuster films of the late 1970s, from *The Godfather* to *Star Wars*. In fact, *Star Wars*' successful appeal for a wide audience partly hinged on older viewers' appreciation of the film's homage to the aesthetics and narrative pacing of 1930s sci-fi adventure serials. Cook suggests that such nostalgic pastiches "generated a two-tiered system of communication, presenting themselves as fantasy-adventure spectacles for the economically crucial teenage audience, and as tapestries of allusion for an older, more cinematically sophisticated one."

The perceived value of a property like Superman also lay in its potential to act as a bridge between older and younger audiences. A December 9, 1979, *New York Times* article quoted DC Comics president Sol Harrison on Superman's multigenerational popularity: "It is not unusual for grandfather, father and son to share an interest in Superman."[65] Though not necessarily accurate, Harrison's self-interested declaration is part of a broader industrial lore about heritage properties that imagined their appeal as both cross-generational and focalized within the family unit.

Yet as an article in *Businessweek* concluded, "[Superman] must prove that he can win over an audience of adults as well as children to justify an investment of $50 million in his first feature film."[66] As the cautionary tone of the statement suggests, this was also the greatest risk associated with the property. Superman had undergone a process of juvenilization in the late 1940s and 1950s, so that by the late 1970s, it was perceived as a children's property that didn't necessarily resonate with the current generation of kids, but was also too childish to appeal to adults, even those who had grown up paying avid attention to the Man of Steel's exploits. Though director Richard Donner would claim that he was "making a picture for adults that kids will go see,"[67] the film's success hinged on activating parental nostalgia while making Superman feel modern and relevant, and even somewhat rebellious, for younger audiences.

Even as the film placed Superman in a contemporary setting, it also drew upon a combination of generic cues, design elements, and casting choices to give it both a glimmer of classical Hollywood and a selective air of reverence toward Superman's own history. Clark Kent and Lois Lane's interactions drew inspiration from the screwball comedies of the 1930s and 1940s. Costuming and set design also harkened back to the 1940s, with Lois Lane banging away at a typewriter instead of a word processor. Even the decision to make Lois and Clark newspaper reporters was retro. In the comic book, both had become television reporters in 1970. The producers cast iconic 1940s actor Glenn Ford as Superman's adopted father, Jonathan Kent, and Kirk Alyn and Noell Neill, who had portrayed Superman and Lois Lane in the 1948 film serial, in brief cameos as Lois Lane's parents.

While gesturing backward for a ciné-and-pop-culture-literate crowd, the film also changed large chunks of Superman's backstory that were at the time considered canonical, including eliminating his crime-fighting career as Superboy while growing up in Smallville. These changes were intended both to simplify the mythos for a more general audience, as well as to eliminate parts of the Superman backstory that might be perceived as too juvenile. Despite this omission, the film still presented Superman's origin as a coming-of-age story common to many blockbusters of the era, following his path from awkward teen to untested hero to savior. This transition required him at film's end to reject his Kryptonian father's warnings not to interfere with the course of human history by reversing time in order to save Lois Lane's life. Though clearly a metaphorical nod to youthful rebellion intended to complicate Superman's overgrown Boy Scout reputation, the scene also reveals the film's fairly apolitical efforts to engage the youth market by ultimately depicting the character's history-changing actions as rooted in individualism and romance: he defies his father to save the woman he loves, not the world.

Superman was the second-highest-grossing film in 1978, generating $82.6 million in domestic box office revenues.[68] Now a division of WCI, the Licensing Corporation of America (LCA) went to work adding forty new licensees to the fold before the film reached the theaters.[69] *Superman*'s box office and merchandising success kicked off a cycle of comic book and comic strip adaptations in the late 1970s and early 1980s, as Hollywood studios optioned the rights to classic properties like Flash Gordon (De Laurentis/Universal), Little Orphan Annie (Columbia), Alley Oop (Columbia), Terry and the Pirates (Embassy), Sheena, Queen of the Jungle (Embassy), and Popeye (Paramount/Disney), many of which were still in circulation in their original medium but had long since become more valuable as licensable IP.[70] For example, the King Features Syndicate (KFS), which owned the rights to Popeye, saw its earnings from licensing the rights to the character increase by 60–70 percent in the late 1970s, a return far greater than monies earned by the internationally distributed comic strip.[71]

Robert Altman's *Popeye* (1980) provides an interesting contrast to Superman's successful blockbuster adaptation. In 1979, Popeye was celebrating its fiftieth anniversary as a character with a merchandising blitz, ranging from ceramic collectible figurines to pop art–style T-shirts. A year earlier, KFS had commissioned Hanna Barbera to produce a new animated TV series, *The All New Adventures of Popeye*, which was intended to sanitize a property that had come under attack in the early 1960s by parent groups concerned with the level of violence in the cartoon. The combination of a new kid-friendly TV series and a promotional campaign that called explicit attention to Popeye's long-standing popularity made the property particularly appealing to Hollywood. Robert Evans licensed the film rights from KFS. Evans convinced Paramount to distribute the film despite the studio's concerns over his choice of Robert Altman as director. Paramount's interest in the project partly stemmed from the fact that the studio still owned the distribution rights to the 1940s and 1950s *Popeye* cartoon series and partly from the film's star, Robin Williams, whose TV series *Mork and Mindy* was produced by Paramount for ABC TV. Still, to offset the risk associated with Altman, who'd had a string of recent flops, Paramount sold off the international distribution rights to the live-action film to Disney.[72]

Altman's *Popeye* placed the iconic sailor into a live-action revisionist musical that played up the characters' cartoonishness (when punched, they might fly fifty feet in the air or have their bodies twist and contort in inhuman ways) and had them sing and dance poorly in intentionally atonal sloppy numbers. The film also featured many of Altman's signature techniques, including dense soundscapes and a sprawling cast of characters that overshadowed the characters of Popeye and Olive Oyl. Screenwriter Jules Feiffer expressed concern that during preproduction for the film, Altman "talked about [the people of Sweethaven, the town where Popeye was set] a lot more than he talked about the characters of Popeye and Olive Oyl." The film's poor box office convinced Hollywood insiders that art cinema was incompatible with the blockbuster's broad-based appeal.[73]

Yet Altman's approach to reworking Popeye as a heritage brand actually fits quite nicely with the retro-strategies of its day. Altman drew inspiration from Popeye's early adventures in the E. C. Segar Thimble Theatre (1919–) comic strips, which were often chaotic and fantastical in their plotting, engaged in social satire that skewered commercial culture and middle-class virtues, and featured a large ensemble cast. Indeed, the town of Sweethaven and the Oyl family had been in existence for over ten years before Popeye made his first comic strip appearance in 1929. Consequently, in dropping the live-action Popeye into a preestablished story world and positioning him as an interloper on events already in motion before his arrival (Oyl's engagement to Bluto, for example), Altman not only took the character back to its pre-iconic roots but also managed to tell a coming-of-age story. Popeye's arrival in town is motivated by his search for his pappy, whom he subsequently discovers is the tyrannical commodore taxing Sweethaven's residents for every possible infraction. Over the course of the film, Popeye embraces his individuality—including learning to appreciate spinach—by rejecting his father, while becoming a surrogate dad to Swee'Pea. The film's aesthetics and characterization nostalgically evoke the Depression-era comic strip while the story ultimately reaffirms Popeye's mythic status as an everyman seeking to assert his individuality in a conformist society. All of these strategies were widely perceived at the time as acceptable means for reviving heritage brands.

Moreover, to call *Popeye* a commercial failure is somewhat a misnomer. Costing $20 million, *Popeye* earned over $49 million at the box office domestically and was the twelfth largest earner in 1980.[74] The presold nature of the character and Williams's popularity certainly made these numbers seem disappointing, especially compared with the success of the *Star Wars* sequel, *The Empire Strikes Back*, which earned $141.7 million,[75] but it was likely the film's unrealized merchandising potential that actually earned it the reputation as a failure. While *Popeye* made money at the box office, its merchandise—including a Milton Bradley board game, a Colorforms playset, eight-inch vinyl dolls and six-inch bendables, as well as a lunchbox—wasn't flying off the shelf.

Of course, it could also be argued that licensees failed to adapt tie-in products to the film's emphasis on character over plot, story world over goal-driven protagonist. For instance, the Milton Bradley board game redrew Sweethaven's richly textured landscape as a linear grid that players advanced through—rather than explored—on their way toward accomplishing the task of delivering baby Swee'Pea from the docks into town. Similarly, dolls focused exclusively on the main characters (Popeye, Olive Oyl, Bluto, Wimpy, Swee'Pea) while providing no context for them to interact with one another. While both of these tie-in ideas might seem better suited to the contemporary media environment, I have already demonstrated in a previous chapter how the Lone Ranger Frontier Town encouraged exploration of the Masked Man's story world through play. Meanwhile, *Star Wars* action figures—in stores at the same time as *Popeye* merchandise—offered children opportunities to flesh out the backstories of hundreds of minor characters that populated the film universe.

Hollywood would eventually brand *Popeye* a "failure," but the very fact that the studios (reluctantly) backed an Altman-directed blockbuster to begin with reveals the multiplicity of tactics embraced to revive heritage brands. Rather than a mistake or aberration, the movie had its place within an industrial context that saw heritage brands as valuable resources but was often uncertain about how to strike the balance between nostalgia and relevance needed to successfully revive them. It is within this environment that JWC sought to further extend the Lone Ranger's career.

The Legend of the Lone Ranger

On January 5, 1978, JWC entered into a joint venture agreement with UK-based ITC to produce a new Lone Ranger film.[76] Throughout the 1960s and 1970s, ITC had gained a reputation for producing cult British TV series—*The Saint*, *The Persuaders*, and *The Prisoner*. In the 1970s, the company ventured into film production, and was connected with critical and financial successes like *On Golden Pond*, *The Boys from Brazil*, *Sophie's Choice*, *The Dark Crystal*, and the first two Muppet films, which it coproduced with the Jim Henson Company. Notably, in 1980, in the midst of preproduction for *The Legend of the Lone Ranger*, ITC also released the colossal blockbuster bomb *Raise the Titanic*, which would effectively bankrupt the company and have considerable repercussions on the Lone Ranger's cinematic comeback (a point I return to at the end of this section).

The Legend of the Lone Ranger (*LLR*) was both a commercial and a critical failure. Costing $21 million to produce, the film only grossed $13 million domestically.[77] Comparatively, other heritage brand blockbusters fared anywhere from mildly to wildly better. *Flash Gordon* (1980) and *Annie* (1982) cost $20 million and $50 million respectively, and both films eked out small profits, earning $27 million and $57 million domestically.[78] Meanwhile, *Superman*'s budget clocked in at over $55 million, though this included the costs of shooting the sequel, which was filmed simultaneously. *Superman 2* would go on to earn $300 million internationally during its theatrical run.[79] Though critiques of *LLR* encompassed everything from the poor acting to the stultifying pacing of the action sequences, a common refrain among several film critics was that the film tried—and failed—to replicate *Superman*'s formula.[80]

In some ways, *LLR*'s narrative structure was very similar to that of *Superman*. Both films began with preludes that explored their respective hero's childhood: Clark Kent growing up in Smallville; John Reid meeting Tonto following the murder of Reid's parents. Both films dedicated nearly one-third of their screen time to developing the characterizations of their protagonists' alter egos: Clark Kent as journalist and John Reid as lawyer. Both films featured arch nemeses (Lex Luthor and Butch Cavendish) involved in convoluted real estate crime: Luthor plans to destroy the California coastline in order to create new oceanfront housing; Cavendish kidnaps President Grant and holds him for ransom in exchange for the title to the state of Texas.

And to the extent that both films were envisioned as high concept blockbusters based on presold properties with long histories of successful merchandising and multigenerational appeal, *LLR* was a lot like *Superman*. In packaging and marketing the film, JWC and its partners pursued many of the same tactics that Warner Communications had with *Superman*. Poster art reduced the film down to a single iconic image of a gloved hand holding up a glistening silver bullet accompanied by a catchy yet familiar slogan—"the Lone Ranger Rides Again" (see Figure 6.6). Originally scheduled for a Christmas release in seven hundred theaters nationwide, the film featured state-of-the-art camera effects to render larger than life the Masked Man's lightning-fast trigger finger reflexes and Silver's mighty gallop.[81] And it would cast established actors in key supporting roles—Christopher Lloyd as Butch Cavendish and Jason Robards as President Ulysses S. Grant—while seeking a fresh face for the central hero. Indeed, a 1977 report in the *Hollywood Reporter* stated that Wrather was "now determined to cast an unknown . . . [and] cast at least two superstars to give the unknown the same prestige support the 'Superman' title star is getting."[82] Much as *Superman*'s casting of Kirk Alyn and Noell Neil in cameo roles as Lois Lane's parents offered an intertextual nod to longtime aficionados, *LLR* cast former Lone Ranger John Hart in the role of the current Lone Ranger's potential love interest's uncle. But notably, the film did not have a part for Clayton Moore, the man most closely associated with the Masked Man.

From the onset, however, there seemed to be a lack of clarity over the target audience for the film. Through merchandising and third-party licenses, *LLR* was positioned as kid-friendly. Among seventy-nine items it licensed, JWC commissioned Gabriel to manufacture a toy line, Aladdin to create a metallic lunch box, and Milton Bradley to develop a board game and puzzles based on the film.[83] JWC partnered with Edgar Rice Burroughs, Inc. in colicensing the rights for Filmation to produce the animated *Tarzan/Lone Ranger Adventure Hour*, which ran on CBS from 1980 to 1982. JWC also commissioned the New York Times Syndicate to

Figure 6.6. High concept poster art for *The Legend of the Lone Ranger.*

launch a new Lone Ranger comic strip, which ran from 1981 to 1984. The timing suggests that JWC was hoping to use the comic strip and cartoon to extend the Lone Ranger's merchandising window beyond the film.

Radio promotions, however, targeted 18-to-25-year-olds and attempted to construct the Masked Man as a cult figure among the college crowd. One promotion called for radio deejays to host a Lone Ranger cocktail contest, in which local bartenders would compete for who could invent an alcoholic beverage that lived up to the slogan, "One shot and you're a legend."[84] Such contests represented a radical departure from LRI's Lone Ranger rules, in which imbibing alcohol was at the top of the list of "Don'ts." Other initiatives devised to attract college-age viewers included convincing over three hundred university marching bands to incorporate the William Tell Overture—the Lone Ranger's signature theme music—into their set lists, culminating in the piece being featured during the halftime ceremony of the nationally televised USC–Notre Dame football game in 1980.[85] As Wrather explained, the goal was to give the film an "in" image with teenagers and young adults, who would advocate on its behalf, telling others, "Hey, Man, you gotta see this."[86]

Moreover, despite recommendations made by the National Center for Survey Research that JWC "forgo at least part of the old traditional Lone Ranger audience for a new one,"[87] the company remained cognizant of "changes that could be a source of comment or criticism from some of the died-in-the-wool fans," even going so far as to maintain a list of proposed story departures from the original Lone Ranger mythos.[88] As a result of this uncertainty, from February 1978 to January 1980, seven different writers were commissioned to produce scripts for the film, which varied in tone from irreverent and lighthearted to epic and action-packed.[89]

Though it was understood that the film would deal with the Lone Ranger's backstory, including a childhood encounter between John Reid and Tonto, and would recount the Masked Man and Tonto's first adventure together, multiple story variations were generated. Some versions featured a young John Reid saving Tonto's life, others had Tonto's tribe taking in the Reid brothers after their parents had been killed. In some scripts, John Reid is revealed to be a natural talent with both guns and horses long before he takes on his masked identity; in other scripts—including the version eventually produced—Tonto teaches Reid how to shoot and how to tame Silver. Wrather et al. repeatedly debated whether or not the scripts they vetted captured the essence of the character, often evoking their understanding of an imagined audience as the ultimate arbiter of such matters. For instance, after rejecting an initial script by Ben Roberts as "light, fast, glib, but also shallow and ordinary . . . [lacking] the extraordinary elements we want and must have for a Lone Ranger picture," Stunell proposed that JWC pursue an epic story, arguing that "general reaction to the Lone Ranger, as I have observed it, places him somewhere above a Joe Namath, or a John Wayne, and below a superman—identifiably human, bigger than all of us, but not possessed of magical powers. I believe that is the way the public wants and will accept him."[90] Stunell was still expressing similar concerns two years later, this time over Michael Kane's script: "My chief concern goes to the primary objective as a whole: The audience should leave with a sense of awe, respect, and utterly memorable impact of this character, the Lone Ranger. Jack [Wrather] hit on two key reasons why it doesn't come off yet: Cavendish and Amy. He's not a large enough adversary, she's not woman enough."[91]

Confusion over how to reposition the Lone Ranger for a contemporary market extended beyond debates over plot points to include decisions about the above-the-line talent hired to work on the film. Despite the nods to high concept marketing, the man hired to oversee the actual production of the film, Walter Coblenz, was more readily known for his work on political fare like *All The President's Men* (1976) and *The Onion Fields* (1978), which had attained both critical and countercultural acclaim. In turn, Coblenz hired William A. Fraker to direct. Fraker was an accomplished cinematographer coming off three consecutive Academy

Award nominations for *Looking for Mr. Goodbar* (1977), *Heaven Can Wait* (1978), and *1941* (1979), but had virtually no prior experience as a director, let alone in mounting a blockbuster production. Martin Starger was also an odd choice as executive producer. While at ABC, Starger had been responsible for initiating the network's pursuit of highly touted miniseries like *Roots*. He was also executive producer on Robert Altman's *Nashville* (1975). These key personnel in decision-making roles suggest that a planned Lone Ranger feature likely drew inspiration from the art cinema movement even as it sought to replicate the appeal and success of popcorn blockbusters like *Jaws* or *Star Wars*.

Perhaps the greatest confusion came from casting virtual unknown Klinton Spilsbury in the title role. While Spilsbury's poor acting—necessitating that all of his dialogue be overdubbed by Stacey Keach in postproduction—has become the stuff of Hollywood legend, it was the performer's bad-boy image and his vocal ambivalence toward the Lone Ranger's unsullied heroic status that were particularly incongruent with the way JWC wanted the character to be interpreted. Film reviewers repeatedly seized upon Spilsbury's lack of intensity, his apparent disinterest in carrying on or living up to the Lone Ranger's ideals, and his reputation as a troublemaker on the set, which included having an altercation with a local waitress and starting a bar brawl. These reports were presented as damning evidence that Spilsbury was the antithesis of the character he was portraying on screen and a poor substitute for the man whose boots he was essentially filling, the by-then 65-year-old Clayton Moore. As Gary Deeb reported, "Whenever [Spilsbury] was chided for his childish rampages, he explained the behavior by yelling: 'Hey, I'm the Lone Ranger!' This sort of carousing and pratfalling probably wouldn't raise many eyebrows under ordinary circumstances. [But] he was playing the role of an all-American hero, and he was following in the footsteps of an actor who had extended the Lone Ranger credo into his personal life since 1949."[92]

Where JWC sought to cast a youthful, handsome Lone Ranger who would carry on the mantle of his predecessors, going so far as to reject scripts that depicted him as brash, impetuous, or rebellious,[93] Spilsbury openly expressed suspicion toward Cold War heroes:

> It's scary to think of these people saying the world needs a new hero . . . that's the mentality of the '50s that led us into the '60s. When are we gonna learn? I think that if anything went wrong with our country in the '50s and '60s . . . it was our tendency to expect our heroes to be perfect. I find that to be a rather immature way of looking at things because all you

> can eventually do is destroy your heroes. There comes a time when we find out that our heroes are not perfect and become disillusioned. That's why people like make believe heroes . . . if you dig behind the Lone Ranger, you're just going to find a story that someone made up. . . . I found myself rebelling against the idea that I should behave like the character I was playing. I'm an actor, not a hypocrite.[94]

Spilsbury's antiestablishment persona clashed not only with the nostalgic sentiments JWC sought to tap into, but also with the popcorn blockbuster JWC ultimately sought to assemble. Had JWC pursued a more rebellious depiction of the Masked Man in *LLR*, Spilsbury's antics might have been successfully recast as helping to define the Lone Ranger's new laid-back and antiauthoritarian persona. But because the film purported to maintain the qualities long associated with the Lone Ranger even as it explored his younger years, Spilsbury's moral lapses were de facto equated with JWC's managerial failings.

Of course, it is easy to speculate about what might or might not have happened had either Spilsbury been better behaved or the Lone Ranger been reimagined as a more brash and flawed character. Of greater interest is how debates over Spilsbury's lack of worthiness as a replacement for Clayton Moore speak to the challenges in updating a heritage brand. Attempting to balance the desires of established fans with the perceived tastes of younger consumers, JWC's casting choices were driven by concerns that the Lone Ranger not appear to be old, but that he also continue to come across as old-fashioned. In the end, *LLR* missed the mark with both younger and older viewers. One *Washington Post* film reviewer lamented that the enthusiasm and excitement expressed by politicos at a special Kennedy Center screening of the film underscored *LLR*'s disconnect with younger audiences: "At a Kennedy Center invitational preview last weekend, an audience dominated by elderly buckaroos whooped it up whenever the movie evoked a familiar cliché: the first appearance of the hero in his mask; the sound of the William Tell Overture; catch lines like 'Hi-yo Silver. Away!' or 'Who was that Masked Man?' Indeed, 'Legend' may be a cult turkey for oldtimers. Unfortunately, there's no compelling reason for moviegoers a generation or two younger to get similarly carried away. If anything, the most pertinent question for uninitiated customers is likely to be, 'Who are these hopeless amateurs?'"[95]

At the same time, many critics also postulated that the film would be equally disappointing to long-term Lone Ranger fans expecting to see the Masked Man's legacy passed on to a worthy recipient. Critics noted that

Spilsbury and Michael Horse, cast as Tonto, were both outwardly very pretty men who lacked the inner conviction to truly embody their parts. Wrote the *New York Times'* Janet Maslin: "WELCOME to the Land of the Perfect Profile, where the only thing prettier than a cowboy is his horse. It is here that the latest Lone Ranger rides—in slow motion, through a parade of pastel sunsets, to the accompaniment of soothing music that might otherwise turn up in a life insurance ad. Beside him is the handsome Tonto, who has silky hair and a voice that ought to be teaching yoga or pitching Perrier. Because both characters have become part of American folklore, they wear the outfits with which they have always been associated. Too bad. They belong in Calvin Klein jeans . . . the Ranger keeps remarking that he feels things in his gut. Since everything about him appears to be made of sawdust, it's hard to believe that either the gut or the feelings are real."[96]

Significantly, Spilsbury's vacuous and insincere performance was almost always contrasted with that of Moore's, who was repeatedly identified by critics as both a Lone Ranger acolyte and the hero's living embodiment: "Moore says he identified with the Lone Ranger's philosophy. 'This is part of my code of life. The silver bullets stood for law and order, fair play and honesty. I never took advantage of people. Even fighting an outlaw on the show, I never kicked him when he was down.'"[97] It was JWC's mishandling of Clayton Moore that would prove most damaging to its efforts to revive the Lone Ranger brand.

The Legend of Clayton Moore

Throughout the 1970s, Clayton Moore continued to make public appearances as the Lone Ranger, charging $1,000 per performance and averaging one hundred public appearances each year.[98] JWC would claim that it turned a blind eye to these unsanctioned appearances out of respect for the acclaim Moore had brought to the role. As Stunell explained, "Clayton Moore has made a fine living for himself over the years portraying the Lone Ranger. We allowed him to do it, even though legally we could have stopped him. I guess it was our way of expressing appreciation for past services rendered."[99]

In actuality, Moore's public appearances existed in a symbiotic relationship with JWC's pursuit of markets for its Lone Ranger back catalog and its efforts to tap into nostalgia for the character's 1950s exploits. In addition to continued syndication of *Lone Ranger* television episodes both locally and internationally, JWC found new outlets for *The Lone Ranger* radio programs in the emerging Old-Time-Radio segments featured on oldies stations and in the audiocassette market. While the radio ranger had been voiced by Brace Beemer (among others), the marketing materials JWC circulated to potential radio stations featured Moore's likeness, and Moore's public appearances certainly helped activate nostalgic memories for those "days of yesteryear." JWC also used Moore's likeness on the covers of Dell comic books that reprinted stories of the Masked Man's 1950s exploits as well as in advertisements employing the Lone Ranger as product spokesperson, such as a series of ads for Colorado Springs cologne that featured famous cowboy heroes from the 1950s.[100] As mentioned above, JWC also employed Moore to make public appearances at their Lone Ranger restaurant franchises. Moore's continued appearances in Lone Ranger reruns, on merchandise, and in public settings prolonged consumer association with him as the Lone Ranger, making JWC's decision in 1979 to "retire" him seem all the more abrupt.

In the two years leading up to *LLR*'s release, JWC took Moore to court to legally prevent him from appearing in public as the Lone Ranger, citing concerns about audience confusion over the existence of two Lone Rangers. Moore rebutted that if such concern was legitimate the company would surely also pull all the TV episodes and other licensed ephemera featuring his likeness out of circulation as well.[101] JWC's concern wasn't so much with Moore, though, as with the perception that the Lone Ranger was aging and out of touch with a new generation of consumers. Press coverage of Moore's public appearances in the mid-1970s often pointed to the actor's dyed hair and slight paunch, but perhaps more damning was the intimation that Moore's Lone Ranger did not resonate with younger audiences in the same way that it did with their parents. Describing an appearance Moore made at a Chrysler dealership in 1973, Polly Paddock of the *Charlotte Observer* noted, "Few of the youngsters shoved towards Moore by their camera-toting parents seemed to understand all the fuss. But none of them muttered the immortal words, 'who was that Masked Man?'"[102]

In some ways, JWC's actions in trying to rid the Lone Ranger property of its perceived stodginess mimicked the strategies employed by many heritage brand owners looking to revive interest in their properties. Russell Baker humorously lamented that the Lone Ranger's fate was similar to those of other aging icons like Buck Rogers, Little Orphan Annie, and Flash Gordon.[103] But where characters like Popeye had previously existed exclusively in cartoon form and actor George Reeve's death in

1958 meant that the producers of *Superman: The Motion Picture* did not have to contend with an existing star's close association with the part, Clayton Moore was still very much alive, and in the eyes of the public, was the performer who defined the Lone Ranger. As Moore's lawyer, Bob Michaels, explained, "Clayton Moore, in the hearts and minds of America *is* the Lone Ranger. They use his picture and his voice to promote their product. All he has to do is open his mouth. He *is* the Lone Ranger."[104]

Concerns about audience overidentification with particular performers had previously led companies like LRI and DC Comics to try to suppress the identities of the actors portraying their iconic characters on the radio and in the film serials. Columbia's *Superman* (1948) serial lists "Clark Kent," not Kirk Alyn, as its star. Meanwhile, the sudden death of the radio's first Lone Ranger, Earl Graser, in an automobile accident in 1941 did not even interrupt scheduled broadcasts. Trendle simply had Striker concoct an elaborate story in which the Lone Ranger was gravely wounded and unable to speak for several weeks while then-announcer Brace Beemer was groomed for the role. When the Lone Ranger regained use of his vocal cords, his altered voice was explained away as a permanent effect of his injury. No public announcement of Graser's demise or Beemer's debut was ever made. Television changed all this. The public was not only presented with a face and body with which to associate a character; the ritual of the weekly schedule ensured repeat viewing and habit formation.

Of course, Clayton Moore's 1950s TV contract forbade him from making public appearances as the Lone Ranger unless previously sanctioned by LRI.[105] These instances were supposedly reserved for appearances of national importance, as befit the Lone Ranger's status. Furthermore, Moore was warned not to draw attention to himself as performer, whether in or out of costume. As Trendle firmly reminded the actor in an August 15, 1949, letter, "Theoretically the Lone Ranger is a mythical character. I have told Mr. Beemer that many, many times. When Mr. Beemer is on set in costume or before the microphone playing the Lone Ranger, then we assume that he is the Lone Ranger. The minute he is off the mike or out of costume, then he is just Brace Beemer and the mythical character, the Lone Ranger, carries on."[106] These documents played a hand in JWC's successful injunction against Moore in the late 1970s.

Despite the court ruling in JWC's favor, however, Moore refused to go quietly into the night. He swapped his mask for a pair of thick-rimmed sunglasses and vowed to continue making public appearances. Through the press, Moore also took the battle to the court of public opinion. Appearing on nearly one hundred radio talk shows over a two-week period, Moore successfully mobilized hardcore Lone Ranger fans, who, according to Chadwick Allen, collected nearly one million signatures for a petition to boycott *LLR*.[107] Moore's successful outreach efforts were partly built on his appearances throughout the decade at dozens of nostalgia conventions, which at the time served as hubs for fans to form a community outside of corporate reach and offered them intimate access to the former stars of their favorite programs. Long before events like the San Diego Comic-Con became industry promotional platforms, comic book and nostalgia conventions served as important sites for challenging corporate creative authority and control.

Moore leveraged his popularity not only to resist JWC's efforts to shut him down, but also to actively challenge the company's cultural authority as the Lone Ranger's proper stewards. As Moore explained to *New York Times* reporter Robert Lindsey, "I have no animosity toward the Wrather people, but I just hope and pray they live up to the moral code of Clayton Moore for the last thirty years."[108] Similarly conflating Moore with the character he portrayed, one protest letter described him as "more than a character or a role, he is a symbol of what our American ideals strive to be—fair, just, heroic, brave, and courageous against all evil, negative forces regardless. One other man is in this lofty category, the Duke (John Wayne), AMERICAN. Certainly when Wayne reached the age Clayton Moore is more or less, no one proposed a younger John Wayne—to fit some ridiculous youth oriented junior executive's idea of what would sell movies."[109]

JWC responded to fan protest letters by asserting its corporate authorial responsibility to protect both the public and the property from harm. Denying the claim that they were "simply callous 'property owners,'" JWC instead described themselves as "custodians of a precious part of American history, of mythology deeply rooted in and profoundly affecting the lives of Americans for the past fifty years."[110] Acknowledging public sympathy for Moore by spuriously comparing the backlash to that encountered by Moore himself in the 1950s when he took over the Lone Ranger role from Brace Beemer, JWC sought to chastise long-standing fans for their unwillingness to let their children have their own version of the hero: "Yet, can we deny the children of today . . . *their* Lone Ranger? Surely they deserve to grow up with the example before them of a youthful, virile man whom they can strive to emulate, one who seeks justice, who fights for law and order, who speaks out for what is right and fair. It is not the man behind the mask, it is the *Lone Ranger* and *what he stands for* that is important."[111]

JWC attempted to position itself as an intermediary capable of speaking on behalf of the property and its stakeholders and translating their respective values for one another. Yet public rejection of JWC's paternalism speaks to the tenuous cultural authority corporate authors possess when they stray too far from their own stated objectives. Brown, Kozinets, and Sherry Jr. argue that current retro-branding strategies require brand managers to co-create meanings with an active and participatory brand community.[112] Similarly, Adam Arvidsson suggests that brand managers must shift away from trying to teach consumers about appropriate uses for particular products and properties toward finding ways to monetize the meanings that community members assign to brands.[113] Whereas Trendle and LRI worked to create controlled environments for Lone Ranger brand participation, JWC encountered a community of brand loyalists seeking a more active say in how the Masked Man was to be interpreted and willing to boycott product extensions that they felt sullied their investment in the brand.

As such, it might be argued that *LLR*'s failure was not so much a sign that the Lone Ranger's popularity was declining, but rather, a demonstration of its brand community's efforts to hold JWC accountable for its mismanagement of the property. In an article celebrating the delayed release of the film as a sign that the "Good Guys [were] Winning the 'Lone Ranger' Battle," Gary Deeb asserted, "The Wrather Corp.'s cavalier treatment of Moore is the major cause of the poor box office expectations for the movie."[114] Though it is clear that JWC was deeply invested in maintaining the Lone Ranger's brand essence on screen, their casting decisions coupled with their mishandling of Clayton Moore reframed the corporation as untrustworthy and disloyal to both the Lone Ranger ethos and those who were invested in upholding it, namely Moore and his fan base. Or, as Deeb exclaimed, "Who the devil wants to see some 25-year-old punk playing the Lone Ranger—especially when the people who hired him have done everything possible to hurt Clayton Moore?"[115]

Most press coverage described the battle between Moore and JWC as akin to an entrepreneurial David versus a greedy corporate Goliath. As Walter Coblenz would later note while reflecting on the bad publicity that surrounded *LLR*'s release, "The Wrather organization won their day in court, but sometimes that's not how things work in America. Clayton became almost a folk hero."[116] Deeb elaborated, "The little guy, in the guise of an aging journeyman actor, is berating the pants off the Giant, in the guise of a nasty corporation. And as the story plays out, a nationwide audience of millions sits back and watches Good triumph over Evil."[117] In the midst of an economic recession, with jobless rates reaching a high of 10.8 percent in 1982 and many corporations cutting ties with long-term employees in order to keep profit margins high by pursuing cheaper labor abroad, the JWC/Moore struggles were repeatedly reframed as a test of the American workers' ability to retain their rights. One article even recounted how demand for Moore's labor had significantly increased during the scandal, with multiple commercials in the works for Jeno's Pizza, Ford pick-ups, the Texas Rangers baseball club, and Corning Optical sunglasses. While *LLR* struggled at the box office, Moore was able to triple his public appearance fee to $3,000.[118]

Hence, it might be concluded that Moore and his advocates were able to accomplish what JWC could not: namely, to channel nostalgia for a heritage brand while successfully updating its meanings to reflect contemporary concerns. Through Moore's continued embodiment of the character, the Lone Ranger was transformed—from an advocate for corporate America into a champion for workers' rights, entrepreneurial labor, and fans' struggles to wrestle control over their hero from the clutches of greedy businessmen—all the while appearing unaltered from his past depictions. Moore was able to parlay this image into multiple endorsements for companies seeking to tap into anticorporate and populist sentiment. JWC eventually dropped the injunction in 1984, allowing Moore to once again don the Lone Ranger mask in public appearances.

LLR's box office troubles were certainly exacerbated by the bad PR heaped on the film and its producers because of the poorly handled transition from Moore to Spilsbury. But ITC's financial troubles in the wake of *Raise the Titanic* also played a significant part in *LLR*'s quick exit from theaters. To stay solvent, ITC sold the distribution rights to its most prominent productions, including *LLR*, to Universal Studios.[119] JWC complained that the deal ITC struck placed *LLR* in a precarious position because Universal was not required to invest any capital in marketing the film but was still guaranteed 30 percent of every dollar *LLR* grossed.[120] That meant the studio had no reason to keep the film afloat if it did not immediately yield positive returns, since it earned revenue no matter what the box office take was. Indeed, while Universal initially released *LLR* into 1,018 theaters, the studio also quickly abandoned promoting the film in the face of the negative attention it received, pulling the movie after only five weeks.[121]

While JWC barely recouped its financial investment in the film, the company was quick to differentiate the character's value from the managerial errors made in rebooting it. Stunell explained, "I'm fond of saying, 'The Lone Ranger' is bigger than all of us, and he'll live longer than all of us. Just as I'm the, so to speak, current 'caretaker,' I imagine when I'm long-gone there'll still be somebody performing this function."[122]

Conclusion

Throughout this chapter, I've argued that heritage brands, while lucrative, also pose complex managerial challenges because of their need to consistently strike the right balance between nostalgia and innovation. In focusing on 1960s television and 1970s Hollywood blockbusters, I've also suggested that the rewards and pitfalls associated with heritage brands are not new phenomena.

The Lone Ranger's apparent decline in popularity at a moment when nostalgia brands were otherwise quite popular might be attributed to a general loss of interest in the Western genre among consumers. Michael Cimino's epic Western *Heaven's Gate*, released one year prior to *LLR*, reportedly earned back less than 10 percent of its $44 million budget.[123] In 1981, the year *LLR* was released, only five Westerns were produced by Hollywood studios, as compared to twenty-three a decade earlier. Indeed, only sixteen traditional Westerns would be released by Hollywood over the course of the 1980s, though there were several comedic (*Draw!* [1984], *Lust in the Dust* [1985], *Three Amigos!* [1986], *Sunset* [1988]), contemporary (*Urban Cowboy* [1980], *Hard Country* [1983], *The Milagro Beanfield War* [1988]), and sci-fi (*The Aurora Encounter* [1986]; *Near Dark* [1987]) variations.

But as I have also demonstrated, much of the difficulty JWC encountered in revitalizing the property resulted either from limitations placed on how the Lone Ranger could be adapted or from the company's unintended antagonism toward its brand community. Though JWC was quite open to reworking the property, it was unsuccessful either in proposing Lone Ranger concepts that gelled with network programming and scheduling practices or in mobilizing the Masked Man's fan base. Thus, the property's difficulties might be attributed to both structural constraints placed on innovations and shifting power dynamics between corporate owners, creative labor, and brand loyalists. This resulted in a rejection of *LLR* but not necessarily the Lone Ranger.

Indeed, a similar case might be made for the 2002 Lone Ranger backdoor pilot that aired on the WB network. The Lone Ranger was, by then, under new management by Classic Media Incorporated (CMI) (see next chapter), and its owners entered into a development deal with Warner Brothers Television to produce an updated Lone Ranger series as part of Warner's new multiplexing strategy. Warner wanted to create programming that could be recycled across its cable holdings, and in particular, could be viewed on both the WB and TNT channels. Since they catered to two very different audiences, tweens and adults 18–49 respectively, Warner sought out heritage brands that could appeal on different levels to these dual demographics. *Smallville* was the gauge used in measuring success, or, as *Variety* (April 1, 2002) explained, "The strong numbers behind WB's 'Smallville' prove that even musty old franchises can still hit, but only if you can come in with a fresh take."[124]

Like its predecessor, CMI was open to updating the property and approved changes that brought the Lone Ranger more in line with the product conventions favored by WB. The pilot depicted an unproven Lone Ranger in his late teens predominantly without his trademark mask; played up romantic tensions between the protagonist and Tonto's sister, including a seminude romp in a makeshift nineteenth-century hot tub; incorporated thematic references to contemporary teen culture, such as having the hero go on a "spirit quest" that looked a lot like getting stoned; and featured a pop/rock soundtrack drawn from Warner's music catalog. In other words, it faithfully mimicked *Smallville*'s formula, and was largely panned by critics for doing so, with one reviewer mockingly referring to the pilot as "Dawson's Reservation," a reference to the WB's *Dawson's Creek*, which patented the network's programming style.[125]

Not a single review claimed that the Lone Ranger was unsellable—quite the opposite. Several argued that renewed patriotic verve in a post-9/11 America made the moment ripe with opportunity for heroes steeped in Americana.[126] Ultimately, the Lone Ranger pilot was deemed a failure because of its tonal inconsistencies, its "ham-fisted attempts to be 'cool' and relevant to the network's teen-age core audience" at the expense of staying true to the character's brand essence.[127] The failed WB pilot, much like *LLR* two decades before, was perceived to be a misalignment of brand and product conventions that failed to resonate with an existent or emergent Lone Ranger fan community.

JWC's difficulties also point to a shifting relationship between corporate overseers and consumers, wherein the rise to prominence of more formalized and organized fan communities in the 1970s generated new expectations that corporations should be as beholden to the brand communities they serviced as they were to the properties they managed. Ultimately, it was JWC's failure to take the Lone Ranger's core fan base into account that proved detrimental to extending the brand's reach with new consumers, not its unwillingness to innovate the Lone Ranger formula. In many ways, JWC's encounters with the Lone Ranger's fan community are indicative of contemporary efforts to revitalize heritage brands, wherein a long history of consumer loyalty is often both boon and bane to managerial attempts to rejuvenate a property. Many contemporary heritage brand owners have found the reboot path laden with anxieties over balancing the desires of older and newer consumers, in turn producing new tactics for navigating fan expectations.

Star Trek fan loyalty is legendary, but it has not always extended to the purchase of officially licensed merchandise or the embrace of corporate-sanctioned texts. A great deal of Star Trek community consumption revolves around fan-created content, whether fan fiction or homemade props. This has left the property's owners, CBS and Universal Studios, trying to figure out how to translate the franchise's value with fans into actual monetary value.

The 2009 *Star Trek* reboot borrowed heavily from fan-inspired works, telling an alternate timeline story that played up both action and romance. The hope was that this strategy would both appease Trekkers and allow the franchise to shed a lot of continuity baggage. In so doing, director J. J. Abrams skillfully positioned himself in media interviews as a non-Trekker with a distinct appreciation for fan cultures. Abrams neither claimed to know better than Trek fans, nor to be a guardian of Trek lore (as JWC mistakenly did with the Lone Ranger), but rather self-identified as someone with fannish sensibilities who could give consumers the kind of story they had been clamoring for. As Abrams opined, "The whole point was to try to make this movie for fans of movies, not fans of 'Star Trek,' necessarily. . . . If you're a fan, we've got one of the writers who's a devout Trekker, so we were able to make sure we were serving the people who are completely enamored with 'Star Trek.' But we are not making the movie for that contingent alone."[128]

Universal and Abrams were also quick to cast actor Leonard Nemoy in a significant role and seek his opinion in casting his successor. As Nemoy later explained, "I could see Zach [Quinto] had an internal life as an actor, which is important to the Spock character, because there's so little to show physically. . . . I called J. J. and immediately told him he was going to work."[129] While such claims clearly serve the interests of Star Trek's franchise owners in publicizing the film, they are also the product of shifting industrial lore when it comes to imagining what consumers want from their entertainment experiences. Industry insiders now define their relationship to fandom quite differently than in previous eras. Where JWC sought to scold and educate fans on how to appreciate the Lone Ranger's value, many contemporary brand managers are far more open to (regulated) fan participation, and are also much more likely to self-identify as fans themselves, as members (with benefits) of the very communities they are seeking to engage and exploit.

CHAPTER 7

The Lone Ranger and the Mouse House Together at Last? New Twenty-First-Century Partnerships in the Licensing Biz

Introduction

On March 7, 2012, superstar executive producer Jerry Bruckheimer tweeted, "What's coming will show you why this isn't going to be your grandfather's Lone Ranger and Tonto. . . ."[1] A day later, Bruckheimer tweeted, "Tonto and the Lone Ranger ride again!" along with a publicity photo taken on location in Albuquerque, New Mexico, of actors Johnny Depp and Armie Hammer dressed in full regalia on their first day of shooting.[2] Shot from a low angle, the image depicts Hammer as the Lone Ranger clad in a black suit and mask, white Stetson hat, and Texas Ranger star badge, looking statuesque and staring off into the distance astride Silver.

Beside him is Depp as Tonto, face painted in white and black stripes with a stuffed crow sitting atop his head. Tonto is eying the Lone Ranger with a look that seems to express a cross between disdain and distrust. Depp's appearance quickly became an online sensation. According to Google, the image was filtered to over 1.6 million web pages, many specializing in entertainment and celebrity news (see Figure 7.1).[3]

On the surface, this bit of promotional buzz seems completely in line with contemporary viral marketing practices that make use of social media to conscript brand enthusiasts to help spread the gospel. Of course, as I've argued throughout this book, the use of promotional paratexts to cultivate investment in particular character brands is not new, nor is the attempt to get a brand community to engage in free forms of publicity. Indeed, even Bruckheimer's claim that the latest version of the Lone Ranger is a far cry from the one revered by the silent generation seems like a classic retro-branding tactic: evoking the past to call attention to dissimi-

Figure 7.1. On March 8, 2012, Jerry Bruckheimer tweeted this promotional image for the 2013 *The Lone Ranger* motion picture.

larities, which in turn also highlight the property's longevity and brand essence. Indeed, the tweeted image differentiated Bruckheimer's Masked Man from his predecessors' largely through intertextual nods to the property's most iconic representatives, Clayton Moore and Jay Silverheels. To understand how this was *not* grandpa's Lone Ranger, the image purposely referenced grandpa's Lone Ranger (see Figure 7.2).

A common practice since the late 1930s, by the early 1950s most promotional stills for the Lone Ranger featured him accompanied by Tonto and Silver, often keenly observing something happening just beyond the frame. As noted in Chapter 5, these images were carefully orchestrated to depict the Lone Ranger as a man of action, as well as to highlight the loyal partnership he had with Tonto. The Bruckheimer image was carefully selected to simultaneously recall and subvert this storied set of associations. In this regard, Bruckheimer successfully brought to the foreground both brand continuity and differentiation by showcasing key Lone Ranger attributes while hinting at a shift in the relationship between these elements. The component parts of the Lone Ranger formula remained intact yet reordered.

Of course, George Trendle would have likely been aghast at the less than reverent look Tonto gives the Lone Ranger, not to mention Bruckheimer's "gaffe" in giving Tonto top billing in his tweet. Trendle vehemently objected to Lone Ranger publicity photos that challenged the Masked Man's carefully cultivated image as mythic hero, which he perceived as a challenge to the authority exercised by LRI in managing the Lone Ranger's publicity. As such, to focus solely on continuity in the licensing game not only runs counter to the overarching argument of this book—that what looks similar on the surface is, in fact, historically contingent—but it also overlooks several profound changes to the fields of character licensing and merchandising that have produced new occupational purviews for brand managers and new challenges to their creative, cultural, and institutional authority.

That Bruckheimer acknowledged Tonto's primacy captures two fundamental changes in how the twenty-first-century Lone Ranger is being managed: First, and in more than one way, the Lone Ranger is not the star of *The Lone Ranger*. As portrayed by Johnny Depp, there can be little doubt that in Bruckheimer's "take" on the Masked Man's adventures, Tonto was the film's bona fide star. Not only did Depp's celebrity status outweigh Hammer's, but marketing for the film repeatedly emphasized both Depp's and Bruckheimer's attachment to the project as key promotional devices. In comparison, LRI and JWC sought to diminish Clayton Moore's association with the role, and to elevate the Lone Ranger above the performer

Figure 7.2. Bruckheimer's tweeted photo clearly evokes previous Lone Ranger publicity stills even as it seeks to distinguish the current iteration from its predecessors. These two promotional stills were used by LRI and JWC in marketing the 1950s *Lone Ranger* TV series.

who acted out his adventures. And while these efforts were largely unsuccessful in severing Moore's association with the role, they nonetheless participated in a mythologizing process that granted greater significance to the Lone Ranger as symbolic brand than to Moore's embodiment of the role. Simply put, though a lot of fans saw Clayton Moore as the Lone Ranger, the Lone Ranger was never thought to be Clayton Moore. Yet today, there appears to be little qualm about privileging Depp's star persona as key to revitalizing Tonto.

Second, Bruckheimer had far greater leeway in promoting the Lone Ranger than did Jack Chertok in the 1950s or even Walter Coblenz in the 1980s, when all publicity was filtered through LRI and JWC. A star persona in his own right, Bruckheimer as licensee (he optioned the film rights in 2007) was given a great deal of creative and managerial authority in shaping public perception of the brand's value by the Lone Ranger's then IP owner, Classic Media Incorporated (CMI). CMI was an entertainment rights firm with an established portfolio of characters, including the Lone Ranger, The Green Hornet, Lassie, Gumby, Felix the Cat, Where's Waldo, VeggieTales, Harvey Entertainment Properties (Casper the Friendly Ghost, Richie Rich, Baby Huey), the Jay Ward Productions characters (Rocky and Bullwinkle, George of the Jungle, Dudley Do-Right), and Rankin/Bass's pre-1974 library (Rudolph the Red-Nosed Reindeer, Frosty the Snowman), plus dozens of other brands.[4] In 2010 CMI earned \$19.2 million in profits based on \$82.2 million in royalty revenues generated from \$325 million in retail sales of licensed merchandise based on these properties.[5] The company ranked 67th on *License Global!*'s list of the top 125 licensing operations.[6] CMI made no pretense to having "created" any of its properties, or to "producing" anything with them, but rather, defined its role strictly as managing, facilitating, and overseeing their continued circulation and extension through licensing.[7] CMI ceded creative and merchandising control of the Lone Ranger to Bruckheimer and long-time distributor Disney as part of the licensing arrangement.

On the one hand, this apparent shift in power from licensor to licensee points to a reconfiguration in the relationship between IP owners and the talent they employ to extend character brands. Whereas LRI in the 1930s sought to facilitate localizable and customizable encounters between the Lone Ranger and its investors and in the 1950s redefined its role as policing how licensees translated the property, licensors today like to play matchmaker, pairing properties with the best available talent—in essence, surrounding them with "good people/partners" with preestablished star/authorial personas and brand recognition. CMI actively promoted Bruckheimer's and Depp's attachment to the project as key indicators of the property's renewed relevance. This is the essence of "creative management" practices designed to increase brand equity by generating opportunities for talent to invest their labor and then seeking to monetize those inspirations.

On the other hand, CMI's ceding its creative authority to Bruckheimer also potentially points to the diminished position held by independent IP brokers within an increasingly conglomerated entertainment complex. Pierre Bourdieu has suggested that one's position within the field of cultural production influences both the tactics one is likely to employ—what Bourdieu calls "position-takings"—and one's perceived occupational identity, or disposition.[8] Most character-licensing operations are now divisions within horizontally integrated media conglomerates. In contrast, CMI was almost entirely dependent upon licensees with significant production and distribution resources to place its properties in front of consumers, which in turn necessitated a renegotiation of its creative authority. CMI assigned the Walt Disney Corporation all distribution and merchandising rights for *The Lone Ranger* in exchange for its financing Bruckheimer's film. In turn, Disney partnered with powerful licensees like Lego, who also exercised some degree of influence over film production.

CMI's hands-off approach to Bruckheimer's tweet is indicative of a softening of managerial oversight toward licensees as well as consumers. Even as Bruckheimer's efforts to build anticipation for a Lone Ranger feature film borrowed from tactics employed by LRI decades earlier, there can be little doubt that as he encouraged followers to retweet and circulate the publicity photo online, control over the meanings and interpretations of this image slipped from his and CMI's hands and were taken up by an eclectic network of evaluators, tastemakers, and other intermediaries. Partly a response to convergence culture's celebration of "participation" and "spreadability,"[9] these sorts of social media marketing campaigns can be fraught with tensions for IP owners who see fan communities as possessing a "contested utility,"[10] useful in generating seemingly "authentic" buzz about brand extensions but also in need of managerial guidance to bring their activities "under capital."[11]

In this chapter, I situate CMI's practices within the current character-licensing field. I argue that while the objectives of character licensing and brand management remain similar, with many of the tactics introduced over the past eighty years now being industrial norms, the field as a whole has experienced tremendous change in status and impact on creative decision making within Hollywood. In particular, I explore the shifting power dynamics between licensors, licensees, retailers, and social media influencers, which have, in turn, led to an embrace of new creative management tactics on the parts of brand managers. As befits the Lone Ranger's diminished status in the contemporary era, the property and its owners make few appearances in this broad overview. In the second half of the chapter, however, I situate adjustments made to the Lone Ranger brand over the past decade within shifting licensor-licensee relations. I argue that these new partnerships engage in a type of co-branding between property and talent that is essential to promoting both parties. I end with a case study on the prerelease promotion for *The Lone Ranger*, looking at how marketing for both film and merchandise attempted to position the property's reputation in relation to those of its current brand partners, in turn redefining the Lone Ranger's cultural value and brand equity. I must also note that in the midst of my drafting this chapter, CMI was acquired by DreamWorks for $155 million.[12] I explore the broad implications of this deal in the conclusion to this chapter.

The Current State of the Field

Character licensing and merchandising are essential components of how the contemporary entertainment industries operate, generating and sustaining cross-media franchises and cultivating investments among globally dispersed brand communities. Rather than seeing them emerging as by-products of media conglomeration and convergence, I have argued throughout this book that such industrial restructuring partly builds on the groundwork laid by earlier generations of brand managers and IP owners. Yet as licensing becomes more commonplace as an industry driver, the contemporary character-licensing environment has become far more comprehensive and complex than at any prior time, with new configurations of authority emerging in response to the cultural and industrial particularities of the current moment.

Retail sales of licensed goods in the United States and Canada in 2011 totaled $109.3 billion and earned IP owners $5.316 billion in royalty revenue.[13] Globally, licensed merchandise is estimated to account for $187 billion, or 5 percent of all retail sales, with many experts believing those numbers to be underreported.[14] Character and entertainment brand licensing accounted for 43.86 percent of all retail sales of licensed merchandise at $48 billion, while earning property owners $2.48 billion in

Table 7.1. Top Twenty Licensed Franchises, 2011

Franchise	*Retail Sales of Licensed Merchandise in the U.S.*
1. Disney Princess (Disney)	$1.60 billion
2. Star Wars (Lucasfilm)	$1.50 billion
3. Pooh (Disney)	$1.09 billion
4. Cars (Disney)	$1.05 billion
5. Hello Kitty (Sanrio)	$800 million
6. Mickey & Friends (Disney)	$750 million
7. WWE (WWE)	$700 million
8. Toy Story (Disney)	$685 million
9. Peanuts (Iconix, Peanuts Worldwide)	$600 million
10. Sesame Street (Sesame Workshop)	$515 million
11. Disney Fairies (Disney)	$435 million
12. Thomas the Tank Engine (Hit Entertainment)	$390 million
13. Garfield (Paws Inc.)	$370 million
14. Dora the Explorer (Nickelodeon)	$330 million
15. SpongeBob (Nickelodeon)	$330 million
16. Spider-Man (Marvel/Disney)	$325 million
17. Ben 10 (Cartoon Network)	$295 million
18. Angry Birds (Rovio)	$250 million
19. Batman (DC/Warner)	$245 million
20. Barbie (Mattel)	$242 million

royalty revenue.[15] Unsurprisingly, kids' properties continue to dominate the character-licensing field. In 2005, children under 14 spent $40 billion annually and pressured their parents to spend an additional $500 billion annually on merchandise.[16] Brand-licensed toy sales alone accounted for $22.3 billion in consumer spending.[17] If children's properties dominate the character-licensing business, then heritage brands continue to be perceived as key to cultivating new consumers through nostalgic appeals to parents.

Table 7.1 lists the top twenty entertainment brand licenses by sales in 2011. In total, thirty-seven licensed franchises earned at least $100 million, with four franchises exceeding the $1 billion mark (Disney Princesses, Star Wars, Winnie the Pooh, Disney's Cars), three of which at the time were Disney properties (now all four are). Indeed, seven of the top twenty licensed franchises were Disney brands. As *Forbes*'s Jenna Goudreau notes, the majority of the properties on the list are at least twenty-five years old, making them "culturally entrenched characters that people grew up with and then introduced to their children."[18] The Lone Ranger's absence from this list is an indication of the property's declining value among consumers, though not necessarily among licensees.

The "evergreen," or the property that never loses its value, is reified within industry lore as both timeless and ever-adaptable to changing trends, possessing qualities that transcend generation, and it can also be refurbished without losing its brand essence. Or, as Deborah Forte, president of Scholastic Media, owners of classic IP like Clifford the Big Red Dog, I Spy, and The Magic School Bus, explains, "Particularly in the kids' market, if you have a stable of evergreen brands, it's like having an annuity. You are not starting from scratch in terms of your investment or your relationship with your customer and you always have a new crop of consumers coming in."[19]

The More Things Change . . .

As in the past, product extensions require careful mediation, especially when children are involved. According to the Nick Jr. website, Dora the Explorer "teaches children how to observe situations and solve problems as they explore Dora's world with her. Along the way, kids learn basic Spanish words and phrases, as well as math skills, music, and physical coordination."[20] The property repeatedly finds ways to infuse its educational and cultural diversity messages into every product that is licensed using its image. A photo on the website of a young girl adorned in a Dora T-shirt explains to parents how such items can "help your kids learn the lessons of sharing & caring."[21] Meanwhile, the more overtly commercial Cars franchise not only sells certain types of products (action figures, DVDs, video games, and clothing, to name just a few), it also sells certain types of images related to boys' play culture and masculinity. For example, the "Lightning McQueen Mechanics Shirt for Toddler Boys," which is *only* available for boys, inspires its wearers to become "budding mechanics" as well as "Disney *Cars* fan[s]."[22] Though media scholars might question either the ideological efficacy of these claims or how well they translate into what children actually "do" with these properties, what cannot be denied is corporate management's attempt to align the economic and social values of these properties under its purview. Though such practices date back decades, as evidenced by LRI's attempts to market the Lone Ranger's virtues in helping to promote healthfulness in children (whether through the Lone Ranger Safety Clubs or as a form of psychosomatic medicine), it is also important to note how IP value is reconfigured according to pervading social mores.

For example, in 2007, American Greetings Properties, owners of Strawberry Shortcake, decided to give their property a "fruit-forward" makeover when they began encountering difficulties selling the relevance of their candy-obsessed bloomer-wearing character. While Brooks Barnes claims that Strawberry Shortcake was not connecting with modern girls, it is probably more accurate to say that it was not connecting with potential licensees seeking to tap into that market.[23] Licensees feared that the nutritionally and fashion-challenged character did not resonate with prevailing discourses on child rearing that stressed the importance of healthy eating and the desirability of toys that help children learn the value of personal expression through commodity consumption. So, American Greetings modernized Strawberry Shortcake's wardrobe and replaced her calico cat accessory with a cell phone. The licensor also decided to downplay the character's sugary shortcake junk food associations and instead emphasize its all-natural strawberry goodness. They also redrew the curvature of her body, transforming her from a diminutive girl with baby fat into a slim fashionista-in-training. In order to test out the character's new look, American Greetings organized focus groups consisting of its licensing partners (as opposed to consumers) to determine which changes were likely to inspire future investment in the brand.[24]

And misalignment of entertainment-based properties and merchandise can still elicit consumer ire. A 2003 Hulk plush doll licensed by Play-by-Play Toys came under fire from consumers because it featured an exaggeratedly large bulge in the green monster's genital area (measured at 2 inches on a 12-inch tall doll), which was seen as inappropriate for children and led to demands that the product be taken off the shelf.[25] Similarly, Disney was taken to task for licensing *High School Musical* underwear for young girls with the slogan "Dive In" emblazoned on them.[26] When character brands become overly associated with products or companies that have fallen out of consumer favor, licensors must work to distance their properties from these negative associations or risk sharing in their tainted reputations. Many IP owners have backed away from licensing arrangements with confectioners as that industry has come under heavy scrutiny from the Food and Drug Administration for contributing to childhood obesity. Since 2001, character-licensed foods and drinks have been halved.[27] In 2008, Nickelodeon introduced a no-junk-food policy for its licensed characters, following Disney's lead two years earlier.[28] While licensors have sought to transform the dissipating market for sweets by rebranding their properties as embodying healthful qualities—Looney Tunes characters have been featured on "Eating Right Kids" foods and beverages[29]—this is not always an easy fit, particularly when character brands have long-established histories with unhealthy sweets. Hence, Disney's efforts to license Mickey Mouse as the face of Tesco's fresh fruit snacks was generally regarded as a failure; the association "lacked an element of credibility because of Disney's strong associations with confectionary."[30]

Similarly, managing evergreen properties is continually framed by licensors as needing to carefully strike a balance between innovation and preserving brand essence. As Forte explains, "What people remember about Scholastic products is trust: parents believe in them, teachers rely on them, kids enjoy them. . . . It's a big responsibility and our customers hold us to a higher standard."[31] Rhetorically, this often means gesturing to the past as both an assurance of quality and an indicator of the brand's long history of being forward thinking. An ad placed by I Love Lucy IP licensor Unforgettable Licensing appearing in the trade magazine *License Global!* captures this convergence of past and future success, stating, "Many say that the comedy made famous by LUCY was ahead of its time, and the brand stays on trend by expanding into new platforms like social media . . . after all, who's more social than Lucy and Ethel?"[32] In 2008, more than eight hundred *I Love Lucy* items were available for sale, ranging from key chains to collector-edition Barbie dolls and DVD sets.[33] In 2012, the number of products had risen to over two thousand, largely marketed to women aged 18–54.[34]

Trade talk will also play up how the universal qualities possessed by evergreen brands supposedly transcend generational boundaries. These qualities are positioned as part of a property's unchanging brand essence, whereas design, product, or platform changes are merely intended to provide updated ways of connecting consumers with those qualities. For example, Rich Magallanes, senior vice president for Nickelodeon Animation, gave the following explanation for Viacom's decision to reboot the Teenage Mutant Ninja Turtles property; it was less an admission that earlier iterations were not resonating with target consumers than a desire to improve on an already universally revered concept: "The TMNT series has always had buzz—it never really died . . . we're not resurrecting this property, we're just hitting the reset button. We are trying hard to keep the integrity of the property and at the same time take it to the next level. . . . The Turtles are teenage brothers who are still kids and who are learning and growing into their shells . . . it's about being a kid and about not being perfect, but being OK with yourself."[35] Similarly, Jordan Sollitto, executive vice president of International Licensing for Warner Brothers Consumer Products (WBCP), predicted the success of the 2013 *Man of Steel* merchandising campaign precisely for the reason that "Superman is such an enduring superhero because what he represents is universal and timeless . . . the notion of standing up for what's right crosses borders, and never goes out of style."[36]

While John Caldwell reminds us that all of these self-serving public disclosures are primarily intended to improve brand position and should not, therefore, be taken as evidence of a property's true consumer appeal, the repeated discursive focus on universality and balancing past and future iterations is nonetheless significant in revealing how licensors imagine the qualities required of successful evergreens in order to be championed by licensees, retailers, and consumers.[37] Thus, it is perhaps unsurprising that marketing for the 2013 Lone Ranger film also seized hold of a series of universal truisms supposedly embodied by the Masked Man. Distributed via social media like Facebook and Twitter, the "Lone Ranger Code" included, "Fight for what's right: mind, body, and spirit," and "Respect the land. You'll be part of it one day."[38] These creeds purposely elided specific references to formula (as opposed to Tonto's infamous "Kemosabe" or the Lone Ranger's "Hi-Yo Silver! Away!"), while positioning the Lone Ranger as espousing values that would resonate with any potential filmgoer. Of course, what constitutes shared values is historically contingent. In the 1950s, the Lone Ranger stood for the American Heritage of corporate capitalism, not individualism and environmentalism. Typically, the focus on promoting universality obfuscates the many ways in which character brands are refurbished to meet prevailing standards of what constitutes shared value systems.

Licensors continue to position themselves as intermediaries tasked with speaking on behalf of the property and translating its core attributes. Much as LRI and JWC sought to explain to licensees, creative labor, and consumers what made the Lone Ranger tick, Brian Deputy, vice president of Worldwide Creative for WBCP, explains, "We were held to a very high standard to faithfully and authentically communicate Superman's true essence in our creative approach for the *Man of Steel* style guide. . . . The approach was unique in that instead of starting out with the question, 'what does Superman look like?,' we had to ask, 'Who is he?'"[39]

Institutionalizing Licensors and Centering in on Brands

It is not simply that character licensing is a lucrative component of the current media mix, but that IP management has become central to how the contemporary entertainment industry operates. This is particularly the case within certain industry subsets where IP value has eclipsed product value, though increasingly, entertainment conglomerates are being reorganized in ways that place brands at the core of their business. For example, the comic book industry has seen steady sales declines since the collectors market bust in the early 1990s.[40] But as of 2011, the DC Comics library alone has generated $16 billion in revenue for WBCP.[41] According to its 2007 Annual Report for stockholders, Marvel Entertainment, while still the top-selling comic book publisher in the United States, is actually "one of the world's most prominent character-based entertainment companies, with a proprietary library of over 5,000 characters."[42] Recognizing that their intellectual property holdings are their "most valuable asset," Marvel's "growth strategy" now revolves around increasing the exposure of its characters through various media outlets (films, television, video games, comic books), which in turn generates revenue opportunities through the increased toy and merchandise licenses accompanying each new release.[43]

Inverting the common assumption that licensed merchandise is an ancillary profit source, Marvel views the various stories told about its characters as primarily a means for generating new merchandising opportunities for its various IP brands. In 2007, over 70 percent of the company's revenue, at $343.6 million, was earned through licensing.[44] In September 2009, Disney bought Marvel for $4 billion with the intention of exploiting Marvel's stable of superhero characters to make greater inroads with young male consumers, perceived to be more interested in Spider-Man than Mickey Mouse.[45] In 2010, Marvel ranked sixth in the world in character/entertainment brand licensing, with Marvel licenses accounting for $4.9 billion in retail sales.[46] In 2011, Marvel licenses generated $6 billion in retail sales, though the company's earnings were now listed as part of Disney's top-ranking $37.5 billion.[47]

In 2012, Disney's consumer products division underwent a significant restructuring indicative of how brands rather than products now drive the entertainment industry business model. Newly appointed head of consumer products, Bob Chapek, reorganized the division around particular franchises as opposed to product categories. Where before there had been

Table 7.2. Media Conglomerate Rankings in Sales of Licensed Merchandise

Company	*2011 Rank*	*Global Sales Licensed Merch.*	*Key Properties*
Disney	1	$37.5 billion	Mickey Mouse & Friends, Princess Line, Winnie the Pooh, Pixar characters (Cars, Toy Story), Marvel Universe
Warner Brothers	5	$6 billion	DC Comics characters, Looney Tunes
Nickelodeon	6	$5.5 billion	Dora the Explorer, SpongeBob SquarePants
DreamWorks	14	$3 billion	Shrek, Kung Fu Panda, Madagascar
Cartoon Network	19	$2.9 billion	Adventure Time, Dexter's Laboratory, The Powerpuff Girls
Twentieth Century Fox	24	$2.2 billion	Family Guy, The Simpsons
BBC	27	$1.7 billion	Doctor Who, Sherlock Holmes
NBC Universal	34	$1.3 billion	Law & Order, Tonight Show, Community, The Office
Sony	47	$1 billion	Jeopardy, Seinfeld, The Sing-Off
ITV	66	$410 million	Coronation Street, Hell's Kitchen
ABC	67	$400 million	Castle, Scandal, Grey's Anatomy
CBS	77	$300 million	The Amazing Race, NCIS, Two and a Half Men
Food Network	86	$212 million	Chopped, Restaurant Impossible
ESPN	107	$125 million	ESPN brand

teams responsible for licensing the rights to toys, food, or clothing bearing Disney characters, now Disney's consumer products teams are organized around franchises like Disney Princesses, Classic Characters, Pixar animated films, and Marvel Entertainment. The new organization is intended to foster both closer relationships with production units at Disney in order to coordinate media and merchandising initiatives at the development phase, and to promote integrated merchandising campaigns that place brands rather than products at their center.[48]

A glance at the 2011 list of the top 125 global licensors reveals that all the major film studios and most television networks now operate their own in-house licensing division (see Table 7.2).[49]

Additionally, several top licensing operations are housed within companies that produce content for film and television, such as fifteenth-ranked Lucasfilm, which generated $3 billion in Star Wars merchandise sales (Star Wars still ranked #1 in boys toys and #2 overall in licensed toy sales in 2011, partly contributing to Disney's acquisition of the company in 2012), and twenty-eighth-ranked Sesame Street Workshop, whose merchandise sales were $1.7 billion.[50]

While content producers and distributors have developed in-house licensing operations designed to leverage their brands, the other type of organizational configuration popular among contemporary character brand owners focuses exclusively on IP extension and management. Though reliant upon media tentpoles (usually a film or TV series) to provide coverage for merchandising campaigns, such companies are also set up to be flexible in pursuing deals not tied directly to existing production infrastructures. Whereas most consumer product divisions linked to major studios and networks oversee dozens of properties, most independent IP companies tend to focus on only a handful of properties (CMI was somewhat of an exception in this regard), allowing these operations to focus on cultivating brand loyalty by generating more intimate relationships with licensees and brand communities (see Table 7.3).

While the tendency of late has been for large conglomerates to acquire independent IP companies, tying brand extension more directly to production and distribution chains, the consumer products divisions of these same conglomerates have also increasingly sought to emulate the flexible and intimate organizational cultures of the independents they are gobbling up. As such, Disney's Chapek explained the value of acquiring Marvel Entertainment not only in terms of adding popular IP that might attract male demographics, but also in terms of allowing Disney Consumer Products to absorb and re-create the organizational culture of a (relatively) smaller IP holder: "We are the largest licensor in the world—and size, scale and scope is important—but I want to be as nimble as a small company . . . that's the cultural value of our Marvel brand."[51]

Similarly, when Viacom acquired the Teenage Mutant Ninja Turtles property from the now defunct 4 Kids Entertainment for $60 million in 2009, this was done in the midst of a reorganization of Nickelodeon's consumer products division designed to make the division feel "small and agile," in turn fostering better relationships with its licensees.[52] As Michael Connolly, Viacom's head of International Consumer Products and Brand Licensing operations, explains, "We believe that our licensees know what they are doing. We can't go out there and design toys."[53] I will return to the shifting power dynamics between licensors and licensees later in the chapter.

Table 7.3. Top Independent Character-Licensing Operations Based on Merchandise Sales, 2011

Company	*2011 Rank*	*Global Sales Licensed Merch.*	*Key Properties*
Iconix	2	$11 billion	Peanuts, fashion
Sanrio	8	$5 billion	Hello Kitty
Rainbow	11	$3.8 billion	Winx, Pop Pixie
MGA Entertainment	29	$1.65 billion	Bratz, Lalaloopsy
Pokemon Company	30	$1.6 billion	Pokemon
Giochi Prezios	31	$1.5 billion	Gormiti
Nelvana	48	$1 billion	Babar
Marathon Media	55	$710 million	Redakai, Totally Spies
Classic Media	69	$376 million	Where's Waldo, Gumby, VeggieTales, Casper the Friendly Ghost, Lone Ranger, Green Hornet, Lassie, and many more
Saban Brands	70	$375 million	Mighty Morphin' Power Rangers
Studio 100	74	$334 million	Maya the Bee, Vicky the Viking
C3 Entertainment	87	$200 million	Three Stooges, Grizzly Adams
Entertainment One	88	$200 million	Peppa Pig
Viz Media	92	$200 million	Naruto
Big Tent Media	94	$182 million	Domo
The Wiggles	95	$180 million	The Wiggles
Ludorum	97	$157 million	Chuggington
Mind Candy	108	$125 million	Moshi Monsters
Suzy's Zoo	125	$60.4 million	Suzy's Zoo

Constituting Creativity

In the contemporary era, licensing and merchandising opportunities have also become increasingly constitutive of the kinds of creative decisions made in developing entertainment properties.

While brand extension has been crucial to Marvel's reconfiguration as an entertainment IP company (as opposed to just a comic book publisher), licensing agreements can also prove restrictive when it comes to franchise building, especially in managing the cross-media careers of character brands. After all, licensing contracts specify who gets to (legally) tell what kinds of stories involving preexisting characters or brands, under what conditions, and in what forms. Licensing agreements precede the production of many texts and delineate production terms. They stipulate both product and production conventions that either ensure brand consistency or spell out terms of deviation across markets. They set the parameters of textual and extra-textual innovation, enabling certain forms of storytelling while constraining others. For example, the film rights for two of Marvel's most successful properties, Spider-Man and the X-Men, are currently licensed to two different studios, Sony and 20th Century Fox, making it highly unlikely that these characters will team up with one another or with other unlicensed Marvel characters in their cinematic adventures. In comic book form, Marvel has developed an interwoven story world inhabited by all of its characters, which "permits [the company] to use the popularity of characters to more fully develop existing but lesser-known characters."[54] Such storytelling possibilities are interrupted by Marvel's licensing agreements with Sony and Fox, which allow all three companies to use only particular characters in their films.

These agreements were signed prior to Marvel's foray into film production, but continue to impact how the company translates its superhero universe to the screen. The rights to Spider-Man and the X-Men characters will not revert back to Marvel unless Sony and Fox miss their production deadlines. In fact, Sony scrapped plans to produce a fourth installment of the popular Spider-Man franchise because of negotiation delays with the project's director, Sam Raimi, that would have caused the studio to miss its license renewal deadline.[55] Instead, Sony opted to reboot the series with a new cast and creative team, exemplifying yet another way in which contemporary licensing agreements structure storytelling possibilities.

Licensing agreements are particularly pertinent in shaping stories that attempt to bring together properties from different owners. There are countless anecdotes of children combining discrete toy brands into shared story worlds through play, whether by having GI Joe date Barbie (or blow her up) or by pitting Transformers against GoBots. While the melding of discrete universes holds tremendous appeal for fan communities, such combining of separate IPs can pose challenges (as well as opportunities) to property owners.

In 1988, producer Stephen Spielberg, director Robert Zemeckis, and Disney's Touchstone Pictures successfully adapted Gary K. Wolf's novel *Who Censored Roger Rabbit?* The film, much like the book, is set in a world where famous cartoon characters not only coexist with humans, but also live together in a shared space called Toon Town. While the film was hailed at the time for its technological ingenuity, its true feat was in negotiating hundreds of licensing agreements with dozens of property owners that permitted these animated properties to share screen time. Legend has it that Spielberg convinced rival property owners to see the mutual benefit of working together by leasing out their characters for cameo appearances in the film for as little as $5,000.[56] In reality, hard-nosed negotiations shaped the film's development from storyboard to screen. Disney and Spielberg were unable to work out a deal with either the King Features Syndicate or Harvey Entertainment, resulting in the absence of iconic properties like Popeye and Casper the Friendly Ghost and the elimination of a key scene in the film.[57] Meanwhile, Warner's agreement with Disney stipulated that Bugs Bunny and Daffy Duck be given equal screen time with their cartoon rivals Mickey Mouse and Donald Duck. Hence, one of the centerpiece scenes in the film, where Bob Hoskins's private eye character, Eddie Haskell, first encounters Jessica Rabbit, showcases Donald and Daffy as dueling piano players at a nightclub. Mickey Mouse and Bugs Bunny also share a single scene in which they each fail to assist Haskell as he is plummeting off a cartoon skyscraper.[58]

Disney's Pixar Studios would encounter similar creative challenges in producing *Toy Story* (1995). Toy giants Mattel and Hasbro refused to license the rights to their Barbie and GI Joe properties (Hasbro did give permission for its Mr. Potato Head property).[59] Mattel reasoned that Barbie's appeal with young girls was the doll's lack of definable personality, which allowed girls to see older versions of themselves in it. Thus, Barbie's inclusion in the film risked undermining its perceived market appeal because it would assign the doll a particular voice.[60] Mattel's refusal necessitated a script rewrite since Barbie had been slated to make a key heroic appearance, helping Buzz Lightyear and Woody escape from toy torturer Sid.[61] Seeing the incredible box office and merchandising success generated by the film (*Toy Story* earned $361 million worldwide at the box office while 25 million Buzz and Woody action figures have been sold over the past 15 years[62]), Mattel would shift its corporate philosophy when it came time for the Toy Story sequels, and Barbie has featured prominently in *Toy Story 2* and *3*. Meanwhile, Hasbro declined to license the right to GI Joe because *Toy Story* featured a scene in which Sid blows up the toy soldier, which was seen as antithetical to the property's brand image.[63]

CMI's 2005 deal with comic book publisher Dynamite Entertainment gave the licensee complete creative freedom to tinker with the Lone Ranger formula, including pairing the property with some of its other licensed characters, eventually leading to the 2011 *Lone Ranger: The Death of Zorro* miniseries, which featured the Lone Ranger investigating Zorro's murder, linking together the timelines of two properties owned by different companies (Zorro is owned by Zorro Productions). It bears mentioning that Dynamite's creative freedom was less a result of its standing within the comic book industry than its relative position vis-à-vis particular property owners. While CMI's deal with Dynamite allowed the latter to pair the Lone Ranger with any Dynamite character, the arrangement Dynamite signed with Universal Studios for *Battlestar Galactica* comics explicitly prevented the publisher from linking the BSG universe with any other licensed properties, making an Adama-Tonto crossover highly unlikely.[64] Simply put, Universal felt it had more to lose than CMI. In all instances, the creative authority vested in licensees is either constrained or enabled (and sometimes both) by the licensing agreements they enter into.

Licensee Power and Creative Management

In the contemporary era, it is increasingly difficult to distinguish between companies that fall under the category of "licensor" versus "licensee," as many take on both roles, operating both inbound and outbound licensing programs, while others serve as licensing agents for other IP owners. For example, in 2012, Sony licensing division ranked forty-seventh worldwide, generating $1 billion in retail sales for properties like the Green Hornet, actually owned by CMI, and the Smurfs, owned by Belgium-based IMPS.[65] Sony licensed the film rights to both properties, as well as the merchandising rights, based on the film adaptations, and then proceeded to take on the role of consumer product licensor, sharing profits with both IP owners, but ultimately making all executive decisions about product extensions. Meanwhile, even as it privileged the outbound extension of its own IP, Marvel Entertainment operated an inbound licensing division that acquired comic book adaptation rights to popular franchises like Stephen King's *Dark Towers* or the ABC/Disney TV series *Castle*.[66]

Many of the world's leading toy licensees are also ranked among the world's top licensors. While competitors Mattel and Hasbro paid out over $400 million combined in licensing and royalty fees to the IP owners they worked with in 2012,[67] the companies also combined to generate $12.2 billion in licensed merchandise sales based on the outbound licensing of their own IP (i.e., merchandise based on properties like Barbie and Transformers that were manufactured by companies other than Mattel and Hasbro).[68] Mattel holds the global master toy license for all WBCP properties (Batman, Superman, The Hobbit, Looney Tunes, etc.), as well as exclusive deals to create toys and games based on properties owned by Disney,

DreamWorks, Nickelodeon, and the WWE.[69] It also generates tremendous revenue from licensing out the rights to Barbie, Hot Wheels, and Monsters High in categories like apparel, publishing, and sporting goods, earning the company fourth place on the 2012 Top Global Licensors list.[70] Mattel also acquired HIT Entertainment's Barney and Thomas the Train properties in 2012 for $680 million, after serving as their primary toy licensee for nearly a decade.[71] Evidencing how many large-scale manufacturers have also restructured their businesses around IP extension, Jessi Dunne, senior vice president, Consumer Products for Mattel, has sought to recast the company's image, stating, "I want to play a part in changing people's perception of what Mattel can be beyond toys. . . . if there comes a time when we can create a brand that doesn't have to be a toy expression, that would be an interesting market. If the company has the appetite to go down that path, I think there is massive opportunity there."[72] Perhaps less ambitious in scope but equally invested in moving Mattel beyond the toy category, Rosa Zeegers, senior vice president, Global Consumer Products for Mattel, revealed the company's current plans for its Hot Wheels line as "turning it from a toy brand to a boy brand, developing content and online gaming, creating racing events worldwide and focusing on sportswear, outdoor, gaming and online categories . . . we have to be stronger in a lifestyle positioning to gain credibility."[73]

In an era when licensors and licensees are often one and the same and licensing programs involve collaborations between powerful partners, tactics for cultivating and managing shared investment in IP extension have also grown more complex. While LRI certainly sought to promote shared investment in the Lone Ranger property and to encourage licensees to seek creative inspiration from the Masked Man's core attributes and formulaic plotting (as well as advice from LRI on how best to tap into these resources), in many ways this process has become far more intense in recent times, with companies like Mattel hosting an annual Global Licensing Summit attended by seven hundred of its licensees, where the objective is "to showcase all our licensees' products [to one another] and . . . get all of our partners working together and sharing ideas."[74] While the summit's objective is partly to teach licensees how to collaborate in promoting Barbie and Hot Wheels, in order to generate a coordinated brand identity across product lines, Mattel also uses these moments to foster a sense of exclusivity and specialness among its licensees, treating them to a Barbie fashion show and a Hot Wheels–sponsored reception featuring race care superstars Mario Andretti and Danica Patrick.[75]

While licensors typically have held an upper hand in the licensor/licensee dyad, powerful licensees have begun to exercise greater creative authority not only over product extensions but also branded content. Take Lego, for example. As of 2012, it was the world's most valuable toy company at $15 billion, bringing in $4.09 billion in revenue and $981 million in profits.[76] Lego holds an 85 percent share of the building-block market, which also happens to be the fastest-growing consumer toy subcategory for both boys and girls (video games are considered a separate product category altogether).[77] Though the company came to the licensing game rather late, only accepting its first inbound license in 1999 when it partnered with Lucasfilm to produce Lego replicas based upon *Star Wars: The Phantom Menace*,[78] its unique position and reputation has allowed the company to develop licensing partnerships unlike those of many of its competitors, negotiating nonexclusivity deals with major IP holders, for shorter terms and smaller upfront fees and royalty guarantees. For example, Hasbro's deal with Marvel prohibits the company from licensing rights to DC Comics characters or by extension other WBCP properties. Hasbro is locked into this deal for eight years (through 2017) and had to pay Marvel an upfront fee of $100 million and up to $140 million in royalty fees based on retail sales.[79] Comparatively, Lego was able to negotiate deals with both WBCP/DC and Disney/Marvel to create construction sets based on their properties. Lego's deal with Disney would expire after two years and only cost the company a $1.5 million guarantee. Disney also agreed to halve the royalty fees if Lego agreed to carry key property extensions in their Lego stores (as opposed to just placing them at other retail outlets like Walmart and Toys-R-Us).[80] One such property is the Lone Ranger, which Disney hoped would benefit from placement in front of Lego enthusiasts who frequent the specialty stores (something I'll return to later in the chapter).

Lego's market share and its stalwart embrace of a brand essence focused upon getting kids to build things are what attract brand partners willing to compromise on exclusivity and royalty rates. At a moment when industry lore dictates that building strong brand communities necessitates providing creative participation opportunities, Lego's building ethos seems worth sharing shelf space with competitors. Indeed, Lego employs this credo in all of its negotiations with licensors, emphasizing, "[Lego] are not looking for brand extension, but merely to supply other things that the Lego core consumer might like . . . everything has to link back to the bricks and the building ethos of Lego."[81]

By insisting that all of its licensing partnerships have to add value to the Lego brand, Lego challenges the typical efforts of licensors to convince licensees to subsume product identity under the licensed IP. Lego is also able to dictate product extension terms by insisting that it will only enter into a licensing partnership if the media franchise will provide "settings that fit into themes around which Lego designs its toys."[82] As such, Lego justified its initial foray into licensing with Lucasfilm as complementary to its existing line of spaceship and rocket kits.[83] This framing mechanism rhetorically reinforces the notion that Lego as licensee is highly selective even as its insistence on nonexclusivity allows it to partner with all of the major entertainment conglomerates simultaneously.

Lego has been able to leverage its position and reputation to impact franchise tentpoles. In the case of the Lone Ranger, Lego decided to manufacture a stagecoach set piece even though there was no such scene in the film. In what might be theorized in terms of Jean Baudrillard's notion of the simulacra,[84] upon seeing Lego's design, Disney instructed Bruckheimer and director Gore Verbinski to add a stagecoach scene in postproduction so that the film accurately matched the Lego replicas that were supposed to faithfully re-create existing scenes in the film.[85]

Disney's decision to retroactively insert a stagecoach into the Lone Ranger blockbuster to better align the film with the not-so-ancillary licensed merchandise manufactured by Lego should not necessarily be taken as evidence that (some) licensees have gained the upper hand on licensors. Instead, it might be looked upon as a shift in managerial tactics away from policing licensee investment in character brands toward enabling creative engagement with licensed properties that taps into licensee expertise within designated product categories. Eschewing romantic conceptualizations of creativity as rooted in talented individuals, scholars like Chris Bilton and Philip Schlesinger have demonstrated how creativity remains a managed process within organizations, albeit one that is seemingly more open to ideas pitched from the peripheries that might then be absorbed and commercialized by the overall brand.[86] Derek Johnson makes a similar claim about franchise management, wherein franchisees within discrete markets are given leeway to experiment, with the most successful ideas folded back into the central franchise node[87] (while failures can presumably be laid at the feet of "entrepreneurial" licensees, not the brand itself). All three scholars suggest that such managerial approaches emerge in response to both the unpredictability of global markets and the global dispersal of labor. As such, according to Bilton, creative management is less about allowing creative individuals to do their thing, than it is about creatively managing networks of individuals within organizations, allowing for contradictory ideas to circulate, and then developing value via commercialization.[88] Evidencing this tactical shift, Disney's Chapek explains how the reorganization of the consumer products division reduced its product oversight role, now seen as redundant, and instead better positioned Disney to coordinate and integrate licensee ideas into the overall brands they managed: "In the past, category alignment was a shadow function of our licensees that sort of replicated how our licensees were organized and how they were structured. . . . What we do best is create and sustain these franchises and commercialize them, and what our licensing partners do best is be category experts."[89]

Of course, the degree to which Disney is willing to entrust its IP to its licensees is also dependent upon the reputations the latter have already established in their particular fields. Tellingly, Chapek adds, "We would be kidding ourselves to ever think we can ever become greeting card experts like Hallmark."[90] In other words, in championing a "creative management" approach to brand extension, IP owners like Disney have tended to favor partnerships with established and reliable licensees, who tend to be less innovative but better positioned to get consumer and, more importantly, retailer buy-in for the products they bring to market. Or, as Doug Wadleigh, senior vice president of Franchise Development at Mattel, explains the company's successful partnership with WBCP, "The best way to characterize the WBCP/Mattel relationship—and the reason it works—is because we understand each other and have established global processes that allow us to proactively manage the business. There aren't too many things that surprise us at this stage of the relationship."[91]

In turn, Mattel is brought into the creative development process as early as eighteen months before a film reaches market, often when a project is still in preproduction, to pitch toy ideas that might be worked into the production.[92] Or, as Brad Globe, president of WBCP, explains, "Yes, we're the studio and we're the closest to the people making the movie, but we integrate Mattel at the earliest stage with the film's producers, the director and the art director. . . . We both know the important thing is to translate the movie's elements into something the kids can play with."[93]

Consolidation of the Retail Market

In many respects, recent changes in the approach that licensors have taken with licensees can be explained by the rise to power of a third crucial member of the licensing chain, the retailer.

Retail has always been an integral part of the licensing chain. In the

1930s, LRI devised merchandising strategies to help licensees get Lone Ranger branded products into stores and to incentivize retailer participation in pushing branded goods (see Chapter 3). But while these early "shop concepts" were designed to help licensees,[94] today they are more likely to be applied at the behest of powerful retailers like Target and Walmart, whose control of shelf space has placed them in positions of authority able to influence licensor decisions over product extensions and licensee partnerships. As Tony Lisanti, editor-in-chief of *License Global!*, explains, "The challenge for many brand licensing executives, regardless of the inherent popularity or potential for any particular property, is finding the opportunities available at retailers worldwide."[95]

While chain stores and discount department stores emerged in the United States in the mid-1940s, it wasn't until the early 1990s that chains like Target and Walmart began to position themselves as one-stop-shopping outlets and started squeezing out regional competitors and local mom-and-pop stores.[96] As of 2011, Walmart operated 8,970 stores in fifteen countries. Target operated 1,763 stores.[97] A 1990 retail study predicted that 50 percent of all retail stores would be out of business by 2000. Many regional chains, from Ames to Woolworth, have indeed folded.[98] These regional chains represented the core business for midsized manufacturers, and their demise made it increasingly difficult to place products on store shelves, in turn contributing to a disinvestment on the part of many licensors in partnering with regional licensees. Meanwhile, the consolidation of the retail market has given corporations like Walmart greater leverage in negotiating price point and supply chain procedures, demanding higher quality items at lower gross retail prices while refusing to stock items in bulk. All of this places further pressure on manufacturers to curb profit margins and to be prepared to roll out distribution or sit on stock.

The pressure placed by retail giants on manufacturers partly explains why licensors have increasingly sought out large-scale licensees, who are best positioned to meet retailer demands. More to the point, the consolidation of the retail market has led many licensors to put the proverbial cart in front of the horse, prioritizing retailer needs and knowledge in devising merchandising campaigns over those of licensees. If, historically, licensees were expected to identify viable retail outlets for branded products, Mattel now "[asks] retailers who are the key licensees they wanted to work with [for Barbie and Hot Wheels merchandise] and matche[s] them up."[99] Similarly, a key component of Disney's reorganization was a recasting of its sales staff from product experts to retailer specialists: "If you talked to our sales people three months ago, they would say they were either music sales people, games sales people, movies sales people, publishing sales people, or licensing sales people. . . . Now they say we are Walmart sales people or Target sales people. . . . That's a key difference because now they represent the total breadth of the Walt Disney Company for their customer base."[100]

Arguably, Disney's reorganization around franchises was motivated by the one-stop-shopping experience touted by megastores, which necessitates greater cohesion across branded merchandise simply by virtue of having a wide array of products, from apparel and home furnishing to toys and food items, being available on adjacent shelves. Disney CEO Bob Iger intimated as much when he stated, "As the retail market becomes more centralized, it is important to provide the consumer with an array of choices in a seamless, coordinated way."[101]

Moreover, retailers like Walmart and Target are increasingly capable of exercising tremendous influence over how character brands are extended simply by virtue of standardized floor plans and consumer profiling. Across the United States, these stores feature similar layouts that divide product categories by gender, age, and household location (kitchen, bathroom, yard, etc.), while providing licensors with data on consumer taste preferences that further refine product extension possibilities. As Mattel's Zeegers explains, "The retailer is usually the first to know whether [a brand] is . . . driving traffic into stores and leveraging that momentum over it into home décor, apparel, stationery, party and other categories."[102]

Online Shopping, Social Media Marketing, and Internet Influencers

If the consolidation of the retail market constitutes one of the key areas of transformation in how contemporary licensing operates, then the expansion of Internet and social media usage constitutes the other unprecedented terrain shaping industry practices. Even as megastores squeeze out smaller retailers, the retail industry as a whole is looking to online trends as radically altering the consumer experience. In 2012, online retail totaled $210 billion, or 7 percent of total retail sales.[103]

Online shopping not only recalibrates how retailers go about their business, but how licensors imagine the borders and boundaries that have constituted markets and product categories historically. Licensing contracts delineate the territory within which licensees are permitted to sell licensed products, but online stores like Amazon.com greatly expand the geographic parameters of consumer searches, often creating conflicts when licensees manufacturing similar items begin encroaching on one another's territory. Meanwhile, licensing categories have largely been a by-product of how retailers have historically specialized and then divided up limited shelf spaces. Online stores potentially challenge such categorization (though many merely replicate traditional categories), as search engines deploying Boolean algorithms and tagging allow consumers to customize categories or invent new ones. As of this writing many of these categorization issues remain unresolved.

Despite these confusions, however, IP owners have begun looking at ways to extend existing properties into virtual spaces. This can range from developing online games and mobile apps to undertaking innovative product integration initiatives like Mattel's deal with StarDoll to sell virtual Barbie fashions to the platform's community of "paper doll" enthusiasts. StarDoll members can visit the Barbie store in the StarDoll mall and purchase virtual clothing off the rack using virtual currency. Every time they do so, StarDoll pays Mattel a small royalty extracted from the membership fee that is required to access these online shopping features. Virtual fashions correspond with real clothing, and StarDoll members are given the opportunity to acquire real Barbie-themed merchandise, with Mattel paying StarDoll a small royalty every time a user makes a "real world" purchase at the virtual Barbie store.

For the most part, however, IP owners have made use of online spaces and social media platforms as resources for cultivating brand communities and conscripting them into providing free promotional labor—and sometimes, actual product extension and revenue-generating labor—in exchange for managed participation opportunities in shaping brand meaning. Facebook, Pinterest, and Tumblr pages for character brands are set up not only to share the latest information with consumers, but to encourage brand loyalists to spread the word by sharing, retweeting, pinning, and blogging about the brand. Since most forms of fan sharing include adding personalized sentiments about the latest product release, film, episode, etc., these activities can potentially serve to authenticate the brand through the apparent circulation of grassroots support, though in reality, many of these campaigns are carefully choreographed.

Of course, once fans are given the opportunity to share their thoughts and feelings about a property, IP owners potentially relinquish control over defining the attributes and meanings that give these properties their social and economic capital. Simone Murray refers to the "contested utility" that fans possess for media institutions precisely because their desire to participate in spreading the gospel for their favorite properties can result in translations that differ greatly from those prescribed and promoted in brand bibles.[104] Adam Arvidsson suggests that brand managers today must abandon the notion that they can shape how consumers invest in particular branded products, and instead must seek to mold consumer investment into monetizable product extensions.[105] Mattel's Zeegers explained the company's stance on cultivating parental investment in its Fisher Price line of toys as follows: "Today's mom doesn't want to be told what to do. . . . They talk to one another in online communities and make decisions based on advice from other moms."[106] Mattel maintains a list of four hundred influential mommy bloggers to whom it sends free advance samples of its toys in the hopes of getting a positive write-up.[107] In other words, social media platforms are important intelligence-gathering sites for IP owners in crafting future product campaigns as well as alliance-building spaces between brand owners and key online influencers with developed followings, capable of focusing fan investment in branded content and products. The hope is that if these influencers feel included in shaping discourse surrounding the brand, they in turn will sing its praises. As Lauren Kurzu of Cepia LLC, owners of Zhu Zhu Pets, explains, "Bloggers can be really great evangelists for the brand, but you have to be invested in listening to what they say to you. . . . You can't just throw something out there and expect gratuitous support."[108]

Of course, such recruitment efforts can backfire. Mattel recently hosted a summit for influential mommy bloggers designed to "teach" them why boys loved car-themed toys. Though it was billed as an open dialogue, many bloggers found Mattel's efforts condescending and openly criticized the company. On their blog *The Mouthy Housewives*, bloggers wrote, "Thank you, Mattel. . . . Thank you for knowing that as women we are incapable of playing with our male children."[109]

Bruckheimer and Disney engaged in a similar gambit in attempting to build excitement for the Lone Ranger motion picture and its accompanying merchandising campaign. As of May 6, 2013, *The Lone Ranger* Facebook page had 386,742 "likes" and 33,265 "friends" talking about the film on the social network site (in comparison, *Man of Steel* had 617,632 "likes" and 75,824 "friends" talking about that film).[110] While *The Lone Ranger* Facebook page provided a resource hub for fans looking to share GIFs and other news about the film, only admins were permitted to upload materials, and negative comments were quickly removed (as opposed to allowing other fans to rebut). Still, Disney could not control how the Lone Ranger's "friends" "talked" about him once they left the fan page, and while the film's producer and distributor sought to selectively create online buzz, the film was also subjected to a tremendous amount of buzzkill. A Google search revealed that the term "Lone Ranger" when combined with the word "skeptical" brought up over thirty million pages.[111] As I discuss below, online marketing for the Lone Ranger sought to transform skepticism into anticipation, with mixed results.

In turning my attention to the latest efforts to reboot the Lone Ranger, I argue that attempts to cultivate investment in the property reveal the extent to which contemporary brand management practices have been reshaped in accordance with the shifting positions held by licensors, licensees, retailers, and consumers within the licensing field today, but also in relation to the asymmetrical power possessed by independent IP owners vis-à-vis their horizontally and vertically integrated licensing partners.

The Lone Ranger Rides Again?

Industry buzz in 2012 about the possibility of a new Lone Ranger feature film, following on the heels of a critically acclaimed comic book series (2006–2011) published by Dynamite Entertainment, might have led one to conclude that the Masked Man was about to make a comeback. This, of course, presumes that the Lone Ranger ever went away. Though JWC's fortunes took a turn for the worse following the box office failure of *Legend of the Lone Ranger*,[112] the Lone Ranger property continued to garner interest. In 1985, JWC sold off its television properties to the Southbrook International Television Company Limited for $10 million.[113] This was a significant loss compared to the $7.75 million JWC initially spent acquiring the properties from 1954 to 1957, which in 1985 dollars was the equivalent of slightly over $29.5 million.[114] The Lone Ranger property has since exchanged hands three more times, having been acquired by Lorne Michaels's Broadway Video in 1993, CMI in 2000, and in 2012 by DreamWorks, which bought CMI.[115]

While not the merchandising cash cow it used to be, the Lone Ranger continued to be licensed to various toy and memorabilia manufacturers. From 1997 to 2000, Hallmark manufactured and sold Lone Ranger lunch boxes as part of its "School Days" line, and also released a miniature version of the lunch box as a Christmas ornament.

During that same period, Playing Mantis released Lone Ranger and Tonto action figures as part of its retro "Captain Action" line. Captain Action was a popular toy in the late 1960s and 1970s. Its gimmick was that Captain Action could transform himself into other popular heroes, licensed from other companies. In the late 1990s, Playing Mantis revised the concept by tying the character to heritage brands like the Lone Ranger, the Green Hornet, Flash Gordon, and the Phantom. Tellingly, DC and Marvel refused to grant licenses to produce Superman, Batman, and Spider-Man action figures, though they had been a part of the original Captain Action line. Neither company wanted to associate their properties with a product targeting nostalgia enthusiasts.

In 2001, in celebration of the sixtieth anniversary of their initial partnership, General Mills released a box set titled "The Lone Ranger Rides Again" that included reprinting a vintage 1941 Lone Ranger Cheerios box cover and a retro mini lunch box featuring a vintage Lone Ranger image. Also in 2001, CMI entered into a partnership with Vandor, a manufacturer of retro-themed products, to manufacture a slew of Lone Ranger items, including salt and pepper shakers, magnets, coffee mugs, coasters, and wall clocks. Vandor makes similar items for various classic and heritage brands including Marilyn Monroe, Elvis Presley, Star Trek, I Love Lucy, and Gone With the Wind.

Even as the majority of Lone Ranger licensed merchandise reinforced the brand's nostalgia status by emphasizing iconic images and vintage styles, the property was also licensed to third-party media producers tasked with updating and reviving it. In 1994, The Topps Company acquired the rights to publish a Lone Ranger miniseries as part of its newly launched comic book line. The four-part story incorporated supernatural elements and rewrote the character of Tonto as intelligent, sarcastic, and well aware of how he had been misrepresented in popular media. The miniseries was well received, and an accompanying trading card set also sold well, but Topps did not renew its license, possibly due to stagnating comic book sales.[116] In 1996, Broadway Video optioned the Lone Ranger film rights to Fox Family Films, which intended to "reconfigure the film for the '90s, hoping for a big action adventure in the spirit of the Indiana Jones films" while adding "Lethal Weapon–like banter between the Lone Ranger and Tonto . . . who gets disgruntled when the Ranger tries to hog the spotlight."[117] The film was never produced, possibly because Fox Family Films president Chris Meledandri, who negotiated the deal, shifted positions to head up Fox Animation in 1997. In 2002, CMI optioned the Lone Ranger film rights to Columbia, which envisioned making a film similar to its 1998 hit *Mark of Zorro*, combining humor, romance, and action, with the possibility that "a lithe, buxom female might even play the part of Tonto."[118] Once again, the film failed to move beyond the development stage and underwent several rewrites before the project was eventually abandoned. It is possible that Columbia executives changed their minds about a cheeky take on the Lone Ranger following the poorly received 2002 WB pilot, which also engaged in several of these proposed formula tweaks. Nevertheless, the deal Columbia made with CMI guaranteed the licensor six figures against $1.5 million, revealing the value of the property for both parties.[119]

The inability to transform interest in the Lone Ranger into a motion picture speaks to the challenges of reviving any heritage brand, wherein striking the right balance between nostalgia and innovation can be a daunting task that both intrigues and frightens off investors. Take the Batman franchise. Following the success of the *Batman* TV series in the mid-1960s, William Dozier produced a motion picture starring Adam West as Batman in 1969, which maintained—and even ramped up—the television show's campy tone and aesthetics. The film became a cult hit and a moderate box office success, but its low-end special effects, comedic tone, and television-inspired casting were out of sync with the direction Hollywood blockbusters were taking. As industry perceptions of the audience for superhero fare shifted, the franchise languished for over a decade. Unsure what to do with the property, CBS considered optioning the rights to a Batman in outer space film in the late 1970s, possibly in hopes of cashing in on the Star Wars phenomenon.[120] In 1979, Michael Uslan and Benjamin Melnicker optioned the film rights and set out to produce a darker version of Batman, but all of the major studios rejected their script, "Return of the Batman," because it was not considered campy enough to attract consumers who had grown up watching the TV series.[121]

In 1983, Jon Peters and Peter Guber came on board as producers and reconceived the Batman project so that it followed the formula for *Superman: The Motion Picture* (1978), retelling Batman and Robin's origins as a family-friendly and nostalgic pastiche of older iterations of the characters.[122] Instrumental on *Superman*, Tom Mankiewicz was hired to pen the script, though uncertainties about tone led to nine additional rewrites by nine separate screenwriters over the next three years.[123] Tim Burton became attached to the project in 1986, and the screenplay underwent four additional rewrites, each screenwriter tasked with making the property darker.[124] Along with the success of Frank Miller's gritty *Dark Knight Returns* graphic novel (1985), which sold well with non-comic-book readers, Burton's reputation for dark and quirky family comedies like *Pee Wee's Big Adventure* (1985) and *Beetlejuice* (1988) likely played a hand in convincing the studios that a darker Batman film could still strike a chord with audiences accustomed to watching campy Adam West reruns. The gambit paid off, with *Batman* grossing over $400 million at the box office. Nevertheless, as Eileen Meehan has noted, the film's phenomenal merchandising success was built on a two-pronged marketing campaign that offered products to consumers that featured either the dark Batman or his family-friendly 1970s incarnation.[125] Ultimately, it was not a lack of interest in Batman that caused more than two decades to pass between films, but deep anxiety over failing to meet consumer expectations that might in turn undermine the property's iconic value.

The Batman franchise encountered these paralyzing misgivings despite being a flagship property within a major media conglomerate.[126] The Lone Ranger's fate was far more precarious precisely because CMI did not possess its own production arm. While this minimized CMI's risk, it also lessened the IP holder's creative input in shaping how the Lone Ranger might be updated. Despite possessing a significant amount of control over the Lone Ranger, licensees inevitably passed on the project in favor of "safer bets," usually properties they owned outright or ones that had a more recent track record with consumers. Unlike Batman, where rejected script ideas would at least inform (for better or worse) the next set of decisions made by Warner executives about the property, Lone Ranger options would ultimately expire before nervous studio heads were prepared to green-light production, and the rights would revert to CMI, beginning the process over again.

Thus, while there have been few new Lone Ranger stories told over the past three decades (the Topps comic book perhaps being an exception), the property has clearly remained in demand behind the scenes. So when CMI reached deals with Dynamite Entertainment in 2005 to launch a new Lone Ranger comic book series and with Jerry Bruckheimer in 2007 to produce a new Lone Ranger feature film, these were not unprecedented events but business as usual. That these two productions would eventually reach market while others failed to do so speaks more to the corporate cultures of these licensees than CMI's role in managing the property.

Dynamite Entertainment primarily engages in license farming by leasing the rights to presold commercial properties and adapting them to comic book form. Dynamite currently holds the rights to publish comic books based on film franchises (*Robocop*, *Terminator*), cult films (*Army of Darkness*, *Highlander*, *The Man With No Name*, *Total Recall*, *The Warriors*), cult and nostalgia television series (*BattleStar Galactica*, *A Game of Thrones* [itself an HBO adaptation of a literary fantasy series by George R. R. Martin], *Warehouse 13*, the *Stargate* franchise, *The Bionic Man*, *Xena*), classic literary characters (*Sherlock Holmes*, *Zorro*), and heritage properties from old-time comic strips and radio (*Buck Rogers*, *Dan Dare*, *The Green Hornet*, *The Lone Ranger*, *The Phantom*).[127] Dynamite's modus operandi is to pair classic properties with cutting-edge artists and writers who offer fresh takes on classic fare. As I discuss further below, the excitement for many readers rests in the pairing of beloved characters and in-demand talent, placing important emphasis on auteurism as key to brand revival.

Given its corporate strategy, the Lone Ranger was a low-risk and logical property for Dynamite to license, with the first issue of the series debuting September 15, 2006. The issue quickly sold out of the ten thousand copies that were initially printed and received a second printing.[128] In 2007, *The Lone Ranger* was nominated for an Eisner award for Best New Series.[129] Despite the small-scale distribution, it is likely that the buzz surrounding the comic book series partly contributed to Bruckheimer's decision to option the film rights.

Bruckheimer was able to leverage his success with the *Pirates of the Caribbean* franchise to convince Disney in 2009 to finance and distribute the film, though Disney's interest was also partly spurred by its larger goal of expanding male demographics for its brand.[130] Disney's investment in the Lone Ranger came at a middle point in its efforts to "masculinize" its brand, prior to its purchase of Marvel and Lucasfilm and the failure of *John Carter* at the box office. Had Bruckheimer approached the company three years later than he did, it is unlikely Disney would have agreed to the deal, despite Bruckheimer's reputation and past success for them. Indeed, in December 2012, Disney threatened to shut down production on *The Lone Ranger* unless the budget was slashed from $260 million to $213 million.[131]

Retro Reboot

Both Bruckheimer and Dynamite sought to exploit the malleability of the Lone Ranger formula to simultaneously distance their productions from the property's perceived shortcomings, better align it with successful contemporary genre categories, and exploit the Masked Man's heritage status in order to position their takes on the character as obvious outgrowths of qualities already inherent to the Lone Ranger's brand essence.

Among the first things noticeable about efforts to revive the Lone Ranger brand was how rarely licensees mentioned that it is a Western. Detailing Dynamite Entertainment's interest in adapting the Lone Ranger, spokesperson J. Allen stated, "After all, the Lone Ranger is THE archetype of the modern superhero, he is THE definition of 'Americana,' a crusader for truth, justice and the American way. This is *the first* superhero we're talking about, the first man to put on a mask and right the wrongs of the age! The inspiration for all others."[132] In shifting the Lone Ranger's status from cowboy to superhero and retroactively identifying him as a precursor to all modern-day superheroes, Allen sought to reposition the property for the contemporary comic book market, in which the superhero genre not only dominates but is viewed as rich source material for developing cross-media franchises.

In retroactively situating the Lone Ranger among the superhero pantheon, Allen engaged in a bit of cultural (re)branding tied directly to the Lone Ranger's heritage status. It was not enough to simply declare the Lone Ranger a superhero; he was given the hyperbolic status of the *first* superhero, a legacy character that has inspired all future creations. Rather than updating the character for twenty-first-century sensibilities, Allen attempted to revise the Lone Ranger's meanings without abandoning its core features. In some ways this is not that dissimilar from LRI's efforts in the postwar era to reposition the Lone Ranger as a defender of an American Heritage suddenly harmonious with—rather than at odds with—corporate capitalist ideals. Similarly, Dynamite's focus on the Lone Ranger's historical significance (even as the company played fast and loose with that history) fits perfectly with earlier efforts to locate the property's current value within both its fictional past and past market appeal.

Meanwhile, Bruckheimer repeatedly described *The Lone Ranger* as an action/adventure film with comedic elements.[133] Even when describing the impact of Disney's budget cuts on the story, Bruckheimer took the opportunity to distance the film from its Western heritage, explaining, "We cut a sequence involving a coyote attack—supernatural coyotes—and a small animated segment. The train [scenes] are intact. We trimmed it a little bit. [Verbinski] made some sacrifices creatively, but nothing that would hurt the film. We had to work it out. The studio set a number, and it was always our responsibility to get to the number."[134]

Perhaps of even greater significance than the careful repositioning of the Lone Ranger's status as *not* a Western hero was the emphatic focus on the casting of Depp as Tonto. The media attention given to Bruckheimer's optioning of the Lone Ranger film rights, to Johnny Depp being cast as Tonto, and to speculation over who would be cast as the Masked Man (George Clooney was rumored for a while, then Ryan Gosling, before Armie Hammer was finally cast[135]) may seem like business as usual in today's celebrity buzz- and spoiler-driven promotional climate. But it is actually quite new in marketing character brands.

Creative Partnerships

Historically, property owners have been reluctant to foreground the creative labor involved in popularizing character brands. LRI and National Periodicals Press went to great lengths to suppress the identities of the actors portraying the Lone Ranger and Superman on the radio and in the film serials. Trendle contemplated and eventually rejected a possible agreement with David O. Selznick in the early 1940s to produce a Lone Ranger film starring Gary Cooper partly because he was reluctant to over-associate the property with such recognizable star power.[136] Such attempts at secrecy were undone by television, but property owners largely maintained an ambivalent relationship to the creative talent associated with their properties, as evidenced by decisions to cast relative unknowns in leading roles for both *Legend of the Lone Ranger* and *Superman: The Motion Picture*. Even recently, when rumors circulated prior to *Superman Returns* that Nicholas Cage was interested in the role, Hollywood insiders expressed concern that Cage's star persona would overwhelm the character. Casting for the latest *Batman* and *Spider-Man* franchise installments have favored known commodities who were not A-list stars (Tobey Maguire, Christian Bale). And while Depp's casting might be seen as an extension of the blockbuster logic in place since the late 1970s, wherein Hollywood stars have repeatedly been slotted in key supporting roles (usually as villains), all the promotion for *The Lone Ranger* emphasized that Tonto/Depp *was* the star of the film. As a promotional piece on the *Huffington Post* summarized, "As Johnny Depp's film adaptation of 'The Lone Ranger,' continues to seek out its masked cowboy, perhaps the job description is scaring some potential co-stars off: the titular character is actually going to be the sidekick."[137] Similarly, the title of Julie Miller's *Vanity Fair* piece, "Of Course Johnny Depp Can Make *The Lone Ranger* Remake Look Cool," made plain how casting a bankable star persona like Depp granted the project a degree of legitimacy and "freshness" it might otherwise have lacked.[138]

Whereas previously IP owners sought to promote the idea of characters like Superman and Batman selling themselves, now marketing rhetoric enthusiastically endorses (and rejects) particular creative "takes" on existing properties. Whether it is Bryan Singer's vision for the X-Men franchise or Christopher Nolan's interpretation of the Batman universe, what is celebrated is the pairing of "auteur" and brand.

In the case of *The Lone Ranger*, early promotional rhetoric not only played up Bruckheimer's and Depp's involvement, but also repeatedly reminded stakeholders—presumably both potential consumers and licensees—of the pair's previous success with the *Pirates of the Caribbean* franchise. Miller described Depp's Tonto as a "spirit warrior, with his goth face paint and Keith Richards–ian hair ornaments, look[ing] like a cross between Brandon Lee's *The Crow* and Captain Jack Sparrow."[139] This connection is significant for several reasons: prior to the release of the first *Pirates of the Caribbean* (2003) film, skeptics argued that swashbuckling films were untenable in an age of futuristic sci-fi and, moreover, that a film based on an outdated 1967 Disney theme park attraction would fail to capture the interest of the crucial 14-to-24-year-old demographic. *Pirates of the Caribbean* became a huge box office success, earning $653 million worldwide (combined, the four franchise installments have grossed over $4 billion).[140] *Pirates* also proved to be a hugely successful merchandising phenomenon, finding particular niches for extending the franchise experience by focusing on costume and set design, as well as the gamesmanship between the main characters. The first three installments generated $1.6 billion in toy, video game, clothing, and other product sales.[141] *Pirates*' success was largely attributed to Depp's quirky performance and Bruckheimer's penchant for spectacle. Thus, playing up Bruckheimer's and Depp's ability to beat the odds positioned them as capable of doing the same for *The Lone Ranger* (see Figure 7.3).

Indeed, in interviews Bruckheimer played up his own reputation for reviving supposedly dead genres as a kind of trade story that established his career capital and served as an authorial calling card: "Don't forget eight years ago the media was saying we were crazy to do a pirate movie, that they'd all failed and especially a pirate movie about a theme park ride. You can't do that. And look what happened."[142] In this manner, the Lone Ranger was positioned as benefiting from Bruckheimer's "touch," but also worthy of it, providing him with a challenge that would either extend or undermine his own star persona.

And indeed, when franchise installments don't succeed, blame is often now attributed to auteurs. Where JWC was faulted in its handling of Clayton Moore and casting of Klinton Spilsbury, the blame for *Superman Returns*'s disappointing box office was placed on Bryan Singer's somber approach and misplaced homage to the first two Superman franchise

Figure 7.3. All three film trailers for the 2013 *The Lone Ranger* identified the film as "From the Team that Brought You . . . ," followed by the Pirates of the Caribbean skull-and-bones logo. This is a screen grab from trailer #3.

installments. Meanwhile, only the proven talent of two more auteurs, Christopher Nolan and Zach Snider—a self-proclaimed comic book fan—were touted as capable of righting the franchise ship. A new Superman wasn't needed, just a new take on him.

Since the mid-1980s, the comic book industry has also invested in marketing authorial takes on established properties.[143] Dynamite repeatedly seeks to pair iconic properties with name-brand talent offering unique perspectives on these characters. Thus, filmmaker and comic book enthusiast Kevin Smith has penned *The Green Hornet* and *Bionic Man* comic books, while acclaimed artist Alex Ross has been employed to draw covers for *Buck Rogers* and *The Phantom*. With the *Lone Ranger* comic book, Dynamite emphasized the involvement of John Cassaday as both cover artist and art director. Still, in interviews, Cassaday always spoke of the Lone Ranger's influence on him as a child rather than the influence he exerted over the property, suggesting that even as character-talent pairings are becoming essential marketing tools, inspiration still emanates from the brand itself. As Cassaday explains, "Each time I sit down to do a Lone Ranger cover, it feels like a day off. The Masked Man is one of my all-time favorite characters."[144] Similarly, series writer Brett Matthews—a collaborator with Joss Whedon on *Buffy the Vampire Slayer* and *Firefly*—explained his violent take on the Masked Man's origins as inspired by his desire to introduce a new generation of readers to a timeless character, rather than reinvent the Lone Ranger:

> I think it's okay if things *evolve*. But you know what?—the characters you love and the stories you remember from back when you were a kid, they're not going anywhere. Nothing can or ever will take them away.

> And so I thinks it's okay—actually a really good thing, when more people get to discover something you find so special . . . if the core of the thing remains that same, on some level you're all responding to the same thing, which is probably what made the Lone Ranger an icon in the first place. And why he should always remain one. . . . That said, some re-interpretations are just about getting back to basics or the roots of a character, set in a world that is applicable to the audience of today.[145]

But not all creative inspiration for updating the property drew from the Lone Ranger's revered past. Depp was quite vocal—even critical—of the Lone Ranger's previous representation of Native Americans, stating, "I remember watching it as a kid, with Jay Silverheels and Clayton Moore, and going: 'Why is the f——ing Lone Ranger telling Tonto what to do?' I liked Tonto, even at that tender age, and knew Tonto was getting the unpleasant end of the stick here. That's stuck with me. And when the idea came up [for the movie], I started thinking about Tonto and what could be done in my own small way to try to—'eliminate' isn't possible—but re-invent the relationship, to attempt to take some of the ugliness thrown on the Native Americans, not only in the Lone Ranger, but the way Indians were treated throughout the history of cinema, and turn it on its head."[146] While such critique would have been impermissible at prior moments—JWC was none too happy with Klinton Spilsbury's disparaging remarks about the titular character he portrayed in *Legend of the Lone Ranger*—in an era defined by creative management, where debate and disagreement over a property's core attributes is seen as essential for monetizing the brand, Depp's comments were positioned as just one more form of inspiration drawn from the Lone Ranger's storied past that could be reconfigured as a selling point for the new film. Much of the promotional focus on how the Lone Ranger property had been "evolved" was placed on Tonto's reinvention; a tacit recognition perhaps that the brand's earlier iterations largely inspired skepticism and embarrassment for contemporary consumers over its anachronistic racial politics. Bruckheimer, Depp, and Disney largely sought to acknowledge—rather than overlook—these negative associations, and reconfigured them as a mode of brand differentiation.

In some ways, Depp's skepticism about Tonto's previous depictions was positioned as a shared affinity between producers and consumers who were part of the same maligned Lone Ranger brand community. If a typical online response to the film was Lauren Humphries-Brooks's "From the very moment it was announced, I have been both skeptical and excited for *The Lone Ranger*. . . . The original TV show was so embedded in its time, and became so iconic, that it was difficult to imagine how Disney and Gore Verbinski would go about bringing it up to date without offending just about everyone,"[147] then Depp's outspoken critiques seemed less concerned with assuaging those concerns, than provocatively suggesting that they served as a challenge that inspired the reboot. Rather than clamp down on the skepticism, Bruckheimer, Depp, and Disney seemingly embraced it in trying to build anticipation for the film. In so doing, they focused a lot of attention on challenging rather than channeling past Lone Ranger lore, while still using the source material as inspirational fodder. If this attempt was successful, consumers would flock to the theaters not in spite of their skepticism, but precisely because they wanted to see whether Bruckheimer, Depp, and Disney could rise above it. Or, as the *Examiner* reviewer proclaimed after the release of the film's third trailer, "When *The Lone Ranger* was announced, I have to admit I was skeptical. But the trailers look like a lot of fun, and who can resist Johnny Depp in a kid-friendly summer action film? The box office numbers will agree."[148] This epitomizes how creative management has reconfigured dissent and uncertainty within brand communities as monetizable opportunities.

Where JWC chastised fans for opposing its brand revival efforts, Bruckheimer and Disney were content to let Internet chatter take its course without interceding. This might in part be attributed to the Lone Ranger's diminished status as a cultural commodity, but it was also likely a by-product of a shifting set of definitions over what constitutes effective brand management in the so-called "experience economy."[149] Joseph Pine and James Gilmore have argued that in addition to producing products and providing services, businesses must now orchestrate memorable events for consumers, and that over time these events *become* the actual brand essence rather than just a value-added opportunity.[150] As such, promotional fodder like Bruckheimer's tweeted photo worked to both build anticipation for the Lone Ranger motion picture and to let social media influencers become part of the process of building anticipation, whether positive or negative.

Licensing Reputation

Efforts to cultivate investment in the Lone Ranger encompassed more than just associating the property with brand name celebrities. They also involved associating the Lone Ranger with brand name consumer products manufacturers. Though Disney engaged in only a limited amount of product licensing for the film—an issue I return to in the conclusion to this chapter—the company's choice of licensing partners was both indicative of the imagined audience for the property as well as how consumer products and other paratextual materials like film trailers and set photos create buzz for the brand.

Only two major licensees were announced prior to *The Lone Ranger*'s release: Lego, which released six Lone Ranger–themed play sets, and National Entertainment Collectibles Association (NECA), which manufactured action figures, bobble heads, and costumes. By comparison, *Man of Steel* had dozens of items for sale, ranging from T-shirts, candies, cups, and thermoses to sticker books, thumb drives, cell phone covers, and a product tie-in with Norton's antivirus software. There were also three Superman Lego play sets and over half a dozen different types of action figures, manufactured by Mattel. On the one hand, the disparity in merchandise between these two blockbusters might be read as an indication of how industry insiders viewed their respective market potential. On the other hand, it suggests a very different imagined consumer for each property.

Simply put, while *Man of Steel* merchandise was meant to be played with, *The Lone Ranger* merchandise was meant to be collected. *Man of Steel* merchandise seemed primarily geared toward a child market; *The Lone Ranger*'s to an older fan base, though one more likely to recall the failed *Legend of the Lone Ranger* blockbuster than the property's mid-twentieth-century heyday. Many of these adult fans came of age in the 1980s, when it was common for children's TV series to promote toy lines, and have embraced the action figures, play sets, and ironic T-shirts and posters that extend current television experiences. Of course, these new toys aren't marketed as toys at all, but as art, with emphasis placed less on play than display. Enhancing this trend is the fact that young adults choose to get married and have children later in life, leaving them with disposable income that can be spent on products that help bridge childhood and adult consumer tastes.

NECA is widely regarded as a manufacturer of quality action figures for adult collectors, with an emphasis on sculpting detail and points of articulation, or the number of movable parts that allow consumers to pose the figures in hundreds of different ways.[151] NECA's 7-inch Lone Ranger figure retailed for $18–25 and its 18-inch figure retailed for $75–80 (see Figure 7.4).[152] Most of Mattel's figures retailed for $7–13 and were quite literally designed to be touched, as pressing on Superman's foot triggered the doll to perform an action like pulling apart a bank vault door or lifting an oversized wheel (see Figure 7.5).[153]

Figures 7.4, 7.5. NECA's Lone Ranger and Tonto action figures and Mattel's Man of Steel "Bank Breaker" action figure. The level of craftsmanship in NECA's toys is top-notch, while Mattel's toys are designed for "playability." Author's collection.

Even the Lego sets seemed tailored to different audiences, with the price point for *Man of Steel* sets ranging from $12.99 to $49.99 (though two of the three retailed for under $20), while three of six *Lone Ranger* play sets retailed for over $50 (four of six for over $30), with the train set costing nearly $100 to purchase.[154]

Given the Lone Ranger's relative absence from public life for the past thirty years, Disney's merchandising approach appeared cautious, focused primarily on associating the property in the eyes of both consumers and future licensees with manufacturers known for their exclusivity and quality. Whereas partnering with Mattel or Hasbro might signal that an IP owner is developing a major (and mainstream) merchandising campaign around a property, partnering with NECA and Lego allowed Disney to tap into the reputations these licensees have for being highly selective with their licensed product deals. As *Adweek* columnist Sam Thielman summarizes, "All that serves to illustrate that Lego is a particularly desirable partner in the toy-licensing world, not only because kids like the product but also because Lego is very selective about who it chooses to sign deals with."[155] Of course, selectivity does not equal obscurity, as both Lego and NECA work almost exclusively with established entertainment franchises, Lego favoring multi-installment blockbusters (Star Wars, Batman, Harry Potter, Pirates of the Caribbean) and NECA a combination of blockbusters (Lord of the Rings, Star Trek, The Smurfs) and cult properties (Donnie

Darko, Sweeney Todd, The Walking Dead). Rhetorically, this communicates to potential investors that there must be something about the property worthy of attention.

If these licensing arrangements were partly intended to convey the Lone Ranger's elite status to other licensees, they were also designed to generate buzz, offering intentionally leaked "spoilers" of key scenes in the upcoming film that worked hand-in-hand with the film trailers and publicity stills in providing consumers with materials to deconstruct and reconstruct. All three official trailers for *The Lone Ranger* focused considerable attention on an elaborate train heist action sequence,[156] which Bruckheimer claimed was the most ambitious chase sequence ever shot.[157] In part because the film trailers hyped the train sequence, the most anticipated Lone Ranger Lego play set was the train heist packet, deemed by Thielman "the envy of all AFOLs—adult fans of Lego."[158] In other words, the film trailers served as paratexts both for the film and for the branded merchandise. Both the trailer and the play set encouraged the kinds of "forensic fandom" that Jason Mittell suggests are essential in maintaining fan investment in popular entertainment, encouraging them to piece together—quite literally in the case of Lego—the larger story from the selective plot elements offered up as clues by marketers.[159] Thus, in addition to describing the product, online Lego reviewers and fans speculated about the goings-on in the film. For example, the host of *The Brick Show*, a Youtube series dedicated to reviewing construction toys, speculated that the Lone Ranger's nephew, Danny Reid, played an important role in the train sequence because the character's mini-fig came with a slingshot accessory. He also speculated that archnemesis Butch Cavendish might be a corrupt lawman in the film because his character's mini-fig had a sheriff's badge. Finally, in describing the content of the train itself, which included a stash of silver alloy, the reviewer speculated that in the film, the train sequence might follow on the heels of the silver mine shootout, another play set available from Lego (see Figures 7.6 and 7.7).[160]

The prerelease of toys like the Lego sets were designed to harness fan excitement about the product/property mix. The objective was to get Lego fans to invest in the Lone Ranger as much as to offer merchandise to Lone Ranger fans as part of the promotional buildup for the film. *The Brick Show*'s Youtube channel has 71,934 subscribers and its videos have been viewed 67,882,248 times.[161] The Lone Ranger train set review was viewed 48,891 times.[162] The channel's core audience comprises Lego fans, not Lone Ranger enthusiasts, but product reviews could definitely have enticed those consumers to see the motion picture, especially when an in-

Figure 7.6. Frame grab from *The Lone Ranger* trailer #3 featuring the titular hero riding Silver through a train car.

Figure 7.7. Lego's The Lone Ranger Constitution Train Chase box. These paratexts work hand-in-hand to build anticipation for the film and the merchandise. Author's collection.

trinsic part of the review hypothesized on how best to re-create the movie scene upon which the train set was based.

However, building a Lone Ranger fan community through a coalition with Lego's existing brand community can be tricky. Online influencers like the Lego reviewers at *The Brick Show* can shape consumer discourse around a branded product in ways that shift value away from the licensed property. Where much online buzz about the film had been skeptical, reviews of the Lone Ranger Lego sets were almost unanimously positive. The primary focus, however, was about their Western theme, not the Lone Ranger. Indeed, even as Bruckheimer and Disney purposely veered away from describing the film as a Western, Lego embraced the genre head-on, and so did Lego fans. Lego brand relations director Michael McNally explained the company's interest in the Lone Ranger as allowing it to revisit a popular play set theme: "We look at how to rotate themes in, to have novelty and drive enthusiasm . . . and we hadn't expressed the Western theme for a while."[163] Similarly, the *Brick Show* review for the Lone Ranger train set identified it as highly anticipated because it featured a train with tracks and offered the first Western-themed Lego set in nearly five years. The Lone Ranger was largely a means to an end: "A lot of fans were pumped for that . . . they wanted a pure Lego-based non-licensed western theme, but we got Lone Ranger . . . we'll take it."[164]

Another review on Blockset.com, which boasts 7,754,012 members, declared the Lone Ranger Comanche Camp set a success, not because of how well it replicated an anticipated scene from the film or tied in with the Lone Ranger mythos, but because "the set has a lot of play possibilities for the target age range—in and out of the teepee, paddling the canoe, ejecting the scorpions and so on—and also looks good on display for those of us less inclined to play with our finished models."[165] While creative management strategies now seek to harness and monetize fan meaning-making practices, it is unclear how Disney might have cultivated investment around the Lone Ranger when the property's presence was largely tangential to the desires and objectives of its investors.

Conclusion

Licensing, merchandising, and character brand management have now become core, commonsense, and critical practices within the contemporary entertainment industry. While clearly not a new approach, the reliance on these processes has arguably intensified over the past quarter century, raising the stakes considerably for investors. Paradoxically, character brand licensing's ascent has actually created new challenges for IP owners over creative authority, with powerful licensees, retailers, and social media influencers increasingly demanding and exerting greater control over how properties are extended across product and production categories and made meaningful within them. In turn, these new configurations have given rise to an embrace of creative management tactics, designed to be responsive to a dispersed and empowered network of stakeholders demanding to be heard rather than told what to do with branded IP.

How is all this working out for the Lone Ranger? Very clearly, CMI took a backseat to powerful licensees like Dynamite, Bruckheimer, and Disney, even ceding merchandising rights to these partners. In turn, Bruckheimer and Disney deferred to powerful product manufacturers like Lego in shaping both production and promotional buzz for the film. Though all parties involved continued to pay rhetorical lip service to drawing inspiration from the Lone Ranger's brand essence, even if said inspiration was to "evolve" the property in ways that radically altered and undermined its original conceptualization, it is also more than evident that the Lone Ranger's resurrection was dependent upon associating it with reputable partners whose star power might rub off on the property.

Potential trouble emerged when those partners put forth conflicting visions of what the Lone Ranger's associative value was: an action-adventure romp featuring the world's "first" masked superhero versus a big-budget Western that can help extend a popular theme for block building enthusiasts. While creative management tactics are intended to embrace rather than resolve contradictions of this sort, the oddly tangential role played by the Lone Ranger brand as linking pin within this network amplified the challenge. Simply put, the Lone Ranger seemed a means to an end for Lego to extend its Western-themed play set line, all the while positioned by Bruckheimer and Disney as an opportunity for fans of *Pirates of the Caribbean* to see how the same creative team would rise to the challenge of reviving another forgotten brand. Very little about the promotion for the film seemed to argue for the property's continued relevance for contemporary consumers beyond witnessing Bruckheimer, Depp, and Verbinski's creative bravado.

Would this have been the case had DreamWorks acquired the rights to CMI's properties before the deal with Bruckheimer and Disney was struck? Certainly, joining a horizontally and vertically integrated media conglomerate would have expanded in-house options for the property. As DreamWorks CEO Jeffrey Katzenberg expained, "Classic Media brings a large and diverse collection of characters and branded assets that is extremely complementary to DreamWorks Animation's franchise business, and we plan to leverage it across our motion picture, television, home entertainment, consumer products, digital theme park and live entertainment channels."[166]

While DreamWorks Classic possesses what CMI did not in terms of in-house production capabilities, it is abundantly clear that DreamWorks did not see the Lone Ranger as the star property in the CMI buyout. Almost all the press about the purchase emphasized the significance of CMI's animation holdings, including Casper the Friendly Ghost and Rocky & Bullwinkle. Moreover, as I've suggested throughout the chapter, while CMI was perhaps disadvantaged by the dispositional shift within the licensing field toward empowering licensees and retailers, this tactical recalibration was not reserved for smaller players alone. Disney, WBCP, and other giants have also reorganized their consumer products divisions accordingly.

Speculation aside, what was ultimately needed for the Lone Ranger to be resurrected as a meaningful character brand were partners who saw the property's value existing beyond their particular product silos. Regardless of the comparisons that were repeatedly made between *The Lone Ranger* and *Pirates of the Caribbean*, it is the difference between these two properties that remains key. From the outset, brand extension for *Pirates* was envisioned as tying products not only to the movie, but to an integrated brand experience that pushed consumers in various directions, whether video games, theme park rides, or a line of tween adventure books. Owning neither the television, animation, attraction, or syndication rights to the Lone Ranger, Disney's licensing campaign focused on merchandise that only promoted engagement with the motion picture, rather than the brand. No attempt was made to push its partnership with Lego further to include a Lego Lone Ranger video game, even though such arrangements are a staple of Disney's other licensing partnerships with Lego like Pirates, Cars, or the Avengers. And though I earlier suggested that the deal with NECA strategically offered the potential to associate the Lone Ranger brand with quality action figures, in turn elevating its status among collectors and cult film buffs, the flip side is that failure to procure a more playable toy deal with a licensee targeting kids also potentially made it harder to adapt the property into an animated television series even if the film turned out to be successful with that demographic. Where Disney's consumer product division lacked incentive to be thinking about the Lone Ranger as a character brand, CMI lacked the clout to insist upon a brand-based merchandising approach, resulting in an oddly unbalanced campaign lacking in both breadth and scope.

Tellingly, at the 2012 Licensing Expo, the major showcase for IP extension into consumer products, neither Disney nor CMI had a single Lone Ranger item or teaser on display (though both booths were well represented in terms of their star properties). When I asked the person manning the CMI booth about the Lone Ranger, I was informed that Disney was handling all licensing for the new film. When I inquired at the

Figures 7.8–7.11. Note the complete absence of the Lone Ranger as IP at either the CMI (top left) or Disney (top right) booths at the 2012 Licensing Expo, especially when compared with WBCP's efforts to promote both *Man of Steel* (bottom) and the Superman brand to would-be licensees (left). Author's collection.

Disney booth, I was told that they were only handling consumer products based on the film and that the Lone Ranger merchandising campaign had not gotten underway yet (the Lego deal was announced only in January 2013). Disney's reps referred me back to CMI for any non-film-related brand extensions. Neither CMI nor Disney seemed to conceptualize the property as possessing value beyond the film, and both seemed eager to pass the buck when it came to cultivating investment in it. In comparison, WBCP's booth not only showcased the *Man of Steel* costume in a glass display and encouraged passersby to take photographs of it, but the Superman brand was featured in numerous forms, from Lego mini-figs to *Smallville*-inspired fashions (see Figures 7.8–7.11).

While Disney would eventually attempt to integrate the Lone Ranger into its broader leisure-inspired convergence and world-building strategies, such efforts were not timed to build buzz for *The Lone Ranger*, occurring instead concomitantly with the film's release. Mere weeks before the release, and amid increasingly negative buzz, Disney proposed to revamp its Adventureland theme park ride to include the Masked Man and Tonto. It also included those characters among the first play packs available for the Disney Infinity video game, which featured an immersive environment where characters from Disney properties ranging from Cars and Monsters, Inc. to Pirates of the Caribbean could interact with one another. Such efforts would prove too little too late. *The Lone Ranger* was a colossal box office failure, despite positive reviews of the video game and merchandise produced by Lego.

In the next chapter, I review the fallout from the film's flop and the accompanying lessons "learned" by Hollywood. Though I have argued throughout this chapter that failed tactics deployed in attempting to cultivate investment and generate buzz for the film inevitably contributed to its poor showing, it is not at all clear that industry executives or film reviewers saw these connections. While the lessons Hollywood seems to learn from failures certainly inform future production and promotional strategies, those lessons rarely seem to reflect upon the strategies that contributed to failure in the first place.

CHAPTER 8

Parting Shots

Introduction

The Lone Ranger (2013) will likely go down as one of the biggest box office bombs in recent blockbuster history. Costing $225 million to produce and tens of millions more to promote, the film earned only $49 million during its July 4th holiday weekend premiere, or about $20 million less than analysts predicted (and those predictions were already low).[1] A month into its release, *The Lone Ranger* had grossed only $89 million domestically and an additional $156 million overseas.[2] In September 2013, Disney seemed to wash its hands of the project, announcing that the company would lose up to $190 million on the film.[3] There would be no Lone Ranger sequel, no alteration of the Adventureland theme park ride to incorporate the Masked Man and Tonto's adventures, and despite positive reviews from video game critics, there will likely be no incorporation of the Lone Ranger play set into the Disney Infinity core game.[4] Lone Ranger merchandise at the Disney online store was discounted up to 66 percent, including NECA Halloween costumes marked down from $45 to $17, indicating both initial expectations and subsequent reassessment of the film's market longevity.[5] Less than a month later, Disney ended its "first look" deal with Jerry Bruckheimer, which had been in place for nearly two decades and resulted in twenty-seven productions.[6]

This brief conclusion is less concerned with what went wrong than with how critics and Hollywood insiders made sense of the film's poor performance. While the lessons Hollywood has learned will undoubtedly shape future strategies for rebooting heritage brands and crafting tentpole-driven transmedia franchises (not to mention the short- and long-term viability of the Lone Ranger IP), those lessons seem oddly incongruent with the logics (and missteps) that contributed to the advance marketing campaign to mobilize Lone Ranger stakeholders prior to the film's release. Likewise, critical response to the film demonstrated an acutely selective memory of the Lone Ranger's prior exploits, framing the contemporary film's shortcomings as resulting from both radical departures from a tried-and-true formula and also, contradictorily, failure by the creative team to modernize said formula. Neither perspective approached the Lone Ranger formula as a flexible and fluid equation subject to numerous historical reconfigurations.

Critical Response

Critics lambasted the film. *The Lone Ranger* received only a 31 percent approval rating on Rotten Tomatoes.[7] Though there were many things that critics found wrong with *The Lone Ranger*, a general pattern began to emerge, which focused primarily on the film's tonal inconsistencies and production excesses.[8] The most common criticism of *The Lone Ranger* was that it was too violent for a PG-13 film distributed by Disney and featuring a golden-age hero known for his fair play.[9] As one reviewer summarized, "Wholesale slaughter of Native Americans, a human organ-eating bad guy, harshly treated indentured Chinese laborers, corporate boardroom maneuvering . . . *bring the kids*! . . . Riding what must be the limits of PG-13, and certainly the edgiest Disney movie in ages, the film's desire to make a point about the bloody path history left in its wake when it came to building the West, belongs in an entirely different movie."[10]

Beyond questioning *The Lone Ranger*'s kid-friendliness, much critical attention focused on the film's production excesses: its length (2.5 hours); its dalliances with supernatural elements like flesh-eating rabbits, which seemingly served no overt plot purpose; its clunky framing device, which featured an old and weathered Tonto working as a living statue of the "noble savage" at a carnival in 1933 and recounting his first adventure with the Lone Ranger to a young boy dressed up in a cowboy suit and mask.[11] As Kirsten Acuna of *The Business Insider* summarized, "There was a good story to be told about American greed and the consequences that come with making a naive, impulsive decision in youth. Unfortunately, 'The Lone Ranger' was so dragged down by unnecessary, weird moments (the killer rabbits, horse humor, and narration from an aged Tonto that the film could have done without) that the point fell short of hitting home."[12]

A lot of attention was also focused on Depp's portrayal of Tonto.[13] While Depp's performance was commended, many critics still found the blatant disregard for the significance of casting a white actor in red face distasteful: "There's really no way the film or Depp himself can clear the hurdle of casting a white actor in a role that has largely defined the screen image of Native Americans for decades. That's not to imply that the actor's japery is in any way malicious (which it isn't) or that the filmmakers don't bend over backwards to ensure that Tonto emerges as a hero in his own right (which they do). Regardless, watching Depp mince about in a headdress and war paint and roll his eyes at the gawky white man by his side can't help but feel vaguely uncomfortable, not to mention exploitative."[14]

Of course, none of these criticisms necessarily explains *The Lone Ranger*'s failure. After all, *Man of Steel* was also accused of being excessively long and overly violent (the final battle between Superman and Zod likely killed millions of Metropolis citizens), hampered by awkward flashbacks that distracted from the central action, and laden with unnecessary stylistic elements like Jor-El's flying horse-dragon.[15] *Man of Steel* grossed $662,839,585 in domestic and global box office.[16] *The Wolverine* endured numerous negative reviews for its stereotypical portrayal of Japanese culture and society so as to earn $370,508,000.[17] Both films' revenues tripled their production budgets.

Indeed, *The Lone Ranger* received many of the same criticisms lobbed at most contemporary heritage brands, from Batman to Zorro.[18] In their attempt to strike a balance between tapping into/manufacturing a retro nostalgia for childhood icons while updating their brand image for contemporary sensibilities, many of these properties are seen by critics as suffering from "origin-story-itis,"[19] whose symptoms include too much time spent rehashing a backstory that far too few filmgoers remember to begin with, and too much effort spent trying to offer novel twists on a canonical yet outdated formula in order to appease diehard fans who will likely be displeased in any event by changes made to the original concept. Though there is a constant recognition on the part of critics that the dated aspects of the original source material must be overcome in order to resuscitate a given heritage brand, there is often also an immediate pushback against efforts to mess with the perceived brand essence of a property. Hence, even as the Lone Ranger is assessed as too corny, *The Lone Ranger* is too serious and violent. Even Matt Zoller Seitz, one of the few reviewers to give *The Lone Ranger* a positive review, notes, "The film portrays its setting as a PG-13 version of Sergio Leone and Clint Eastwood's every-man-for-himself hellscape. Granted, this has been the Western's default worldview since the seventies, but it's still startling to see it applied to 'The Lone Ranger.'"[20]

Without supporting or refuting critical assessments of *The Lone Ranger*, I must note that film critics only selectively engaged the property's long and complex textual and extra-textual history in their efforts to make sense of the film. For example, critics saw the film as detouring from the Lone Ranger's historical appeal to children. As I've argued throughout this book, however, the Lone Ranger was conceptualized from the outset as a property that would draw both adults and children. While the radio Ranger never shot to kill (and neither does the current version), *The Lone Ranger* radio series was quite violent, regularly featuring stories about murder and lynching. LRI was quite explicit in its Lone Ranger guidelines about aiming for realism in storytelling and in deflecting acts of violence onto Tonto rather than eliminating them entirely from the formula. While by today's standards, the 1950s TV series is seen as quaint and tame, merely looking at *TV Guide* listings from the era reveal that the highly rated show typically aired in prime time when more than just children watched. In the 1960s and 1970s, JWC considered numerous Lone Ranger projects that were adult themed, and the 2005 critically acclaimed Dynamite comic book series was decidedly dark, gory, and violent.

Critical response to *The Lone Ranger* also fits Nicolas Sammond's assertion that Disney is regularly policed by its own fan base whenever it seeks to venture beyond the "kid-friendly" market it has historically claimed stewardship over. Sammond argues that Disney's rhetorical mastery of the claim that it produces positive and appropriate children's media has also handcuffed the company in its pursuit of older audiences, since the expectation among critics and parents is for all Disney fare to live up to those standards.[21] Or, as media analyst Phil Contrino explained, "It hurts that word is getting out pretty quickly that it's actually pretty violent for a Disney movie. . . . The idea that a Disney movie might not be kid friendly is going to hurt it the most at this point."[22]

My point here is not to suggest that critics got it wrong, that *The Lone Ranger* isn't tonally inconsistent in its attempts to draw in multigenerational audiences or overly violent for a PG-13 rated film (though the benchmark for "overly violent" certainly isn't a stable one). Rather, it is to suggest that selective understandings of both Disney and the Masked Man's historical appeal provided a habitual framing mechanism for addressing the current film's supposed misfires.

Conversely, discussions of Depp's portrayal of Tonto neither acknowledged the historical continuity between the current misrepresentation and the Lone Ranger's long-troubled depiction of Native Americans, nor the ways that Depp, Bruckheimer, and Verbinski's attempts to "correct" Tonto's stereotypical portrayal fit within a broader effort to reconstitute the character's racial otherness. From the outset, non-Native Americans have portrayed Tonto. The radio voice for Tonto throughout the series' twenty-one-year run was Irish American actor John Todd (though LRI would employ real Native Americans for public appearances). Moreover, the character's tribal affiliation has always been problematic. On radio and television, Tonto was identified as a member of the Potawatomi nation. However, the Potawatomi nation did not reside in the Southwest where the Lone Ranger adventures took place, nor did their appearance resemble Tonto's dress. Beginning with *Legend of the Lone Ranger* (1981), Tonto's tribal affiliation changes to Cherokee, which is geographically more proximate, but also illustrative of how tribal affiliation has largely been understood as an interchangeable dimension of the character. Ultimately, there is nothing that marks the character as historically or culturally either Potawatomi or Cherokee.

Though other actors portraying Tonto have been Native Americans, their tribal affiliations have never matched the character. Chief Thundercloud, who played Tonto in the Republic film serials, was either Cherokee or Muskogee. Jay Silverheels was a member of the Canadian Mohawk First Nations. *LLR*'s Michael Horse is mixed Yaqui, Mescalero Apache, Zuni, and Latino. Depp has guessed that he might have some Cherokee or Cree ancestry.[23] In 2012, LaDonna Harris of the Cherokee nation adopted Depp as an honorary son.[24] Harris is president of Americans for Indian Opportunity. While the adoption was seen by many as a cynical and exploitative attempt to drum up publicity and appease Native American critics,[25] it does ironically represent the closest Tonto's casting has gotten to tribal accuracy—though in the film Tonto is identified as Comanche.

It is also worth noting that Depp has been explicit in distancing his portrayal of Tonto from any claims to authenticity. He admits to drawing inspiration for Tonto's look from a painting by Kirby Sattler called *I am Crow*, which is neither historically nor anthropologically accurate.[26] Sattler's website explicitly states: "I am not a historian, nor an ethnologist. . . . [I hope to] satisfy my audience's sensibilities of the subject without the constraints of having to adhere to historical accuracy."[27] In the film, Chief Big Bear notes that Tonto's appearance is out of sync with Comanche culture, which he attributes to Tonto's mental breakdown following the slaughter of his village when he was a boy. In other words, where previous representations of Tonto—even those designed to recuperate the character—have all made claims to depicting Native Americans authentically, the current iteration makes no such claim. Instead, Depp, Bruckheimer, and Verbinski depict Tonto as an unreliable narrator and idiosyncratic oddball.

None of this should be read as an attempt to redeem the film's depictions of Native Americans or to excuse casting a white actor in a Native American role. Rather, my intent is to demonstrate how critics rarely historicized *The Lone Ranger*'s racial politics in their attempts to explain the current film's missteps. Had they done so, they might have produced a more sophisticated assessment of how and why Depp's Tonto challenged earlier representations even as it reinforced certain hegemonic notions about Native American identity. One need only look to NECA's line of Tonto Halloween costumes, marketed as allowing consumers to tap into their "inner spirit warriors," to see how the film's attempts at presenting an inauthentic Tonto are translated into merchandise that allows for the appropriation and performance of "nativeness" as commodity fetish.[28]

Lessons Learned

So, what lessons did the Lone Ranger's shooting blanks at the box office teach Hollywood? Very little with regard to racial sensitivity or historical relativity. Predictably, the number one lesson learned—or rather, reinforced—was that Westerns are an unprofitable genre in the contemporary movie landscape, and certainly incapable of holding up a franchise tentpole. Over and over again, industry analysis compared *The Lone Ranger* to other big-budget Western flops dating back over a decade, including *Wild Wild West* (1999), which cost $190 million to produce and banked only $27 million during its opening weekend, and *Cowboys & Aliens* (2011), which cost $163 million and took in just $36 million.[29] Analysts further pointed to the challenge Westerns faced overseas, making them an even greater risk for Hollywood since global markets could not offset sluggish domestic returns (this in spite of the fact that *The Lone Ranger* grossed $171,200,000 in overseas box office, or 65.7 percent of its total box office draw of $260,502,115).[30] Despite efforts by Bruckheimer and Disney to market *The Lone Ranger* as an action film set in the West rather than a Western per se, Hollywood insiders were inclined to believe that audiences were unwilling to accept the historical setting as conducive to large-scale action and adventure.

Of course, this is a selective interpretation of comparable data. Arguably, *Wild Wild West* and *Cowboys & Aliens* both failed because they weren't Western enough for audiences. Or, *The Lone Ranger* might have been compared with other summer 2013 box office flops like *White House Down* and *R.I.P.D.*, leading to the conclusion that the buddy film was cycling out of popularity with filmgoers. Ultimately, blaming the film's box office failure on its generic trappings affirms a popular rationalization that undoubtedly contributes to the devaluation of the Western genre even as it claims merely to be observing it. Contemporary Westerns are expensive to produce because they require specialized costumes, props, and sets, and productions are often tied to location shooting in ways that those of other genres are not. This is an inversion of the historical argument in favor of producing Westerns, which were once considered cash cows because of how cheaply they could be made. Claiming their unpopularity among filmgoers belies another truth: Westerns are unpopular among Hollywood executives because they are not cost-effective.

The other lesson hammered home by *The Lone Ranger*'s failure is one that I've argued throughout this book: namely, that the fault rests with those tasked with cultivating investment in the property rather than with the IP itself. Though many analysts noted that the Lone Ranger simply was not recognizable enough among younger filmgoers to serve as a tentpole production, never once was there the suggestion put forward that the Masked Man ought to be put out to pasture. Instead, blame was placed squarely on the shoulders of those tasked with drawing inspiration from the Lone Ranger's brand essence in order to monetize the property's inherent value. As Disney's head of distribution Dave Hollis explained, "The frustrating part for us is that we had all the ingredients here. You take a classic franchise, team the world's most successful producer, an award-winning director and the biggest movie star in the world and you think your chances of success are pretty good. But we just didn't make it work."[31]

Whereas prior to the film's release, analysis and marketing (and as Caldwell reminds us, these are often one and the same when it comes to the industry's semipublic disclosures[32]) had focused on Bruckheimer's history of success in breathing new life into dead genres like the swashbuckling film,[33] post-release analysis noted his recent string of box office duds like *Prince of Persia* and *The Sorcerer's Apprentice* as well as his penchant for going well over budget, and questioned his understanding of what contemporary filmgoers wanted to see.[34] As Brandon Gray noted, "Domestically, Mr. Bruckheimer's pictures, outside of his 'Pirates of the

Caribbean' movies, have not been blockbusters. . . . I don't know if it's fair to say a person's taste is out of sync with the public, but I would argue the choices made here have not been the most universally appealing ones."[35]

Likewise, while Depp and Verbinski had earlier been lauded for their quirkiness and stylistic flair, which were seen as potential boons that would help *The Lone Ranger* rise above its generic trappings,[36] post-release assessment of their creative contributions pointed to audience fatigue with Depp's shtick and, in a manner reminiscent of how Hollywood made sense of *Popeye*'s (1980) failure three decades prior, Verbinski's flair was reinterpreted as a distracting excess that undermined the film's blockbuster aspirations.[37] Perhaps most interestingly, Armie Hammer was also called out for his role in tanking the film, though criticism did not focus on his on-screen performance, but rather, his off-screen antics, or more accurately, the lack thereof. When Hammer was initially cast as the Lone Ranger, industry buzz was largely positive, seeing him as possessing an all-Americanness that combined ruggedness with aw-shucks naiveté that fit the character's profile.[38] After the film fizzled, analysts focused on Hammer's lack of social media presence. As *Variety*'s Justin Kroll and Rachel Adams reported, "So far, Armie Hammer has followed a conventional media strategy that some marketing experts would argue ignores the current zeitgeist. . . . In today's overexposed media landscape, where celebs are under the constant eye of cellphone cameras, bloggers and the TMZs of the world, Hammer has managed to keep his personal life below the radar. If anything, that has made him appear somewhat mysterious and elusive."[39]

Critics noted that in spite of the controversy caused by Depp's casting, *The Lone Ranger* trended well among Depp's Facebook friends and Twitter followers.[40] Hammer's desire to protect his privacy and apparent lack of tech savvy became sticking points despite their seeming to gel with the qualities that had previously made him a good fit for the film.

The criticism Hammer received is noteworthy for two reasons: First, it demonstrates a significant shift in industry thinking on prerelease PR. Where *LLR*'s Klinton Spilsbury was attacked by critics for his inappropriate off-screen behavior, which was understood as casting a negative pall on his portrayal of such a revered icon as the Lone Ranger, Hammer was dinged for the opposite: he was not public or vocal enough during his time on-set to attract the attention of either entertainment journalists or potential fans. If Spilsbury was expected to keep his private life private, Hammer was expected to be more available and engaged during his off hours. In other words, a trend can be detected toward opening up productions to public scrutiny in ways heretofore deemed potentially troublesome (though as I note below, this is not without its perceived risks).

Second, the expectation that Hammer would help drum up excitement for *The Lone Ranger* with his fan base through social media points to the increased reliance the industry has on talent assuming the role of self-promoters. Rosalind Gill and Elizabeth Ellcessor have both pointed to the growing expectation that celebrities manage their brand image through social media as well as engage more directly with their fans. In so doing, the expectation is for talent to mobilize their followers as promotional resources as well as box office attendees.[41] If nothing else, industry focus on Hammer's shortcomings when it came to selling *The Lone Ranger* reinforces this aspect of contemporary lore and potentially contributes to an institutionalization of such practices. Or, as publicist Kelly Bush summarized, "Building a social presence is very important, because it's rapidly becoming the source of news and information across all key demos. Social media allows actors to establish a direct relationship with their fans . . . that they can nurture from project to project."[42]

The creative team behind *The Lone Ranger* responded to these criticisms by blaming the film critics, whom they claimed had been out to ruin the film ever since word had broken of Disney's temporarily shutting down production in 2011 because of budgetary concerns.[43] Critics lambasted this conspiratorial claim by pointing to the box office success of many panned films, like *Grown Ups* and its sequel, *Grown Ups 2*.[44]

Though there is clearly a certain amount of desperation and damage control that can be detected in these assertions, they also reveal the flip side of the industry's push for more advanced promotion through social media networking. Even as analysts pointed to Armie Hammer's failure to be on Facebook as a contributing factor in *The Lone Ranger*'s lame performance, Hammer et al. expressed anxiety over their inability to sufficiently control spin when—in Verbinski's assessment—online entertainment sites were reporting standard operating procedure within Hollywood as if it were breaking news.[45] Both Bruckheimer and Verbinski dismissed the Disney shutdown as a common tactic by studios looking to rein in budgets and asserted that this event was massively blown out of proportion by online entertainment news sites needing to fill content quotas.

Many such sites exist at the interstices of professional journalism and fan spoiler outlets, and are increasingly utilized by Hollywood as part of their advanced PR. While it is doubtful that reports of on-set troubles alone would dissuade audiences from seeing the film—even Hammer admitted that *World War Z* made bank despite repeated reports of creative differences between the studio and the film's above-the-line talent[46]—it is certainly true that the vast majority of stories about *The Lone Ranger* appearing both prior to and post-release referenced the Disney shutdown,[47] framing how the film was marketed and requiring Bruckheimer and his creative team to repeatedly defend—rather than celebrate—the film's merits. In the end, film critics may have served as convenient patsies for *The Lone Ranger*'s beleaguered talent, but their tactical finger pointing taps into a broader industry anxiety over the "contested utility"[48] that fan-journalists possess in extending brand reach.

Perhaps the most significant bit of industry theorization to emerge in the wake of *The Lone Ranger*'s box office bust was a refinement of what fits within the "blockbuster" and "tentpole" categories. Slippery concepts to begin with, the blockbuster has lately been characterized by its production scale and large marketing budgets, while the tentpole film is understood as the central piece of a multimediated and merchandise-driven franchise. Typically, blockbusters are tentpole films intended to generate tremendous buzz that will then drive filmgoers to seek out ways to extend the franchise experience. Shortly after *The Lone Ranger*'s release, industry analysts started to question whether the blockbuster film remained a viable business strategy for Hollywood: "But there's a separate, larger question inherent to the 'Lone Ranger' conversation having to do with blockbusters and moviemaking generally. Essentially it's this: With attempts at new franchises like Disney's 'The Lone Ranger' and Sony's 'White House Down' failing, will studios in the coming years double down on the established franchises they already know work, making fewer movies on an ever-narrower band of subjects?"[49]

Shortly thereafter, Disney CEO Bob Iger affirmed his belief that tentpole strategies were essential to that corporation's goals for creating cross-platform entertainment experiences, but also indicated that the studio would be more selective in identifying potential source material that could be effectively exploited in this manner. Iger then identified upcoming sequels to *Finding Nemo* and *Star Wars* as two such examples.[50] In other words, Disney would double down on sequels to proven fare as tentpole productions rather than try to develop original content. Some analysts suggest this strategy has built-in limitations for a corporation whose business model is still focused on driving consumers to purchase vacation packages (how many new Nemo rides can be built regardless of the number of film installments produced?).[51] Others have suggested that Disney must recognize that its strengths in developing new IP are now found in television and that the company should look to develop film franchises that extend the Disney Channel experience rather than the other way around.[52]

Regardless, the key dimension of the argument as far as I am concerned centers on the designation of "originality" when it comes to blockbusters. One of the most interesting rebuttals that Bruckheimer provided to critiques of *The Lone Ranger* was the following: "Critics keep crying out for original movies. You make one and they don't like it. What can I tell you?"[53]

Bruckheimer's differentiation of *The Lone Ranger* from other blockbusters because of its original content remains an ambiguous and intriguing proposition. Obviously, the Lone Ranger is not a new character, so how can a film based on his exploits—and essentially updating his origin story without too much variance from either the 1948 or 1981 versions—be considered original? At best, it might be considered an original take on preexisting content. To some extent, Bruckheimer's statement seems to offer a troublesome glimpse into the discourse of "originality" that permeates Hollywood, wherein new ideas are essentially understood as new perspectives on old ones. But there is another way to interpret Bruckheimer's comments, wherein Bruckheimer was not referring to the source materials as original, but rather, to the creative flourishes brought to the production by Verbinski and Depp. In an era when some critics lament the decline of auteurist cinema as displaced by a blockbuster mentality in Hollywood,[54] Bruckheimer's comments seem designed to accuse critics of hypocritical complicity by disparaging *The Lone Ranger* precisely for its artistic digressions from the blockbuster formula. While the veracity of Bruckheimer's self-serving claims is debatable, they do point to a potential shift within industry strategy away from entrusting franchises to visionary filmmakers/producers toward creative teams who can reproduce the genre efficiently as opposed to innovatively. Or, as one review of *The Wolverine* summed up the choice of James Mangold as the film's director following the departure of auteur filmmaker Darren Aronofsky: "A skilled technician as opposed to a master artist, Mangold's chief selling point as a filmmaker is his adaptability to different genres . . . he closely studies the conventions of the genre in question to craft a well-made—if sometimes a little *too* square—piece of mainstream studio entertainment that gives audiences what they want."[55]

And what is to become of the Lone Ranger? This is harder to predict. While no one suggested that the Masked Man was responsible for his own box office fate, the property's perceived alignment with the Western genre and its failure to draw in younger crowds are likely to discourage stakeholders from "following the leader" as they did in droves in the early 1950s.[56] That said, one of the most repeated concerns expressed about the property both before and after the film's release was that the Lone Ranger had been out of the spotlight for too long, making it a challenge to attract younger viewers without roping in parents and grandparents as intermediaries. In turn, this may have contributed to the tonal inconsistencies noted by critics. Perhaps in anticipation of this concern, on June 17, 2013, DreamWorks brokered a deal with Netflix to develop three hundred hours of children's content, much of which would be drawn from the recently formed DreamWorks Classic unit that oversees properties like Fat Albert, Mister Magoo, Rocky and Bullwinkle, and the Lone Ranger.[57] Whether the film's poor performance will sour DreamWorks and Netflix on developing an animated Lone Ranger series remains to be seen, but the deal seems intended to increase the visibility of DreamWorks Classic properties among young children, thus setting up future franchises as well as extending existing ones.

Lacking Ammunition

One last piece of business remains to be addressed regarding the film and its merchandising campaign: where the heck were the Lone Ranger silver-rimmed six-shooters? As noted in Chapter 2, George Trendle saw the potential for Lone Ranger silver bullet premiums even before the radio series launched. The radio series' very first giveaway was a toy gun, which received 24,607 write-in requests from listeners. Every iteration of the property has featured an accompanying toy gun license, and even during those periods when there was no Lone Ranger film, television, or comic book series, there have been Lone Ranger toy guns. Yet among the dozen or so licenses granted for *The Lone Ranger*, none were for guns. One could purchase a Lone Ranger mask, hat, badge, and even handkerchief from NECA, but no pistols. Why not?

Neither Bruckheimer nor Disney has an explicit policy prohibiting toy gun licenses, although Disney has exhibited some selectivity in this area. Bruckheimer and Disney issued licenses to manufacture *Pirates of the Caribbean* toy gun muskets. The *Toy Story* franchise has produced Buzz Lightyear ray guns as well as an array of water guns with other branded characters, but Disney has never licensed a Woody popgun, despite the obvious connection with the toy sheriff character. Indeed, Woody costumes for boys come complete with gun belt and holster, but no weapons.

Perhaps the age differential between the imagined audiences for *Pirates of the Caribbean* and *Toy Story* as well as the fanciful versus realistic nature of ray guns and pistols contributed to Disney's reluctance to license a Woody gun. Uncertainty over *The Lone Ranger*'s target audience might have created a situation where the character's most merchandisable attribute was deemed too realistic for the boy toy market, and too pedestrian for the teen toy market, where it would compete with military-grade weaponry replicas from franchises like GI Joe.

It is also quite possible that Disney decided against issuing Lone Ranger gun licenses in the wake of the November 2012 Sandy Hook elementary school shooting, which resulted in a public outcry against gun violence in America (especially when it involved affluent suburban children, who comprise Disney's primary consumer base).[58] If this is the case, however, then it should be noted that the moratorium on guns is selective at best. Lone Ranger Lego minis, NECA action figures, and the Disney Infinity play set all feature the hero with weapons drawn; the latter allows players to shoot bandits in the chest and head with the Masked Man's silver-rimmed popgun. This is a far cry from LRI's purposeful efforts to allay parental concerns about violence by always having the Lone Ranger shoot opponents in the hand.

Whatever the reason for not issuing a Lone Ranger toy gun license, the decision radically alters the perceived brand equity of the property. From the outset, the Lone Ranger was positioned as a healthy alternative to other blood and thunder radio programs. Yes, the radio series was violent, and yes, the Lone Ranger was an expert marksman. But LRI's ability to sell toy guns was predicated on selling the public on the Lone Ranger as a responsible hero unwilling to use his guns unless absolutely necessary and always in the least deadly way possible. In other words, the character's merchandisable attributes were intimately connected to a brand essence rooted in promoting violence as a last resort. In spite of criticism noting the current film's excessive violence, the Lone Ranger depicted on screen still stands for those qualities, seeking to bring his brother's murderer to justice while rejecting vengeance. Yet at times the film also presents this worldview as naive as the narrative arc builds toward a final showdown culminating in the villains' deaths. If the Lone Ranger's refusal to kill is no longer positioned as an asset to be exploited then, of course, a Lone Ranger toy gun makes little sense in a climate critical of gun culture. As a parent of young children, I am somewhat relieved to have one less violent weapon as play object to contend with in the toy aisles, but as a scholar, I wonder, was this a missed opportunity to teach about responsible gun use by tapping into and extending the Lone Ranger's brand essence through merchandising?

Silver Bullet Syndrome?

Recently, the phrase "Silver Bullet Syndrome" has entered marketing-speak as a warning against embracing a single-pronged approach to brand management. The Lone Ranger is now looked upon by the business world as an outmoded example that should not be followed. To put it simply, the "Silver Bullet Syndrome" negatively associates single-mindedness in the business arena with the Lone Ranger's naive approach to problem solving, suggesting that the latter will inevitably lead to failure. Beth Hawks, founder of CoreComm PR, bluntly states, "Folks, there is no silver bullet. Your customers are out there communicating in a variety of methods just like you. If you want to reach them you must incorporate a variety of communication tools into your communications plan. The Lone Ranger totally missed the train, the silver bullet didn't work, Silver the horse is going to be put out to pasture. Please don't be the Lone Ranger. We'd like the train to reach its destination."[59]

The trouble with this metaphor is that it contributes to the erroneous assumption that earlier forms of brand management were somehow myopic in their strategic execution. I've hopefully complicated that assumption by demonstrating the multifaceted tactics employed by LRI and JWC in extending the Lone Ranger across platforms and in popularizing the property among potential stakeholders operating under very different sociohistorical and industrial conditions. By using the Lone Ranger as an example of why the old ways no longer work, the "Silver Bullet Syndrome" participates in the erasure of a dynamic brand management history that continues to resonate in the contemporary media environment.

Beyond the Lone Ranger, this book has offered an in-depth exploration of licensing as a key site of cultural labor. While one aim of this project was to shine a light on what licensors "do," an important intervention given the invisibility of this type of work, I also sought to maintain a critical sensibility by reconstructing how licensors at different historical junctures came to understand their labor and define their particular occupational worth, status, and identity.

Building on Pierre Bourdieu, I have explored how licensors developed particular position-taking tactics and occupational dispositions in response to their shifting position within the media industries. Cultivating

IP investment requires constant attention to the alignment of economic and cultural values and an awareness of how IP can and cannot be adapted to varying products. To do this, licensors take on roles as cultural intermediaries capable of translating brand essence into both merchandisable attributes and consumer investments. Licensors stake their authority and reputation on their translation skills. This was clearly LRI's role throughout the 1930s, when it acted as go-between among franchisees in local markets, and in the 1950s, when the company prioritized its role in policing licensees to ensure coherence across media and merchandising platforms and adherence to a set of conformist cultural values.

An early example of a franchisable and localizable cross-media lifestyle brand that offered fans both immersive world-building experiences and participatory opportunities through commodity consumption, LRI cultivated a loyal brand community that was essential to spreading the Lone Ranger gospel. Importantly, the Lone Ranger's brand community included its licensees and work-for-hire talent, all of whom participated in extending the property's reach and expanding the Masked Man's mythos. LRI's efforts in guiding, inspiring, and policing these myriad subcommunities attest to the complexities of IP management. Though it is doubtful that actual licensors today would recall LRI's early investment in customization, localization, and participation as tactics for transforming the Lone Ranger into a national icon, the field is currently revisiting many of these practices as commonsense strategies for building global multiplatform brands. Regardless of whether or not the Lone Ranger leads the way, today's character licensors continue to follow in LRI's footsteps.

Notes

Chapter One

1. "Lone Ranger Enters Field of Merchandise," *Advertising Age*, May 23, 1938.

2. "Manufacturers Licensed to Produce Lone Ranger Articles," February 13, 1939. George W. Trendle Papers (henceforth "Trendle Papers"), Detroit Public Library, Series II (Business Papers), Subseries C (Productions), Box 69, Folder 20.

3. "Mask vs. Beard," *New Yorker*, December 17, 1938, 12–13.

4. *"The Lone Ranger": Details of Procedure in Handling the Exploitation of the Program for Maximum Retail Results*, ca. 1939, 8. Trendle Papers, Series II, Subseries C, Box 69, Folder 20.

5. Eileen Meehan, "'Holy Commodity Fetish, Batman!': The Political Economy of a Commercial Intertext," 47–65.

6. Jonathan Gray, *Show Sold Separately: Promos, Spoilers, and Other Media Paratexts*.

7. Lee Felbinger, *Collector's Reference and Value Guide to the Lone Ranger*; Dick Osgood, *Wyxie Wonderland: An Unauthorized 50-Year Diary of WXYZ Detroit*; David Rothel, *Who Was That Masked Man? The Story of the Lone Ranger*.

8. For a notable exception, see Chadwick Allen, "Omnimedia Marketing: The Case of the Lone Ranger." Allen traces how the Lone Ranger was marketed across media and merchandising platforms from the late 1930s through the early 1980s, arguing that the property predated Star Wars as a multimedia franchise. Though Allen's work is informative and detailed, it is primarily descriptive and makes little effort to contextualize these generative precursors.

9. Valerie Wee, *Teen Media: Hollywood and the Youth Market in the Digital Age*; Sharon Marie Ross, *Beyond the Box: Television and the Internet*.

10. "World's Fair Crowd Meets Buck Rogers."

11. Robert Lesser, *A Celebration of Comic Art and Memorabilia*, 179.

12. Neal Gabler, *Walt Disney: The Triumph of the American Imagination*, 275–277.

13. John D. Schwartz, "Buck Rogers: Interplanetary Multi-Media Hero," 11.

14. "Winnie the Pooh Goes on the Air," *Playthings*, May 1933; "Shirley Slesinger Lasswell."

15. Gregory J. Battersby and Charles W. Grimes, *2010 Licensing Update*, 5.

16. Ibid.

17. *Licensing Industry Survey*, 2012.

18. Yana Polikarpov, "From Apparel to Home Décor, Disney Revamps Licensing Biz," Brandweek.com, March 23, 2009.

19. Jane Gaines, *Contested Culture: The Image, The Voice, and the Law*, 214.

20. Norma Odom Pecora, *The Business of Children's Entertainment*, 56.

21. St. Claire McKelway, "The Literary Character in Business & Commerce," 74.

22. Karen Raugust, *The Licensing Business Handbook*, 5.

23. Stephen J. Sansweet and Peter Vilmur, "From dog food to film, look inside 'Star Wars,'" *Billings Gazette*, November 3, 2007.

24. Gary Cross, *Kids' Stuff: Toys and the Changing World of American Childhood*; Jane Gaines, "The Queen Christina Tie-Ups: Convergence of Show Window and Screen"; Ian Gordon, *Comic Strips and Consumer Culture, 1890–1945*; Mark C. Rogers,"License Farming and the American Comic Book Industry," *International Journal of Comic Art* 1, no. 2 (1999): 132–142.

25. Christopher Anderson, *Hollywood TV* (Austin: University of Texas Press, 1994); Catherine Johnson, "Trading Auntie: The Exploitation and Protection of Intellectual Property Rights during the BBC's Monopoly Years," 441–458; Michael Kackman, "Nothing On But Hoppy Badges: *Hopalong Cassidy*, William Boyd Enterprises, and Emergent Media Globalization," 76–101; Mary Kearney, "Recycling Judy and Corliss: Transmedia Exploitation and the First Teen-Girl Production Trend," 264–295; Jason Scott, "The Character-Oriented Franchise: Promotion and Exploitation of Pre-Sold Characters in American Film, 1913–1950," 34–55.

26. Gray, *Show Sold Separately*; Henry Jenkins, *Convergence Culture: Where Old and New Media Collide* (New York: New York University Press, 2006); Derek Johnson, *Franchising Media Worlds: Content Networks and the Collaborative Production of Culture*; Barbara Klinger, *Beyond the Multiplex: Cinema, New Technologies, and the Home*; Jason Mittell, "To Spread or to Drill?"

27. Johnson, *Franchising Media Worlds*, 64.

28. Ibid., 93.

29. Bernard Miège, *The Capitalization of Cultural Production*.

30. Paul Du Gay, "Introduction," in *Production of Culture/Cultures of Production*, ed. Paul Du Gay, 7.

31. Contract with Republic Pictures, 1938. Trendle Papers, Series II, Subseries C, Box 69, Folder 3.

32. "Appendix B, 1952 television production contract." Trendle Papers, Series II, Subseries C, Box 69, Folder 6.

33. Arthur Myers, "They Bought the Rights to Get Rich."

34. Personal interview with Jay Emmett, April 17, 2005.

35. Nicole Garrison-Sprenger, "Dynamic duo saving Superman."

36. Pierre Bourdieu, *The Field of Cultural Production: Essays on Art and Literature*, 76.

37. Timothy Havens, "The Evolution of Industry Lore in African American Television Trade."

38. Bourdieu, *Field of Cultural Production*; Raymond Williams, *Marxism and Literature*.

39. "Mickey Mouse Emerges as Economist,"

40. "Manufacturers Licensed to Produce Lone Ranger Articles," February 13, 1939. Trendle Papers, Series II, Subseries C, Box 69, Folder 20.

41. The History of The Lone Ranger. Anonymous unpublished manuscript, ca. 1954, Chapter 2, page 5. Trendle Papers, Series II, Subseries C, Box 69, Folder 20.

42. Miège argues that cultural industries are sites of struggle between asymmetrical occupational groups vying for creative and economic power. See *Capitalization of Cultural Production*.

43. John Thornton Caldwell, "Cultures of Production: Studying Industry's Deep Texts, Reflexive Rituals, and Managed Self-Disclosures," 199–212.

44. Tim Havens, Amanda Lotz, and Serra Tinic, "Critical Media Industry Studies: A Research Approach," 234–253.

45. John T. Caldwell, *Production Culture: Industrial Reflexivity and Critical Practice in Film and Television*; Miranda Banks, "My Media Studies: Off-Screen Stories," 20–22; Vicki Mayer, *Below the Line: Producers and Production Studies in the New Television Economy*.

46. Liz McFall, "What about the Old Cultural Intermediaries? An Historical Review of Advertising Producers," 532–552.

47. Paul Du Gay and Michael Pryke, "Introduction," in *Cultural Economy: Cultural Analysis and Commercial Life*, 8.

48. Caldwell, *Production Culture*.

Chapter Two

1. *The History of the Lone Ranger*. Anonymous unpublished manuscript, ca. 1954, 2–3. Trendle Papers, Series II, Subseries C, Box 69, Folder 20.

2. Ibid.

3. Wayne Morgan, "'If Your Grocer Does Not Keep the Ivory Soap': Palmer Cox, The Brownies, and Nineteenth Century Marketing," 22–29.

4. Ibid., 25.

5. Ibid., 25–26.

6. Ibid., 26.

7. Gary Cross, *Kids' Stuff: Toys and the Changing World of American Childhood*, 89.

8. Ibid., 88.

9. Ian Gordon, *Comic Strips and Consumer Culture, 1890–1945*, 82.

10. Donald Crafton, *Before Mickey: The Animated Film 1898–1928*, 40.

11. Jason Scott, "The Character-Oriented Franchise: Promotion and Exploitation of Pre-Sold Characters in American Film, 1913–1950," 40.

12. Richard DeCordova, "The Mickey in Macy's Window: Childhood, Consumerism, and Disney Animation," 203–213.

13. Gordon, *Comic Strips*; Cross, *Kids' Stuff*.

14. *Comic Strips*, 49.

15. *Kids' Stuff*, 39.

16. Stefan Kanfer, *Serious Business: The Art and Commerce of Animation in America from Betty Boop to Toy Story*, 48.

17. Giannalberto Bendazzi, *Cartoons: One Hundred Years of Cinema Animation*, 53.

18. Scott, "Character-Oriented Franchise," 41.

19. Morgan, "If Your Grocer"; Gordon, *Comic Strips*.

20. "If Your Grocer," 25.

21. Avi Santo, "A Teenie Weenie Amount of 'Goodwill': Cross-Media Character Brand Merchandizing in the 1920s," *Journal of Consumer Culture* 12 (2012), 283–305.

22. Ibid.

23. Letter from Borgfeldt Assistant Treasurer George Pfeiffer to William Donahey, 11 March 1921. William Donahey Papers, Wisconsin Historical Society, Box 1, Folder 2. Quoted in Santo, "A Teenie Weenie Amount."

24. *Comic Strips*, 44–45.

25. *Kids' Stuff*; Lisa Jacobson, *Raising Consumers: Children and the American Mass Market in the Early Twentieth Century*.

26. Gregory J. Battersby and Danny Simon, *Basics of Licen$ing: How to Extend Brand and Entertainment Properties for Profit*, 19.

27. *Kids' Stuff*, 94.

28. Ibid., 91.

29. Charles Eckert, "The Carole Lombard in Macy's Window," 1–[illegible]

30. Tom Kemper, *Hidden Talent: The Emergence of Hollywood Agents*.

31. "Veiled Vindictive Annie,"; "Hooverism in the Funnies."

32. Trendle would buy out Kunsky by decade's end.

33. See TLS (typed letter signed), Jewell to Striker, February 15, 1933, and TLS, Striker to Jewell, February 20, 1933. Raymond J. Meurer Papers (henceforth "Meurer Papers"), Detroit Public Library, Box 16.

34. Butch Cavendish was first introduced on radio in 1940, following the 1938 Republic film serials' telling the Masked Man's origin as the lone survivor of an ambush. Prior to 1938, the Lone Ranger had no official origin. Tonto and the Lone Ranger's first encounter is told on radio in 1938, though only in 1949, as part of the Lone Ranger TV series' premiere episode, is that origin story retroactively altered from its original continuity, or ret-conned, so that Tonto saves the Lone Ranger's life following the Cavendish gang ambush. I discuss both events in greater detail in Chapter 5.

35. J. A. Aberdeen, *Hollywood Renegades: The Society of Independent Motion Picture Producers*.

36. *The History of the Lone Ranger*, 6–7.

37. J. Bryan III, "Hi Yo Silver," 20.

38. *The History of the Lone Ranger*, Chapter 2, page 7.

39. Dick Osgood, *Wyxie Wonderland: An Unauthorized, 50-Year Diary of WXYZ Detroit*, 92.

40. *Buck Jones v. Republic Productions Inc.* Transcription of deposition. April 4, 1939, p. 31. Meurer Papers, Box 16.

41. Tino Balio, *Grand Design: Hollywood as a Modern Business Enterprise, 1930–1939*, 326, 334.

42. Ibid., 334.

43. Scott Bruce and Bill Crawford, *Cerealizing America: The Unsweetened Story of American Breakfast Cereal*, 80–82.

44. Lone Wolf Tribe, accessed March 17, 2013, http://scoop.diamondgalleries.com/Home/4/1/73/1016?articleID=43573.

45. Bruce and Crawford, 80.

46. *Kids' Stuff*, 114.

47. "Radio's Most Spectacular Incident." Promotional pamphlet, June 1933. Trendle Papers, Series II, Subseries C, Box 69, Folder 20.

48. *The History of the Lone Ranger*, Chapter 2, 22.

49. Lone Ranger chronology ca. 1953. Trendle Papers, Series II, Subseries C, Box 79, Folder 12.

50. "Our Best Salesman Rides a Horse." Ad for Gordon Bakery.

51. *The History of the Lone Ranger*, Chapter 2, 8–9.

52. Michele Hilmes, *Hollywood and Broadcasting: From Radio to Cable*, 82–83.

53. LRI Shareholder Reports, 1940–1954. Trendle Papers, Series II, Subseries C, Box 79, Folders 12–13.

54. Robert Heide and John Gilman, *Disneyana: Classic Collectibles, 1928–1958*, 37–38.

55. Douglas Gomery, "Disney's Business History: A Reinterpretation," in *Disney Discourse: Producing the Magic Kingdom*, 71–86; DeCordova, "The Mickey in Macy's Window," 205 (quote from letter written by Roy Disney to Disney's toy licensee, Borgfeldt & Co., on March 4, 1931).

Chapter Three

1. *The Lone Ranger: Transcribed Half-Hour Dramas.* Sales booklet, ca. 1938. George W. Trendle Papers (henceforth "Trendle Papers"), Detroit Public Library, Series II (Business Papers), Subseries C (Productions), Box 69, Folder 20.

2. Henry Jenkins, *Convergence Culture: Where Old and New Media Collide*, 279. Young first coined the term in a May 2003 interview with Jenkins.

3. John Dunning, *The Encyclopedia of Old-Time Radio*; Jim Harmon, *The Great Radio Heroes* (City: McFarland, 2001); Harvey Sheldon, *The Golden Age of Radio and History*, 2013).

4. Jonathan Gray, *Show Sold Separately: Promos, Spoilers, and Other Media Paratexts.*

5. Michele Hilmes, *Radio Voices: American Broadcasting, 1922–1952*, 13.

6. Gary Cross, *Kids' Stuff: Toys and the Changing World of American Childhood*, 101.

7. Ibid., 68.

8. Kate Lacey, "Radio in the Great Depression: Promotional Culture, Public Service, and Propaganda," 24.

9. Roland Marchand, *Advertising the American Dream: Making Way for Modernity, 1920–1940*, 109.

10. Cross, *Kids' Stuff*, 103.

11. Ibid., 102.

12. Ibid., 102.
13. Ibid., 100–101.
14. "Annie's Big Surprise Party," October 18, 1935.
15. Scott Bruce and Bill Crawford, *Cerealizing America: The Unsweetened Story of American Breakfast Cereal*, 84–87.
16. Marilyn Lawrence Boemer, *The Children's Hour*; Lisa Jacobson, *Raising Consumers: Children and the American Mass Market in the Early Twentieth Century.*
17. Jacobson, *Raising Consumers*, 10.
18. Nicholas Sammond, *Babes in Tomorrowland: Walt Disney and the Making of the American Child, 1930–1960*, 2.
19. Warren Susman, *Culture as History: The Transformation of American Society in the Twentieth Century.*
20. Little Orphan Annie's Treasure Hunt. Game produced and distributed by Blackett, Sample & Hummert for the Wander Company, 1933.
21. *Kids' Stuff*, 107.
22. See "'Hi-Yo Silver!' Cowboy Honors for East Side Boy," originally printed in *Roanoke News*, September 9, 1938. Reprinted in LRI marketing binder. Trendle Papers, Appendix B (Business Papers—Publicity).
23. A notable exception occurred in 1938 following the accidental death of actor Earl Graser, the voice of the Lone Ranger. A serialized storyline was devised to distract listeners as the company searched for a new Lone Ranger. In the story, the Lone Ranger is ambushed, shot, and left to die. Tonto searches for his companion for several weeks and then nurses him back to health. LRI worked with series sponsors to turn Graser's death into a marketing opportunity, tying the storyline to a map that radio listeners could acquire to follow along with Tonto as he searched for the missing hero.
24. Gray, *Show Sold Separately*, 177–188.
25. Amanda Lotz, *The Television Will Be Revolutionized*, 171–173.
26. "'The Lone Ranger' Mask: A Give-Away that 'Cleans House' for Retailers and Door-to-Door Salesmen," ca. 1939. Trendle Papers, Series II, Subseries C, Box 69, Folder 20.
27. Airdate February 2, 1938.
28. *Babes in Tomorrowland*, 171.
29. *Kids' Stuff*, 107.
30. J. Bryan III, "Hi Yo Silver," 20.
31. David Rothel, *Who Was That Masked Man? The Story of the Lone Ranger*; Bruce Smith, *The History of Little Orphan Annie*; John D. Schwartz, "Buck Rogers: Interplanetary Multi-Media Hero."
32. Susan Smulyan, *Selling Radio: The Commercialization of American Broadcasting, 1920–1934*, 37.
33. Victoria Johnson, *Heartland TV: Prime Time Television and the Struggle for U.S. Identity*, 41.
34. Alexander Russo, *Points on the Dial: Golden Age Radio beyond the Networks*, 64.
35. James Schwoch, "A Failed Vision: The Mutual Television Network," 3–11.
36. Christopher Sterling and John Kittross, *Stay Tuned: A Concise History of American Broadcasting*, 2nd ed., 122.

37. "Radio's Most Spectacular Incident." Promotional pamphlet, June 1933. Trendle Papers, Series II, Subseries C, Box 69, Folder 20.

38. Ibid.

39. Ibid.

40. *The Lone Ranger: Transcribed Half-Hour Dramas.*

41. Schwoch, "A Failed Vision."

42. *Baker's Helper*, August 20, 1938.

43. J. Bryan III, October 14, 1939.

44. Michele Hilmes, *Hollywood and Broadcasting: From Radio to Cable*, 144.

45. Christopher Anderson, "Ziv Television Programs, Inc.," *The Encyclopedia of Television*, 2nd ed., 2626–2629.

46. Hilmes, *Hollywood and Broadcasting*, 145.

47. *The Lone Ranger: Transcribed Half-Hour Dramas*, 56.

48. Thomas S. Dicke, *Franchising in America: The Development of a Business Method, 1840–1980*, 2.

49. Derek Johnson, *Franchising Media Worlds: Content Networks and The Collaborative Production of Culture*, 447, 453.

50. Koichi Iwabuchi, "How 'Japanese' is Pokemon?" in *Pikachu's Global Adventure: The Rise and Fall of Pokémon*, ed. Joseph Tobin, 53–79.

51. Albert Moran, *Copycat TV: Globalisation, Program Formats, and Cultural Identity.*

52. Michael Kackman, "Nothing On But Hoppy Badges: *Hopalong Cassidy*, William Boyd Enterprises, and Emergent Media Globalization," 76.

53. Moran, *Copycat TV*, 22.

54. Ibid.

55. Tim Hollis, *Hi There, Boys and Girls! America's Local Children's TV Shows.*

56. *The Lone Ranger Merchandising Exploitation Publicity Supplement*, ca. 1938. Trendle Papers, Series II, Subseries C, Box 69, Folder 20.

57. *The Lone Ranger: Transcribed Half-Hour Dramas*, 8.

58. *Detroit Saturday Night*, October 23, 1937. Reprinted in LRI marketing binder. Trendle Papers, Appendix B.

59. C. B. Boutell, "Hi-Yo Silver Lining."

60. TLS, Sehl Advertising Agency, Inc., to Trendle, October 17, 1935. Raymond J. Meurer Papers (henceforth "Meurer Papers"), Detroit Public Library, Box 16.

61. Marketing Binders, Trendle Papers, Appendix B.

62. A "Quick" Question from One of Our New Sponsors in the Southwest: "Is the 'Lone Ranger' Program Effective During Summer Months?" 1939. Trendle Papers, Series II, Subseries C, Box 69, Folder 20.

63. *The Lone Ranger: Transcribed Half-Hour Dramas*, 12.

64. "Who's Asleep at the Switch," *Grocers Spotlight Newspaper*, ca. 1934.

65. *Kids' Stuff*, 108.

66. *"The Lone Ranger": Details of Procedure in Handling the Exploitation of the Program for Maximum Retail Results.* Manual, ca. 1939, 2. Trendle Papers, Series II, Subseries C, Box 69, Folder 20.

67. Ibid., 6.

68. Ibid., 3.

69. Ibid., 10.

70. TLS, Lloyd George Venard, Director of Sales, WCKY, to Chas C. Hicks, April 28, 1938. Trendle Papers, Appendix B.

71. *The Lone Ranger*, 7.

72. Ibid.

73. *Baker's Helper*, August 20, 1938.

74. Lone Ranger Comic Strip Newspaper Syndication List, ca. 1938. Trendle Papers, Series II, Subseries C, Box 69, Folder 20.

75. Dick Osgood, *Wyxie Wonderland: An Unauthorized 50-year Diary of WXYZ Detroit*, 135.

76. Synopsis Lone Ranger Contract with Republic Productions, June 1937. Trendle Papers, Series II, Subseries C, Box 69, Folder 3.

77. *The History of The Lone Ranger*, ca. 1954, Chapter 2, p. 24. Trendle Papers, Series II, Subseries C, Box 69, Folder 20.

78. Transcription of deposition by George W. Trendle. *Buck Jones v. Republic Productions Inc.* March 31, 1939, 55. Meurer Papers, Box 16.

79. *The Lone Ranger*, 8.

80. Ibid.

81. Ibid.

82. Ibid., 9.

83. Republic Pictures Presents: The Motion Picture Version of The Lone Ranger. Merchandising packet, ca. 1938. 1. Trendle Papers, Series II, Subseries C, Box 69, Folder 3.

84. Robert S. Lynd and Merrill Lynd, *Middletown: A Study in Contemporary American Culture* (New York: Harcourt, Brace, 1931); Robert S. Lynd and Merrill Lynd, *Middletown in Transition: A Study in Cultural Conflicts* (New York: Harcourt, Brace, 1937).

85. *Babes in Tomorrowland*, 138.

86. Sharon Marie Ross, *Beyond the Box: Television and the Internet*, 9.

87. Republic Pictures merchandising packet, 7.

88. Ibid., 5.

89. Jacobson, *Raising Consumers*, 42–46.

90. *The History of The Lone Ranger*, Chapter 2, 21–22.

91. TLS, Striker to Jewell, January 6, 1933. Meurer Papers, Box 16.

92. *The Lone Ranger: Transcribed Half-Hour Dramas*, 37.

93. *Babes in Tomorrowland*, 165.

94. Richard DeCordova, "The Mickey in Macy's Window: Childhood, Consumerism, and Disney Animation," 208.

95. Republic Pictures merchandising packet, 1.

96. "The Mickey in Macy's Window," 209.

97. Albert M. Muniz and Thomas C. O'Guinn, "Brand Community," 412.

98. Ibid.

99. Henry Jenkins, "Affective Economics 101," on FlowTV.org, September 20, 2004, accessed March 17, 2013. http://flowtv.org/2004/09/affective-economics-101/.

100. James H. McAlexander, John W. Schouten, and Harold F. Koenig, "Building Brand Community."

101. Muniz Jr. and O'Guinn, "Brand Community," 418.
102. McAlexander, Schouten, and Koenig, "Building Brand Community," 38.
103. Ibid.
104. Muniz Jr. and O'Guinn, "Brand Community," 412.
105. Jenkins, "Affective Economics 101."
106. "Brand Community."
107. Viviana Zelizer, *Pricing the Priceless Child: The Changing Social Value of Children*, 33–36.
108. *Raising Consumers*, 10.
109. "The Lone Ranger," 6.
110. Ibid., 12.
111. "Hi Yo Silver Lining," *New Republic*, January 11, 1941.
112. Republic Pictures merchandising packet, 1.
113. Thanks to Michael Kackman for suggesting the "bland" descriptor as capturing the seemingly disengaged nature of how brands approached politics.
114. *Weber's Lone Ranger Safety Club Official Manual*, 1939, 15. Trendle Papers, Series II, Subseries C, Box 69, Folder 20.
115. Daniel Czitrom, *Media and the American Mind: From Morse to McLuhan*.
116. *Weber's Lone Ranger Safety Club Official Manual*, 8.
117. *Babes in Tomorrowland*, 184–185.
118. *Weber's Lone Ranger Safety Club Official Manual*, 4–5.
119. Ibid., 7.
120. Ibid., 9.
121. Ibid., 13.
122. Ibid., 30.
123. Christopher Anderson, *Hollywood TV*, 155.
124. Republic Pictures merchandising packet, 1.
125. *Weber's Lone Ranger Safety Club Official Manual*, 25.
126. Republic Pictures merchandising packet, 3.
127. *Weber's Lone Ranger Safety Club Official Manual*, 14–15.
128. David Itzkoff, "The Movie Industry's New Playthings.

Chapter Four

1. Lawrence Lessig, *Free Culture: The Nature and Future of Creativity*, 233.
2. Peter Jaszi, "Toward a Theory of Copyright: The Metamorphoses of 'Authorship,'" 455–502; Jane Gaines, *Contested Culture: The Image, The Voice, and the Law*; Peter Jaszi, "On the Author Effect: Contemporary Copyright and Collective Creativity," 293–320; Siva Vaidhyanathan, *Copyrights and Copywrongs: The Rise of Intellectual Property and How It Threatens Creativity.*
3. W. T. Jaeger, "Copyright: Misappropriation of a Character," 1780–1798; D. B. Feldman, "Finding a Home for Fictional Characters: A Proposal for Change in Copyright Protection," 687–720; M. T. Helfand, "When Mickey Mouse Is as Strong as Superman: The Convergence of Intellectual Property Laws to Protect Fictional Literary and Pictorial Characters," 623–674.
4. Gaines, *Contested Culture*; Jaszi, "Toward a Theory of Copyright"; Jaszi, "On

the Author Effect"; Martha Woodmansee, "The Genius and the Copyright: Economic and Legal Conditions of the Emergence of the 'Author,'" 425–448; Mark Rose, *Authors and Owners: The Invention of Copyright.*

5. Dr. Seuss Enterprises is currently one of the most litigious IP owners. From 2006 to 2010, the company sent out cease and desist notices for supposed copyright infractions to a range of entities from musician Kevin Ryan, whose 2007 mash-up "Dylan Gives a Who" remixed Seuss lyrics with Dylan songs, to Lorax AG, a green company working on clean coal. They also went after the city of Louisville in 2008 for attempting to temporarily rename a small section of town "LouWhoVille" as part of the annual Christmas celebration.

6. *Contested Culture*; "Toward a Theory of Copyright"; "On the Author Effect"; Vaidhyanathan, *Copyrights and Copywrongs*; Rosemary Coombe, *The Cultural Life of Intellectual Properties: Authorship, Appropriation and the Law.*

7. *Cultural Life of Intellectual Properties*, 10.

8. Nicholas Sammond, *Babes in Tomorrowland: Walt Disney and the Making of the American Child, 1930–1960.*

9. Thomas Donaldson, T. Preston, and Lee E. Preston, "The Stakeholder Theory of the Corporation: Concepts, Evidence, and Implications," 68.

10. Article I, Section 8, Clause 8 of the United States Constitution.

11. Woodmansee, "The Genius and the Copyright"; Rose, *Authors and Owners.*

12. Michel Foucault, "What Is an Author?" in *Language, Counter-Memory*, 113–139.

13. "Genius and the Copyright," 426.

14. *Authors and Owners*, 4.

15. "On the Author Effect," 297.

16. *Contested Culture*, 61.

17. Matt Stahl, "Privilege and Distinction in Production Worlds: Copyright, Collective Bargaining, and Working Conditions in Media Making," 54–68.

18. "Privilege and Distinction," 56.

19. "On the Author Effect," 298.

20. "Toward a Theory of Copyright," 489.

21. The United States did not sign the Berne Convention agreement until 1988 and has continued to exclude discussion of moral rights.

22. Ian Gordon, *Comic Strips and Consumer Culture, 1890–1945*, 31–32.

23. Ibid., 31.

24. Dick Osgood, *Wyxie Wonderland: An Unauthorized 50-year Diary of WXYZ Detroit*, 92.

25. Ibid., 75.

26. Heidi MacDonald, "Inside the Superboy Copyright Decision."

27. Siegel and Shuster did win the right to require DC to identify them as Superman's creators (though not the moral right to determine how the character is utilized).

28. Michael Dean, "An Extraordinarily Marketable Man: The Ongoing Struggle for Ownership of Superman and Superboy," 16.

29. Harold Gray to J. M. Patterson, January 17, 1931; J. M. Patterson to Harold Gray, January 18, 1931, Joseph Medill Patterson Papers, 1879–1946, Box 9, Folder 1. Donnelley Library, Lake Forest College, Lake Forest, Illinois.

30. Bob Levin, *The Pirates and the Mouse: Disney's War Against the Counterculture*.

31. Quoted in Helfand, "When Mickey Mouse Is as Strong," 644.

32. Paul du Gay and Michael Pryke, "Introduction," in *Cultural Economy: Cultural Analysis and Commercial Life*, 2.

33. Avi Santo, "A Teenie Weenie Amount of 'Goodwill': Cross-media Character Brand Merchandising in the 1920s," 283–305.

34. Brian Cronin, "Comic Book Legends Revealed #198," accessed April 5, 2013, http://goodcomics.comicbookresources.com/2009/03/12/comic-book-legends-revealed-198/.

35. Gaines, *Contested Culture*, 214.

36. *Chaplin v. Amador*, Court of Appeal of California, First Appellate District, Division Two, July 30, 1928.

37. *Prouty v. National Broadcasting Company*, 1939.

38. "When Mickey Mouse Is as Strong," 646.

39. Quoted in ibid., 640.

40. Rosemary Coombe, "Tenth Anniversary Symposium: New Direction: Critical Cultural Legal Studies," 61.

41. Feldman, "Finding a Home for Fictional Characters," 706.

42. TLS, Trendle to Raymond Meurer, April 13, 1967. George W. Trendle Papers (henceforth "Trendle Papers"), Detroit Public Library, Series II (Business Papers), Subseries C (Productions), Box 46, Folder 13.

43. Quoted in *Wyxie Wonderland*, 386.

44. TLS, James Jewell to Fran Striker, January 21, 1933. Raymond J. Meurer Papers (henceforth "Meurer Papers"), Detroit Public Library, Box 16.

45. Quoted in *Wyxie Wonderland*, 193.

46. Ibid., 400.

47. Jeff Verona, "Heroes and Villains: Ventures and Adventures in the Comic Book Industry," in *Science Fiction and Market Realities*, 185.

48. Alexander Russo, "A Dark(ened) Figure on the Airwaves: Race, Nation and *The Green Hornet*" in *Radio Reader: Essays in the Cultural History of Radio*, ed. Michele Hilmes and Jason Loviglio (New York: Routledge, 2001), 257–276.

49. *Wyxie Wonderland*, 163.

50. David Bordwell, Janet Staiger, and Kristin Thompson, *The Classical Hollywood Cinema: Film Style and Mode of Production to 1960*; Thomas Schatz, *The Genius of the System: Hollywood Filmmaking in the Studio Era*; Kyle Edwards, "Brand-Name Literature: Film Adaptation and Selznick International Pictures' Rebecca," 32–58.

51. Schatz, *The Genius of the System*.

52. *Writers Guide to the Lone Ranger Program*, reprinted in David Rothel, *Who Was That Masked Man? The Story of the Lone Ranger*, 86–89.

53. Ibid.

54. Ibid.

55. TLS, Hank Ketcham to Sandy McGowan, January 31, 1968. Hank Ketcham Papers, Howard Gotlieb Archival Research Center, Boston University, Box 20, Folder 2.

56. Helfand, "When Mickey Mouse Is as Strong," 647n138.

57. Ibid., 648–649.

58. Quoted in ibid., 649.
59. Gaines, *Contested Culture*, 47.
60. In addition to the two cases discussed here, LRI was also concerned with "copycat" properties that might cut into its market share, such as *The Lone Rider* comic book, which also starred a masked cowboy riding a "super horse" (Lightning) accompanied by a Native American sidekick (Swift Arrow). Though the Lone Rider characters did not physically resemble the Lone Ranger, Silver, or Tonto, in 1951, LRI accused its creators of copying the basic formula for Lone Ranger adventures, while also objecting to the use of the word "Lone" in the character's name. Regardless of whether the Lone Rider was a Lone Ranger knock-off, LRI's litigious response indicates how corporate owners utilize IP law to gain competitive advantage over a possible rival.
61. *Helen Kane v. Max Fleischer and Others*. Supreme Court of New York, Appellate Division First Department, May 1936.
62. The film won the 1938 Exhibitor Award for Best Serial of the Year.
63. *Contested Culture*, 107.
64. *Buck Jones v. Republic Productions Inc*. Transcription of deposition. March 31–April 4, 1939, 80. Meurer Papers, Box 16.
65. Ibid., 20.
66. "On the Author Effect," 1992.
67. *Buck Jones v. Republic*, 12.
68. Ibid., 66.
69. Ibid., 28.
70. Ibid., 86.
71. Ibid., 31.
72. Ibid., 110.
73. *Contested Culture*, 68.
74. Ted Striphas, "Harry Potter and the Simulacrum: Contested Copies in an Age of Intellectual Property," 1–17.
75. I found only one brief mention of the case in Dorothy J. Howell's *Intellectual Properties and the Protection of Fictional Characters.*
76. Judge Parker, ruling on *The Lone Ranger Incorporated v. O. C. Cox Operating as Wallace Brothers Circus and Lee Powell*, U.S. Circuit Court of Appeals, 4th Circuit, January 5, 1942, 2. Meurer Papers, Box 18.
77. Due to a plot contrivance, several different actors, including Powell, portrayed the Lone Ranger in the film serial.
78. LexisNexis Academic's legal database shows that the case has been cited in twenty-six other court decisions, including landmark copyright and trademark cases such as *Warner Bros. Pictures, Inc. v. Columbia Broadcasting System, Inc.* (1951), *Columbia Broadcasting System, Inc. v. Decosta* (1967), and *Ideal Toy Corp. v. Kenner Products Div. of General Mills Fun Group, Inc.* (1977).
79. *Dr. Seuss Enterprises v. Penguin Books* is a groundbreaking case because the court distinguished between parody and satire, ruling that satire was not covered by fair use. The court found that *The Cat NOT in the Hat! A Parody by Dr. Juice* did not transform Geisel's initial work through social commentary, but rather, used Geisel's style to satirize the O. J. Simpson murder trial.
80. *Lone Ranger, Inc. v. O. C. Cox*, 4.

81. Ibid., 5.

82. Ibid., 2–3.

83. *Contested Culture*, 214.

84. *Lone Ranger, Inc. v. O. C. Cox*, 6–7.

85. *Wyatt Earp Enterprises v. Sackman, Inc.*, (1958).

86. *CBS v. DeCosta* (1967).

87. *Lone Ranger, Inc. v. O. C. Cox*, 7.

88. Jaeger, "Copyright: Misappropriation of a Character," 1783.

89. Rosemary Coombe, "Tenth Anniversary Symposium: New Direction: Critical Cultural Legal Studies," 473.

90. "DC fires lawyers in Siegel Superman case." *Newsarama*, accessed April 28, 2010, http://blog.newsarama.com/2010/02/28/dc-fires-lawyers-in-siegel-superman-case/.

91. Subject: Lone Ranger Anniversary Story, ca. 1953, 10. Trendle Papers, Series II, Subseries C, Box 69, Folder 20.

92. *Penguin Books USA, Inc., et al. v. Dr. Seuss Enterprises, L.P.*, Supreme Court of the United States, September 22, 1997.

93. "About Us," *Seussville*, accessed April 5, 2013, http://www.seussville.com/faq/about_us.php.

Chapter Five

1. *The History of The Lone Ranger*, anonymous unpublished manuscript, ca. 1954, Chapter 2, p. 2. George W. Trendle Papers (henceforth "Trendle Papers"), Detroit Public Library, Series II (Business Papers), Subseries C (Productions), Box 69, Folder 20.

2. Ibid., Chapter 2, pp. 3–4.

3. Ibid., Chapter 2, pp. 4–5.

4. *General Mills: 75 Years of Innovation, Invention, Food & Fun*, 16, accessed Apri 8, 2013, http://www.generalmills.com/~/media/Files/history/history_book.ashx.

5. *The History of The Lone Ranger*, Chapter 2, p. 5.

6. Tim Brooks and Earle Marsh, *The Complete Dictionary to Prime Time Network and Cable TV Shows, 1946–Present*, 1353–1354.

7. *The History of The Lone Ranger*, Chapter 2, p. 3.

8. Douglas Holt, *How Brands Become Icons: The Principles of Cultural Branding*.

9. *The History of The Lone Ranger*, Chapter 2, p. 5.

10. TLS Trendle to Harry Poppe, February 14, 1950. Trendle Papers, Series II, Subseries C, Box 66, Folder 3.

11. Ibid.

12. Elizabeth Edwards Spalding, *The First Cold Warrior: Harry Truman, Containment, and the Remaking of Liberal Internationalism*.

13. Elaine Tyler May, *Homeward Bound: American Families in the Cold War Era*.

14. Ibid.

15. Lizabeth Cohen, *A Consumers' Republic: The Politics of Mass Consumption in Postwar America*, 7.

16. Henry Jenkins, "Revenge of the Origami Unicorn: The Remaining Four Principles of Transmedia Storytelling" on *Confessions of an Aca-Fan*, December 12, 2009, accessed April 8, 2013, http://henryjenkins.org/2009/12/revenge_of_the_origami_unicorn.html.

17. Holt, *How Brands Become Icons*, 23.

18. J. Clarke Mattimore and Hanibal Coons, "The Fighting Funnies," 24–41.

19. *The Lone Ranger Standards and Background*, 1952, 4. Trendle Papers, Series II, Subseries C, Box 69, Folder 20.

20. Lone Ranger's National Defenders Secret Portfolio, 1941, 6, http://www.thrillingdays.com/premiums/pr-lrnd-page6.html, accessed April 8, 2013.

21. Lee Felbinger, *Collector's Reference and Value Guide to the Lone Ranger*, 105.

22. Lone Ranger's National Defenders Secret Portfolio, 5.

23. Cohen, *A Consumers' Republic*, 7.

24. Greg Castillo, *Cold War on the Home Front: The Soft Power of Midcentury Design*.

25. Will Herberg, *Protestant, Catholic, Jew: An Essay in American Religious Sociology*, 79.

26. Jackson Lears, *Fables of Abundance: A Cultural History of Advertising in America*, 248.

27. Ibid., 249.

28. Herberg, *Protestant, Catholic, Jew*, 264.

29. *Subject: Lone Ranger Anniversary Story*, ca. 1953, 1. Trendle Papers, Series II, Subseries C, Box 69, Folder 20.

30. The episodes in question aired between February 14, 1944 and August 7, 1944. "The Lone Ranger meets Teddy Roosevelt" aired on May 19, 1944. "The Lone Ranger meets Annie Oakley" aired on May 8, 1944.

31. TLS draft, December 21, 1951. Trendle Papers, Series II, Subseries C, Box 43, Folder 5.

32. "Western Union Story" aired July 9, 1952. "Union Pacific, No3" aired November 12, 1947.

33. *The Lone Ranger Standards and Background*, 4.

34. Ibid., 1.

35. Ibid.

36. George Lipsitz, "The Meaning of Memory: Family, Class, and Ethnicity in Early Network Television," in *Private Screenings: Television and the Female Consumer*, 92–93.

37. Ad in *Saturday Evening Post*, November 1949.

38. "Our Best Salesman Rides a Horse."

39. Michael Kimmell, *Manhood in America: A Cultural History*, 240.

40. *Suggested Lone Ranger Interview For Late Evening Programs at Parent Level*, ca. 1951. Trendle Papers, Series II, Subseries C, Box 70, Folder 6.

41. *A Consumers' Republic*, 185–188.

42. Doug Batemma, "Pictures of a Bygone Era: The Syndication of Amos 'n' Andy, 1954–66," 3–39.

43. *The History of The Lone Ranger*, 55.

44. In a July 31, 1950 memo from George Trendle to Alan Campbell, Trendle complains that the ABC standards person is suddenly cracking down on the

show's description of Tonto as a half-breed. Trendle states that LRI had used the term for eighteen years without remark. Trendle Papers, Series II, Subseries C, Box 66, Folder 1.

45. *The Lone Ranger Standards and Background*, 2.

46. "The Origin of Tonto," December 7, 1938.

47. "Enter the Lone Ranger," September 15, 1949.

48. *The Lone Ranger Standards and Background*, 5.

49. Amy Kiste Nyberg, *Seal of Approval: The History of the Comics Code.*

50. Signed contract, Apex Film Productions and Lone Ranger Inc., 1952. Schedule B. Trendle Papers, Series II, Subseries C, Box 69, Folder 6.

51. Bradford Wright, *Comic Book Nation: The Transformation of Youth Culture in America*, 157–172.

52. Quoted in Steven Mintz, *Huck's Raft: A History of American Childhood*, 293.

53. Nyberg, *Seal of Approval*, 1998.

54. *Comic Book Nation*, 60.

55. Umberto Eco, "The Myth of Superman," 14–22.

56. Teen scientist Lex Luthor blames Superboy for an experiment that caused him to lose all his hair. See *Adventure Comics* No. 271 (April 1960). Superboy's teen crush, Lana Lang, makes her first appearance in *Superboy* No. 10 (Sept.–Oct. 1950). A decade later, the adult version of Lana Lang showed up in Metropolis and competed for Superman's affections with Lois Lane. See *Action Comics* No. 272 (January 1961).

57. Henry Jenkins, "The Revenge of the Origami Unicorn: Seven Principles of Transmedia Storytelling (Well, Two Actually. Five More on Friday)," Confessions of an Aca-Fan, December 12, 2009, http://www.henryjenkins.org/2009/12/the_revenge_of_the_origami_uni.html, accessed April 8, 2013.

58. "Mr. & Mrs. Clark (Superman) Kent," *Superman's Girlfriend, Lois Lane* #19 (1961); "Superman & Batman: Brothers," *World's Finest* #172 (December 1967).

59. *Tonto* debuted in 1951 and lasted thirty-one issues. *The Lone Ranger's Famous Horse Hi-Yo Silver* debuted in 1952 and lasted thirty-four issues. In comparison, Dell's *Lone Ranger* title, which launched in 1948, ran until issue 145, published in 1962.

60. *Superman's Pal Jimmy Olsen* debuted October 1954 and lasted 163 issues until March 1974. *Superman's Girlfriend, Lois Lane* debuted March/April 1958 and lasted 137 issues until September/October 1974.

61. Jenkins, December 12, 2009.

62. *The Lone Ranger Standards and Background*, 3.

63. John Thornton Caldwell, *Production Culture: Industrial Reflexivity and Critical Practice in Film and Television*, 7.

64. Dick Osgood, *Wyxie Wonderland: An Unauthorized 50-year Diary of WXYZ Detroit*, 177.

65. Signed contract, LRI and General Mills, March 3, 1941. Trendle Papers, Series II, Subseries C, Box 83, Folder 9.

66. Signed contract, LRI and General Mills, May 16, 1947. Trendle Papers, Series II, Subseries C, Box 83, Folder 9.

67. James L. Baughman, *The Republic of Mass Culture: Journalism, Filmmaking, and Broadcasting in America since 1941*, 65.

68. Michele Hilmes, *Hollywood and Broadcasting: From Radio to Cable*, 146–147.

69. Michael Kackman, "Nothing On But Hoppy Badges: *Hopalong Cassidy*, William Boyd Enterprises, and Emergent Media Globalization," 77–78.

70. TLS Trendle to Chertok, July 11, 1949, and TLS Trendle to Chertok, July 12, 1949. Trendle Papers, Series II, Subseries C, Box 66, Folder 1.

71. Signed Second Television Production Agreement between Apex Film Corporation and Lone Ranger Inc., February 25, 1952, clause 16. Trendle Papers, Series II, Subseries C, Box 69, Folder 6.

72. Brooks and Marsh, *Complete Dictionary*, 1355–1364. Beginning in 1955, CBS scheduled *Sergeant Preston of the Yukon* against *The Lone Ranger*. Ironically, George Trendle once owned both properties. Trendle sold the Lone Ranger to the Jack Wrather Corporation in 1954. He would sell Sergeant Preston to Wrather in 1957.

73. *The History of The Lone Ranger*, Chapter 2, p. 2.

74. *Complete Dictionary*, 1455.

75. Ibid.

76. Ibid., 1456.

77. Ibid.

78. Hilmes, *Hollywood and Broadcasting*, 146.

79. General Mills and LRI stuck with ABC, despite its limited coverage, to cross-market the radio and television series, and because of ABC's investment in attracting "youthful families," where CBS and NBC targeted highbrow viewers. Chris Anderson notes, "ABC chose to align itself with small-ticket advertisers, those selling the types of products that young families might be more likely to need and afford." This fit with General Mills' product lines as well as LRI's merchandising endeavors. Christopher Anderson, *Hollywood TV*, 140.

80. Resume General Mills, Inc—Show Productions—Lone Ranger, Inc Contract, February 1, 1949, clauses 9 and 13.

81. TLS, Trendle to Fralik, April 11, 1949. Trendle Papers, Series II, Subseries C, Box 66, Folder 14.

82. Quoted in letter from Trendle to Chertok, May 12, 1949, Trendle Papers, Series II, Subseries C, Box 65, Folder 10.

83. Alexander Russo, "A Dark(ened) Figure on the Airwaves: Race, Nation and *The Green Hornet*," in *Radio Reader: Essays in the Cultural History of Radio*, ed. Michele Hilmes and Jason Loviglio (New York: Routledge, 2001), 257–276.

84. TLS, Trendle to Fralik, April 11, 1949. Trendle Papers, Series II, Subseries C, Box 66, Folder 14.

85. Trendle correction, April 30, 1952. Trendle Papers, Series II, Subseries C, Box 69, Folder 20.

86. Ibid.

87. Signed contract between The Lone Ranger Incorporated and Republic Productions, Incorporated, June 22, 1937. Trendle Papers, Series II, Subseries C, Box 69, Folder 3.

88. TLS, Trendle to Chertok, April 11, 1950. Trendle Papers, Series II, Subseries C, Box 66, Folder 3.

89. Quoted in letter from Trendle to Chertok, June 20, 1949. Trendle Papers, Series II, Subseries C, Box 65, Folder 10.

90. TLS, Trendle to Chertok, December 18, 1949. Trendle Papers, Series II, Subseries C, Box 66, Folder 2.

91. Michele Hilmes, *Radio Voices: American Broadcasting, 1922–1952*, 20–22.

92. Derek Johnson, "Will the Real Wolverine Please Stand Up? Marvel's Mutation from Monthlies to Movies," in *Film and Comic Books*, 64–85.

93. TLS Striker to Chertok, May 22, 1949; TLS Trendle to Chertok, August 25, 1949; TLS Trendle to Chertok, December 9, 1949. Trendle Papers, Series II, Subseries C, Box 65, Folder 10; Box 66, Folder 1; Box 66, Folder 2.

94. TLS Trendle to Chertok, May 23, 1949. Trendle Papers, Series II, Subseries C, Box 65, Folder 10.

95. Quoted in letter from Striker to Chertok, May 22, 1949. Trendle Papers, Series II, Subseries C, Box 65, Folder 10.

96. TLS Chertok to Trendle, July 10, 1950. Trendle Papers, Series II, Subseries C, Box 66, Folder 4.

97. Signed Television Production Agreement between Apex Film Corporation and The Lone Ranger, Inc., March 22, 1949, clause 16. Trendle Papers, Series II, Subseries C, Box 69, Folder 6.

98. Signed Television Production Agreement between Apex Film Corporation and The Lone Ranger, Inc., clauses 5, 6, 8, 11, and 14.

99. *The Origin and Development of the Lone Ranger*, ca. 1953, 2. Trendle Papers, Series II, Subseries C, Box 69, Folder 20.

100. Jason Mittell, "To Spread or to Drill?" on JustTV.wordpress.com, February 25, 2009, http://justtv.wordpress.com/2009/02/25/to-spread-or-to-drill/, accessed April 8, 2013.

101. "Revenge of the Origami Unicorn."

102. The story unfolded January 15–22, 1947, in four installments titled: "From Outer Space" (Jan. 15, 1947), "The Butterfield Stage" (Jan. 17, 1947), "The Silver Bullet" (Jan. 20, 1947), and "Rays of the Sun" (Jan. 22, 1947).

103. *Hollywood TV*, 153.

104. Signed contract, LRI and General Mills, May 16, 1947. Trendle Papers, Series II, Subseries C, Box 83, Folder 9.

105. Trendle had asked Campbell to conduct a study of successful nonfilmed television series to see if this added expense was cutting into the licensor's profits. Campbell's response revealed that as of January 1950, most nonfilmed series were actually more costly than the Lone Ranger. Interoffice memo, Trendle to Campbell, January 6, 1950; Interoffice memo, Campbell to Trendle, January 19, 1950. Trendle Papers, Series II, Subseries C, Box 43, Folder 13.

106. Ibid. Campbell argued that the show had simply been sold too cheaply and could not be renewed for less than $8,000 per episode.

107. In 1948, all four networks (ABC, CBS, NBC, and Dumont) offered relatively complete prime-time lineups for the first time. *The Lone Ranger* remained a prime-time radio series airing at 7:30 p.m. and thus faced increased competition.

108. *Collector's Reference*, 92–93.

109. Draft of contract between The Lone Ranger, Inc., and Variety Club of Greater Miami, Tent no. 33, January 12, 1951. Raymond J. Meurer Papers (henceforth "Meurer Papers"), Detroit Public Library, Box 9.

110. Lynn Spigel, *Welcome to the Dreamhouse: Popular Media and Postwar Suburbs.*

111. Sean Griffin, "Kings of the Wild Backyard: Davy Crockett and Children's Space," in *Kids' Media Culture*, ed. Marsha Kinder (Durham, NC: Duke University Press, 1999), 102–121.

112. Ibid., 107.

113. Ibid., 104–109.

114. "Liggett's Young Set 'Out West.'"

115. Dorothy J. Howell, *Intellectual Properties and the Protection of Fictional Characters*, 109.

116. Gary Cross, *Kids' Stuff: Toys and the Changing World of American Childhood*, 164.

117. Quoted in Peter Caranicas, "Bibles Hold Tentpole Revivals," 5.

118. "Game On! Intelligent Designs or Fan Aggregators?" April 8, 2011. A video of the symposium is available on Henry Jenkins's blog, accessed April 8, 2013, http://henryjenkins.org/2011/07/transmedia_hollywood_2_videos.html.

119. "Will the Real Wolverine Please Stand Up?," 69.

120. David Aaker, *Building Strong Brands*.

121. David Aaker, "How CMOs Build Brands by Collaborating Across Silos," on HBR Blog Network, May 31, 2011, http://blogs.hbr.org/cs/2011/05/five_collaboration_routes_for.html, accessed April 8, 2013.

Chapter Six

1. *Esquire* magazine, February 1973.

2. *Berry's World*, July 29, 1965.

3. Andy Nairn, "Nostalgia—it ain't what it used to be," *The Guardian*, May 13, 2009, accessed March 17, 2013, http://www.guardian.co.uk/commentisfree/2009/may/13/advertising-nostalgia.

4. David Aaker, *Building Strong Brands*, 231.

5. Brooks Barnes, "Beloved Characters as Reimagined for the 21st Century."

6. In Alexandra Bruell, "Modern Branding Campaigns Develop a Nostalgic Feeling," *PR Week*, July 6, 2010, accessed March 17, 2013, http://www.allbusiness.com/marketing-advertising/marketing-techniques/14768827-1.html.

7. Paul Earle, "The Real Reason Brand Revival Works," *Brand Channel*, February 16, 2004, accessed March 17, 2013, http://www.brandchannel.com/brand_speak.asp?bs_id=78.

8. Barnes, "Beloved Characters."

9. Marilyn Liebrenz-Himes, Hamed Shamma, and Robert F. Dyer, "Heritage Brands—Treasured Inheritance or 'Over the Hill,'" 140.

10. *The Lone Ranger: A Planned Pattern*. Report, 1958. Wrather Papers, Series 5 (Wrather Entertainment and Business Interests), Box 1, Folder 8.

11. In a 1980 letter to a disgruntled stockholder, Jack Wrather waxed poetic about his company's legacy, claiming, "I suppose in some small way we started the 'conglomerate' craze back in the early 60s when we bought and owned television and radio stations, the Lone Ranger and Lassie, built the Disneyland hotel, bought Muzak, WNEW, Stephens Marine, and even, God save the mark, A. C. Gilbert, among other things." TLT, Jack Wrather to Thomas L. Kepner, Octo-

ber 27, 1980. Jack and Bonita Granville Wrather Papers (henceforth "Wrather Papers"), Loyola Marymount University Archives, Series 5 (Wrather Entertainment and Business Interests), Box 6, Folder 5.

12. Lone Ranger Television Series Promotional Kit, May 20, 1964. Wrather Papers, Series 5, Box 1, Folder 1.

13. "Wrather Corp.'s Last Roundup," 68.

14. Ibid.

15. *A View of Wrather Corporation in 1975 and a Look at 1976*, Confidential—For the Board of Directors, January 19, 1976. Wrather Papers, Series 1, Subseries B (Subject Files), Box 3, Folder 4.

16. Wrather Papers, Series 1, Subseries B, Box 1, Folder 12.

17. Olga Neville, "For Your Holiday . . . Why Not a Nice Bank Hold-Up?" *Olga Neville's Hollywood Report*, ca. 1957. Wrather Papers, Series 5, Box 1, Folder 8.

18. "Wrather Corp.'s Last Roundup."

19. Jerry Buck, "Masked Man Still Cries 'Hi Ho' in 48 Countries."

20. "Wrather Corp.'s Last Roundup."

21. Ibid.

22. Ibid.

23. *Looking Back and Looking Ahead: JWC Mission*, ca. 1977, 3. Wrather Papers, Series 1, Subseries B, Box 3, Folder 5.

24. *The Lone Ranger: A Planned Pattern.*

25. Hal Humphrey, "Lone Rangers Never Die."

26. *The Lone Ranger: A Planned Pattern.*

27. "The Lone Ranger Fact Sheet." *News from the Lone Ranger*, ca. 1960. Wrather Papers, Series 5, Box 1, Folder 2.

28. Derek Kompare, *Rerun Nation: How Repeats Invented American Television*, 69.

29. Olga Neville, "The Marshal Who Drank Only Milk!" *Olga Neville's Hollywood Report*, ca. 1957. Wrather Papers, Series 5, Box 1, Folder 8.

30. Jason Mittell, "The Great Saturday Morning Exile: Scheduling Cartoons on Television's Periphery in the 1960s," 33–54.

31. By the late 1950s, General Mills was primarily sponsoring animated TV series like *Rocky and His Friends*, starring Rocky and Bullwinkle. Of greater significance, the company had invested considerable resources into developing its own slate of animated characters featured during commercials on Saturday mornings, including Trix the Rabbit, Lucky the Leprechaun, Count Chocula, etc. *General Mills: 75 Years of Innovation, Invention, Food & Fun*, accessed April 8, 2013, http://www.generalmills.com/~/media/Files/history/history_book.ashx.

32. Eric Schaefer, *"Bold! Daring! Shocking! True!" A History of Exploitation Films, 1919–1959.*

33. "The Top Box-Office Hits of 1956."

34. Wrather Papers, Series 5, Box 1, Folder 4.

35. Jonathan Gray, *Show Sold Separately: Promos, Spoilers, and Other Media Paratexts.*

36. Henry Jenkins, "'The All-American Handful': Dennis the Menace, Permissive Childrearing and the Bad Boy Tradition."

37. Benjamin Holcomb, *Mego 8" Super-Heroes: World's Greatest Toys!*

38. *The Lone Ranger Rides Again!* Toy Catalog, Gabriel Industries, 1973. Wrather Papers, Series 5, Box 1, Folder 4.

39. Stan Stunell to Stuart Christenfeld, May 16, 1980. Wrather Papers, Series 1, Subseries C (The Legend of the Lone Ranger Film Production), Box 1, Folder 1.

40. JWC interoffice memo, Stan Stunell to Jack Wrather, August 10, 1977. Wrather Papers, Series 1, Subseries C, Box 2, Folder 7.

41. JWC interoffice memo, Stan Stunell to Jack Wrather, November 16, 1977. Wrather Papers, Series 1, Subseries C, Box 2, Folder 7.

42. Stan Stunell to Stuart Christenfeld, May 16, 1980. Wrather Papers, Series 1, Subseries C, Box 1, Folder 1.

43. *The Lone Ranger: A Treatment for a Television Series*, 1976. Wrather Papers, Series 1, Subseries C, Box 4, Folder 6.

44. Todd Gitlin, *Inside Prime Time*, 203–220.

45. *Lone Ranger Television Series Possible Formats*, n.d. Wrather Papers, Series 1, Subseries C, Box 2, Folder 7.

46. Ibid.

47. Ibid.

48. Ibid.

49. *In Search of the Lone Ranger Starring Lassie: A Television Series Outline*, September 19, 1975. Wrather Papers, Series 1, Subseries C, Box 3, Folder 8.

50. The Lone Ranger had made a previous guest appearance on *Lassie* in the episode "Peace Patrol" (1959). Timmy and Lassie try to apprehend a thief who has stolen money for Lone Ranger–sponsored government bonds.

51. *In Search of the Lone Ranger Starring Lassie: A Television Series Outline*, September 19, 1975.

52. *Lone Ranger Resume*, marketing document draft, June 8, 1977. Wrather Papers, Series 1, Subseries C, Box 3, Folder 8.

53. Justin Wyatt, *High Concept: Movies and Marketing in Hollywood.*

54. Ali was the world heavyweight boxing champion at the time casting decisions were being made, and had taken on the popular nickname Black Superman after a Johnny Wakelin song written about him. Recognizing Ali's popularity among adult males and within the African American community, demographics that were not perceived at the time to be avid comic book readers, DC Comics sought to capitalize on the cross-promotional possibilities to extend their market reach, including publishing an oversized *Superman versus Muhammad Ali* comic in 1978, which featured Ali and Superman teaming up to thwart an alien invasion. Though it is unlikely that DC or parent company TWI would have ultimately approved casting Ali as Superman, the buzz generated by leaking the possibility that he might be considered for the role seems to fit with the company's overall brand association and extension strategies.

55. Thomas Schatz, *Old Hollywood/New Hollywood: Ritual, Art, and Industry*, 189–216.

56. Ibid.

57. John Cawelti, "*Chinatown* and Generic Transformation in Recent American Films," 288.

58. Ibid., 294.

59. Ibid., 289.

60. Ibid., 295.

61. Schatz, *Old Hollywood/New Hollywood.*

62. David A. Cook, *Lost Illusions: American Cinema in the Shadow of Watergate and Vietnam, 1970–1979*, 58.

63. "Hoping to Soar with Superman," 150.

64. Ibid.

65. Miles Beller, "Hollywood Is Banking on the Comics."

66. "Hoping to Soar with Superman," 147.

67. Ibid., 151.

68. *Box Office Mojo*, April 8, 2013.

69. "Hoping to Soar with Superman," 150.

70. Beller, "Hollywood is Banking."

71. Ibid.

72. Robert Evans, *The Kid Stays in the Picture*, 302.

73. Kimberly Ann Owczarski, *Batman, Time Warner, and Franchise Filmmaking in the Conglomerate Era*, PhD diss., University of Texas at Austin, 2008, 215–218.

74. "Box office statistics for *Popeye* (1980)," *The Numbers*, accessed April 8, 2013, http://www.the-numbers.com/movies/1980/0PPY.php.

75. Cook, *Lost Illusions*, 97.

76. Marstar Productions interoffice memo, Stuart Mandel to Martin Starger, January 5, 1978. Wrather Papers, Series 1, Subseries C, Box 2, Folder 6.

77. "Box office statistics for *Legend of the Lone Ranger* (1981)," *The Numbers*, accessed April 8, 2013, http://www.the-numbers.com/movies/1981/0LOLR.php.

78. "Box office statistics for *Flash Gordon* (1980)," *The Numbers*, accessed April 8, 2013, http://www.the-numbers.com/movies/1980/0FLGO.php; "Box office statistics for *Annie* (1982)," *The Numbers*, accessed April 8, 2013, http://www.the-numbers.com/movies/1982/0ANNI.php.

79. "Box office statistics for *Superman* (1978)," *The Numbers*, accessed April 8, 2013, http://www.the-numbers.com/movies/series/Superman.php.

80. Richard Freedman, "Bite the Silver Bullet"; Clark Walworth, "New Lone Ranger Rides in Remake."

81. JWC interoffice memo, Jack Wrather to Stan Stunell et al., February 15, 1980. Wrather Papers, Series 1, Subseries C, Box 1, Folder 9.

82. Hank Grant, "Hank Grant Rambling Reporter," *Hollywood Reporter*, July 29, 1977.

83. *Legend of the Lone Ranger Promotional Guide from Universal Pictures*, ca. 1981. Wrather Papers, Series 1, Subseries C, Box 4, Folder 10.

84. Ibid.

85. TLS, John C. Calhoun, Marketing Coordinator for Associated Film Distribution, to Stan Stunell, September 16, 1980. Wrather Papers, Series 1, Subseries C, Box 2, Folder 3.

86. JWC interoffice memo, Bill Shay to Jack Wrather, March 25, 1981. Wrather Papers, Series 1, Subseries C, Box 2, Folder 3.

87. *The Lone Ranger: Concept Development Survey Report*, National Center for Survey Research, 1978. Wrather Papers, Series 1, Subseries C, Box 1, Folder 4.

88. JWC interoffice memo, Stan Stunell to Jack Wrather, January 29, 1980. Wrather Papers, Series 1, Subseries C, Box 3, Folder 8.

89. Robert Enders (1978), William Roberts (1978), Ivan Goff (1979), Ben Roberts (1979), Rob Thompson (1979), Michael Kane (1980), and Gerald Derloshon (1980).

90. JWC interoffice memo, Stan Stunell to Jack Wrather, March 20, 1978. Wrather Papers, Series 1, Subseries C, Box 3, Folder 8.

91. JWC interoffice memo, Stan Stunell to Jack Wrather, April 4, 1980. Wrather Papers, Series 1, Subseries C, Box 3, Folder 8.

92. Gary Deeb, "Good Guys Winning the 'Lone Ranger' Battle," 23.

93. Interoffice memo, Stan Stunell to Jack Wrather, February 21, 1978. Wrather Papers, Series 1, Subseries C, Box 3, Folder 8.

94. Quoted in M. Greco, "Clayton Moore for Fair Play," 3–4.

95. Gary Arnold, "Endangered Ranger," F7.

96. Janet Maslin, "The Lone Ranger Rides Again Once More," C8.

97. April Mansfield, "Disquiet on the Western Front: Who Was That Masked Man I Saw You With?," F1.

98. David Rothel, *Who Was That Masked Man? The Story of the Lone Ranger*, 242.

99. Quoted in Mansfield, "Disquiet on the Western Front."

100. Moore objected to this particular ad because, first, he received no royalties for it, and second, he felt that associating the Lone Ranger with aftershave besmirched the Masked Man's masculinity.

101. Quoted in Deeb, "Good Guys Winning."

102. Polly Paddock, "Lone Ranger Rides Again—In Sleek Car," 1E, 4E.

103. Russell Baker, "The Lone Ranger Bites the Silver Bullet.

104. Quoted in Mansfield, "Disquiet on the Western Front."

105. TLS Trendle to Moore, August 15, 1949. George W. Trendle Papers (henceforth "Trendle Papers"), Detroit Public Library, Series II (Business Papers), Subseries C (Productions), Box 68, Folder 12.

106. Ibid.

107. Chadwick Allen, "Omnimedia Marketing: The Case of the Lone Ranger," 478–479.

108. Quoted in Rothel, *Who Was That Masked Man?*, 248, 250.

109. TLS, Edna Gayle Cunningham to Bonita Wrather, August 12, 1980. Wrather Papers, Series 1, Subseries C, Box 5, Folder 4.

110. *Who Was That Masked Man?*, 250.

111. Ibid.

112. Stephen Brown, Robert V. Kozinets, and John F. Sherry Jr., "Teaching Old Brands New Tricks: Retro Branding and the Revival of Brand Meaning," *Journal of Marketing* 67 (July 2003): 19–33.

113. Adam Arvidsson, "Brands: A Critical Perspective," 235–258.

114. "Good Guys Winning."

115. Ibid.

116. Quoted in "Q&A: How Bad Publicity Hit 'Legend of the Lone Ranger,'" A1–A2.

117. "Good Guys Winning."

118. *Who Was That Masked Man?*, 248.

119. JWC interoffice memo, Jack Wrather to Stan Stunell, November 8, 1981. Wrather Papers, Series 1, Subseries C, Box 4, Folder 4.

120. Ibid.

121. Ibid.

122. See unpublished chapter draft by David Rothel, *Who Was That Masked Man?*, 251. Jack and Bonita Granville Wrather Papers, Loyola Marymount University Archives, Series 5 (Wrather Entertainment and Business Interests), Box 2, Folder 4.

123. "Box office statistics for *Heaven's Gate* (1980)," *The Numbers*, accessed April 8, 2013, http://www.the-numbers.com/movies/1980/0HVGT.php.

124. The WB also announced plans to create a series based on L. Frank Baum's *Oz* books as well as updated versions of *MacGyver*, *The Courtship of Eddie's Father*, and *Tarzan*.

125. Rob Owen, "New 'Lone Ranger' pales in comparison to the original."

126. Gail Pennington, "Hi-Yo! Lone Ranger Rides Again—on the WB."

127. Owen, "New 'Lone Ranger.'"

128. Quoted in Lev Grossman, "*Star Trek*: Back to the Final Frontier," *Time*, April 23, 2009, accessed March 17, 2013, http://www.time.com/time/magazine/article/0,9171,1893488,00.html.

129. Ibid.

Chapter Seven

1. Tweet from Jerry Bruckheimer, March 7, 2012, accessed March 11, 2012.

2. Tweet from Jerry Bruckheimer, March 8, 2012, accessed March 11, 2012.

3. Google search for "Lone Ranger + Bruckheimer + Twitter" conducted on March 11, 2012.

4. "Portfolio," *Classic Media Website*, accessed April 14, 2010, http://www.classicmedia.tv/.

5. Richard Verrier, "DreamWorks Animation buys 'Casper,' 'Lassie' parent Classic Media."

6. "2011 Top 125 Global Licensors," T1–T30.

7. "About US," Classic Media, accessed April 14, 2010, http://www.classicmedia.tv/.

8. Pierre Bourdieu, *The Field of Cultural Production: Essays on Art and Literature*.

9. Henry Jenkins, *Convergence Culture: Where Old and New Media Collide*; Henry Jenkins, Sam Ford, and Joshua Green, *Spreadable: Creating Value and Meaning in a Networked Culture*.

10. Simone Murray, "'Celebrating the Story the Way It Is': Cultural Studies, Corporate Media and the Contested Utility of Fandom," 7–25.

11. Adam Arvidsson, "Brands: A Critical Perspective," 235–258.

12. Verrier, "DreamWorks Animation."

13. *Licensing Industry Survey, 2012*.

14. Amanda Peabody, "Brazil Steps Up Its Licensing Game," 34–38; Tony Lisanti, "Global Licensors: New, Noteworthy and the Impressive," 8.

15. *Licensing Industry Survey, 2012*.

16. James McNeal, quoted in "BuyBabies"; K. Campbell and K. Davis-Packard, "How ads get kids to say I want it!" *Christian Science Monitor*.

17. D. Hayes, "Invasion of the Techie Tots," 1.
18. Ibid.
19. Quoted in Bernadette Casey, "A Brand that Endures," 40–42.
20. "Dora the Explorer Curriculum," NickJr.com, accessed May 11, 2013, http://www.nickjr.com/dora-the-explorer/about-dora-the-explorer/dora-the-explorer-curriculum.html.
21. Ibid., accessed April 14, 2010.
22. http://www.Disneystore.com, accessed April 14, 2010.
23. Brooks Barnes, "Beloved Characters as Reimagined for the 21st Century."
24. Ibid.
25. Thomas Whitaker, "Hulk Doll's Monster Willy," *The Sun* [London], August 1, 2007, http://www.thesun.co.uk/sol/homepage/news/81124/Hulk-dolls-monster-willy.html.
26. David Thomas, "Fury over Asda's 'sexually suggestive' Disney underwear for young girls," *The Telegraph*, August 14, 2008, http://www.telegraph.co.uk/news/2556204/Fury-over-Asdas-sexually-suggestive-Disney-underwear-for-young-girls.html.
27. Nick Hughes, "Character assassination: health crusaders have hit character licensing—and particularly confectionery—hard, but the likes of Lazy Town's healthy hero Sporticus offer some hope."
28. Ibid.
29. Lynn Truong, "Looney Toons Eating Right Kids Review," Parentingsquad.com, September 11, 2009, accessed April 14, 2010, http://parentingsquad.com/looney-toons-eating-right-kids-review.
30. Hughes, "Character assassination."
31. Quoted in Casey, "A Brand that Endures."
32. "*I Love Lucy*: No Splainin' Necessary," *Global Licence!*, 2–3.
33. Karen Raugust, *Merchandise Licensing in the Television Industry*.
34. "*I Love Lucy*: No Splainin' Necessary."
35. Quoted in Tony Lisanti, "Turtle Power," *Global Licence!* (September/October 2012): 42–48.
36. Quoted in Amanda Cioletti, "Man of Steel," *Global Licence!* (February 2013): 50–51.
37. John Thornton Caldwell, *Production Culture: Industrial Reflexivity and Critical Practice in Film and Television* (Durham, NC: Duke University Press, 2008).
38. "The Lone Ranger Code" was used as a promotional device, May 15–31, 2013, on Facebook and Twitter.
39. Quoted in Cioletti, "Man of Steel."
40. Jonathan V. Last, "The Crash of 1993," *The Daily Standard*, vol. 16, no. 37, June 13, 2011, accessed May 7, 2012, http://www.weeklystandard.com/articles/crash-1993_573252.html?nopager=1.
41. Tony Lisanti, "Toy Power Rises," *Global Licence!*, 80.
42. *Marvel Entertainment Annual Report for Stockholders*, 3.
43. Ibid.
44. *Marvel Entertainment Annual Report for Stockholders*, 3.
45. Patrick Goldstein, "Disney's purchase of Marvel is a super deal."
46. "2010 Top 125 Global Licensors," T5.

47. "2011 Top 125 Global Licensors," T4.
48. Tony Lisanti, "Disney's New Character," 48–54.
49. "2011 Top 125 Global Licensors."
50. Ibid.
51. Quoted in "Disney's New Character."
52. Lisanti, "Turtle Power."
53. Ibid.
54. *Marvel Entertainment Annual Report for Stockholders.*
55. "Specific deadline timetables for Marvel's licensed films," *Superhero Hype*, August 2012, accessed September 11, 2012, http://forums.superherohype.com/showthread.php?t=452113.
56. Norman Kagan, *The Cinema of Robert Zemeckis*, 93–117.
57. Jeffrey Price and Peter S. Seaman, *Who Shot Roger Rabbit.*
58. Kagan, *Cinema of Robert Zemeckis.*
59. "Toy Wonder."
60. Ibid.
61. David Price, *The Pixar Touch*, 128.
62. Karen Paik, *To Infinity and Beyond! The Story of Pixar Animation Studios*, 104.
63. "Toy Wonder."
64. Derek Johnson, *Franchising Media Worlds: Content Networks and the Collaborative Production of Culture*, PhD diss., University Of Wisconsin, Madison, 2009.
65. "2011 Top 125 Global Licensors."
66. "Marvel's Greatest Licensed Comics," *Comic Book Resources*, July 14, 2010, accessed May 12, 2013, http://forums.comicbookresources.com/showthread.php?330648-Marvel-s-greatest-Licensed-comics.
67. Sam Thielman, "How Lego Became the Most Valuable Toy Company in the World," Adweek, April 15, 2013, accessed May 12, 2013, http://www.adweek.com/news/advertising-branding/how-lego-became-most-valuable-toy-company-world-148578.
68. "2011 Top 125 Global Licensors."
69. Ibid.
70. Ibid.
71. "Mattel Completes Acquisition of HIT Entertainment," HitEntertainment.com, February 1, 2012, accessed May 12, 2013, http://www.hitentertainment.com/corporate/newsdetail.aspx?nid=9.
72. Tony Lisanti, "Jessi Dunne Brings New Magic to Mattel, 24–25.
73. Quoted in Tony Lisanti, "Barbie's Wow Factor," 72–74.
74. Ibid.
75. Ibid.
76. Thielman, "How Lego Became the Most Valuable."
77. Ibid.
78. Ibid.
79. Ibid.
80. Ibid.
81. "How Lego Handles Licensing," *Managing Intellectual Property*, April 1, 2012.
82. "How Lego Became the Most Valuable."

83. Ibid.

84. Jean Baudrillard, *Simulacra and Simulation (The Body, In Theory: Histories of Cultural Materialism)* (Ann Arbor: University of Michigan Press, 1995).

85. "How Lego Became the Most Valuable Toy Coompany."

86. Chris Bilton, *Management and Creativity: From Creative Industries to Creative Management*; Philip Schlesinger, "The most creative organization in the world? The BBC, 'Creativity' and 'Managerial Style,'" *International Journal of Cultural Policy* 16, no. 3 (2010): 271–285.

87. *Franchising Media Worlds.*

88. Bilton, *Management and Creativity.*

89. Quoted in Lisanti, "Disney's New Character."

90. Ibid.

91. Tony Lisanti, "Jessi Dunne Brings New Magic to Mattel," 24–25. .

92. Allie Townsend, "*Green Lantern* and Mattel: Friends with Benefits."

93. Ibid.

94. "Why the Licensing Surge?—Because it Sells!!" (ca. 1976), accessed April 14, 2010, http://megomuseum.com/megolibrary/adarchive/1976/licensing.html.

95. Tony Lisanti, "The Retail Reality," 8.

96. *History of Retailing in North America.*

97. 2010 Walmart and Target annual reports.

98. *History of Retailing in North America.*

99. Quoted in Lisanti, "Barbie's Wow Factor."

100. Quoted in Lisanti, "Disney's New Character."

101. Quoted in ibid.

102. Quoted in Lisanti, "Barbie's Wow Factor."

103. *History of Retailing in North America.*

104. Murray, "'Celebrating the Story.'"

105. Arvidsson, "Brands: A Critical Perspective."

106. Quoted in "Barbie's Wow Factor."

107. Mae Anderson, "Toymakers aggressively court mommy bloggers," NBC News.com, December 20, 2011, accessed May 12, 2013, http://www.nbcnews.com/id/45742380/ns/business-holiday_retail/t/toymakers-aggressively-court-mommy-bloggers/#.UY_m1q7QY1p.

108. Quoted in ibid.

109. Quoted in Harry Bradford, "Mattel Faces Backlash After Toy Company Tries To Teach Moms How To Play With Hot Wheels.

110. Stats from *Lone Ranger* and *Man of Steel* Facebook pages, May 6, 2013, accessed May 12, 2013, http://www.facebook.com/TheLoneRanger?ref=ts&fref=ts; http://www.facebook.com/manofsteel?ref=ts&fref=ts.

111. Search performed on March 6, 2013.

112. Though JWC recouped its investment in *Legend of the Lone Ranger* from foreign box-office receipts, a loss of stockholder faith and Jack Wrather's declining health led to the company's dissolution in the mid-1980s.

113. "Wrather Corp. Announces Agreement to Sell its TV and Motion Picture Properties to Southbrook Television Corp."

114. Figures ascertained using Measuring Worth converter, accessed May 12, 2013, http://www.measuringworth.com/uscompare/.

115. David J. Fox, "Hi Yo! Salute to the Lone Ranger Set in Lone Pine"; "DreamWorks buys Classic Media for $155 million."

116. Topps entered the comic book market in 1993 to create synergies between its trading cards and other media. At the time, the comic book industry was booming. In addition to the Lone Ranger, Topps also published the X-Files and Xena comic books. Within two years, the comic book boom went bust. Topps ceased publishing comic books in 1998.

117. Michael Fleming, "Fox Family Wrangles Ranger," 1.

118. Claude Brodesser, "'Ranger' Rides to Columbia."

119. Ibid.

120. "Interview with Michael Uslan—Part 1," November 8, 2005, accessed May 12, 2013, http://www.batman-on-film.com/interview_muslan_2.html.

121. Ibid.

122. Nancy Griffin and Kim Masters, *Hit & Run: How Jon Peters and Peter Guber Took Sony For A Ride In Hollywood*.

123. Ken Hanke, *Tim Burton: An Unauthorized Biography of the Filmmaker* (New York: Renaissance Books, 1999).

124. Ibid.

125. Eileen Meehan, "'Holy Commodity Fetish, Batman!' The Political Economy of a Commercial Intertext," 47–65.

126. In 1967, Kinney National acquired DC Comics parent company National Periodicals Press. Four years later, Kinney CEO Steve Ross would change the company's name to Warner Communications following the purchase of Warner Brothers studios.

127. "Characters," Dynamite Entertainment website, accessed May 12, 2013, http://www.dynamite.com/htmlfiles/infoDB.html?index=characters.

128. "Lone Ranger #1 Sells Out!," Dynamite Entertainment, press release, accessed May 12, 2013, http://www.dynamiteentertainment.com/htmlfiles/lone rangerpress091506.html.

129. "Your 2007 Eisner Award Nominees," *The Comics Reporter*, April 19, 2007, accessed May 12, 2013, http://www.comicsreporter.com/index.php/your_2007_eisner_award_nominees/.

130. Diane Mermigas, "Disney's Superhero Bid for Elusive Young Males," *CBS News Moneywatch*, September 1, 2009, accessed May 12, 2013, http://www.cbsnews.com/8301–505123_162–33243927/disneys-superhero-bid-for-elusive-young-males/.

131. Alex Billington, "Disney Stops Production on Verbinski's 'The Lone Ranger' with Depp," FirstShowing.net, August 13, 2011, http://www.firstshowing.net/2011/disney-stops-production-on-verbinskis-the-lone-ranger-with-depp/; Kyle Buchanan, "Those *Lone Ranger* Budget Cuts Didn't Work," *Vulture*, June 13, 2012, http://www.vulture.com/2012/06/those-lone-ranger-budget-cuts-didnt-work.html. All sites accessed May 12, 2013.

132. "Cassaday Joins the Lone Ranger," IGN.com, December 12, 2005, accessed May 12, 2013, http://www.ign.com/articles/2005/12/13/cassaday-joins-lone-ranger.

133. "About the Film," *Lone Ranger* website, accessed May 12, 2013, http://disney.go.com/the-lone-ranger/#/about.

134. Kim Masters, "Jerry Bruckheimer Breaks His Silence on Disney's $215 Million 'Lone Ranger' Compromise."

135. Jeff Ames, "Johnny Depp Likes Brad Pitt or George Clooney to Play the Lone Ranger," *Collider*, December 1, 2010, http://collider.com/the-lone-ranger-brad-pitt-george-clooney/; "Ryan Gosling In 'The Lone Ranger'? Star In Talks For Johnny Depp Classic," *Huffington Post*, April 16, 2011, http://www.huffingtonpost.com/2011/04/16/ryan-gosling-in-the-lone-ranger_n_850011.html. All sites accessed May 12, 2013.

136. Correspondence between David O. Selznick, Raymond Meurer, Katherine Brown, and Daniel O'Shea, Executive VP Selznick Productions, March 18–April 15, 1942. Selznick Papers, Box 842, Harry Ransom Humanities Research Center.

137. "Johnny Depp's 'Lone Ranger' Seeks To 'Reinvent' Tonto, Native American Treatment," *Huffington Post*, May 9, 2011, accessed May 12, 2013, http://www.huffingtonpost.com/2011/05/09/johnny-depps-lone-ranger-tonto-native-americans_n_859279.html.

138. Julie Miller, "Of Course Johnny Depp Can Make *The Lone Ranger* Remake Look Cool," VanityFair.com, March 8, 2012, accessed May 12, 2013, http://www.vanityfair.com/online/oscars/2012/03/johnny-depp-armie-hammer-the-lone-ranger-preview.

139. Ibid.

140. *Box Office Mojo*. Data retrieved April 18, 2012.

141. *Disney Corporation Report to Shareholders, 2007.*

142. Quoted in Rebecca Keegan, "'Lone Ranger': Masked man need not be a star, says Bruckheimer."

143. Paul Lopes, *Demanding Respect: The Evolution of the American Comic Book*.

144. "Looking Ahead With The Lone Ranger," Newsarama.com, April 23, 2007, accessed May 12, 2013, http://www.dynamite.com/boards/showthread.php?874-Newsarama-Ranger-Article.

145. Quoted in Cliff Biggers, "The Lone Ranger Rides Again," 1.

146. Quoted in Anthony Breznican, "Johnny Depp wants 'The Lone Ranger' to back off Tonto: 'Why is the f——ing Lone Ranger telling Tonto what to do?,'" EW.com, May 8, 2011, accessed May 12, 2013, http://insidemovies.ew.com/2011/05/08/johnny-depp-tonto-lone-ranger/.

147. Lauren Humphries-Brooks, "New Trailer For The Lone Ranger Hypes The Plot, The Actors And The Trains," Wegotitcovered.com, April 15, 2013, accessed May 12, 2013, http://wegotthiscovered.com/movies/ne-trailer-lone-ranger-hypes-plot-actors-trains/.

148. "'The Lone Ranger'—Most anticipated movies of summer 2013: Fandango's Top 10," Examiner.com, April 16, 2013, accessed May 12, 2013, http://www.examiner.com/list/most-anticipated-movies-of-summer-2013-fandango-s-top-10/8-the-lone-ranger.

149. Joseph Pine and James Gilmore, *The Experience Economy*.

150. Ibid.

151. "Hot Toys or NECA?," SideshowCollectors.com forum, August 8, 2010, http://www.sideshowcollectors.com/forums/showthread.php?t=81195; "Collector's Spotlight" on NECA website, http://necaonline.com/category/blog/collector-spotlight/. Both sites accessed May 12, 2013.

152. Prices gathered from Amazon.com, Toysrus.com, Walmart.com, Target .com, EntertainmentEarth.com, Mattel.com, and Lego.com on May 2, 2013.

153. Ibid.

154. Ibid.

155. "How Lego Became the Most Valuable Player."

156. The first *Lone Ranger* trailer debuted October 2, 2012. The second trailer debuted December 11, 2012. The third trailer debuted April 17, 2013.

157. Kevin Jaggernauth, "Latest 'Lone Ranger' Draft Ditches Supernatural Elements, But Set Pieces Will Need To Be Scaled Back," *Indie Wire*, August 17, 2011, http://blogs.indiewire.com/theplaylist/lastest_lone_ranger_draft_ditches_supernatural_elements_but_setpieces_will_; Drew Taylor, "Jerry Bruckheimer Says Supernatural Coyotes Out, Train Sequences Stay In Scaled Down 'Lone Ranger,'" *Indie Wire*, October 19, 2011, http://blogs.indiewire.com/theplaylist/jerry_bruckheimer_explains_how_he_trimmed_the_budget_of_lone_ranger_by_doin. Both sites accessed May 12, 2013.

158. "How Lego Became the Most Valuable Player."

159. Jason Mittell, "To Spread or to Drill?," *Just TV*, February 25, 2009, accessed May 12, 2013, http://justtv.wordpress.com/2009/02/25/to-spread-or-to-drill/.

160. "LEGO Lone Ranger Constitution Train Chase Review: LEGO 79111," *BrickShow*, March 29, 2013, accessed September 6, 2010, http://www.youtube.com/watch?v=yKBC3AYDFJQ.

161. Ibid.

162. Ibid.

163. "How Lego Became the Most Valuable Player."

164. "LEGO Lone Ranger Constitution."

165. "Review: 79107 Comanche Camp," Brickset.com, March 19, 2013, accessed May 12, 2013, http://www.brickset.com/news/article/?ID=6026.

166. "Dreamworks Animation Agrees to Acquire Classic Media." Press release, July 23, 2012, accessed May 12, 2013, http://ir.dreamworksanimation.com/releasedetail.cfm?ReleaseID=694144.

Chapter Eight

1. George Szalai, "Disney Analysts Peg 'Lone Ranger' Loss at up to $190 Million, Remain Bullish on Stock," *Hollywood Reporter*, August 9, 2013, accessed October 2, 2013, http://www.hollywoodreporter.com/news/disney-analysts-peg-lone-ranger-581961.

2. "The Lone Ranger," Boxofficemojo.com, accessed October 2, 2013, http://www.boxofficemojo.com/movies/?id=loneranger.htm.

3. Marc Grasser, "'The Lone Ranger' Could Cost Disney Up to $190 million in Losses," *Variety*, August 13, 2013, accessed October 2, 2013, http://variety.com/2013/film/news/the-lone-ranger-could-lose-disney-up-to-190-million-1200574995/.

4. Playlist Staff, "What Went Wrong? The Good, The Bad & The Weird Of Disney's 'The Lone Ranger,'" IndieWire.com, July 8, 2013, accessed October 2, 2013, http://blogs.indiewire.com/theplaylist/after-the-dusts-settled-the-good-the-bad-and-the-weird-of-disneys-the-lone-ranger-20130708?page=2.

5. http://www.disneystore.com/the-lone-ranger/mn/1018202/?searchRedirect =1&searchTerm=Lone+Ranger&catalogFromSearch=10002, accessed October 2, 2013.

6. Sharon Waxman, "Disney to End First-Look Deal With Jerry Bruckheimer," *The Wrap*, September 19, 2013, accessed October 2, 2013, http://www.thewrap .com/disney-to-end-first-look-deal-with-jerry-bruckheimer/.

7. "The Lone Ranger," Rottentomatoes.com, accessed October 2, 2013, http:// www.rottentomatoes.com/m/the_lone_ranger/.

8. Jonathan Kim, "ReThink Review: The Lone Ranger—Tonto Redeemed, Disney Unchained?," *Huffington Post*, July 11, 2013, accessed October 2, 2013, http://www.huffingtonpost.com/jonathan-kim/rethink-review-emthe-lone_b _3578405.html; Claudia Puig, "'Lone Ranger' masks its fun behind bloated action tale," *USA Today*, July 2, 2013, accessed October 3, 2013, http://www .usatoday.com/story/life/movies/2013/07/01/lone-ranger-review/2438235/;

"Review—In 'Lone Ranger,' excess completely runs off the rails," Associated Press, July 3, 2013, accessed October 3, 2013, http://www.starnewsonline.com /article/20130703/ENT/130709864; Bob Grimm, "The Lowest Depp," Newsreview.com, July 11, 2013, accessed October 3, 2013, http://www.newsreview .com/reno/lowest-depp/content?oid=10560365.

9. John Frost, "The Lone Ranger Falls Flat At Box Office," *The Disney Blog*, July 8, 2013, accessed October 2, 2013, http://thedisneyblog.com/2013/07/08 /the-lone-ranger-falls-flat-at-box-office/; Roger Moore, "Some moments thrill, others too violent to enjoy 'The Lone Ranger,'" *The Gazette*, July 3, 2013, accessed October 2, 2013, http://gazette.com/movie-review-some-moments-thrill -others-too-violent-to-enjoy-the-lone-ranger/article/1503087; Kate Erbland, "'The Lone Ranger' May Be The Most Bizarre Blockbuster Yet," *Film School Rejects*, July 3, 2013, accessed October 2, 2013, http://www.filmschoolrejects.com /reviews/review-the-lone-ranger.php.

10. Playlist Staff, July 8, 2013.

11. Mike Ryan, "'The Long Ranger': The Oddest Movie Of The year?" *Huffington Post*, July 2, 2013, accessed October 3, 2013, http://www.huffington post.com/mike-ryan/the-lone-ranger-review_b_3530610.html; Kenneth Turan, "Not even Johnny Depp can rescue 'The Lone Ranger,'" *Los Angles Times*, July 3, 2013, accessed October 3, 2013, http://www.latimes.com/entertainment/movies /moviesnow/la-et-mn-lone-ranger-20130703,0,3532050.story; David Edelstein, "Edelstein on The Lone Ranger: An Uncomfortable Mix of Silliness and Sadism," *Vulture*, July 3, 2013, accessed October 3, 2013, http://www.vulture .com/2013/07/movie-review-the-lone-ranger.html.

12. Kristen Acuna, "'The Lone Ranger' Is Lining Up To Be Disney's Next 'John Carter' Bust," *Business Insider*, July 3, 2013, accessed October 3, 2013, http:// www.businessinsider.com/the-lone-ranger-looks-like-it-bomb-2013–7.

13. "Johnny Depp as Cultural Appropriation Jack Sparrow . . . I mean Tonto," Nativeappropiations.com, March 8, 2012, accessed October 3, 2013, http:// nativeappropriations.com/2012/03/johnny-depp-as-cultural-appropriation-jack -sparrow-i-mean-tonto.html; Aisha Harris, "Johnny Depp's Tonto: Not as Racist as You Might Think. But Still Kind of Racist," *Slate*, July 3, 2013, accessed October 3, 2013, http://www.slate.com/blogs/browbeat/2013/07/03/johnny_depp

_as_tonto_lone_ranger_movie_pushes_against_racism_but_reinforces.html; Marley Brown, "Tonto Racist: '"Lone Ranger' Johnny Depp Character Understandably Offends Native Americans," Policymic.com, July 2013, accessed October 3, 2013, http://www.policymic.com/articles/51443/tonto-racist-lone-ranger-johnny-depp-character-understandably-offends-native-americans; Ria Kristina Torrente, "'The Lone Ranger' Gets Mixed Reviews: Is Johnny Depp's Tonto Racist?" *International Business Times*, July 4, 2013, accessed October 3, 2013, http://au.ibtimes.com/articles/486393/20130704/lone-ranger-johnny-depp-racist-lena-dunham.htm#.Uk2C3Mlig3I.

14. Ethan Atler, "The Lone Ranger Hi-Yo Stinker Away," Televisionwithoutpity.com, July 3, 2013, accessed October 2, 2013, http://www.televisionwithoutpity.com/mwop/moviefile/lights-camera-action-jackson/2013/07/the-lone-ranger-hi-yo-stinker-away/.

15. Chris Nashawaty, "Review: 'Man of Steel' is joyless," CNNentertainment.com, June 16, 2013, accessed October 2, 2013, http://www.cnn.com/2013/06/14/showbiz/ew-man-of-steel/index.html; Rachel Edidin, "Grim, violent Man of Steel sells Superman's soul for spectacle," Wired.uk.com, June 17, 2013, accessed October 2, 2013, http://www.wired.co.uk/news/archive/2013–06/17/man-of-steel-review; Playlist Staff, "The Best & Worst of 'Man of Steel,'" Indiewire.com, June 17, 2013, accessed October 2, 2013, http://blogs.indiewire.com/theplaylist/the-best-worst-of-man-of-steel-20130617?page=3#blogPostHeaderPanel.

16. "Man of Steel," Boxofficemojo.com, accessed October 2, 2013, http://www.boxofficemojo.com/movies/?id=superman2012.htm.

17. Matt Rimer, "The Wolverine Is A Racist Buzzkill: A Review," Fourpins.com, July 29, 2013, accessed October 2, 2013, http://four-pins.com/life/the-wolverine-is-a-racist-buzzkill-a-review/; "The Wolverine," Boxofficemojo.com, accessed October 2, 2013, http://boxofficemojo.com/movies/?id=wolverine2.htm.

18. For a discussion of efforts to balance Batman's retro appeal with a need to update the brand, see Eileen Meehan's "Holy Commodity Fetish, Batman! The Political Economy of a Commercial Intertext," in *The Many Lives of the Batman: Critical Approaches to a Superhero and His Media*, ed. Roberta E. Pearson and William Uricchio (New York: Routledge, 1991), 47–65. For a discussion of audience struggles to reconcile nostalgic memories of Batman with contemporary renditions of the character, see Lynn Spigel and Henry Jenkins, "Same Bat Channel, Different Bat Times: Mass Culture and Popular Memory," in *The Many Lives of The Batman*, ed. Roberta E. Pearson and William Uricchio (New York: Routledge, 1991). On a more populist front, see reviews of the early-1990s Zorro television series (A&E, 1990–1993) and turn-of-the-twenty-first-century film franchise (1998, 2005), which often complain of the character being too juvenile for contemporary tastes: Chris Hick, "DVD review: 'Zorro' slashes his way onto DVD," *Deseret News*, January 10, 2011, accessed October 2, 2013, http://www.deseretnews.com/article/700102101/Zorro-slashes-his-way-onto-DVD.html; Matt Anderson, "The Legend of Zorro," *Movie Habit*, October 28, 2005, accessed October 2, 2013, http://www.moviehabit.com/review.php?story=leg_j805.

19. Playlist Staff, July 8, 2013.

20. Matt Zoller Seitz, "The Lone Ranger," Rogerebert.com, July 3, 2013, ac-

cessed October 2, 2013, http://www.rogerebert.com/reviews/the-lone-ranger-2013.

21. Nicholas Sammond, *Babes in Tomorrowland: Walt Disney and the Making of the American Child, 1930–1960* (Durham, NC: Duke University Press, 2005).

22. Acuna, "'The Lone Ranger' Is Lining Up."

23. Anthony Breznican, "Johnny Depp wants 'The Lone Ranger' to back off Tonto: 'Why is the f——ing Lone Ranger telling Tonto what to do?,'" *Entertainment Weekly*, May 8, 2011, accessed October 2, 2013, http://insidemovies.ew.com/2011/05/08/johnny-depp-tonto-lone-ranger/.

24. Jorge Rivas, "Johnny Depp Made Honorary Member Of Comanche Nation," Colorlines.com, May 30, 2012, accessed October 2, 2013, http://colorlines.com/archives/2012/05/johnny_depp_made_honorary_member_of_comanche_nation.html.

25. Scott Johnson, "Johnny Depp's Native American Heritage Informed His Tonto Role in the Lone Ranger," Comicbook.com, June 30, 2013, accessed October 2, 2013, http://comicbook.com/blog/2013/06/30/johnny-depps-native-american-heritage-informed-his-tonto-role-in-the-lone-ranger/; Dodai Stewart, "Johnny Depp Takes Tonto Character from Racist to Merely Culturally Insensitive," *Jezebel*, March 9, 2012, accessed October 2, 2013, http://jezebel.com/5891904/johnny-depp-takes-tonto-character-from-racist-to-merely-culturally-insensitive.

26. Caity Weaver, "Johnny Depp's Tonto is Based on a White Man's Painting of an Imaginary Native American," *Gawker*, May 1, 2012, accessed October 2, 2013, http://gawker.com/5906868/johnny-depps-tonto-is-based-on-a-white-mans-painting-of-an-imaginary-native-american.

27. Kirby Sattler website, accessed October 2, 2013, http://kirbysattler.sattlerartprint.com/artist.html.

28. NECA website, accessed October 2, 2013, http://necaonline.com/40955/licenses/movies/the-lone-ranger/the-lone-ranger-mens-tonto-costume.

29. Geoff Boucher, "'The Lone Ranger': 'Metaphorical universe' or just 'Wild Wild West' without Will Smith?," *Entertainment Weekly*, April 14, 2013, accessed October 2, 2013, http://insidemovies.ew.com/2013/04/14/lone-ranger-tom-wilkinson/; Bilge Ebiri, "'The Lone Ranger' and the Curse of the Blockbuster Western," *Bloomberg Businessweek*, July 8, 2013, accessed October 2, 2013, http://www.businessweek.com/articles/2013–07–08/the-lone-ranger-and-the-curse-of-the-blockbuster-western.

30. Pamela McClintock, "Box Office Report: 'Lone Ranger' Marks Third Big-Budget Bomb of Summer," *Hollywood Reporter*, July 6, 2013, accessed October 2, 2013, http://www.hollywoodreporter.com/news/box-office-report-lone-ranger-581303.

31. Todd Cunningham, "Johnny Depp Can't Save 'Lone Ranger' From Being 'John Carter'-Sized Bomb For Disney," *The Wrap*, July 7, 2013, accessed October 2, 2013, http://www.thewrap.com/movies/article/just-48m-5-day-holiday-weekend-lone-ranger-john-carter-sized-bomb-101526.

32. John T. Caldwell, *Production Culture: Industrial Reflexivity and Critical Practice in Film and Television* (Durham, NC: Duke University Press, 2008).

33. Chris Nashawaty, "Box Office Buccaneer," *Entertainment Weekly*, July 25,

2003, accessed October 2, 2013, http://www.ew.com/ew/article/0,,465481,00.html.

34. Dawn C. Chmielewski and Richard Verrier, "'The Lone Ranger' is out of the saddle," *Los Angles Times*, August 16, 2011, accessed October 2, 2013, http://articles.latimes.com/2011/aug/16/entertainment/la-et-lone-ranger-20110816; Dawn C. Chmielewski and Steven Zeitchik, "After 'Lone Ranger,' Disney may not be willing to take risks," *Los Angles Times*, July 9, 2013, accessed October 2, 2013, http://articles.latimes.com/2013/jul/09/entertainment/la-et-ct-lone-ranger-20130709; Eric Eisenberg, "Disney To End Its Deal With Jerry Bruckheimer," Cinemablend.com, September 20, 2013, accessed October 3, 2013, http://www.cinemablend.com/new/Disney-End-Its-Deal-With-Jerry-Bruckheimer-39493.html.

35. Chmielewski and Zeitchik, "After 'Lone Ranger.'"

36. Marc Grasser, "Disney, Jerry Bruckheimer See 'Lone Ranger' as New Genre-Bending Superhero," *Variety*, June 25, 2013, accessed October 2, 2013, http://variety.com/2013/film/news/disney-jerry-bruckheimer-see-lone-ranger-as-new-genre-bending-superhero-1200501501/.

37. Owen Gleiberman, "After the dismal debut of 'The Lone Ranger,' has Johnny Depp's craft turned to shtick?," *Entertainment Weekly*, July 15, 2013, accessed October 3, 2013, http://insidemovies.ew.com/2013/07/15/johnny-depp-career-lone-ranger/; Victoria Pavlova, "Jerry Bruckheimer—Lone Ranger Flop Marks Jerry Bruckheimer's Fall From Grace At Disney," Contactmusic.com, July 12, 2013, accessed October 3, 2013, http://www.contactmusic.com/news/jerry-bruckheimer-jeopardy-disney_3759133.

38. Justin Kroll and Rachel Abrams, "Will 'Lone Ranger' Be Armie Hammer's Magic Bullet?," *Variety*, June 25, 2013, accessed October 2, 2013, http://variety.com/2013/film/news/cover-story-will-lone-ranger-be-armie-hammers-magic-bullet-1200501482/.

39. Ibid.

40. Graeme McMillan, "Why Aren't More People Talking About 'The Lone Ranger?,'" *Hollywood Reporter*, July 2, 2013, accessed October 3, 2013, http://www.hollywoodreporter.com/heat-vision/johnny-depps-lone-ranger-why-578731.

41. Rosalind Gil, "'Life is a Pitch': Managing the Self in New Media Work," *Managing Media Work*, ed. Mark Deuze (Thousand Oaks, CA: Sage, 2010), 249–262; Elizabeth Ellcessor, "Tweeting @feliciaday: Online Social Media, Convergence, and Subcultural Stardom," *Cinema Journal* 51, no. 2 (Winter 2012): 46–66.

42. Kroll and Abrams, June 25, 2013.

43. Hilary Lewis, "'Lone Ranger' Stars Say Critics Bashed Movie Before They Saw It," *Hollywood Reporter*, July 6, 2013, accessed October 2, 2013, http://www.hollywoodreporter.com/heat-vision/lone-ranger-stars-say-critics-600290.

44. Sean O'Neal, "*The Lone Ranger* crew blames enormously powerful movie critics for conspiring to kill *The Lone Ranger*," *A. V. Club*, August 6, 2013, accessed October 2, 2013, http://www.avclub.com/articles/the-lone-ranger-crew-still-cant-believe-critics-cr,101242/.

45. Sandy Schaefer, "'Lone Ranger' Encounters More Budget Woes; Production Behind Schedule," Screenrant.com, 2012, accessed October 2, 2013, http://screenrant.com/lone-ranger-budget-production-problems-sandy-179446/.

46. Lewis, "'Lone Ranger' Stars Say Critics Bashed Movie."

47. Matthew Belloni and Borys Kit, "Johnny Depp's 'The Lone Ranger' Shut Down By Disney," *Hollywood Reporter*, August 12, 2011, accessed October 3, 2013, http://www.hollywoodreporter.com/news/johnny-depps-lone-ranger-shut-222777; Dawn C. Chmielewski, "Disney shuts down production of 'Lone Ranger,'" *Los Angeles Times*, August 12, 2011, accessed October 3, 2013, http://latimesblogs.latimes.com/entertainmentnewsbuzz/2011/08/disney-lone-ranger.html; Peter Rainer, "'The Lone Ranger' is wit-free and derivative," *Christian Science Monitor*, July 2, 2013, accessed October 3, 2013, http://www.csmonitor.com/The-Culture/Movies/2013/0702/The-Lone-Ranger-is-wit-free-and-derivative.

48. Simone Murray, "Celebrating the story the way it is: Cultural studies, corporate media and the contested utility of fandom," *Continuum: Journal of Media & Cultural Studies* 18, no. 1 (2004): 7–25.

49. Steven Zeitchik, "Is 'The Lone Ranger' debacle an end-of-the-empire sign?," *Los Angeles Times*, July 9, 2013, accessed October 3, 2013, http://articles.latimes.com/2013/jul/09/entertainment/la-et-mn-lone-ranger-hollywood-blockbusters-box-office-disney-20130709.

50. Grasser, "'The Lone Ranger' Could Cost Disney."

51. Chmielewski and Zeitchik, "After 'Lone Ranger.'"

52. Derek Thompson, "Disney Is Not a Movie Company; It's a Television Company," *The Atlantic*, July 10, 2013, accessed October 2, 2013, http://www.theatlantic.com/business/archive/2013/07/disney-is-not-a-movie-company-its-a-television-company/277680/.

53. Garry McConnachie, "Box office disasters—just who should the finger be pointed at?" *Daily Record*, August 7, 2013, accessed October 3, 2013, http://www.dailyrecord.co.uk/entertainment/movies/movie-news/box-office-disasters-just-2136381.

54. "The Summer of Failure—How Hollywood Can Eliminate its Blockbuster Mentality," *Corner Critic*, August 4, 2013, accessed October 3, 2013, http://thecornercritic.wordpress.com/2013/08/04/the-summer-of-failure-how-hollywood-can-eliminate-its-blockbuster-mentality/; Gilbert Cruz, "*The Lone Ranger* Represents Everything That's Wrong With Hollywood Blockbusters," *The Vulture*, July 5, 2013, accessed October 3, 2013, http://www.vulture.com/2013/07/lone-ranger-is-everything-wrong-with-hollywood.html?test=true.

55. Ethan Alter, "The Wolverine: Pain Is for Chumps, Bub," *Television Without Pity*, July 26, 2013, accessed October 2, 2013, http://www.televisionwithoutpity.com/mwop/2013/07/the-wolverine-pain-is-for-chumps-bub/.

56. LRI Lone Ranger ad in *Variety*, ca. 1951.

57. Matt Brain, "Netflix signs exclusive deal for over 300 hours of original DreamWorks Animation content," *The Verge*, June 17, 2013, accessed October 2, 2013, http://www.theverge.com/2013/6/17/4437404/netflix-dreamworks-exclusive-deal.

58. Talk at Old Dominion University by Dr. Eduardo Bonilla-Silva, September 17, 2013.

59. Beth Hawks, "The Silver Bullet," *PR for a Pro*, August 7, 2011, accessed October 3, 2013, http://corecomprblog.blogspot.com/2011/06/silver-bullet.html.

Bibliography

Scholarly Works

Aaker, David. *Building Strong Brands*. Philadelphia: Free Press, 1995.

———. "How CMOs Build Brands by Collaborating Across Silos." HBR Blog Network, May 31, 2011. http://blogs.hbr.org/cs/2011/05/five_collaboration_routes_for.html.

Aberdeen, J. A. *Hollywood Renegades: The Society of Independent Motion Picture Producers*. Cobblestone Enterprises, 1999.

Allen, Chadwick. "Omnimedia Marketing: The Case of the Lone Ranger." In Nicolas S. Witschi, ed. *A Companion to the Literature and Culture of the American West*. New York: Wiley-Blackwell, 2011, 462–482.

Anderson, Christopher. *Hollywood TV*. Austin: University of Texas Press, 1994.

———. "Ziv Television Programs, Inc." *The Encyclopedia of Television*. 2nd ed., ed. Horace Newcomb. New York: Routledge, 2006, 2626–2629.

Arvidsson, Adam. "Brands: A Critical Perspective." *Journal of Consumer Culture* 5, no. 3 (2005): 235–258.

Balio, Tino. *Grand Design: Hollywood as a Modern Business Enterprise, 1930–1939. History of the American Cinema*, vol. 5. Los Angeles: University of California Press, 1995.

Banks, Miranda. "My Media Studies: Off-Screen Stories." *Television & New Media* 10 (2009), 20–22.

Batemma, Doug. "Pictures of a Bygone Era: The Syndication of Amos 'n' Andy, 1954–66." *Television & New Media* 7, no. 1 (February 2006): 3–39.

Baudrillard, Jean. *Simulacra and Simulation (The Body, In Theory: Histories of Cultural Materialism)*. Ann Arbor: University of Michigan Press, 1995.

Baughman, James L. *The Republic of Mass Culture: Journalism, Filmmaking, and Broadcasting in America since 1941*. 3rd ed. Baltimore: Johns Hopkins University Press, 2005.

Bendazzi, Giannalberto, *Cartoons: One Hundred Years of Cinema Animation*. London: John Libbey, 1994.

Bilton, Chris. *Management and Creativity: From Creative Industries to Creative Management*. Hoboken, NJ: Wiley-Blackwell, 2006.

Bordwell, David, Janet Staiger, and Kristin Thompson. *The Classical Hollywood Cinema: Film Style and Mode of Production to 1960*. New York: Columbia University Press, 1985.

Bourdieu, Pierre. *The Field of Cultural Production: Essays on Art and Literature*. New York: Columbia University Press, 1993.

Brown, Stephen, Robert V. Kozinets, and John Sherry Jr. "Teaching Old Brands New Tricks: Retro Branding and the Revival of Brand Meaning." *Journal of Marketing* 67 (July 2003): 19–33.

Caldwell, John Thornton. "Cultures of Production: Studying Industry's Deep Texts, Reflexive Rituals, and Managed Self-Disclosures." In *Media Industries: History, Theory and Method*, ed. J. Holt and A. Perren. Sussex, UK: Wiley-Blackwell, 2009, 199–212.

———. *Production Culture: Industrial Reflexivity and Critical Practice in Film and Television*. Durham, NC: Duke University Press, 2008.

Castillo, Greg. *Cold War on the Home Front: The Soft Power of Midcentury Design*. Minneapolis: University of Minnesota Press, 2010.

Cawelti, John. "*Chinatown* and Generic Transformation in Recent American Films." In *Film Genre Reader 4*, ed. Barry Keith Grant. Austin: University of Texas Press, 2012, 279–297.

Cohen, Lizabeth. *A Consumers' Republic: The Politics of Mass Consumption in Postwar America*. New York: Alfred A Knopf, 2003.

Cook, David A. *Lost Illusions: American Cinema in the Shadow of Watergate and Vietnam, 1970–1979*. Berkeley: University of California Press, 2002.

Coombe, Rosemary. *The Cultural Life of Intellectual Properties: Authorship, Appropriation and the Law*. Durham, NC: Duke University Press, 1998.

———. "Tenth Anniversary Symposium: New Direction: Critical Cultural Legal Studies." *Yale Journal of Law & the Humanities* 10 (1998).

Crafton, Donald. *Before Mickey: The Animated Film 1898–1928*. Chicago: University of Chicago Press, 1993.

Cross, Gary. *Kids' Stuff: Toys and the Changing World of American Childhood*. Cambridge, MA: Harvard University Press, 1997.

Czitrom, Daniel. *Media and the American Mind: From Morse to McLuhan*. Chapel Hill: University of North Carolina Press, 1983.

DeCordova, Richard. "The Mickey in Macy's Window: Childhood, Consumerism, and Disney Animation." In *Disney Discourse: Producing the Magic Kingdom*, ed. Eric Smoodin. New York: Routledge, 1994, 203–213.

Dicke, Thomas S. *Franchising in America: The Development of a Business Method, 1840–1980*. Chapel Hill: University of North Carolina Press, 1992.

Donaldson, Thomas T., and Lee E. Preston. "The Stakeholder Theory of the Corporation: Concepts, Evidence, and Implications." *The Academy of Management Review* 20, no. 1 (1995).

Du Gay, Paul. "Introduction." In *Production of Culture/Cultures of Production*, ed. Paul Du Gay. London: Sage, 1997.

Du Gay, Paul, and Michael Pryke. "Introduction." In *Cultural Economy: Cultural Analysis and Commercial Life*, ed. Paul Du Gay and Michael Pryke. London: Sage, 2002.

Eckert, Charles. "The Carole Lombard in Macy's Window." *Quarterly Review of Film Studies* 3, no. 1 (Winter 1978): 1–22.

Eco, Umberto. "The Myth of Superman." *Diacritics* 2, no. 1 (Spring 1972): 14–22.

Edwards, Kyle. "Brand-Name Literature: Film Adaptation and Selznick International Pictures' *Rebecca*." *Cinema Journal* 45, no. 3 (Spring 2006): 32–58.

Ellcessor, Elizabeth. "Tweeting @feliciaday: Online Social Media, Convergence, and Subcultural Stardom." *Cinema Journal* 51, no. 2 (Winter 2012): 46–66.

Feldman, D. B. "Finding a Home for Fictional Characters: A Proposal for Change in Copyright Protection." *California Law Review* 78 (1990): 687–720.

Foucault, Michel. "What Is an Author?" *Language, Counter-Memory, Practice: Selected Essays and Interviews by Michel Foucault*, ed. Donald F. Bruchard. Oxford: Blackwell, 1977, 113–139.

Gaines, Jane. *Contested Culture: The Image, The Voice, and the Law*. Chapel Hill: University of North Carolina Press, 1991.

———. "The Queen Christina Tie-Ups: Convergence of Show Window and Screen." *Quarterly Review of Film and Video* 11, no. 1 (1999).

Gil, Rosalind. "'Life is a Pitch': Managing the Self in New Media Work." *Managing Media Work*, ed. Mark Deuze. Thousand Oaks, CA: Sage, 2010, 249–262.

Gitlin, Todd. *Inside Prime Time*. New York: Pantheon, 1985.

Gomery, Douglas. "Disney's Business History: A Reinterpretation." In *Disney Discourse: Producing the Magic Kingdom*, ed. Eric Smoodin. New York: Routledge, 1994, 71–86.

Gordon, Ian. *Comic Strips and Consumer Culture, 1890–1945*. Washington, DC: Smithsonion, 1998.

Gray, Jonathan. *Show Sold Separately: Promos, Spoilers, and Other Media Paratexts*. New York: New York University Press, 2010.

Griffin, Sean. "Kings of the Wild Backyard: Davy Crockett and Children's Space." In *Kids Media Culture*, ed. Mansha Kinder. Durham, NC: Duke University Press, 1999, 102–121.

Havens, Tim. "The Evolution of Industry Lore in African American Television Trade." Montreal: International Communications Association, 2008.

Havens, Tim, Amanda Lotz, and Serra Tinic. "Critical Media Industry Studies: A Research Approach." *Communication, Culture & Critique* 2 (2009): 234–253.

Helfand, M. T. "When Mickey Mouse Is as Strong as Superman: The Convergence of Intellectual Property Laws to Protect Fictional Literary and Pictorial Characters." *Stanford Law Review* 44, no. 3 (1992): 623–674.

Herberg, Will. *Protestant, Catholic, Jew: An Essay in American Religious Sociology*. Garden City, NY: Doubleday, 1956.

Hilmes, Michele. *Hollywood and Broadcasting: From Radio to Cable*. Urbana: University of Illinois Press, 1990.

———. *Radio Voices: American Broadcasting, 1922–1952*. Minneapolis: University of Minnesota Press, 1997.

Hollis, Tim. *Hi There, Boys and Girls! America's Local Children's TV Shows*. Jackson: University Press of Mississippi, 2001.

Holt, Douglas. *How Brands Become Icons: The Principles of Cultural Branding*. Cambridge, MA: Harvard Business Press, 2004.

Iwabuchi, Koichi. "How 'Japanese' Is Pokemon?" In *Pikachu's Global Adventure: The Rise and Fall of Pokémon*, ed. Joseph Tobin. Raleigh-Durham, NC: Duke University Press, 2004, 53–79.

Jacobson, Lisa. *Raising Consumers: Children and the American Mass Market in the Early Twentieth Century*. New York: Columbia University Press, 2004.

Jaeger, W. T. "Copyright: Misappropriation of a Character." *California Law Review* 56, no. 6 (1968): 1780–1798.

Jaszi, Peter. "On the Author Effect: Contemporary Copyright and Collective Creativity." *Cardozo Arts & Entertainment Law Journal* 10 (1992): 293–320.

———. "Toward a Theory of Copyright: The Metamorphoses of 'Authorship.'" *Duke Law Journal* 2 (1991): 455–502.

Jenkins, Henry. "Affective Economics 101." FlowTV.org, September 20, 2004. http://flowtv.org/2004/09/affective-economics-101/.

———. "'The All-American Handful': Dennis the Menace, Permissive Childrearing and the Bad Boy Tradition." In *The Revolution Wasn't Televised: Sixties Television and Social Conflict*, ed. Lynn Spigel and Mike Curtin. New York: Routledge, 1997.

———. *Convergence Culture: Where Old and New Media Collide*. New York: New York University Press, 2006.

———. "The Revenge of the Origami Unicorn: Seven Principles of Transmedia Storytelling (Well, Two Actually. Five More on Friday)." *Confessions of an Aca-Fan*, December 12, 2009. http://www.henryjenkins.org/2009/12/the_revenge_of_the_origami_uni.html.

———. "Revenge of the Origami Unicorn: The Remaining Four Principles of Transmedia Storytelling." *Confessions of an Aca-Fan*, December 12, 2009. http://henryjenkins.org/2009/12/revenge_of_the_origami_unicorn.html.

Jenkins, Henry, Sam Ford, and Joshua Green. *Spreadable Media: Creating Value and Meaning in a Networked Culture*. New York: New York University Press, 2013.

Johnson, Catherine. "Trading Auntie: the exploitation and protection of intellectual property rights during the BBC's monopoly years." *New Review of Film and Television* 7, no. 4 (2009): 441–458.

Johnson, Derek. *Franchising Media Worlds: Content Networks and the Collaborative Production of Culture*. PhD diss., University of Wisconsin, Madison, 2009.

———. "Will the Real Wolverine Please Stand Up? Marvel's Mutation from Monthlies to Movies." In *Film and Comic Books*, ed. Ian Gordon, Mark Jancovich, and Matthew P. McAllister. Jackson: University Press of Mississippi, 2007, 64–85.

Johnson, Victoria. *Heartland TV: Prime Time Television and the Struggle for U.S. Identity*. New York: New York University Press, 2008.

Kackman, Michael. "Nothing On But Hoppy Badges: *Hopalong Cassidy*, William Boyd Enterprises, and Emergent Media Globalization." *Cinema Journal* 47, no. 4 (2008): 76–101.

Kagan, Norman. *The Cinema of Robert Zemeckis*. Lanham, MD: Rowman & Littlefield, 2003.

Kanfer, Stefan. *Serious Business: The Art and Commerce of Animation in America from Betty Boop to Toy Story*. New York: Da Capo, 2000.

Kearney, Mary. "Recycling Judy and Corliss: Transmedia Exploitation and the First Teen-Girl Production Trend." *Feminist Media Studies* 4, no. 3 (2004): 264–295.

Kemper, Tom, *Hidden Talent: The Emergence of Hollywood Agents*. Los Angeles: University of California Press, 2009.

Kimmell, Michael. *Manhood in America: A Cultural History*. New York: Free Press, 1996.

Klinger, Barbara. *Beyond the Multiplex: Cinema, New Technologies, and the Home*. Los Angeles: University of California Press, 2006.

Kompare, Derek. *Rerun Nation: How Repeats Invented American Television*. New York: Routledge, 2005.

Lacey, Kate. "Radio in the Great Depression: Promotional Culture, Public Service, and Propaganda." In *Radio Reader: Essays in The Cultural History of Radio*, ed. Michele Hilmes and Jason Loviglio. New York: Routledge, 2001, 21–40.

Lears, Jackson. *Fables Of Abundance: A Cultural History Of Advertising In America*. New York: Basic, 1995.

Lessig, Lawrence. *Free Culture: The Nature and Future of Creativity*. New York: Penguin, 2004.

Liebrenz-Himes, Marilyn, Hamed Shamma, and Robert F. Dyer. "Heritage Brands—Treasured Inheritance or 'Over the Hill.'" *Churm* (2007): 140–145.

Lipsitz, George. "The Meaning of Memory: Family, Class, and Ethnicity in Early Network Television." In *Private Screenings: Television and the Female Consumer*, ed. Lynn Spigel and Denise Mann. Minneapolis: University of Minnesota Press, 1992.

Lopes, Paul. *Demanding Respect: The Evolution of the American Comic Book*. Philadelphia: Temple University Press, 2009.

Lotz, Amanda. *The Television Will Be Revolutionized*. New York: New York University Press, 2007.

Lynd, Robert S., and Merrill Lynd. *Middletown: A Study in Contemporary American Culture*. New York: Harcourt, Brace, 1931.

———. *Middletown in Transition: A Study in Cultural Conflicts*. New York: Hartcourt, Brace, 1937.

Marchand, Roland. *Advertising the American Dream: Making Way for Modernity, 1920–1940*. Berkeley: University of California Press, 1985.

Mayer, Vicki. *Below the Line: Producers and Production Studies in the New Television Economy*. Raleigh, NC: Duke University Press, 2011.

McAlexander, James H., John W. Schouten, and Harold F. Koenig. "Building Brand Community." *Journal of Marketing* 66 (January 2002).

McFall, Liz. "What about the Old Cultural Intermediaries? An Historical Review of Advertising Producers." *Cultural Studies* 16, no. 4 (2002): 532–552.

Meehan, Eileen. "'Holy Commodity Fetish, Batman!': The Political Economy of a Commercial Intertext." In *The Many Lives of the Batman: Critical Approaches to a Superhero and His Media*, ed. Roberta E. Pearson and William Uricchio. London: BFI, 1991, 47–65.

Miège, Bernard. *The Capitalization of Cultural Production*. Bagnolet, France: International General, 1989.

Mintz, Steven. *Huck's Raft: A History of American Childhood*. Cambridge, MA: Belknap Press of Harvard University Press, 2004.

Mittell, Jason. "The Great Saturday Morning Exile: Scheduling Cartoons on Television's Periphery in the 1960s." In *Prime Time Animation: Television Animation and American Culture*, ed. Carole A. Stabile and Mark Harrison. New York: Routledge, 2003, 33–54.

———. "To Spread or to Drill?" JustTV.wordpress.com, February 25, 2009. http://justtv.wordpress.com/2009/02/25/to-spread-or-to-drill/.

Moran, Albert. *Copycat TV: Globalisation, Program Formats, and Cultural Identity*. New Barnet, UK: John Libbey, 2005.

Morgan, Wayne. "'If Your Grocer Does Not Keep the Ivory Soap': Palmer Cox, The Brownies and Nineteenth Century Marketing." Charm (2003): 22–29.

Muniz, Albert M., and Thomas C. O'Guinn. "Brand Community." *Journal of Consumer Research* 27 (March 2001).

Murray, Simone. "'Celebrating the Story the Way It Is': Cultural Studies, Corporate Media and the Contested Utility of Fandom." *Continuum* 18, no. 1 (2004): 7–25.

Nyberg, Amy Kiste. *Seal of Approval: The History of the Comics Code*. Jackson: University Press of Mississippi, 1998.

Owczarski, Kimberly Ann. *Batman, Time Warner, and Franchise Filmmaking in the Conglomerate Era*. PhD Diss., University of Texas at Austin, 2008.

Pecora, Norma Odom. *The Business of Children's Entertainment*. New York: Guilford, 2002.

Pine, Joseph, and James Gilmore. *The Experience Economy*. Boston: Harvard Business School Press, 1999.

Rogers, Mark C. "License Farming and the American Comic Book Industry." *International Journal of Comic Art* 1, no. 2 (1999): 132–142.

Rose, Mark. *Authors and Owners: The Invention of Copyright*. Boston: Harvard University Press, 1993.

Ross, Sharon Marie. *Beyond the Box: Television and the Internet*. New York: Blackwell-Wiley, 2008.

Russo, Alexander. "A Dark(ened) Figure on the Airwaves: Race, Nation and the Green Hornet." In *Radio Reader: Essays in the Cultural History of Radio*, ed. Michele Hilmes and Jason Laviglio. New York: Routledge, 2001, 257–276.

———. *Points on the Dial: Golden Age Radio beyond the Networks*. Raleigh-Durham, NC: Duke University Press, 2010.

Sammond, Nicholas. *Babes in Tomorrowland: Walt Disney and the Making of the American Child, 1930–1960*. Durham, NC: Duke University Press, 2005.

Santo, Avi. "A Teenie Weenie Amount of 'Goodwill': Cross-media Character Brand Merchandizing in the 1920s." *Journal of Consumer Culture* 12 (2012): 283–305.

Schaefer, Eric. *"Bold! Daring! Shocking! True!" A History of Exploitation Films, 1919–1959*. Durham, NC: Duke University Press, 2000.

Schatz, Thomas. *The Genius of the System: Hollywood Filmmaking in the Studio Era*. Minneapolis: University of Minnesota Press, 2010.

———. *Old Hollywood/New Hollywood: Ritual, Art, and Industry*. UMI Research Press, 1983.

Schlesinger, Philip. "The most creative organization in the world? The BBC, 'creativity' and managerial style." *International Journal of Cultural Policy* 16, no. 3 (2010): 271–285.

Schwoch, James. "A Failed Vision: The Mutual Television Network." *Velvet Light Trap* 33 (1994): 3–11.

Scott, Jason. "The Character-Oriented Franchise: Promotion and Exploitation of Pre-Sold Characters in American Film, 1913–1950." In *Cultural Borrowings: Appropriation, Reworking, Transformation*, ed. Iain Robert Smith. *Scope: An Online Journal of Film and Television Studies*, 2009, 34–55.

Smulyan, Susan. *Selling Radio: The Commercialization of American Broadcasting, 1920–1934*. Washington, DC: Smithsonian, 1994.

Spalding, Elizabeth Edwards. *The First Cold Warrior: Harry Truman, Containment, and the Remaking of Liberal Internationalism*. Lexington: University Press of Kentucky, 2006.

Spigel, Lynn. *Welcome to the Dreamhouse: Popular Media and Postwar Suburbs*. Durham, NC: Duke University Press, 2001.

Spigel, Lynn, and Henry Jenkins. "Same Bat Channel, Different Bat Times: Mass Culture and Popular Memory." In *The Many Lives of The Batman*, ed Roberta E. Pearson and William Uricchio. New York: Routledge, 1991.

Stahl, Matt. "Privilege and Distinction in Production Worlds: Copyright, Collective Bargaining, and Working Conditions in Media Making." In *Production Studies: Cultural Studies of Media Industries*, ed. Vicki Mayer, Miranda Banks, and John Caldwell. New York: Routledge, 2009, 54–68.

Sterling, Christopher, and John Kittross. *Stay Tuned: A Concise History of American Broadcasting*. 2nd ed. Belmont, CA: Wadsworth, 1990.

Striphas, Ted. "Harry Potter and the Simulacrum: Contested Copies in an Age of Intellectual Property." *Critical Studies in Media Communication* 26, no. 4 (2009): 1–17.

Susman, Warren. *Culture as History: The Transformation of American Society in the Twentieth Century*. New York: Pantheon, 1985.

Tyler May, Elaine. *Homeward Bound: American Families in the Cold War Era*. New York: Basic, 2008.

Vaidhyanathan, Siva. *Copyrights and Copywrongs: The Rise of Intellectual Property and How It Threatens Creativity*. New York: New York University Press, 2001.

Verona, Jeff. "Heroes and Villains: Ventures and Adventures in the Comic Book Industry." In *Science Fiction and Market Realities*, ed. George Edgar Slusser et al. Athens: University of Georgia Press, 1996.

Wee, Valerie. *Teen Media: Hollywood and the Youth Market in the Digital Age*. New York: McFarland, 2010.

Williams, Raymond. *Marxism and Literature*. London: Oxford University Press, 1977.

Witek, Joseph. "From Genre to Medium: Comics and Contemporary American Culture." In *Rejuvinating the Humanities*, ed. Ray Browne and Marshall Fishwick. Bowling Green, OH: Bowling Green University Press, 1992.

Woodmansee, Martha. "The Genius and the Copyright: Economic and Legal Conditions of the Emergence of the 'Author.'" *Eighteenth-Century Studies* 17, no. 4 (1984): 425–448.

Wright, Bradford. *Comic Book Nation: The Transformation of Youth Culture in America*. Baltimore: Johns Hopkins University Press, 2001.
Wyatt, Justin. *High Concept: Movies and Marketing in Hollywood*. Austin: University of Texas Press, 1994.
Zelizer, Viviana. *Pricing the Priceless Child: The Changing Social Value of Children*. Princeton, NJ: Princeton University Press, 1994.

Popular Works

Battersby, Gregory J., and Charles W. Grimes. *2010 Licensing Update*. Sandy, UT: Aspen, 2010.
Battersby, Gregory J., and Danny Simon. *Basics of Licen$ing: How to Extend Brand and Entertainment Properties for Profit*. Norwalk, CT: Kent, 2010.
Boemer, Marilyn Lawrence. *The Children's Hour*. Lanham, MD: Scarecrow, 1999.
Brooks, Tim, and Earle Marsh. *The Complete Dictionary to Prime Time Network and Cable TV Shows, 1946-Present*. 8th ed. New York: Ballantine, 2003.
Bruce, Scott, and Bill Crawford. *Cerealizing America: The Unsweetened Story of American Breakfast Cereal*. London: Faber & Faber, 1995.
Dunning, John. *The Encyclopedia of Old-Time Radio*. New York: Oxford University Press, 1998.
Evans, Robert. *The Kid Stays in the Picture*. Costa Mesa, CA: Phoenix Audio, 1994.
Felbinger, Lee. *Collector's Reference and Value Guide to the Lone Ranger*. Paducah, KY: Schroeder, 1998.
Gabler, Neal, *Walt Disney: The Triumph of the American Imagination*. New York: Vintage, 1997.
Griffin, Nancy, and Kim Masters. *Hit & Run: How Jon Peters and Peter Guber Took Sony For A Ride In Hollywood*. New York: Simon & Schuster, 1997.
Hanke, Ken. *Tim Burton: An Unauthorized Biography of the Filmmaker*. New York: Renaissance Books, 1999.
Harmon, Jim. *The Great Radio Heroes*. New York: McFarland, 2001.
Heide, Robert, and John Gilman. *Disneyana: Classic Collectibles, 1928–1958*. New York: Welcome Enterprises, 1994.
History of Retailing in North America. South Plainfield, NJ: Smyyth LLC, September 27, 2011.
History of the Lone Ranger. Unpublished manuscript. ca. 1954. Trendle Papers, Series II, Subseries C, Box 69, Folder 20.
Holcomb, Benjamin. *Mego 8" Super-Heroes: World's Greatest Toys!* Raleigh, NC: TwoMorrows, 2007.
Howell, Dorothy J. *Intellectual Properties and the Protection of Fictional Characters*. New York: Quorum, 1990.
Lesser, Robert. *A Celebration of Comic Art and Memorabilia*. Portland, OR: Hawthorne Books, 1975.
Levin, Bob. *The Pirates and the Mouse: Disney's War Against the Counterculture*. Seattle: Fantagraphics, 2003.
Osgood, Dick. *Wyxie Wonderland: An Unauthorized, 50-year Diary of WXYZ Detroit*. Bowling Green, OH: Bowling Green University Press, 1981.

Paik, Karen. *To Infinity and Beyond! The Story of Pixar Animation Studios*. San Francisco: Chronicle Books, 2007.
Price, David. *The Pixar Touch*. New York: Alfred A. Knopf, 2008.
Price, Jeffrey, and Peter S. Seaman. Who Shot Roger Rabbit. *Script*. 1986.
Raugust, Karen. *The Licensing Business Handbook*. 7th ed. Portland, OR: EPM Communications, 2008.
———. *Merchandise Licensing in the Television Industry*. Abingdon, Oxon, UK: Focal Press, 1995.
Rothel, David. *Who Was That Masked Man? The Story of the Lone Ranger*. Rev. ed. New York: A. S. Barnes, 1981.
Schwartz, John D. "Buck Rogers: Interplanetary Multi-Media Hero." *Big Little Times*, June 2012.
Sheldon, Harvey. *The Golden Age of Radio and History*. CreateSpace Independent, 2013.
Smith, Bruce. *The History of Little Orphan Annie*. New York: Ballantine Books, 1982.

Newspaper, Magazine, and Trade Press Articles

Arnold, Gary. "Endangered Ranger." *Washington Post*, May 22, 1981, F7.
Baker, Russell. "The Lone Ranger Bites the Silver Bullet." *Los Angeles Herald Examiner*, September 6, 1979.
Barnes, Brooks. "Beloved Characters as Reimagined for the 21st Century." *New York Times*, June 11, 2008.
Beller, Miles. "Hollywood Is Banking on the Comics." *New York Times*, December 9, 1979.
Belloni, Matthew, and Borys Kit. "Johnny Depp's 'The Lone Ranger' Shut Down By Disney." *Hollywood Reporter*, August 12, 2011.
Biggers, Cliff. "The Lone Ranger Rides Again." *Comic Shop News* 995, July 12, 2006, 1.
Boucher, Geoff. "'The Lone Ranger': 'Metaphorical universe' or just 'Wild Wild West' without Will Smith?," *Entertainment Weekly*, April 14, 2013.
Boutell, C. B. "Hi-Yo Silver Lining." *The Nation*, January 11, 1941.
Bradford, Harry. "Mattel Faces Backlash After Toy Company Tries To Teach Moms How To Play With Hot Wheels." *Huffington Post*, March 13, 2013.
Brodesser, Claude. "'Ranger' Rides to Columbia." *Variety*, March 5, 2002.
Bruell, Alexandra. "Modern Branding Campaigns Develop a Nostalgic Feeling." *PR Week*, July 6, 2010.
Bryan, J., III. "Hi Yo Silver." *Saturday Evening Post*, October 14, 1939.
Buck, Jerry. "Masked Man Still Cries 'Hi Ho' in 48 Countries." Associated Press, May 2, 1970.
"BuyBabies." *Economist*, December 9, 2006.
Campbell, K., and K. Davis-Packard. "How ads get kids to say I want it!" *Christian Science Monitor*, September 18, 2000.
Caranicas, Peter. "Bibles Hold Tentpole Revivals." *Variety*, June 29, 2005.
Casey, Bernadette. "A Brand that Endures." *Global Licence!* (May 2011): 40–42.

Chmielewski, Dawn C. "Disney shuts down production of 'Lone Ranger.'" *Los Angeles Times*, August 12, 2011.
Chmielewski, Dawn C., and Steven Zeitchik. "After 'Lone Ranger,' Disney may not be willing to take risks." *Los Angles Times*, July 9, 2013.
Chmielewski, Dawn C., and Richard Verrier. "'The Lone Ranger' is out of the saddle." *Los Angles Times*, August 16, 2011.
Cioletti, Amanda. "Man of Steel." *Global Licence!* (February 2013): 50–51.
Dean, Michael. "An Extraordinarily Marketable Man: The Ongoing Struggle for Ownership of Superman and Superboy." *Comics Journal* 263, November 2004.
Deeb, Gary. "Good Guys Winning the 'Lone Ranger' Battle." *Santa Fe New Mexican*, November 1, 1980.
———. "Lone Ranger Seeks Jury Trial." *Star-News*, September 20, 1979.
"DreamWorks buys Classic Media for $155 million." Associated Press, July 23, 2012.
Fleming, Michael. "Fox Family Wrangles Ranger." *Daily Variety*, January 24, 1996, 1.
Fox, David J. "Hi Yo! Salute to the Lone Ranger Set in Lone Pine." *Los Angeles Times*, May 25, 1993.
Freedman, Richard. "Bite the Silver Bullet." *Spokesman*, May 22, 1981.
Garrison-Sprenger, Nicole. "Dynamic duo saving Superman." *Minneapolis/St. Paul Business Journal*, November 27, 2005.
Gleiberman, Owen. "After the dismal debut of 'The Lone Ranger,' has Johnny Depp's craft turned to shtick?" *Entertainment Weekly*, July 15, 2013.
Goldstein, Patrick. "Disney's purchase of Marvel is a super deal." *Los Angeles Times*, September 1, 2009.
Grant, Hank. "Hank Grant Rambling Reporter." *Hollywood Reporter*, July 29, 1977.
Grasser, Marc. "Disney, Jerry Bruckheimer See 'Lone Ranger' as New Genre-Bending Superhero." *Variety*, June 25, 2013.
———. "'The Lone Ranger' Could Cost Disney Up to $190 Million in Losses." *Variety*, August 13, 2013.
Greco, M. "Clayton Moore for Fair Play." *Calendar*, May 24, 1981.
Grossman, Lev. "*Star Trek*: Back to the Final Frontier." *Time*, April 23, 2009.
Hayes, D. "Invasion of the Techie Tots." *Variety*, February 19, 2007, 1.
"'Hi-Yo Silver!' Cowboy Honors for East Side Boy." *Roanoke News*, September 9, 1938.
"Hi-Yo Silver Lining." *New Republic*, January 11, 1991.
"Hooverism in the Funnies." *New Republic*, July 11,1934.
"Hoping to Soar with Superman." *Businessweek*, December 11, 1978.
"How Lego Handles Licensing." *Managing Intellectual Property*, April 1, 2012.
Hughes, Nick. "Character assassination: health crusaders have hit character licensing—and particularly confectionery—hard, but the likes of Lazy Town's healthy hero Sporticus offer some hope." *Grocer*, September 20, 2008.
Humphrey, Hal. "Lone Rangers Never Die." *Los Angeles Mirror-News*, February 13, 1956.
"*I Love Lucy*: No Splainin' Necessary." *Global Licence!* (May 2012): 2–3.

"In 'Lone Ranger,' excess completely runs off the rails." Associated Press, July 3, 2013.

Itzkoff, David. "The Movie Industry's New Playthings." *New York Times*, June 18, 2009.

Keegan, Rebecca. "'Lone Ranger': Masked man need not be a star, says Bruckheimer." *Los Angeles Times*, May 9, 2011.

Kroll, Justin, and Rachel Abrams. "Will 'Lone Ranger' Be Armie Hammer's Magic Bullet?" *Variety*, June 25, 2013.

Lewis, Hilary. "'Lone Ranger' Stars Say Critics Bashed Movie Before They Saw It." *Hollywood Reporter*, July 6, 2013.

Licensing Industry Survey, 2012. International Licensing Industry Merchandisers' Association, 2012.

"Liggett's Young Set 'Out West.'" *Detroit Times*, October 15, 1939.

Lisanti, Tony. "Barbie's Wow Factor." *Global Licence!* (June 2012): 72–74.

———. "Disney's New Character." *Global Licence!* (June 2012a): 48–54.

———. "Global Licensors: New, Noteworthy and the Impressive." *Global Licence!* (May 2012): 8.

———. "Jessi Dunne Brings New Magic to Mattel." *Global Licence!* (November/December 2012): 24–25.

———. "The Retail Reality." *Global Licence!* (August 2012): 8.

———. "Toy Power Rises." *Global Licence!* (January/February 2012): 36–41.

———. "Turtle Power." *Global Licence!* (September/October 2012): 42–48.

"Lone Ranger Enters Field of Merchandise." *Advertising Age*, May 23, 1938.

MacDonald, Heidi, "Inside the Superboy Copyright Decision." *Publishers Weekly*, April 11, 2006.

Mansfield, April. "Disquiet on the Western Front: Who Was That Masked Man I Saw You With?" *Washington Post*, April 2, 1978, F1.

Marvel Entertainment Annual Report for Stockholders, 2007.

"Mask vs. Beard." *New Yorker*, December 17, 1938, 12–13.

Maslin, Janet. "The Lone Ranger Rides Again Once More." *New York Times*, May 22, 1981, C8.

Masters, Kim. "Jerry Bruckheimer Breaks His Silence on Disney's $215 Million 'Lone Ranger' Compromise." *Hollywood Reporter*, October 19, 2011.

Mattimore, J. Clarke, and Hanibal Coons. "The Fighting Funnies." *Colliers Weekly*, January 29, 1944, 24–41.

McClintock, Pamela. "Box Office Report: 'Lone Ranger' Marks Third Big-Budget Bomb of Summer." *Hollywood Reporter*, July 6, 2013.

McKelway, St. Claire. "The Literary Character in Business & Commerce." *New Yorker*, October 26, 1935, 74.

McMillan, Graeme. "Why Aren't More People Talking About 'The Lone Ranger'?" *Hollywood Reporter*, July 2, 2013.

Mermigas, Diane. "Disney's Superhero Bid for Elusive Young Males." *CBS News Moneywatch*, September 1, 2009.

"Mickey Mouse Emerges as Economist." *New York Times Magazine*, March 10, 1935.

Moore, Roger. "Movie Review: Some moments thrill, others too violent to enjoy 'The Lone Ranger.'" *Gazette*, July 3, 2013.

Myers, Arthur. "They Bought the Rights to Get Rich." *True*, December 1966.
Nairn, Andy. "Nostalgia—it ain't what it used to be." *Guardian*, May 13, 2009.
Nashawaty, Chris. "Box Office Buccaneer." *Entertainment Weekly*, July 25, 2003.
Neville, Olga. "For Your Holiday . . . Why Not a Nice Bank Hold-Up?" *Olga Neville's Hollywood Report*, ca. 1957.
———. "The Marshal Who Drank Only Milk!" *Olga Neville's Hollywood Report*, ca. 1957.
"Our Best Salesman Rides a Horse." *Grocers Spotlight*, ca. 1934.
Owen, Rob. "New 'Lone Ranger' pales in comparison to the original." *Pittsburgh Post-Gazette*, February 23, 2003.
Paddock, Polly. "Lone Ranger Rides Again—In Sleek Car." *Charlotte Observer*, March 16, 1973, 1E, 4E.
Peabody, Amanda. "Brazil Steps Up Its Licensing Game." *Global Licence!* (May 2011): 34–38.
Pennington, Gail. "Hi-Yo! Lone Ranger Rides Again—on the WB." *St. Louis Post-Dispatch*, February 25, 2003.
Polikarpov, Yana. "From Apparel to Home Décor, Disney Revamps Licensing Biz." Brandweek.com, March 23, 2009. http://www.adweek.com/news/advertising-binding-apparel-home-decor-disney-revamps-licensing-biz-105467.
Puig, Claudia. "'Lone Ranger' masks its fun behind bloated action tale." *USA Today*, July 2, 2013.
"Q&A: How Bad Publicity Hit 'Legend of the Lone Ranger.'" *Los Angeles Herald Examiner*, May 23, 1981, A1–A2.
Rainer, Peter. "'The Lone Ranger' is wit-free and derivative." *Christian Science Monitor*, July 2, 2013.
Sansweet, Stephen J., and Peter Vilmur. "From dog food to film, look inside 'Star Wars.'" *Billings Gazette*, November 3, 2007.
"Shirley Slesinger Lasswell." Associated Press, July 20, 2007.
Szalai, George. "Disney Analysts Peg 'Lone Ranger' Loss at up to $190 Million, Remain Bullish on Stock." *Hollywood Reporter*, August 9, 2013. http://www.hollywoodreporter.com/news/disney-analysts-peg-lone-ranger-581961.
Thielman, Sam. "How Lego Became the Most Valuable Toy Company in the World." *Adweek*, April 15, 2013.
Thomas, David. "Fury over Asda's 'sexually suggestive' Disney underwear for young girls." *Telegraph* (London), August 14, 2008. http://www.telegraph.co.uk/news/2556204/Fury-over-Asdas-sexually-suggestive-Disney-underwear-for-young-girls.html.
Thompson, Derek. "Disney Is Not a Movie Company; It's a Television Company." *Atlantic*, July 10, 2013.
"The Top Box-Office Hits of 1956." *Variety Weekly*, January 2, 1957.
Townsend, Allie. "*Green Lantern* and Mattel: Friends with Benefits," *Time*, June 20, 2011.
"Toy Wonder." *Entertainment Weekly*, December 8, 1995.
Turan, Kenneth. "Not even Johnny Depp can rescue 'The Lone Ranger.'" *Los Angeles Times*, July 3, 2013.

"2010 Top 125 Global Licensors." *Global Licence!* (May 2011): T1–T30.
"2011 Top 125 Global Licensors." *Global Licence!* (May 2012): T1–T30.
"Veiled Vindictive Annie." *Time*, September 9, 1935.
Verrier, Richard. "DreamWorks Animation buys 'Casper,' 'Lassie' parent Classic Media." *Los Angeles Times*, July 23, 2012.
Walworth, Clark. "New Lone Ranger Rides in Remake." *Bulletin*, June 5, 1981.
Whitaker, Thomas. "Hulk Doll's Monster Willy." *Sun* (London), August 1, 2007. http://www.thesun.co.uk/sol/homepage/news/81124/Hulk-dolls-monster-willy.html.
"Winnie the Pooh Goes on the Air." *Playthings*, May 1933.
"World's Fair Crowd Meets Buck Rogers." *Youngstown Vindicator*, September 16, 1934.
"Wrather Corp. Announces Agreement to Sell its TV and Motion Picture Properties to Southbrook Television Corp." *Business Wire*, April 24, 1985.
"Wrather Corp.'s Last Roundup." *Businessweek*, September 29, 1973, 68.
Zeitchik, Steven. "Is 'The Lone Ranger' debacle an end-of-the-empire sign?" *Los Angeles Times*, July 9, 2013.

Online Articles and Websites

"About the Film." *Lone Ranger* website. http://disney.go.com/the-lone-ranger/#/about.
"About Us." *Classic Media Website*. http://www.classicmedia.tv/.
"About Us." *Seussville*. http://www.seussville.com/faq/about_us.php.
Acuna, Kristen. "'The Lone Ranger' Is Lining Up To Be Disney's Next 'John Carter' Bust." *Business Insider*, July 3, 2013. http://www.businessinsider.com/the-lone-ranger-looks-like-it-bomb-2013-7.
Ames, Jeff. "Johnny Depp Likes Brad Pitt or George Clooney to Play The Lone Ranger." *Collider*, December 1, 2010. http://collider.com/the-lone-ranger-brad-pitt-george-clooney/.
Anderson, Mae. "Toymakers aggressively court mommy bloggers." NBCNews.com, December 20, 2011. http://www.nbcnews.com/id/45742380/ns/business-holiday_retail/t/toymakers-aggressively-court-mommy-bloggers/#.UY_m1q7QY1p.
Anderson, Matt. "The Legend of Zorro." *Movie Habit*, October 28, 2005. http://www.moviehabit.com/review.php?story=leg_j805.
Atler, Ethan. "The Lone Ranger Hi-Yo Stinker Away." Televisionwithoutpity.com, July 3, 2013. http://www.televisionwithoutpity.com/mwop/moviefile/lights-camera-action-jackson/2013/07/the-lone-ranger-hi-yo-stinker-away/.
———. "*The Wolverine*: Pain Is for Chumps, Bub." *Television Without Pity*, July 26, 2013. http://www.televisionwithoutpity.com/mwop/2013/07/the-wolverine-pain-is-for-chumps-bub/.
Billington, Alex. "Disney Stops Production on Verbinski's 'The Lone Ranger' with Depp." *First Showing*, August 13, 2011. http://www.firstshowing.net/2011/disney-stops-production-on-verbinskis-the-lone-ranger-with-depp/.

Brain, Matt. "Netflix signs exclusive deal for over 300 hours of original DreamWorks Animation content." *The Verge*, June 17, 2013. http://www.theverge.com/2013/6/17/4437404/netflix-dreamworks-exclusive-deal.

Breznican, Anthony. "Johnny Depp wants 'The Lone Ranger' to back off Tonto: 'Why is the f——ing Lone Ranger telling Tonto what to do?'" EW.com, May 8, 2011. http://insidemovies.ew.com/2011/05/08/johnny-depp-tonto-lone-ranger/.

Brown, Marley. "Tonto Racist: 'Lone Ranger' Johnny Depp Character Understandably Offends Native Americans." Policymic.com, July 2013. http://www.policymic.com/articles/51443/tonto-racist-lone-ranger-johnny-depp-character-understandably-offends-native-americans.

Buchanan, Kyle. "Those *Lone Ranger* Budget Cuts Didn't Work." *Vulture*, June 13, 2012. http://www.vulture.com/2012/06/those-lone-ranger-budget-cuts-didnt-work.html.

"Cassaday Joins the Lone Ranger." IGN.com, December 12, 2005. http://www.ign.com/articles/2005/12/13/cassaday-joins-lone-ranger.

"Characters." Dynamite Entertainment. http://www.dynamite.com/htmlfiles/infoDB.html?index=characters.

"Collector's Spotlight." NECA. http://necaonline.com/category/blog/collector-spotlight/.

Cronin, Brian. "Comic Book Legends Revealed #198." *Comic Book Resources*, March 12, 2009. http://goodcomics.comicbookresources.com/2009/03/12/comic-book-legends-revealed-198/.

Cruz, Gilbert. "*The Lone Ranger* Represents Everything That's Wrong With Hollywood Blockbusters." *Vulture*, July 5, 2013. http://www.vulture.com/2013/07/lone-ranger-is-everything-wrong-with-hollywood.html?test=true.

Cunningham, Todd. "Johnny Depp Can't Save 'Lone Ranger' From Being 'John Carter'-Sized Bomb For Disney." *The Wrap*, July 7, 2013. http://www.thewrap.com/movies/article/just-48m-5-day-holiday-weekend-lone-ranger-john-carter-sized-bomb-101526.

"DC fires lawyers in Siegel Superman case." Newsarama. http://blog.newsarama.com/2010/02/28/dc-fires-lawyers-in-siegel-superman-case/.

Disney Store. http://www.Disneystore.com.

"Dora the Explorer Curriculum." NickJr.com. http://www.nickjr.com/dora-the-explorer/about-dora-the-explorer/dora-the-explorer-curriculum.html.

"Dreamworks Animation Agrees to Acquire Classic Media." Press release, July 23, 2012. http://ir.dreamworksanimation.com/releasedetail.cfm?ReleaseID=694144.

Earle, Paul. "'The Lone Ranger' and the Curse of the Blockbuster Western." *Bloomberg Businessweek*, Juy 8, 2013. http://www.businessweek.com/articles/2013-07-08/the-lone-ranger-and-the-curse-of-the-blockbuster-western.

———. "The Real Reason Brand Revival Works." *Brand Channel*, February 16, 2004. http://www.brandchannel.com/brand_speak.asp?bs_id=78.

Edelstein, David. "Edelstein on The Lone Ranger: An Uncomfortable Mix of Silliness and Sadism." *Vulture*, July 3, 2013. http://www.vulture.com/2013/07/movie-review-the-lone-ranger.html.

Edidin, Rachel. "Grim, violent Man of Steel sells Superman's soul for spectacle." Wired.uk.com, June 17, 2013. http://www.wired.co.uk/news/archive/2013–06/17/man-of-steel-review'.

Eisenberg, Eric. "Disney To End Its Deal With Jerry Bruckheimer." Cinemablend.com, September 20, 2013. http://www.cinemablend.com/new/Disney-End-Its-Deal-With-Jerry-Bruckheimer-39493.html.

Erbland, Kate. "Movie Review: 'The Lone Ranger' May Be The Most Bizarre Blockbuster Yet." *Film School Rejects*, July 3, 2013. http://www.filmschoolrejects.com/reviews/review-the-lone-ranger.php.

Frost, John. "The Lone Ranger Falls Flat At Box Office." The Disney Blog, July 8, 2013. http://thedisneyblog.com/2013/07/08/the-lone-ranger-falls-flat-at-box-office/.

"Game On!: Intelligent Designs or Fan Aggregators?" April 8, 2011. A video of the symposium is available on Henry Jenkins's blog. http://henryjenkins.org/2011/07/transmedia_hollywood_2_videos.html.

General Mills: 75 Years of Innovation, Invention, Food & Fun. http://www.generalmills.com/~/media/Files/history/history_book.ashx.

Grimm, Bob. "The Lowest Depp." Newsreview.com, July 11, 2013. http://www.newsreview.com/reno/lowest-depp/content?oid=10560365.

Harris, Aisha. "Johnny Depp's Tonto: Not as Racist as You Might Think. But Still Kind of Racist." Slate, July 3, 2013. http://www.slate.com/blogs/browbeat/2013/07/03/johnny_depp_as_tonto_lone_ranger_movie_pushes_against_racism_but_reinforces.html.

Hawks, Beth. "The Silver Bullet." *PR for a Pro*, August 7, 2011. http://corecomprblog.blogspot.com/2011/06/silver-bullet.html.

Hick, Chris. "DVD review: 'Zorro' slashes his way onto DVD." *Deseret News*, January 10, 2011. http://www.deseretnews.com/article/700102101/Zorro-slashes-his-way-onto-DVD.html.

"Hot Toys or NECA?" Sideshow Collectors forum, August 8, 2010. http://www.sideshowcollectors.com/forums/showthread.php?t=81195.

Humphries-Brooks, Lauren. "New Trailer For The Lone Ranger Hypes The Plot, The Actors And The Trains." Wegotitcovered.com, April 15, 2013. http://wegotthiscovered.com/movies/ne-trailer-lone-ranger-hypes-plot-actors-trains/.

"Interview with Michael Uslan—Part 1." November 8, 2005. http://www.batman-on-film.com/interview_muslan_2.html.

Jaggernauth, Kevin. "Latest 'Lone Ranger' Draft Ditches Supernatural Elements, But Set Pieces Will Need To Be Scaled Back." *Indie Wire*, August 17, 2011. http://blogs.indiewire.com/theplaylist/lastest_lone_ranger_draft_ditches_supernatural_elements_but_setpieces_will_.

"Johnny Depp as Cultural Appropriation Jack Sparrow. . . . I mean Tonto." Native-appropiations.com, March 8, 2012. http://nativeappropriations.com/2012/03/johnny-depp-as-cultural-appropriation-jack-sparrow-i-mean-tonto.html.

"Johnny Depp's 'Lone Ranger' Seeks To 'Reinvent' Tonto, Native American Treatment." *Huffington Post*, May 9, 2011. http://www.huffingtonpost.com/2011/05/09/johnny-depps-lone-ranger-tonto-native-americans_n_859279.html.

Johnson, Scott. "Johnny Depp's Native American Heritage Informed His Tonto Role In The Lone Ranger." Comicbook.com, June 30, 2013. http://comicbook

.com/blog/2013/06/30/johnny-depps-native-american-heritage-informed-his-tonto-role-in-the-lone-ranger/.

Kim, Jonathan. "ReThink Review: The Lone Ranger—Tonto Redeemed, Disney Unchained?" *Huffington Post*, July 11, 2013. http://www.huffingtonpost.com/jonathan-kim/rethink-review-emthe-lone_b_3578405.html.

Kirby Sattler website. http://kirbysattler.sattlerartprint.com/artist.html.

Last, Jonathan V. "The Crash of 1993." *Daily Standard*, June 13, 2011. http://www.weeklystandard.com/articles/crash-1993_573252.html?nopager=1.

"LEGO Lone Ranger Constitution Train Chase Review: LEGO 79111." *Brick-Show*, March 29, 2013. http://www.youtube.com/watch?v=yKBC3AYDFJQ.

"The Lone Ranger." Rottentomatoes.com. http://www.rottentomatoes.com/m/the_lone_ranger/.

"'The Lone Ranger'—Most anticipated movies of summer 2013: Fandango's Top 10." Examiner.com, April 16, 2013. http://www.examiner.com/list/most-anticipated-movies-of-summer-2013-fandango-s-top-10/8-the-lone-ranger.

Lone Ranger National Defenders Select Portfolio. http://www.thrillingdays.com/premiums/pr-lrnd-page6.html.

"Lone Ranger #1 Sells Out!" *Dynamite Entertainment*. Press Release, September 15, 2006. http://www.dynamiteentertainment.com/htmlfiles/lonerangerpress091506.html.

Lone Wolf Tribe. http://scoop.diamondgalleries.com/Home/4/1/73/1016?articleID=43573.

"Looking Ahead With The Lone Ranger." Newsarama.com, April 23, 2007. http://www.dynamite.com/boards/showthread.php?874-Newsarama-Ranger-Article.

"Marvel's Greatest Licensed Comics." *Comic Book Resources*, July 14, 2010. http://forums.comicbookresources.com/showthread.php?330648-Marvel-s-greatest-Licensed-comics.

"Mattel Completes Acquisition of HIT Entertainment." HitEntertainment.com, February 1, 2012. http://www.hitentertainment.com/corporate/newsdetail.aspx?nid=97.

McConnachie, Garry. "Box office disasters—just who should the finger be pointed at?" *Daily Record*, August 7, 2013. http://www.dailyrecord.co.uk/entertainment/movies/movie-news/box-office-disasters—-just-2136381.

Miller, Julie. "Of Course Johnny Depp Can Make *The Lone Ranger* Remake Look Cool." VanityFair.com, March 8, 2012. http://www.vanityfair.com/online/oscars/2012/03/johnny-depp-armie-hammer-the-lone-ranger-preview.

Nashawaty, Chris. "'Man of Steel' is joyless." CNNentertainment.com, June 16, 2013. http://www.cnn.com/2013/06/14/showbiz/ew-man-of-steel/index.html.

NECA website. http://necaonline.com/40955/licenses/movies/the-lone-ranger/the-lone-ranger-mens-tonto-costume.

O'Neal, Sean. "*The Lone Ranger* crew blames enormously powerful movie critics for conspiring to kill *The Lone Ranger*." *A. V. Club*, August 6, 2013. http://www.avclub.com/articles/the-lone-ranger-crew-still-cant-believe-critics-cr,101242/.

Pavlova, Victoria. "Jerry Bruckheimer—Lone Ranger Flop Marks Jerry Bruckheimer's Fall From Grace At Disney." Contactmusic.com, July 12, 2013. http://www.contactmusic.com/news/jerry-bruckheimer-jeopardy-disney_3759133.

Playlist Staff. "The Best & Worst Of 'Man of Steel.'" Indiewire.com, June 17, 2013. http://blogs.indiewire.com/theplaylist/the-best-worst-of-man-of-steel-20130617?page=3#blogPostHeaderPanel.

———. "What Went Wrong? The Good, The Bad & The Weird Of Disney's 'The Lone Ranger.'" IndieWire.com, July 8, 2013. http://blogs.indiewire.com/theplaylist/after-the-dusts-settled-the-good-the-bad-and-the-weird-of-disneys-the-lone-ranger-20130708?page=2.

"Portfolio." Classic Media website. http://www.classicmedia.tv/.

Rimer, Matt. "The Wolverine Is A Racist Buzzkill: A Review." Fourpins.com, July 29, 2013. http://four-pins.com/life/the-wolverine-is-a-racist-buzzkill-a-review/.

Rivas, Jorge. "Johnny Depp Made Honorary Member Of Comanche Nation." Colorlines.com, May 30, 2012. http://colorlines.com/archives/2012/05/johnny_depp_made_honorary_member_of_comanche_nation.html.

Ryan, Mike. "'The Lone Ranger': The Oddest Movie Of The year?" *Huffington Post*, July 2, 2013. http://www.huffingtonpost.com/mike-ryan/the-lone-ranger-review_b_3530610.html.

"Ryan Gosling In 'The Lone Ranger'? Star In Talks For Johnny Depp Classic." *Huffington Post*, April 16, 2011. http://www.huffingtonpost.com/2011/04/16/ryan-gosling-in-the-lone-ranger_n_850011.html.

Schaefer, Sandy. "'Lone Ranger' Encounters More Budget Woes; Production Behind Schedule." Screenrant.com, 2012. http://screenrant.com/lone-ranger-budget-production-problems-sandy-179446/.

"79107 Comanche Camp." Brickset.com, March 19, 2013. http://www.brickset.com/news/article/?ID=6026.

"Specific deadline timetables for Marvel's licensed films." *Superhero Hype*, August 2012. http://forums.superherohype.com/showthread.php?t=452113.

Stewart, Dodai. "Johnny Depp Takes Tonto Character From Racist to Merely Culturally Insensitive." *Jezebel*, March 9, 2012. http://jezebel.com/5891904/johnny-depp-takes-tonto-character-from-racist-to-merely-culturally-insensitive.

"The Summer of Failure—How Hollywood Can Eliminate its Blockbuster Mentality." *The Corner Critic*, August 4, 2013. http://thecornercritic.wordpress.com/2013/08/04/the-summer-of-failure-how-hollywood-can-eliminate-its-blockbuster-mentality/.

Taylor, Drew. "Jerry Bruckheimer Says Supernatural Coyotes Out, Train Sequences Stay In Scaled Down 'Lone Ranger.'" *Indie Wire*, October 19, 2011. http://blogs.indiewire.com/theplaylist/jerry_bruckheimer_explains_how_he_trimmed_the_budget_of_lone_ranger_by_doin.

Torrente, Ria Kristina. "'The Lone Ranger' Gets Mixed Reviews: Is Johnny Depp's Tonto Racist?" *International Business Times*, July 4, 2013. http://au.ibtimes.com/articles/486393/20130704/lone-ranger-johnny-depp-racist-lena-dunham.htm#.Uk2C3M1ig3I.

Truong, Lynn. "Looney Toons Eating Right Kids Review." Parentingsquad.com, September 11, 2009. http://parentingsquad.com/looney-toons-eating-right-kids-review.

Waxman, Sharon. "Disney to End First-Look Deal With Jerry Bruckheimer." *The*

Wrap, September 19, 2013. http://www.thewrap.com/disney-to-end-first-look-deal-with-jerry-bruckheimer/.

Weaver, Caity. "Johnny Depp's Tonto is Based on a White Man's Painting of an Imaginary Native American." *Gawker*, May 1, 2012. http://gawker.com/5906868/johnny-depps-tonto-is-based-on-a-white-mans-painting-of-an-imaginary-native-american.

"Your 2007 Eisner Award Nominees." *The Comics Reporter*, April 19, 2007. http://www.comicsreporter.com/index.php/your_2007_eisner_award_nominees/.

Zoller Seitz, Matt. "The Lone Ranger." Rogerebert.com, July 3, 2013. http://www.rogerebert.com/reviews/the-lone-ranger-2013.

Index